D1614663

Investigations in Universal Grammar

Language, Speech, and Communication

Investigations in Universal Grammar

A Guide to Experiments on the Acquisition of Syntax and Semantics

Stephen Crain and Rosalind Thornton

The MIT Press
Cambridge, Massachusetts
London, England

Second printing, 1999

This book was set in Palatino on the Monotype "Prism Plus" PostScript Imagesetter by Asco Trade Typesetting Ltd., Hong Kong.

Printed and bound in the United States of America.

Library of Congress Cataloging-in-Publication Data

Crain, Stephen, 1947–
  Investigations in universal grammar : a guide to experiments on the
  acquisition of syntax and semantics / Stephen Crain and Rosalind Thornton.
      p.   cm.—(Language, speech, and communication)
  Includes bibliographical references (p.   ) and index.
  ISBN 0-262-03250-3 (hardcover : alk. paper)✓
    1. Language acquisition—Research—Methodology. 2. Grammar,
  Comparative and general—Syntax. 3. Semantics. 4. Competence and
  performance (Linguistics) I. Thornton, Rosalind. II. Title.
  III. Series.
  P118.15.C73   1998
  401'.93—DC21   97-44971
                                                             CIP

To Kermit the Frog

Contents

Acknowledgments

The experimental methods and the model of the language apparatus described in this book were developed over many years, so there are many people to thank. We extend our gratitude first to students and collaborators at the University of Connecticut: Sergey Avrutin, Eva Bar-Shalom, Carole Boster, Paul Gorrell, Anne Halbert, Paul Macaruso, Kazumi Matsuoka, Yoichi Miyamoto, Weijia Ni, Carrie O'Leary, Jaya Sarma, Ana Varela, and especially Cecile McKee, Mineharu Nakayama, and Laura Conway. We also thank more recent students and other collaborators at the University of Maryland at College Park: Peggy Antoinesse, Sharon Armon-Lotem, John Drury, Julien Musolino, Susan Powers, Fred Savarese, Caro Struijke, Spyridoula Varlokosta, and especially Lena Gavruseva.

We are grateful to many colleagues, whose advice we frequently sought and whose encouragement we always received: Gennaro Chierchia, Peter Culicover, Janet Fodor, Teresa Guasti, Henry Hamburger, Norbert Hornstein, Howard Lasnik, Al Liberman, David Lightfoot, Diane Lillo-Martin, Don Shankweiler, Juan Uriagereka, Amy Weinberg, Jurgen Weissenborn, and Edwin Williams. We profited most of all from extensive discussions with Ken Wexler, who deserves much of the credit for developing the Modularity Matching Model.

The true heroes of the piece are the administrators, teachers, and children at the day care centers where we conducted our research. We want to mention in particular the Director, Charlotte Madison, and two of our longtime friends, the teachers Sue Spencer and Margaret Lima, at the Child Development Laboratories at the University of Connecticut. Among our new family at the Center for Young Children at the University of Maryland at College Park, we want to give special recognition to the Director, Fran Favretto, and to the Director of Research, Anne Daniel.

For helping to take the photos, we are indebted to Julien Musolino. An extra-special thanks goes to Laura Conway for drawing many of the illustrations.

There are four people we cannot thank enough, for providing insightful comments on the entire manuscript: Teresa Guasti, William Snyder, Brian Byrne, and Roger Wales.

We end by expressing our heartfelt appreciation to our parents, Garth and Judith Thornton and Bill and Kay Crain, as well as to Stephen's sons, Willis and Austin. Most of this book was written in the year before and the year after the birth of our own LAD, Aurora Luisa Thornton Crain. Not only is Aurora free of responsibility for any mistakes contained herein—she has made the past two years the happiest of our lives.

PART I

The Modularity Matching Model

Chapter 1

Introduction

This book is an introductory guide to research on child language acquisition. It is intended for advanced undergraduates, graduate students, and researchers in cognitive science, especially ones with interest in the psychology of language. Discussion of research methods is couched within the framework of generative grammar, or what is known as the *theory of Universal Grammar*. In part, we chose this framework because of its emphasis on explaining how children acquire natural language. A distinguishing feature of the theory of Universal Grammar is that it postulates principles that are specific to grammar formation, rather than attempting to characterize language acquisition using general principles of learning or cognitive growth (e.g., Chomsky 1971, 1975). Taken together, the linguistic principles of Universal Grammar constitute a theory of the organization of the initial state of the mind/brain of the language learner—that is, a theory of the human faculty for language.

In addition to linguistic competence, performance factors also contribute to the linguistic behavior of both children and adults. In our view, investigations of language acquisition must be framed within a specific model of performance. To assess children's underlying linguistic competence, it is necessary to understand the role of the competence grammar within the performance system. Therefore, we will not focus solely on research on child language acquisition, but will also discuss aspects of the performance system within which the competence grammar resides.

1.1 Experimental Methods: Two Tasks

Our main motivation for writing this book is to help prepare students of language acquisition to conduct experimental investigations of children's linguistic knowledge. We have not chosen to survey a variety of experimental techniques, however.[1] Instead, we discuss research on child language development by explaining the design features of two experimental techniques for assessing children's linguistic competence: one production task and one comprehension task.

The production technique is known as the *elicited production task*. Experiments using this task are designed to evoke particular sentence structures from children. These structures are elicited by devising situations that are uniquely felicitous for a specific kind of sentence. For example, an experimenter might want to elicit declarative sentences that contain a restrictive relative clause. The experimental situations are constructed with the meaning of the target sentence in mind; the result of the experiment is a sentence that corresponds to that meaning in the child's grammar. In some cases, the sentences produced by children will be identical to those produced by adults, but in other cases, children will produce nonadult structures. Children's nonadult productions provide important insight into their grammars, and into the nature of the acquisition process itself.

The elicited production task is also used as a tool for ongoing, in-depth exploration of individual children's grammars. Suppose, for instance, that a linguistic principle is thought to have an effect on five different structures. These five structures could be elicited from the same child subjects, to find out if the principle has the predicted effect on children's grammars. It would be insightful to discover whether or not the principle is in effect in all five structures, as predicted. Just as importantly, from a methodological point of view, the properties of each structure can be further investigated using the elicited production task. In this way, a great deal of evidence can be gathered and a relatively "complete" picture can be assembled of children's emerging grammatical principles.

The comprehension technique is known as the *truth value judgment task*. This task is used to investigate children's understanding of the meanings of sentences. It is often of theoretical interest to know whether or not children assign the same range of interpretations to sentences that adults do. The truth value judgment task can be used to tell if sentences are ambiguous or unambiguous for children and adults. The distinction between unambiguous sentences and ambiguous sentences proves to be crucial in demonstrating children's adherence to certain linguistic principles, known as *constraints*. The demonstration that children know a constraint involves showing that they judge sentences governed by the constraint to be nonambiguous. Children who lack a constraint should find the sentences that are governed by it to be ambiguous; the interpretation ruled out by the constraint should be available to these children. In assessing knowledge of linguistic constraints, therefore, it is essential to understand how children respond to ambiguous sentences. Children's responses to ambiguous sentences are used as a yardstick for measuring their performance in responding to sentences within the jurisdiction of the constraint. In addition, it is sometimes worth knowing if children assign *fewer* interpretations to certain constructions than adults do. Because children are language learners, it is conceivable that they initially hypothesize only a subset of the adult meanings and later extend their interpretive options to include ones that were previously absent. The truth value judgment task is a useful tool for this purpose as well.

There are several reasons for examining child language using these two research methods. First, these two tasks have proven to be especially revealing about children's underlying linguistic competence. These tasks are particularly useful in assessing children's knowledge of principles of Universal Grammar, that is, linguistic principles that are likely to be innately specified. A second reason for discussing these two tasks in particular is that, when used properly, they are relatively free from the influence of performance factors that have been found to mask children's linguistic knowledge in other tasks. Properly designed studies adopting the truth value judgment task and the elicited production task have resulted in extremely consistent and reliable performance by children—indeed, performance that is often on a par with that of adults. Even when children's behavior differs from that of adults, the pattern of children's responses is so consistent that the responses can be confidently attributed to linguistic knowledge and not to performance factors. A final reason for focusing on these two tasks is that they are, in large part, our own inventions; we know them well, and we have refined them over the years to make them better tools for evaluating children's growing linguistic competence. We continue to use these tasks almost exclusively in our own research.

By looking at the methodological prescriptions that have been administered using these tasks in our own prior research, we hope to convince a greater number of students and researchers in child language of the basic correctness of the Innateness Hypothesis and the theory of Universal Grammar. No one will be convinced, or should be, by research that is improperly designed or poorly executed, or by findings that are open to alternative interpretations. The methodological formulas presented in this book are designed to overcome many of these obstacles to the empirical investigation of children's linguistic competence. Research that follows these methodological formulas will therefore have a better chance of being taken seriously, even by critics of the theoretical assumptions that underlie the particular linguistic bent of the researcher. Of course, no single experiment can control every potentially confounding factor or rule out all but one explanation of the findings. However, this should not deter researchers from attempting to conduct sound and tightly controlled empirical investigations of child language. At the very least, the findings from carefully designed studies can be replicated and cannot be dismissed as artifacts of improper procedures or unnatural experimental tasks.

1.2 Structure and Process

The book has three parts. Part I, encompassing chapters 1–16, is an extended discussion of the fundamental assumptions that guide research in child language acquisition. Research does not take place in a vacuum. Both the research questions of interest and the methods that are employed to answer these questions depend on a theoretical framework. This framework includes not only a theory of grammar, but also a set of assumptions about how grammar is embedded in a performance system. As indicated earlier, we will assume that children's linguistic competence is as described by the theory of Universal Grammar. In part I, we outline certain linguistic phenomena as they are viewed within this theoretical framework. The phenomena we describe are characteristic of the research topics in child language that we return to later in the book. We also explain why studies of children are especially pertinent to the investigation of these linguistic phenomena.

In addition to an explicit theory of linguistic competence, part I introduces a model of language processing. In our view, this is essential to the investigation of children's knowledge of linguistic principles. Research findings from studies of child language cannot be properly understood without an appreciation for the language performance system within which linguistic principles operate for children and adults. It is beyond the scope of this book to delve deeply into all aspects of the performance system, but we will present many of its relevant aspects, on the basis of our own conception of the language apparatus and with support from the findings of experimental investigations of both children and adults.

A description of the general operating characteristics of the performance system is crucial to any serious investigation into children's knowledge of linguistic principles. It is frequently lamented that there is an inherent tension between linguistic theory and the kind of performance data that are obtained in experimental research with children (e.g., Cook and Newson 1996, 310). It is commonly held that linguistic theory is "pure" and that performance data are "messy." As a theory of an ideal speaker-hearer's linguistic behavior, it is assumed that a person's competence qualitatively outstrips that person's performance in any task. Without abandoning the competence-performance distinction, we take issue with the notion that there is inherent tension between the competence grammar and the performance system in which it is embedded. According to the model of language processing that we advocate, "messy" data are not anticipated, even in studies with children. On this model, the competence grammar is adversely affected by performance factors only in certain circumstances (see Chomsky 1965, 12–14). Assuming this model, we carefully examine the particular sites of friction between grammatical knowledge and performance factors. One of the goals of the discussion is to explain how the interference of performance factors can be reduced in experimental studies of child language. We discuss strategies that result in optimal performance by subjects, because optimal performance is a fundamental desideratum of experimental research.

1.3 Competing Models of Language Acquisition

We advocate a specific model of the interrelations between linguistic representations and linguistic performance, called the *Modularity Matching Model* (Crain and Wexler, forthcoming). According to this model, children and adults share a common language-processing system. Not only does this model assume that children have knowledge of grammatical principles, just as adults do, but it goes on to make a further, more contentious assumption: that children and adults appeal to the same processing mechanisms of language production and language understanding (see Pinker 1984, 7–8). Finally, owing to the modular architecture of the language apparatus of both children and adults, grammatical knowledge preempts nonlinguistic factors (e.g., extralinguistic knowledge) in most instances. The one exception is ambiguity. When a sentence is ambiguous, nonlinguistic sources of information are sometimes used in resolving the ambiguity. Nonlinguistic factors are not in competition with linguistic knowledge for either children or adults, however, in producing or understanding unambiguous sentences (see chapters 13–14).

According to the Modularity Matching Model, children's linguistic performance in any experimental task is expected to be essentially the same as that of adults, for both ambiguous and unambiguous sentences. The model makes a further empirical prediction as well. If linguistic performance is not typically marred by factors extraneous to language, as the model maintains, then both children and adults should typically behave in conformity with their linguistic knowledge. Of course, both children and adults sometimes make mistakes, and children have been found to perform differently than adults do, both qualitatively and quantitatively. But, because the possible sources of children's nonadult responses are quite limited from the perspective of the Modularity Matching Model, any differences in the performance of children and adults must be explained, or the model is brought into question. It is important, therefore, to describe the ways in which the linguistic performance of children and adults can differ according to the Modularity Matching Model, and to review and reexamine empirical findings that seem, at first glance, to be inconsistent with the model. The relevant findings and the range of possible differences that are consistent with the model are discussed in part I.

The chapters in part I also compare the Modularity Matching Model with two alternative views of the interrelation between linguistic knowledge and other factors that contribute to linguistic behavior: environmental input, extralinguistic knowledge, verbal short-term memory, and so on. One viewpoint that contrasts with the Modularity Matching Model is called the *Input Matching Model*. This model assumes that children's grammars develop largely in response to their linguistic input. Empirical reasons for questioning the Input Matching Model are presented in chapter 5. That chapter presents evidence of both children's nonadult productions and their nonadult interpretations of sentences.

Another alternative view of language and mind is called the *Competing Factors Model*. This model is pervasive in the literature on language acquisition. It is assumed by most researchers working within the generative framework, even by researchers who share with us many fundamental assumptions about the nature of linguistic knowledge, including the Innateness Hypothesis. These researchers do not share our assumptions about the relation between the competence grammar and linguistic performance, however. Researchers who adopt the Competing Factors Model view linguistic knowledge as only one among several components contributing to linguistic behavior in any experimental task. Therefore, on this model, less than perfect performance is expected in studies with children. This viewpoint has become so deeply ingrained that most researchers seem to assume it without argument. On the Modularity Matching Model, by contrast, access to and application of linguistic principles preempts the influence of other factors. On this model, therefore, children's performance should parallel their linguistic competence in many instances.

The Competing Factors Model is presented in detail in chapter 6. Chapter 6 also discusses both areas where the Competing Factors Model and the Modularity Matching Model converge, and areas where they diverge. That chapter explains our reasons for questioning the utility of research designs associated with the Competing Factors Model for the study of child language. Chapters 8 and 9 review many empirical findings that seem to bear out the predictions of the Competing Factors Model; these chapters and the two that follow them, chapters 10 and 11, outline the variety of research designs that have been employed by the model's advocates. Chapters 12 and 13 present our response to the Competing Factors Model. There we argue against the basic assumptions of the model: that memory limitations (chapter 12) and extralinguistic knowledge (chapter 13) interfere with children's access to linguistic principles.

Chapter 14 focuses on one difference between the language apparatus of the child and that of the adult: namely, that children have access to a *language acquisition device* (LAD).[2] This difference leads to some interesting empirical consequences and explains certain apparent differences between child and adult linguistic performance. Finally, part I concludes with a consideration of what can go wrong in assessing children's linguistic knowledge (chapter 15) and a myriad of practical details in administering experiments with children (chapter 16).

We partition models of language and mind into three broad classes largely for purposes of exposition. Making this partition permits us to comment on certain tasks and research strategies that are commonly used in the study of child language, but ones that we argue are inappropriate for studies of child language within the generative framework. In our view, the use of these tasks and research strategies implies the (implicit) acceptance of the Competing Factors Model. Because different research strategies are suggestive of different models, we have chosen to paint in broad strokes those research strategies that are associated with the different models.

We hope to convince researchers who would adopt the Modularity Matching Model that it is also necessary to adopt its methodological assumptions to assess children's knowledge of the principles and parameters of Universal Grammar. It seems to us that many researchers adopt the methodological assumptions of the Competing Factors Model simply because they are not aware of alternatives and because they do not realize that the assumptions of that model are inconsistent with the theoretical framework they embrace. This book is our attempt to clarify the relation between models of child language and research methodology. We argue that many of the research strategies of the past should be abandoned in favor of new research strategies that are more in keeping with a model of language competence and performance that is based on the theory of Universal Grammar. One such model is the Modularity Matching Model.

In making the case for a new set of research strategies, we inevitably take issue with researchers who share our commitment to incorporating insights from the syntax and semantics of generative grammar. We do so precisely because we believe that this commitment demands different research strategies. Through a critical examination of research by those of like concern, we hope to convince investigators "within the family" of the need to adopt alternative research strategies.

Part II of the book (chapters 17–24) covers the elicited production paradigm, and part III (chapters 25–40) covers the truth value judgment task. Because these are dynamic tasks and must be modified to address specific research questions, we provide detailed discussion of a number of experiments using each paradigm. We include discussion of past and present research to illustrate particular design features of these tasks.

A brief disclaimer is called for. Although we review the theoretical background for the syntactic, semantic, and discourse principles that are the subject matter of the experimental investigations we describe, this book is not intended to replace a solid introduction to linguistic theory.[3] Readers without a sufficient theoretical background in linguistics may find that we presuppose a firmer grasp of theory than they have. We do not believe, however, that lack of familiarity with any of the theoretical machinery we employ will interfere with proper understanding of the important points of methodology, and this, after all, is what the book is about.

Chapter 2

Constraints and Universal Grammar

Universal Grammar is a theory of the human biological endowment for language, that is, those aspects of linguistic knowledge that are innately specified. Several empirical hallmarks indicate that a biological property is innately specified. We use the term *hallmarks* because a linguistic property could be innately specified without manifesting certain of the relevant characteristics.

One hallmark of innateness is that a property appears in the absence of decisive evidence from the environment. If children adhere to a linguistic principle for which there is no corresponding evidence in the environment, then the principle is likely to be innately specified. In cases where evidence for a linguistic principle is available in the primary linguistic input, the evidence could actually lead learners astray, should they try to avail themselves of it. We will discuss two such cases in this chapter.

A related hallmark of innate specification is that children acquire a linguistic principle despite considerable latitude in the primary linguistic data they encounter. If all (or at least all normal) children in a linguistic community adhere to a particular principle, despite being exposed to different input, then innate specification is suggested, particularly if the principle is highly complex (from a pretheoretic vantage point).

Another hallmark of innateness is universality. If a linguistic principle is part of the human biological blueprint for language growth, then it is expected to be manifested by children learning any natural language—hence the name Universal Grammar. There are caveats to this expectation, however. In certain instances, an innate linguistic principle will not be expected to be exhibited in all languages. For example, the parameters of natural language (e.g., the null subject parameter) are considered to be innately specified. Although the various settings of a parameter may be innately given, one setting may be manifested by one class of languages, and another setting by another class of languages. Moreover, it is not necessary for every option to be manifested during the course of development in a single language. If the initial value of a parameter is consistent with the target language, then other values will never be adopted; they will simply atrophy, or go wherever unused parameter values go. However, linguistic principles that are not parameterized are expected to appear in all languages, and in all children.[1]

A final hallmark of innateness is sometimes suggested: early emergence. It is not logically necessary for innate principles and parameters to emerge early in the course of development. Just as some properties of physical development are biologically timed to appear months, even years, after birth (e.g., the secondary sexual characteristics), so certain aspects of linguistic knowledge could become operative only at a certain stage of development. In fact, two specific maturation accounts are currently at the forefront of child language research: Borer and Wexler (1987, 1992) propose that the capacity to form A-chains matures in children, and Radford (1990) and others propose that certain functional projections mature. Regardless of the outcome of the debates on these proposals, one should bear in mind that it is consistent with the Innateness Hypothesis for even (seemingly) highly complex linguistic principles to be part of the young child's language faculty. Early emergence of linguistic principles could be construed as additional evidence of innate specification.

The alternative to innateness is learning; yet the early emergence of seemingly complex linguistic principles casts doubt on many learning-theoretic scenarios. This makes child language a good testing ground for innateness: it provides an opportunity to see whether or not particular linguistic principles meet the "early emergence" hallmark of innate specification.

2.1 The Innateness Hypothesis

These joint expectations—that innate principles (a) emerge early, (b) are universal, and (c) appear without decisive evidence from the environment—will be referred to as the *Innateness Hypothesis*. Much of the research reported in this book is concerned with this hypothesis. Because the focus is the study of child language acquisition, the research we discuss examines two of the hallmarks of innateness: early emergence and the mastery of linguistic principles by children in the absence of corresponding experience. We interpret the results of this research as support for the Innateness Hypothesis, generally, and as support for the theory of Universal Grammar in particular.

The remainder of this chapter outlines the kinds of linguistic phenomena that fall within the confines of the theory of Universal Grammar and that are consequently explored in this book.

2.2 Constraints

Unlike much current research, ours will not focus on what children say or on what interpretations they assign to sentences. Instead, the emphasis will be on what children do not say and on what meanings they do not assign to sentences, when there are grounds for thinking that they might say these things and assign these meanings. The Innateness Hypothesis is designed to solve this puzzle—why children do not produce sentences that they might be expected to produce, and why they do not assign meanings that they might be expected to assign. The relevant linguistic knowledge comes in the form of *constraints*, of which this chapter will introduce two kinds. Constraints of both kinds have been investigated using the experimental methods described in subsequent chapters.

Constraints are subject to the argument from the poverty of the stimulus, which concludes that knowledge of constraints cannot be learned and therefore is likely to be innately specified. The argument from the poverty of the stimulus is the topic of the next chapter. The remainder of this chapter will be devoted to constraints.

2.2.1 Sentences and Meanings
To begin the discussion of constraints, we introduce some terminology. Following Aristotle, we view language as pairings of sound and meaning. In more current terms, language is conceived of as a (psychological) mapping between sentences and their

associated meanings. Learning a grammar, then, is learning which sentences are associated with which meanings. We can abbreviate this as follows:

⟨sentence, meaning⟩

In some instances, the mapping between sentences and meanings could be evident to learners based on the *primary linguistic data* (e.g., parental input). For example, consider sentence (1).

(1)   There is an Indian blanket on the couch.

Clearly, a sentence like this is likely to be encountered by learners in situations where there is an Indian blanket on a couch. Although the process is admittedly poorly understood, it is often assumed that "positive" mappings between sentences and meanings can be mastered on the basis of such experience (but see Gleitman 1990 for a critique of this assumption). It is even less clear, however, that knowledge of other aspects of the mapping between sentences and meanings could be attained through experience. One aspect of this mapping is the knowledge that some sentences have more than one meaning; a second is the knowledge that certain sentences are ill formed; a third is the knowledge that, although certain sentences are well formed, they cannot be given a particular meaning. It seems unlikely that these aspects of linguistic knowledge are acquired on the basis of experience. We will consider each of them in turn.

2.2.2 Ambiguity
By the time speakers of English have reached the final state of language development (i.e., the adult grammar), they are able to judge that sentences like (2a) and (3a) are ambiguous (the alternative interpretations are indicated by the paraphrases in (2b) and (3b)).

(2)   a.   We fed her chicken McNuggets.
       b.   We fed her some. vs. We fed it some.

(3)   a.   They seem to enjoy boiling champagne.
       b.   They enjoy doing it. vs. They enjoy drinking it.

We can represent knowledge of ambiguity using the following notation:

⟨sentence, {meaning$_1$, meaning$_2$}⟩

This is read, "A sentence is associated with a set of (in this case, two) semantic representations."

2.2.3 Constraints on Form
Extending the terminology, we can represent the knowledge that certain sentences are ill formed. For example, the verbal elements *want* and *to* may be contracted to form *wanna* in many linguistic contexts, but they cannot be contracted in certain other contexts. In (4)–(7), we provide examples of constructions in which *want* and *to* may be contracted. This is followed by example (8). In (8a), contraction of these elements makes the sentence ill formed; only (8b) is well formed. Notice that much of the evidence available to someone learning English runs counter to the constraint exemplified in (8a). Contraction of *want* and *to* is tolerated in general—(8a) is the exception.

Therefore, if learners were to adopt the traditional principles of induction, they would be tempted to violate the constraint. The relevant empirical facts about children learning English will be reported briefly in chapter 3, and in detail in chapter 21.

(4) a. Who does Arnold wanna make breakfast for?
     b. Who does Arnold want to make breakfast for?

(5) a. Does Arnold wanna make breakfast for Maria?
     b. Does Arnold want to make breakfast for Maria?

(6) a. Why does Arnold wanna make breakfast?
     b. Why does Arnold want to make breakfast?

(7) a. I don't wanna make breakfast for Arnold or Maria.
     b. I don't want to make breakfast for Arnold or Maria.

But:

(8) a. *Who does Arnold wanna make breakfast?
     b. Who does Arnold want to make breakfast?

Knowledge of facts like that in (8a) (i.e., about deviant sentence forms) can be represented as follows:

*sentence

The "star" (*) indicates that the sentence is not well formed—it is deemed to be ungrammatical by some component of grammar. The knowledge that certain sentences are ill formed is represented in the grammar by a constraint. A statement of the constraint on contraction of *want* and *to* is presented in chapter 21.

Because constraints loom large in our discussion of experimental methodology, we will discuss the notion of a constraint in further detail. First, it should be noted that a constraint is a linguistic principle that governs a range of linguistic phenomena, not just a small set of sentences. Any sentence that is similar to (8a) in the relevant respects will be subject to the same constraint. Second, a constraint is a *prohibition* against certain sentence/meaning pairs. The addition of a constraint to a grammar results in an overall reduction in the language (sentence/meaning pairs) that the grammar generates (see Fodor and Crain 1987). To see that constraints are sanctions against certain sentence/meaning pairs, consider what would happen if the constraint on contraction of *want* and *to* was removed from the grammar of English. Let us call the language that results, Shmenglish. Lacking the constraint on contraction of *want* and *to*, Shmenglish would include more sentences, with their associated meanings, than English. Shmenglish would generate sentences like (8a), whereas English does not.[2]

English $\langle$sentence$_1\rangle$
Shmenglish $\langle$sentence$_1$, sentence$_2\rangle$

Children who lacked the constraint would be expected to allow contraction in questions like (8a) roughly as often as they do in questions like (4a), for example. To test the constraint under discussion, the elicited production task has been used to encourage children to produce questions like (8a) as well as ones like (4a). This makes it possible to perform the needed comparison between the proportion of contractions in children's questions like (8a) and the proportion of contractions in questions like (4a).

The findings are briefly summarized in chapter 3, and fuller details of the study are described in chapter 21.

Before we proceed, there is a small wrinkle to iron out. It may be possible in many instances to understand certain sentences that are not well formed, if these were actually produced by a speaker in some conversational context. A speaker who produced (8a), for example, would probably be understood perfectly well, although the utterance itself would sound odd. According to the theory of Universal Grammar, however, such sentences could be produced only by mistake; that is, they would be a product of the performance system, not the grammar. However, grammatical knowledge is embedded within a performance system with a specific architecture, such that there are severe limits on the range of performance mistakes. Whether or not people mistakenly contract *want* and *to*, for example, is an empirical question. Our own research suggests that speakers do not make such performance mistakes (see chapters 13 and 14). The relation between the competence grammar and the performance system will be discussed further as we proceed.

2.2.4 Constraints on Meaning

There are also constraints on the meanings that can be assigned to certain well-formed sentences. In an interesting set of cases, speakers of a language know that some sentences may not be interpreted in a particular way. For example, note that the pronoun *he* and the name *the Ninja Turtle* can pick out a single individual in (9) and (10). By contrast, these same linguistic expressions cannot pick out the same individual in sentence (11). In the examples, if one NP is underlined and another NP is not, they refer to different individuals; if both NPs are underlined, they refer to the same individual.

(9) While he danced the Ninja Turtle ate pizza.
   a. While he danced the Ninja Turtle ate pizza.
   b. While he danced the Ninja Turtle ate pizza.

(10) The Ninja Turtle danced while he ate pizza.
   a. The Ninja Turtle danced while he ate pizza.
   b. The Ninja Turtle danced while he ate pizza.

But:

(11) He danced while the Ninja Turtle ate pizza.
   a. *He danced while the Ninja Turtle ate pizza.
   b. He danced while the Ninja Turtle ate pizza.

Knowledge of what a sentence cannot mean is represented as follows:

⟨sentence, {meaning$_1$, *meaning$_2$}⟩

Since the sentence in question is well formed, we do not attach the asterisk to the sentence portion of the sentence/meaning pair. Rather, we are noting that some particular meaning cannot be assigned to a well-formed sentence; in (11), the pronoun *he* cannot designate the Ninja Turtle—it must pick out some individual who is not mentioned in the sentence. Although (11) is a grammatically well formed sentence, it has only one of the meanings associated with (9) and (10). As the asterisk (*) indicates, the interpretation according to which the pronoun *he* and the name *the Ninja Turtle* have the same referent is ruled out. That is, (9) and (10) are ambiguous; in each case, the pronoun may, but need not, have the same referent as the name. In (10), by contrast, these elements must have disjoint reference; the sentence is unambiguous. It is worth noting that much of the evidence available to learners runs counter to disjoint reference; coreference between pronouns and names is tolerated much of the time, as attested by examples (9) and (10). Example (11) is the exception. Children who adopted the traditional principles of induction, therefore, could easily be misled about the range of interpretations available for sentences like (11).

Noncoreference facts such as the one exhibited in (11) are attributed to a principle known as *Principle C*. This principle prohibits coreference between a pronoun and a name when they are in a certain structural relationship (see chapter 26). Principle C is a constraint. Recall the criterion for deciding whether or not a linguistic principle counts as a constraint: adding a constraint to a grammar results in an overall reduction in the language (sentence/meaning pairs) that it generates. Principle C meets this criterion. To see this, suppose that a dialect of English (i.e., Shmenglish) lacked Principle C. If so, Shmenglish would include more sentence/meaning pairs than English does. Specifically, Shmenglish would generate (11a). Shmenglish would differ from English as follows:

English $\langle$sentence, $\{$meaning$_1$, *meaning$_2\}\rangle$
Shmenglish $\langle$sentence, $\{$meaning$_1$, meaning$_2\}\rangle$

In discussing the constraint on *wanna* contraction, we noted that the utterance of a sentence that violates the constraint would sound odd to the ear; nevertheless, the sentence could be understood. What about violations of Principle C, the constraint on coreference? Clearly, the utterance of a sentence like the one in (11) would not *sound* odd, because the constraint governs the interpretation of (11), not its form. The constraint prohibits interpretation (a).

As we have shown, children who lack the constraint on coreference should find sentences like (12) to be *ambiguous*; both readings, (a) and (b), should be available to these children.

(12)   He danced while the Ninja Turtle ate pizza.
    a.   He danced while the Ninja Turtle ate pizza.
    b.   He danced while the Ninja Turtle ate pizza.

Therefore, these children would be expected to incorrectly accept the coreference interpretation involving the pronoun and the NP in (12). In fact, children should accept this interpretation roughly as often as they accept the corresponding (coreferential) interpretation in sentences like (9) and (10). By contrast, only the noncoreferential (deictic) interpretation of (12) (i.e., (b)) should be available to children who know the constraint. Sentence (12) should be unambiguous for these children just as it is unambiguous for adults. The relevant empirical findings will be reported in chapter 3, and the methodological details of the study itself will be presented in chapters 26 and 27.

2.3 The Importance of Context

The utterance of sentence (12) could be abnormal in another sense: namely, it could be used inappropriately in a conversational context. For example, suppose that some one uses (12) to describe a picture in which there is only one individual, the Ninja

Turtle, who is dancing while he is eating pizza. Although it would be infelicitous for anyone to use (12) to describe such a picture, this kind of infelicity is not uncharacteristic of experimental investigations assessing how children interpret sentences. In such experiments, children would be asked to indicate whether or not sentence (12) correctly describes the picture. On the basis of our own experience, we believe that many children would answer affirmatively, indicating that (12) is an accurate description of such a picture (see chapter 28).

Is such a finding evidence that these children lack Principle C? Not necessarily. It may simply be evidence that these children ignore or override their knowledge of the constraint on coreference in order to comply with the experimenter's request. The constraint on coreference pertains to sentences that are encountered in conversational contexts with (at least) two individuals, the Ninja Turtle and another male character; in such contexts, the pronoun cannot refer to the Ninja Turtle. Notice also that the use of the pronoun *he* implies that the speaker presupposes that the other male individual has previously been introduced into the conversation or is highly salient in the context. Therefore, the application of the constraint in the context of the picture under discussion would require children to accommodate a failed presupposition. Specifically, they would need to modify their mental model of the conversational context by adding the second individual.

What if children are less able than adults to accommodate presuppositional failures (see chapters 12 and 15)? If so, they would be compelled to construct a semantic representation that does not require accommodation—one that is consistent with the context. In the picture we discussed, which was shown in association with (12), the only consistent semantic representation is one in which the pronoun and the name refer to the same individual. This line of reasoning leads to the conclusion that children could be forced to violate the constraint on coreference, not because it is absent from their grammars, but because of the processing difficulty associated with accommodating failed presuppositions.[3]

This hypothetical experiment is no doubt an extreme example of improper experimentation, but it allows us to make a point: that children's failures to comply with a linguistic constraint could arise even if they had mastery of the constraint. Failures could arise because children are not as well versed as adults in recovering from pragmatic infelicities. This should hardly be surprising, given children's more limited experience in such matters, not to mention the fact that both children's and adults' experience largely consists of sentences presented in felicitous contexts. In any event, the observed differences between children and adults would not reside within the language faculty.

These observations underscore the importance of proper experimental design in assessing children's grammatical knowledge.[4] If experimental sentences are presented in inappropriate circumstances, the wrong conclusions might be drawn. In the present example, the researcher could erroneously conclude, from their "Yes" responses, that many children lack Principle C. Just the opposite conclusion might be drawn if children were tested in felicitous circumstances. In an experiment using the truth value judgment task, for example, a sentence like (12) would be presented in circumstances that make it felicitous on both of the readings at issue: (a) the reading that conforms to the constraint on coreference, and (b) the reading that would result if the constraint were absent from a child's grammar. Among the felicitous contexts is one in which someone other than the Ninja Turtle—say, Grover—refused to dance while the Ninja

Turtle ate pizza. In the same context, moreover, the Ninja Turtle could be dancing and eating pizza. On the reading that complies with the constraint, (12) is false; it is incorrect because Grover did not dance while the Ninja Turtle ate pizza. On the non-adult reading, (12) would be true; it would be a correct description of the context, because the Ninja Turtle did dance while he ate pizza. It is worth noting that this part of the context is the same as in the hypothetical experiment in which (12) was used infelicitously. In the judgment experiment, however, children who know the constraint should make the correct judgment—they should respond "No" to sentences like (12)—without having to accommodate any failure of presupposition.

The preceding paragraphs describe the basic properties of the truth value judgment task, although many important details were omitted. For instance, the second character in the (appropriate) experimental context described above played an active role in the story, refusing to dance while the Ninja Turtle ate pizza. What if this character had just stood by, not dancing while the Ninja Turtle ate pizza, but not refusing to dance either—would this affect children's responses? We have found that such seemingly minor differences in the structure of experimental contexts have major consequences on children's responses, largely because these changes alter the felicity of the target sentences. These features of experimental design are the focus of parts II and III of the book.

2.4 Constraints on Discourse

As a final point of clarification, we wish to note that constraints are not limited to sentence grammar, but apply to discourse as well. For example, the singular pronoun *he* in one sentence of a discourse sequence cannot be anaphorically related to certain kinds of quantificational noun phrases (NPs) in a preceding sentence (see Chierchia 1995). Example (13) shows that negative quantificational NPs, such as *no mouse*, are subject to such a constraint. Example (14) shows that the same constraint applies to NPs that contain the universal quantifier *every*.

(13)   No mouse came to Simba's party. He was upset.
    a.   <u>No mouse</u> came to Simba's party. *<u>He</u> was upset.
    b.   No mouse came to <u>Simba</u>'s party. <u>He</u> was upset.

(14)   Every mouse came to Simba's party. He was upset.
    a.   <u>Every mouse</u> came to Simba's party. *<u>He</u> was upset.
    b.   Every mouse came to <u>Simba</u>'s party. <u>He</u> was upset.

However, example (15) demonstrates that a singular pronoun *can* be related to an indefinite NP, *a bear*, that appears in a preceding sentence; that is, the following discourse sequence is ambiguous. This contrasts with the discourse sequences in (13) and (14), which are not ambiguous.

(15)   A bear sleepwalked into Genie's house. He ate the spaghetti.
    a.   <u>A bear</u> sleepwalked into Genie's house. <u>He</u> ate the spaghetti.
    b.   A bear sleepwalked into <u>Genie</u>'s house. <u>He</u> ate the spaghetti.

In addition, it is worth noting that the singular pronoun *he* can be anaphorically related to negatively and universally quantified NPs if these elements appear in the same sentence, as (16) illustrates.

(16) No/Every mouse at Simba's party said that <u>he</u> was upset.
    a. <u>No/Every mouse</u> at Simba's party said <u>he</u> was upset.
    b. No/Every mouse at <u>Simba</u>'s party said <u>he</u> was upset.

Moreover, a *plural* pronoun can be related to preceding quantificational NPs in different sentences in a discourse.

(17) No/Every mouse came to Ernie and Bert's party. They were upset.
    a. <u>No/Every mouse</u> came to Ernie and Bert's party. <u>They</u> were upset.
    b. No/Every mouse came to <u>Ernie and Bert</u>'s party. <u>They</u> were upset.

On the basis of these last three examples, children who lacked the constraint in evidence in (13) and (14) might be expected to permit anaphoric relations between the singular pronoun *he* and the quantificational NPs *every mouse* and *no mouse*. Lacking the constraint, children might find discourse sequences like (13) and (14) to be ambiguous, whereas they are unambiguous for adults. The situation can be depicted as follows:

Child   ⟨discourse sequence, {meaning$_1$, meaning$_2$}⟩
Adult   ⟨discourse sequence, meaning$_1$⟩

Furthermore, children who lacked the constraint on discourse would be expected to allow anaphoric links in discourse sequences like (13) and (14) roughly as often as they do in sentences like (15)–(17). To test children's knowledge of the constraint on discourse binding, the truth value judgment task was used to compare the proportion of anaphora children assigned to discourse sequences like (13) and (14) with the proportion of anaphora they assigned to sentences like (15)–(17). The results are presented in chapter 34.

2.5 Conclusion

This chapter introduced two kinds of linguistic constraints. One kind of constraint encompasses knowledge that certain sentences are ill formed; the other encompasses knowledge that certain well-formed sentences (or discourse sequences) cannot be interpreted in a particular way. Both kinds of constraints can be the exception, rather than the rule, in the linguistic input to children. Children should be expected to violate some linguistic constraints, then, if they learn constraints on the basis of the input. In the next chapter, we will follow up on this observation in order to argue that constraints are part of Universal Grammar. As noted at the beginning of this chapter, Universal Grammar is a theory of the initial state of the human language faculty. The conclusion of the argument presented in the next chapter, therefore, is that constraints are part of the language faculty from its inception.

Chapter 3

The Poverty of the Stimulus

How do speakers acquire knowledge of constraints? Many linguists and psycholinguists have concluded that constraints are innately specified, as part of Universal Grammar. This conclusion is based on the *argument from the poverty of the stimulus,* the topic of the present chapter.

Stated very generally, the argument from the poverty of the stimulus begins with two premises.

(A)   All native speakers know some particular aspect of their language, call it property P.

(B)   Knowledge of property P could not have been learned on the basis of the primary linguistic data.

From premises A and B, we are invited to conclude C.

(C)   Knowledge of property P must be innately specified (i.e., part of Universal Grammar).

This chapter applies the poverty-of-the-stimulus argument to linguistic constraints. It concentrates on the second premise, which has often been challenged in the literature.

3.1 Empirical Coverage

The argument from the poverty of the stimulus can be applied to a range of linguistic phenomena. This is illustrated in the first of the following quotations from Hornstein and Lightfoot 1981:

> People attain knowledge of the structure of their language for which *no* evidence is available in the data to which they are exposed as children. Crucial evidence for such knowledge consists of judgments concerning complex and rare sentences, paraphrase and ambiguity relations, and ungrammatical 'sentences', all of which are available to the linguist but lie outside the primary linguistic data available to the child. Children are not systematically informed that some hypothetical sentences are in fact ungrammatical, that a given sentence is ambiguous, or that certain sets of sentences are paraphrases of each other, and many legitimate and acceptable sentence-types may never occur in a child's linguistic experience. (pp. 9–10)

> If these claims are correct, then it follows as a simple point of logic that inductive theories must be abandoned, because there is no inductive base. If the child's linguistic experience does not provide the basis for establishing some

particular aspect of our linguistic knowledge, there will have to be some other source for that knowledge. That aspect of our linguistic knowledge will have to be a priori in the sense that it arises independently of experience. (p. 12)

Given these facts, it is reasonable to look for a priori knowledge available to the organism, which permits language acquisition to circumvent the environmental deficiencies and thus to take place. (p. 13)

The phenomenon of interest in this chapter is what Hornstein and Lightfoot describe as "judgments concerning ... ungrammatical 'sentences.'" In our terms, these are judgments about linguistic constraints. Let us turn, then, to the application of the poverty-of-the-stimulus argument to linguistic constraints, invoking the two constraints introduced in chapter 2.

3.2 The Innateness of Constraints

The first premise of the argument from the poverty of the stimulus is that native speakers have knowledge that is encoded by constraints. This fact is not contested, as far as we are aware.[1] The second premise is that linguistic constraints could not be learned on the basis of the primary linguistic data. This premise hinges on the claim that there is no information in the environment corresponding to linguistic constraints. This claim merits further discussion.

As stated earlier, constraints are concerned with the ungrammaticality of sentences. They are sanctions against certain ways of putting a message, or sanctions against assigning certain meanings to sentences that are, themselves, well formed.[2] It is conceivable that constraints could be learned by children, assuming the usual mechanisms of induction, only if the relevant kind of evidence is available. This evidence is called *negative evidence* (or *negative data*). Negative evidence is the presentation of ungrammatical sentences, marked as such. If negative evidence were available to children, they could learn constraints on the basis of their experience. When Hornstein and Lightfoot claim that "children are not systematically informed that some hypothetical sentences are in fact ungrammatical," they are claiming that negative evidence of this kind is not systematically available to learners. If Hornstein and Lightfoot are correct in asserting that children lack access to negative evidence, then it follows that children's knowledge about the ungrammaticality of sentences (i.e., constraints) is not learned. Hence, this knowledge is known independently of experience; presumably, it is innately specified.

3.3 Negative Evidence

Other acquisition scenarios are often suggested, however. According to this line of thinking, negative evidence is available, but in more subtle forms than the kind of negative evidence mentioned by Hornstein and Lightfoot—overt negative judgments about hypothetical sentences. A more realistic acquisition scenario is often suggested, which goes as follows: First, children violate a constraint on form, such as the constraint on *wanna* contraction, producing nonadult utterances (e.g., "Who does Arnold wanna make breakfast?"). In response to these errant forms, parents would provide corrective feedback: "No, say, 'Who does Arnold *want to* make breakfast.'"

Negative evidence could be even more subtle. Parents could provide negative feedback simply by failing to understand their children's nonadult utterances; they could supply negative evidence by expanding their children's nonadult utterances; and so on.[3]

Based on these observations, a good deal of research has been conducted, and a great deal of ink has been spilt, on the question of whether some source of negative evidence is available in the primary linguistic input. This question is potentially misleading, however. It is one thing to determine whether or not negative evidence of some relevant kind exists; it is quite another thing to determine whether sufficient negative evidence is available at the relevant time(s) to ensure that all children converge on the target grammar.

Unquestionably, all children master the kinds of linguistic constraints we have described, such as the constraint on contraction, as claimed in the first premise of the argument from the poverty of the stimulus. As far as we know, this premise has not been contested. For negative evidence to guarantee that all children learn all of the linguistic constraints found in the adult grammar, however, it would have to be abundantly available in the primary linguistic data. If negative evidence were scarce, then some learners would not encounter enough of it and would not converge on the target grammar. Since this is contrary to fact (as stated in the first premise), all of the ingredients necessary for convergence must be available in sufficient quantity (see Lasnik and Crain 1985).

As far as we can ascertain, if negative evidence is available to children at all, it is not available in sufficient quantity or at the right times to guarantee that every child converges on the adult grammatical system. Several researchers have reviewed the literature on the availability of negative evidence and have reached the same conclusions that we have: first, that no source of negative evidence is systematically available to all learners; and, second, that the potential substitutes for negative evidence that have been identified (e.g., expansions) are not available throughout the course of development (they may even occur less frequently at those stages of development at which they would be most useful). Here is how Pinker (1990) summarizes the findings:

> [W]hen parents are sensitive to the grammaticality of children's speech at all, the contingency between their behavior and that of their children is noisy, indiscriminate, and inconsistent from child to child and age to age. (p. 217)

For other reviews that reach similar conclusions, see Bowerman 1987, 1988, Brown and Hanlon 1970, Morgan and Travis 1989, Marcus 1993.

Even if negative evidence were available, there is no guarantee that children would use it. Many researchers have pointed out the absence of findings demonstrating that children who are exposed to negative evidence (in experimental settings) use it to jettison incorrect grammatical hypotheses. Studies by Cazden (1972) and by Nelson, Carskaddon, and Bonvillian (1973) found that children who received expanded parental input fared no better through the course of language development than children who did not. Explicit correction is even more rare than expansions (e.g., Brown and Hanlon 1970), and when it does occur, there is little reason to believe that children benefit from it. This is attested by familiar anecdotes that point to children's resistance to correction.

> *Child*   My teacher holded the rabbits and we patted them.
> *Parent*   Did you say your teacher held the baby rabbits?
> *Child*   Yes.
> *Parent*   What did you say she did?
> *Child*   She holded the baby rabbits and we patted them.
> *Parent*   Did you say she held them tightly?
> *Child*   No, she holded them loosely.
> (Cazden 1972)

> *Child*   Nobody don't like me.
> *Parent*   No, say "nobody likes me."
> *Child*   Nobody don't like me.
>
> (Eight repetitions of this dialogue)
>
> *Parent*   No, now listen carefully; say "nobody likes me."
> *Child*   Oh! Nobody don't likes me.
> (McNeill 1970)

> *Child*   Want other one spoon, Daddy.
> *Parent*   You mean, you want the other spoon.
> *Child*   Yes, I want other one spoon, please, Daddy.
> *Parent*   Can you say "the other spoon"?
> *Child*   Other ... one ... spoon.
> *Parent*   Say "other."
> *Child*   Other.
> *Parent*   "Spoon."
> *Child*   Spoon.
> *Parent*   "Other spoon."
> *Child*   Other ... spoon. Now give me other one spoon?
> (Braine 1971)

As these examples illustrate, children are often unable to figure out what adults intend when they explicitly correct their speech. On the basis of current research findings, it seems safe to infer that the universal achievement of language acquisition is accomplished without negative evidence.[4]

The debate surrounding the availability of negative evidence focuses on children's nonadult linguistic behavior—for example, children's overgeneralization of the rule for past tense (resulting in forms like *holded*). We should ask, therefore, whether children violate constraints. The conclusion of the argument from the poverty of the stimulus is that knowledge of constraints is part of the initial state. If this conclusion is correct, then children should not be expected to violate constraints at any stage of language development. If children do not violate constraints in the first place, then the question of the availability of negative evidence is moot.

3.4 Investigating Knowledge of Constraints

Much of our own research has focused on children's knowledge of putatively innate constraints. As far as possible, we have investigated children's knowledge of constraints that would be most susceptible to violations, if these constraints were not part of children's grammars. The two constraints that we introduced in chapter 2 are good examples.

First, consider the constraint on *wanna* contraction. As we noted, there are many constructions in which *want* and *to* may or may not contract, as in (1).

(1) a. Who does Arnold wanna make breakfast for?
     b. Who does Arnold want to make breakfast for?

Children, like adults, should be expected to contract the verbal elements *want* and *to* frequently in such constructions. This tendency toward contraction could follow from the general disposition of speakers to use "reduced" forms as much as possible. This tendency is pitted against the constraint on contraction in the exceptional construction.

(2) a. *Who does Arnold wanna make breakfast?
     b.   Who does Arnold want to make breakfast?

Lacking the constraint, children who applied the common strategies of induction, such as analogy or stimulus generalization, would be expected to produce nonadult questions like (2a) at the stages of language development when they first attempt such questions. It is against this background of what children would be expected to do, given certain theories of learning, that children's behavior will be examined in subsequent chapters. The goal will be to see if children adhere to linguistic constraints or if they instead adopt learning strategies such as analogy or stimulus generalization, consequently producing sentences and assigning meanings that are prohibited by constraints.

Chapter 21 reviews the findings of a study that was designed to investigate how young children form questions with the verbal elements *want* and *to*, using the elicited production methodology. The main findings are these: children showed a general willingness to contract where the constraint is not applicable, but the same children produced almost no contracted forms in constructions like (2a), where a constraint prohibits contraction. This pattern of results is just what the Innateness Hypothesis predicts. It also shows that negative evidence is not relevant in the acquisition of the constraint; children's adherence to constraints obviates the need for negative evidence and argues against the acquisition scenario according to which children learn constraints and make errors in the course of learning.

Consider next the constraint on meaning, Principle C. This constraint limits the interpretations that can be assigned to sentences like (3). Principle C renders (3) deviant when the pronoun and the name are coreferential, as indicated in (a). The only legitimate interpretation of (3) is one in which the pronoun and the name have disjoint reference. Children (and adults) who know Principle C should prohibit coreference in (3).

(3) He danced while the Ninja Turtle ate pizza.
     a. *<u>He</u> danced while <u>the Ninja Turtle</u> ate pizza.
     b.   <u>He</u> danced while <u>the Ninja Turtle</u> ate pizza.

This restriction on interpretation does not hold in other cases, as in (4).

(4) While he danced the Ninja Turtle ate pizza.
     a. While <u>he</u> danced <u>the Ninja Turtle</u> ate pizza.
     b. While <u>he</u> danced <u>the Ninja Turtle</u> ate pizza.

Lacking Principle C, children who apply the usual learning-theoretic strategies would be expected to permit the illicit interpretation of sentences like (3), on analogy with the sentences in (4), assuming that sentences like (4) are part of the primary linguistic data. If so, sentences like (3) would be *ambiguous* for these children, just as (4) is for adults.

It is important, therefore, to observe how children respond to ambiguous sentences like (4) and to compare their pattern of performance on such sentences with their responses to sentences that are governed by the linguistic constraint, as in (3). The pattern of responses to sentences like (4) could be used as a yardstick for sentences like (3). If children know the constraint, then sentences that are governed by the constraint, such as (3), should be unambiguous. In short, the research design we have in mind pits ambiguous control sentences against the (potentially) unambiguous test sentences. The question is whether or not children respond to sentences like (3) on par with ones like (4). To put it another way, the research question is whether or not children find both types of sentences ambiguous.

There are two possible outcomes for any child subject. Children who lack the constraint should find both types ambiguous and should accept coreference in response to both to a similar extent. Children who know the constraint, on the other hand, should not tolerate coreference between the pronoun and the name for sentences like (3), although this interpretation might even be their preferred interpretation of ambiguous sentences like (4). Chapter 26 reviews the findings of a study designed to investigate young children's interpretations of sentences like (3) and (4), using the truth value judgment task. The main findings are that children show a general willingness to assign coreference in sentences like (4), but they consistently reject the coreferential reading of sentences like (3), where a constraint prohibits coreference. This pattern of results is as predicted by the Innateness Hypothesis. These findings also provide another indication that negative evidence may be irrelevant in the acquisition of constraints; as noted earlier, children's consistent adherence to constraints obviates the need for negative evidence. This argues against the acquisition scenario according to which children *learn* constraints, making errors along the way. Because young children consider sentences governed by Principle C to be unambiguous, just as adults do, it follows that negative evidence is not needed for the acquisition of Principle C.

Similar considerations suggest the hypothesis that young children will also adhere to discourse constraints, as illustrated in (5).

(5)   No mouse came to Simba's party. He was upset.
     a.   No mouse came to Simba's party. *He was upset.
     b.   No mouse came to Simba's party. He was upset.

Again, the alternative supposition is that children will judge discourse sequences such as (5) to be ambiguous. The findings are reported in chapter 34.

3.5 An Alternative: Conservative Learning

There is a different way to avoid the conclusion that children's knowledge of constraints is innately specified. This is to abandon the claim that children apply the standard strategies of induction, such as analogy. It has been proposed, for example, that children restrict the sentence forms they produce and the meanings they assign to sentences to ones that they have encountered in the primary linguistic data. According to this viewpoint, learners do not postulate sentence meanings that they have not themselves encountered in the environmental input; similarly, children are seen to avoid producing sentence patterns that they have not yet heard. If children are conservative in this sense, then constraints would not be necessary for language learning. This kind of account of the acquisition of linguistic knowledge (which is encoded in constraints in the framework of Universal Grammar) has been advanced by van Hoek (1995), within Cognitive Grammar.

Interestingly, van Hoek's example involves sentences with a referential NP and a pronoun, as in (6). A constraint on coreference, Principle B, prohibits the (a) interpretation of (6) in the adult grammar; only the (b) interpretation is possible.

(6)   Papa Bear is covering him.
    a.   *Papa Bear is covering <u>him</u>.
    b.   <u>Papa Bear</u> is covering him.

Referring to sentences like (6), van Hoek advances the following proposal:

> Grammaticality judgments constitute judgments that a particular expression is congruent with—or in conflict with—conventionally-established patterns in the language established through schemas. As noted ..., speakers acquire schemas or templates through exposure to actually-occurring expressions, and use those schemas to sanction new expressions.... A sentence such as [(6)] is acceptable if it is judged as an example of a pronominal construction without coreference, but it is unacceptable if it is understood to involve coreference. (p. 337)

On this view, constraints are not innate prohibitions on sentence meanings, but are learned responses to "schemas," linguistic patterns that children internalize on the basis of their experience. A similar proposal is advanced by Rosen and Rosen (1995). They too attempt to circumvent the conclusion of the poverty-of-the-stimulus argument by denying that constraints are statements in the grammars of language learners.

> [P]erhaps the mental grammar actually consists of positive CONSTRUCTS that license sentences, perhaps ample positive evidence is available, and perhaps positive evidence can support learning. If so, then the negative evidence hallmark is irrelevant to questions about innateness.... (Rosen and Rosen 1995, 73)

As Rosen and Rosen point out, according to a conservative learning account children should be inherently unresponsive to sentences until they have built the relevant "construct" for them. That is, children should reject all sentence/meaning pairs that are not consistent with their experience. The findings from studies of child language do not bear out this prediction, however. In a well-known study by Chien and Wexler (1990), children were presented with pictures and were asked questions like (7).

(7)   Is Papa Bear covering him?

The question in (7) would have been presented in the context of a picture in which Papa Bear was shown covering himself, and a monkey was shown standing nearby, watching Papa Bear. First, the experimenter introduced the characters ("This is Papa Bear; this is a monkey"); then children were asked the question in (7).

In response to questions like (7), many young children between the ages of 3 and 6 answered "Yes." Children in Chien and Wexler's study gave this answer roughly half of the time. The correct answer for adult speakers is "No," because the only possible referent for the pronoun in the picture is the monkey, and Papa Bear is not covering the monkey (= *him*). Unlike adults, then, children are apparently able interpret the pronoun *him* as if it were a reflexive pronoun, linked to a preceding, referential NP (its antecedent). It should be noted that these children are also able to assign the correct meaning to pronouns. So if Papa Bear had covered someone else, but not himself, these children answered "Yes" to (7). Because children assign an "extra" meaning, beyond that of adult speakers, the error is one of *semantic overgeneration*. Several attempts have been made to explain children's semantic overgeneration, but we will not review them here.

Let us now return to the conservative learning account of the acquisition of constraints. As Rosen and Rosen (1995) acknowledge, if children's judgments concerning coreference are based on constructs (templates, schemas, etc.), then they should not accept illicit interpretations for sentences for which they have no corresponding construct. Concerning sentences like (6), they remark:

> [T]he child will not be able to construct the coreference interpretation. Because the child cannot interpret the sentence in a way that describes the picture, the child should reject the sentence/picture pairing. (pp. 78–79)

The evidence of children's semantic overgeneration of interpretations in response to questions like (7) undermines the proposal that learners invoke a conservative learning strategy.

Of course, there are possible rejoinders. One is that children fail to respond according to their "constructs" for reasons extraneous to their linguistic knowledge, having to do with the performance system. Rosen and Rosen (1995) appeal to this kind of explanation, stating that "their performance is impaired by unknown factors" (p. 80). Another possible rejoinder is that children simply have not had enough experience with sentences like (6) or questions like (7) to have developed the appropriate schema or template. Without this template, there would be nothing against which to compare such sentences and therefore no reason to reject them.

Neither of these explanations of the recalcitrant findings is plausible, however. First, it should be noted that children make few errors in response to related sentences. For example, it has been found that the same children who incorrectly answered "Yes" to (7) answered "No" to (8), correctly judging (8) to be an inaccurate description of the same context (Thornton 1990).

(8)   I know who covered him. Papa Bear.

Presumably, discourse sequences like (8) are at least as rare as questions like (7). Therefore, it is unlikely that the construct or template corresponding to (8) would develop earlier than the template corresponding to (7). This leaves the account based on unknown performance factors. Being only a promissory note, this account merely stipulates that performance factors conspire to make questions like (7) more difficult than discourse sequences like (8). In the absence of any good reason, based on performance factors, for children to respond differently to examples like (7) and (8), children's semantic overgeneration in questions like (7) represents strong circumstantial evidence against the conservative learning scenarios proposed in the literature. We will further substantiate this view by reporting several examples of children's nonadult productions in chapter 5.

The present example of children's semantic overgeneration illustrates a further point. There are two horns to the dilemma of language learnability: one is how children recover when they have overshot the target language, the other is how children avoid undershooting the target language. One way to resolve the first horn of the dilemma would be for children to be conservative, thereby avoiding the problem associated with syntactic and semantic overgeneration. Such conservative learning models are then left facing the second horn of the dilemma, however. As we show in chapter 5, moreover, children are not conservative learners.

This leaves us to reconsider the solution to the overgeneration problem advanced by the theory of Universal Grammar: overgeneration is held in check by constraints. The second horn of the dilemma is taken care of by general principles, namely, operating principles, such as *move* and *copy*, which are governed by constraints.

3.6 Summary of the Poverty-of-the-Stimulus Argument

This completes the discussion of the argument from the poverty of the stimulus. The argument can be depicted using the notation introduced in chapter 2. The situation confronting the language learner is indicated in the following graphic:

Input (primary linguistic data) → LAD → Final state

⟨sentence, meaning⟩   ⟨sentence, meaning⟩
                      ⟨sentence, {$meaning_1$, $meaning_2$}⟩
                      ⟨sentence, {$meaning_1$, *$meaning_2$}⟩
                      *sentence

As the graphic indicates, certain aspects of the linguistic knowledge mastered by learners are acquired in the absence of input (= primary linguistic data). We have mentioned two linguistic phenomena that bear this property: knowledge that certain linguistic forms are prohibited (as in the case of *wanna* contraction), and knowledge that certain meanings are prohibited (as in the case of disjoint reference (3)). A similar argument can be given for the acquisition of knowledge about ambiguity (e.g., Hornstein and Lightfoot 1981). Each of these aspects of the final state (= adult grammar) is such that it must be mastered in the absence of decisive evidence from the environment. This invites the inference that such facts are not learned, but are part of the human biological blueprint for language acquisition (i.e., the LAD). In short, the logical problem of language acquisition is that the data available to learners underdetermine what they come to know. The solution offered by proponents of the theory of Universal Grammar is that the knowledge is innately given, as part of the LAD itself. Children are preprogrammed to adhere to these principles of linguistic analysis as part of the blueprint for their development. Just as a child cannot help but grow fingers and toes, and not wings or claws, so these linguistic principles, and not others, grow in the child.

3.7 Conclusion

By adulthood, at least, language users have mastered a rich and complex linguistic system. A large amount of the linguistic knowledge encoded in this system is apparently acquired without corresponding evidence from the environment. Among the facts that do not seem to be learned on the basis of experience are knowledge that certain sentence forms and sentence meanings are prohibited. The principles that underlie this knowledge are constraints. In the absence of negative evidence in the primary linguistic data, it is likely that constraints are innately specified. That is, it is likely that constraints are part of Universal Grammar.

If the goal is to investigate which principles are part of Universal Grammar, and which are not, it is now clear why children are ideal subjects. As a consequence of innate specification, the possibility exists that linguistic knowledge may emerge early in the course of development. If children evince knowledge of a principle, knowledge that cannot have been learned from experience, this evidence reinforces the view that the principle is part of Universal Grammar. The theory of Universal Grammar is essentially a biological theory; it is concerned with those aspects of the human biological endowment for language that could emerge early in development, despite the lack of evidence for them in the environment.

Chapter 4
Models of Language Development

Following the logic of the poverty-of-the-stimulus argument, many studies have been designed to investigate linguistic constraints. In the chapters that follow, we examine the design features of such research. For the most part, we focus on the acquisition of syntax, but we also consider aspects of the acquisition of semantics/pragmatics. To clarify certain points of methodology, chapters are divided along methodological lines, with separate descriptions of the methods and results of experimental investigations of children's productions and of their understanding of sentences. Before getting into the details of experimental methodology, however, we need to examine the theory of Universal Grammar from a broader psychological perspective, to make clear its role in the cognitive system that is used to learn and process language.

There are several different conceptions of the interrelations of grammar and the other linguistic and nonlinguistic components of cognition that may be involved in language learning and in language processing. This chapter outlines three models of the language apparatus. Although one of the models is implicit in our earlier work, and that of Wexler, Hyams, and others, the first explicit statement of the operating characteristics of the model we endorse appeared in Crain and Wexler, forthcoming. This model will be contrasted with two other models that have been adopted more generally in the field of developmental psycholinguistics. First, we describe the model we advocate, the Modularity Matching Model.

4.1 The Modularity Matching Model

The *Modularity Matching Model* makes two fundamental assumptions. First, it assumes that the human language-processing system is modular. Broadly speaking, the language apparatus is modular in the sense that the language faculty operates according to principles that are specific to it and not shared by other cognitive systems. According to this conception of modularity, operations within the language faculty are sealed off from other cognitive systems. As a consequence, the construction of syntactic and semantic representations of sentences is not influenced by general cognitive mechanisms—the mechanisms that are used to represent and process real-world knowledge (see Fodor 1983). This explains why considerations about the plausibility of sentences, for example, do not influence the grammatical representations that people construct for them. This is why they can judge sentences to be "funny" or false. To take a simple example, when people read or hear a sentence like *Cats chase dogs*, they do not attempt to put the words together to make the sentence express a true proposition. If they did, they would interpret the sentence *Cats chase dogs* to mean that dogs chase cats. Instead, they take the writer or speaker to have said something false.

Second, the model assumes that the child's language-processing system is essentially the same as that of an adult. For example, if adults do not allow their beliefs and opinions to influence the interpretations they assign to sentences, then, on this model, the same is expected of children. Similarly, both adults and children should invoke the same parsing strategies in resolving ambiguities. Moreover, in the absence of evidence to the contrary, both adults and children are assumed to have similar processing capacity and memory limitations.

Maximizing the similarities between children's cognitive systems and those of adults is needed in part to explain language learnability—why all children successfully converge on an adult linguistic system despite the considerable latitude in their linguistic experience. The model we will consider in section 4.3, the Competing Factors Model, allows children to differ from adults in language processing (possibly, in order to attribute grammatical knowledge to children). This is not the Null Hypothesis, however. It is also unwise. Permitting the characteristics of the child and adult processing systems to differ opens a Pandora's box of possible processing explanations (cf. Atkinson 1996). Moreover, any account of children's performance that attributes different properties to the child and adult processing systems must face a new question: how does the processing system of the child change so as to converge on the adult system? To the extent that the cognitive mechanisms of children and adults are similar, problems of learnability do not arise. For this reason alone it is important to take the assumption of equivalence seriously.

These suppositions jointly form the basis for the Modularity Matching Model. By "modularity matching," we mean that the principles of any component of the language apparatus are the same for children and adults; for example, the principles within the syntactic component are the same, and the principles within the semantic component are the same. Chapters 12, 13, and 14 provide a more complete picture of the language apparatus, according to the Modularity Matching Model. In a nutshell, the language apparatus is a hierarchically organized system in which the results of (partial) analyses at lower levels of linguistic representation are rapidly transferred upward to higher levels for analysis. For example, once (partial) syntactic representations are built, the results are subsequently, and incrementally, shunted to the semantic component, where meaning representations are built; the responsibility of relaying information between levels of representation within the system is undertaken by the verbal working memory system. Only the output from the language faculty makes contact with real-world knowledge. Extralinguistic knowledge, which is not itself contained in a "module," does not influence the construction of linguistic representations at any level, however. The graphic in figure 4.1 illustrates this point.

According to the Modularity Matching Model, *all* of the linguistic abilities of a child are the same as an adult's. Not only do we assume that children have access to Universal Grammar, just as adults do, we also make the more controversial assumption that children are equivalent to adults in the mechanisms they use to process language; that is, they have access to a universal parser. The assumption that the processing capabilities of children and adults are equivalent is not generally accepted even within the generative approach to language acquisition. We take this assumption to be the Null Hypothesis, however.[1]

The Modularity Matching Model borrows heavily from the theory of Universal Grammar. For one thing, the model follows the theory in maintaining that linguistic experience plays only a limited role in grammar formation. According to the Modu-

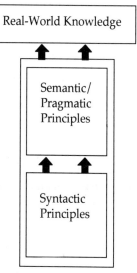

The Language Faculty

Figure 4.1
The Modularity Matching Model

larity Matching Model, innately specified principles of grammar circumscribe the linguistic hypotheses that children formulate. The role of experience is minimal, at least in the acquisition of syntactic and semantic principles; experience simply enables the learner to identify and set the parameters provided by Universal Grammar. That is, experience aids the learner in deciding among grammatical options made available by Universal Grammar. This said, we want to emphasize that it is consistent with both the Modularity Matching Model and the theory of Universal Grammar for children to provisionally select grammatical hypotheses that will later be abandoned on the basis of (positive) evidence from the linguistic community. There is a limit to the possible mismatches between child and adult grammars, however. The limit is stated in the Continuity Hypothesis, according to which children's developing grammars can differ from the target, the adult grammar, only in ways in which adult grammars can differ from each other (see Crain 1991; Pinker 1984).

4.2 The Input Matching Model

The observation that children sometimes hypothesize grammars that differ from the target is important in distinguishing among alternative models of linguistic knowledge and linguistic behavior. For one thing, evidence of children's nonadult behavior indicates that children are not forming grammatical hypotheses based entirely on the input. Therefore, children's nonadult productions and their nonadult interpretations of sentences provide evidence against models that maintain that children's grammatical hypotheses are securely tied to their primary linguistic data. We call this class of models the *Input Matching Model*. The Input Matching Model places little, if any, emphasis on innately specified linguistic knowledge as a source of children's grammatical hypotheses. Instead, general-purpose learning algorithms are assumed to underlie language learning, as well as other cognitive processes.

One example of the Input Matching Model is the *Competition Model* proposed by MacWhinney and Bates (1989) and their colleagues. According to the Competition Model, a learner relies on "cues" from the input to form connectionist networks; these networks are the learner's "grammars." Examples of cues include word order, morphological agreement between linguistic items, and semantic plausibility. The learner comes to place more or less weight on different cues according to their availability in the linguistic environment. According to the Input Matching Model, these differences account for crosslinguistic variation and for variation among speakers of the same language.

Another variant of the Input Matching Model is the *Coalition Model* of Hirsh-Pasek and Golinkoff (1996). As its name suggests, the Coalition Model views grammar formation as the learner's response to a coalition of language-related input sources. Unlike the Competition Model, the Coalition Model admits certain innate knowledge that selectively guides the child to place various "weights" on different sources of input. On the Competition Model, the weights that the child assigns to different cues are strictly determined by the input. By contrast, the Coalition Model of Hirsh-Pasek and Golinkoff maintains that "[t]hese cues are *available* to the child at all times; however, they are not equally *accessible* to the child at different points in development" (p. 189).

On the Coalition Model, there are three different phases of language acquisition. These phases can be characterized according to children's "biases" to attend to different external cues: prosody provides the predominant cues for the child in phase I, semantic cues dominate in phase II, and syntactic cues dominate in phase III. At each phase, the primary source of linguistic knowledge is the environment:

> However, we have suggested that the mechanism for progress within each phase is guided distributional analysis. That is, first the child is primed to selectively attend to certain information *within* each domain that forms the coalition (e.g., prosody, syntax). Second, the child mines these selected inputs *across* domains to construct an interpretation of the linguistic stream and to build mental models. (p. 189) ... Children must learn to exploit the correlations that exist across (as well as within) domains.... (p. 190)

Knowledge of constraints develops in phase III, according to Hirsh-Pasek and Golinkoff. As far as we can tell, however, this knowledge too is based on experience. As the following quotation illustrates, the Coalition Model views the learning of complex syntax as a "discovery" process, in which the child is predisposed to notice co-occurring patterns in the input:

> Finally, in phase III, children learn to comprehend and produce language to represent more complex events that they may not have even witnessed, as well as multipropositional cross-clause constructions. Here, ..., children are biased to rely on *syntactic* cues (although other aspects of the coalition still influence their interpretation of what they hear). With increased capacity to hold more than one event in mind, they are motivated to learn about specific linguistic properties in their language.... (p. 187)

The Coalition Model differs from the Competition Model in that the child's disposition to attend to particular environmental cues changes over time; this is the concession to innateness made by the Coalition Model. It seems clear, however, that this model, like the Competition Model, embraces the fundamental assumptions of input matching and eschews the kind of innately specified linguistic knowledge hypothesized by the Modularity Matching Model.

Another example of the Input Matching Model is Cognitive Grammar, briefly described in chapter 3 (van Hoek 1995). According to this model, language development consists in the acquisition of schemas or templates, based on "exposure to actually-occurring expressions." Rosen and Rosen's (1995) proposal that children build "constructs" from their linguistic experience, rather than being guided by innate knowledge, is still another example of an Input Matching Model.

4.3 *The Competing Factors Model*

There is another view of the relation between mind and behavior. This alternative to the Modularity Matching Model views linguistic behavior as determined by a competition among different factors. According to some advocates of this model, linguistic knowledge is contained in a "module" that is separated from other factors that contribute to linguistic behavior. From the Competing Factors perspective, however, the language module does not have special status, such that its operations preempt the operations of other components. Instead, the principles of grammar can be offset to some degree by other forces contributing to behavior. Linguistic behavior is viewed as a conglomerate of "tendencies," such that the manifestation of knowledge of linguistic principles is seen to be a statistical tendency to act in conformity with these principles. We call this viewpoint the *Competing Factors Model*, represented as in figure 4.2.

It may help to provide examples of factors that are extraneous to the principles of Universal Grammar and yet contribute to linguistic behavior. Researchers commonly refer to "processing difficulties" or "performance factors." For example, Lust, Eisele, and Mazuka (1992) remark, "In the child, these factors may involve a host of independent behavioral and cognitive limitations" (p. 340); and Rosen and Rosen (1995) remark that "several types of methodological errors ... result from failing to recognize the multiplicity of influences on children's behavior" (p. 80). Occasionally, researchers make explicit proposals about the source of processing difficulties. One source of difficulties that has frequently been mentioned is the number of clauses contained in a sentence. It is commonly assumed that children experience greater difficulty

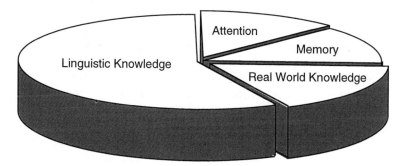

Figure 4.2
The Competing Factors Model

in processing two-clause constructions than in processing one-clause constructions (e.g., McDaniel and Maxfield 1992a, 668–669). To take another example, it has been claimed that processing difficulty increases with the number of (animate) NPs that appear in a sentence (Goodluck 1991, 175–176). It has been maintained that children also experience greater difficulty understanding sentences with three NPs than ones with two NPs (e.g., Goodluck and Tavakolian 1982).

Another factor that has been cited as contributing to children's processing difficulty is "carryover" effects—for example, the similarity of materials across experimental conditions. This, too, has been held responsible for children's errors in comprehension (Philip 1995, 109). As a final example, it has been suggested that young children attempt to interpret constructions in an "order-of-mention" fashion. In comprehending constructions with two clauses, for example, children appear to find it easier to interpret sentences in which the event mentioned in the first clause occurs first in the context. This accounts for the higher proportion of correct responses to sentences like (2) than to sentences like (1) (see Amidon and Carey 1972; Clark 1971; but cf. Crain 1982; Gorrell, Crain, and Fodor 1989).

(1) Before you touch your nose, touch your ears.

(2) After you touch your nose, touch your ears.

According to the Competing Factors Model, factors such as these all compete with children's linguistic knowledge in determining their linguistic behavior in an experimental task.

Proponents of the Modularity Matching Model readily admit that certain factors may sometimes impede the linguistic performance of both children and adults, albeit artifactually. It is easy to make a subject perform poorly (if the instructions to the task are not clear, if a subject is asked to perform two tasks at the same time, etc.). Moreover, there are specific linguistic properties that make some sentences more difficult to cope with than others. It is well known, for example, that adult language users cannot correctly understand deeply center-embedded sentences, in many instances. However, on the Modularity Matching Model children should only be subject to the same "processing difficulties" that curtail adult performance; if adults can process sentences with three animate NPs or sentences with two clauses, or if they are able to respond differently across trials despite being presented with similar materials, then children should be able to also, according to the Modularity Matching Model. It seems evident that adults have little, if any, difficulty interpreting two-clause sentences or ones with three animate NPs. If such sentences fall within the processing capacities of adults, then, by assumption, they should also fall within the processing capacities of children. The observation that children perform less well than adults on such sentences is inconsistent with the Modularity Matching Model, and the differences between children and adults must be explained.

Proponents of the Competing Factors Model cite another kind of factor as interfering with the demonstration of grammatical knowledge. This factor concerns the match between a sentence and the conversational context in which it is used. It is maintained that children (and, to a lesser extent, adults) have a bias to interpret any sentence so as to make it true in the discourse context. For ambiguous sentences, this bias toward interpreting sentences so as to fit the discourse context is eminently reasonable and is consistent with the Modularity Matching Model; however, on the

Competing Factors Model, the bias to make sentences true can also weigh against the interpretation given by grammatical principles for unambiguous sentences. If circumstances are such that a sentence is *not* true on the interpretation that is consistent with the grammatical principle, a conflict arises between grammaticality and the bias to assign a meaning that makes the sentence true in the conversational context. According to proponents of the Competing Factors Model, this conflict can inflate the proportion of errors by children; errors occur on trials where the bias to make a sentence true outweighs children's grammatical knowledge. Similarly, it has been maintained that children (and adults) commit errors in judging whether an answer is or is not appropriate to a question, because they "unconsciously change the word order of the question to match the answer" (McDaniel and McKee 1993, 288).

On the Competing Factors Model, all of these factors are assumed to sometimes suppress the proportion of children's correct responses in a task. This follows only if linguistic behavior is viewed as a probabilistic weighted sum. In the sum total of different probabilistic factors, the influence of factors extraneous to grammar is sometimes enough to make an ungrammatical structure acceptable for children (also see Lust, Eisele, and Mazuka 1992, 338; McDaniel and Maxfield 1992a). This would not happen on the Modularity Matching Model. According to this model, if children know a linguistic principle, then they should behave in conformity with it, just as adults do. In short, the fundamental difference between the Competing Factors Model and the Modularity Matching Model is that grammar has priority over other factors on the Modularity Matching Model; there is no notion of grammaticality in any absolute sense on the Competing Factors Model. Moreover, on the Modularity Matching Model, every child (and adult) is expected to perform perfectly, all things being equal. By contrast, on the Competing Factors Model, a subject's performance depends on the precise mix of contributing variables that influence linguistic behavior at different moments in time. Therefore, a subject's performance may vary from trial to trial; different subjects may perform more or less well; younger children may perform less well than older children; and so on.

4.4 Conclusion

The upshot of this chapter is that different models of language acquisition lead one to expect different patterns of responses by children in experimental tasks that are designed to assess their knowledge of linguistic principles. According to the Modularity Matching Model, children should abide by universal principles at all stages of development. Both children and adults should therefore perform without error on innately specified linguistic principles. If the Continuity Hypothesis is adopted, the differences between children and adults are confined to differences that appear across adult languages. Other divergence in the linguistic behavior of children and adults is not expected.

This contrasts with the predictions of the Input Matching Model and the Competing Factors Model. On the Input Matching Model, children's hypotheses are circumscribed by their experience to a much greater degree. Therefore, there should be a much closer match in the linguistic behavior of children and adults on the Input Matching Model. On the other hand, the Competing Factors Model, like the Modularity Matching Model, may assume that children have access to a grammatical "module." The grammatical module does not have special status (i.e., preempting other determinants of linguistic behavior) on the Competing Factors Model. This model therefore tolerates a much greater mismatch in the linguistic behavior of children and adults than does the Modularity Matching Model (or the Input Matching Model).

It should be understood that the divisions we have made among models of language development are somewhat artificial. For example, the Coalition Model is an Input Matching Model, but it can also be considered a variant of the Competing Factors Model. (According to the Coalition Model, the subsystems of cognition are highly interactive, rather than hierarchically organized.) It should also be understood that the divisions we have made tend to exaggerate differences among researchers who work within the same linguistic framework. As we have indicated, many researchers who adopt the generative enterprise, including its assumptions about innateness and even its assumptions about the modularity of the language faculty, are counted as advocating the Competing Factors Model. The reason is that these researchers adopt the methodological assumptions of that model, rather than the methodological assumptions of the Modularity Matching Model. Assuming the Competing Factors Model, many researchers employ tasks and research strategies that we would deem to be inappropriate for the study of child language within the generative framework. We view our criticisms of the work of these advocates of the Competing Factors Model as a dispute within the family. For this reason, we ignore the vast bulk of child language research, choosing instead to examine the studies of researchers who share our fundamental assumptions about the role of generative grammar in language development but who nevertheless adopt the research strategies of the Competing Factors Model.

We will defend a different set of methodological assumptions, which we believe to be more consistent with the theory of Universal Grammar. We hope to convince those researchers who adopt the basic assumptions of generative grammar that it is also necessary for them to adopt a corresponding set of methodological assumptions in assessing children's linguistic knowledge and to abandon the methodological assumptions of the Competing Factors Model. The argument relies on an explicit statement of the interrelations of grammatical knowledge and performance factors (e.g., short-term memory and extralinguistic knowledge). On the Competing Factors Model, both grammatical knowledge and these and other performance factors contribute to linguistic behavior. On the Modularity Matching Model, grammatical knowledge does not compete with these performance factors on most occasions. Before we examine the differences between these two models more closely, we take a brief excursion to point out some empirical problems with the Input Matching Model and to indicate where the linguistic behavior of children and adults may differ, according to the Modularity Matching Model.

Chapter 5

Continuity versus Input Matching

In conjunction with crosslinguistic research, the study of children's linguistic knowledge is a special source of evidence for deciding whether or not a principle of the theory of Universal Grammar is a viable candidate as a linguistic universal (i.e., likely to be innately specified). As mentioned earlier, one hallmark of innateness is mastery in the absence of experience. Because young children's experience is more limited than that of older children and adults, they can offer relevant data bearing on the "nature/nurture" controversy. Clearly, too, different children encounter different input. This observation leads us to expect different children to adopt different hypotheses, assuming that they are basing their hypotheses on experience. On the other hand, if all children in a linguistic community adopt the same linguistic hypotheses, then we can infer that language development is guided by innate principles, and not by learning-theoretic mechanisms.

The most compelling evidence of innateness probably comes from the observation that children sometimes make nonadult grammatical hypotheses. The Modularity Matching Model readily accepts that children's grammars may differ from those of adults. There are heavy constraints on the different forms that children's grammars can take, however. The model adopts the Continuity Hypothesis—the claim that children's developing grammars can differ from the adult grammar of the linguistic community only in ways in which adult grammars can differ from each other (e.g., Crain 1991; Pinker 1984). According to the Modularity Matching Model, there is one further source of differences in performance between children and adults. Children's nonadult behavior may be derived from the one module that children and adults do not share, the LAD.[1] In chapter 14, we consider how certain nonadult interpretations by children can arise from a principle of the LAD—a principle that governs language development. We postpone that discussion in order to develop the point in detail.

The present chapter offers additional evidence against the Input Matching Model. The evidence consists of children's nonadult linguistic behavior. First we discuss children's nonadult utterances that were discovered using the elicited production task. Then we present evidence of children's nonadult assignments of meanings to sentences that were discovered using the truth value judgment task.

5.1 The Medial-Wh

One source of evidence against the Input Matching Model is based on children's nonadult (but Universal Grammar–compatible) questions. This is the so-called medial-*wh* phenomenon. Using the elicited production task, it was found that some English-speaking children around the age of 3 or 4 consistently insert an "extra" *wh*-word in their long-distance questions, as illustrated in (1) (Thornton 1990; Thornton and Crain 1994).

(1) What do you think what pigs eat?

The appearance of the medial-*wh* in the language of children learning English cannot be explained as children's response to the input. Although these constructions are not grammatically well formed in English, structures like (1) are attested in dialects of German and other languages. Interestingly, even after the medial *wh*-phrase is expunged from children's object extraction questions, it persists in their subject extraction questions. This developmental sequence is consistent with the theory of Universal Grammar. As suggested by Thornton (1990), for example, the extra *wh*-phrase in certain kinds of children's questions may be an overt manifestation of a process that appears in French, for example, in the familiar *que/qui* alternation (Rizzi 1990). English-speaking children's nonadult productions therefore support the Continuity Hypothesis, since both the structures themselves and the course of their development fall within the boundaries established by the theory of Universal Grammar. The medial-*wh* phenomenon constitutes a serious challenge to the Input Matching Model, however.

To conclude this discussion of the medial-*wh* phenomenon, we would add three comments about the nature of children's nonadult productions. First, not all children produce medial *wh*-phrases. Only about one-third of the children we have interviewed produce questions of this form. This shows that there are several possible paths leading from the initial state to the final state of grammar formation. It also eliminates certain explanations of the findings (e.g., accounts based on the maturation of linguistic knowledge). Second, the period during which these children produce medial *wh*-questions persists for several months, perhaps for years. Finally, the explanations that have been offered for grammatical change—that is, for the transition from medial *wh*-questions to adultlike questions—are based on the assumption that negative evidence is not available to children (see chapter 4 and chapter 22).

5.2 Repetition of the Auxiliary

The second example of children's nonadult productions is children's negative questions. It was discovered by Thornton (1993) that children even as old as 5 often form nonadult negative *wh*-object and *wh*-adjunct extraction questions, and nonadult negative yes/no questions. Thus, they ask *wh*-questions like (2b) instead of the adult (2a), and they ask yes/no questions like (3b) instead of the adult (3a) (also see Guasti, Thornton, and Wexler 1995).

(2) a. What doesn't Big Bird like?
     b. What does Big Bird doesn't like?

(3) a. Doesn't Grover like the ice cream?
     b. Does Grover doesn't like the ice cream?

(4) a. What can't Elmo jump over?
     b. What can Elmo can't jump over?
     c. What does Elmo can't jump over?

The (b) and (c) forms in (2)–(4) do not occur in adult English. Of course, there is no a priori reason to expect that children's grammatical hypotheses will be closely tied to their linguistic experience. Not only is the existence of nonadult grammatical structures consistent with Universal Grammar, it can be argued that some of children's nonadult utterances are strong evidence that they are following Universal Grammar. Accordingly, it has been argued that children's negative questions are Universal Grammar–compatible (Thornton 1993; Guasti, Thornton, and Wexler 1995). Although we are not aware of an exact parallel to these negative questions in any other language (besides child English), the process could be related to a doubling construction in the Paduan dialect of Italian, for example (see Guasti, Thornton, and Wexler 1995). On the other hand, children's nonadult questions illustrate another instance in which their grammatical hypotheses are not tied to their primary linguistic data. As such, they pose another challenge for the Input Matching Model.

5.3 The Nature of Wh-Phrases

In recent research on *wh*-questions, linguists distinguish "full" *wh*-phrases (i.e., ones with lexical content, such as *which boys* or *whose food*) and "bare" *wh*-phrases (i.e., ones without lexical content, such as *who* or *what*). The structural properties of children's sentences differ depending on the nature of the *wh*-phrase. For example, in a study of 7 children, using an elicited production task, Thornton (1995) found that 4 children sometimes produced different sentence structures with full *wh*-phrases and bare *wh*-phrases, although the questions were evoked in the same contexts.

The *wh*-questions elicited from children all contained negation. The *wh*-questions with bare *wh*-phrases extracted from object position evoked an "auxiliary-doubling" construction, as illustrated in (5). The auxiliary-doubling structure also appeared in children's questions with full *wh*-phrases; but another structure appeared as well. In children's questions with full *wh*-phrases, an overt *that* complementizer sometimes appeared, as in (6). The complementizer never appeared in children's questions with bare *wh*-phrases, however.[2]

    (5)   What does the Spaceman doesn't like?

    (6)   What food that the Spaceman doesn't like?

Since the structural differences that were observed arose in the same discourse context, they must be imposed by children's grammars. In this case, Thornton suggested that the syntactic component is responsible, with full and bare *wh*-phrases moving to different positions in the structural representations assigned by these children. The theoretical controversy surrounding the nature of these different types of *wh*-phrases is discussed in chapter 23.

5.4 Split Whose-N Questions

In adult English, a full *wh*-phrase in a *wh*-question always moves as a whole to sentence-initial position, as in (7).

    (7)   Whose elephant do you think jumped the best?

Even though the input provides only questions like (7), not all children learning English seem to know that the noun inside a *whose*-N phrase (e.g., *whose elephant*) must be "pied-piped" along with the *wh*-operator *who* and the possessive marker *'s*.

In an elicited production study with 12 child subjects, Thornton and Gavruseva (1996) found 3 children who consistently failed to pied-pipe the noun in forming long-distance *whose*-N questions. Some examples of these children's productions are given in (8).

(8) a. Who do you think's elephant jumped the best?
         (Adult: Whose elephant do you think jumped the best?)
     b. Who do you think's porridge Pocahontas tried?
         (Adult: Whose porridge do you think Pocahontas tried?)

Other kinds of *wh*-phrases are not broken apart in these children's *wh*-questions. For example, *wh*-phrases with the *wh*-operator *which* remain intact in their long-distance questions, as (9) illustrates. (The symbol # indicates that this kind of sentence form is not attested, as far as we know.)

(9) a.   Which dog do you think the boy took for a walk?
     b.   #Which do you think dog the boy took for a walk?

Moreover, *wh*-phrases with the *wh*-operator *whose* also remain intact in the *matrix* *wh*-questions of these children. Example (10) illustrates.

(10) a.   Whose dog do you like?
     b.   #Who do you like's dog?

The 3 children from Thornton and Gavruseva's study apparently hypothesize that the *wh*-word *who* alone is fronted in long-distance questions with possessive *whose*-N phrases. It turns out that there are languages that allow the *wh*-operator 'who' to be extracted out of a possessive NP. Hungarian is one well-documented case (see Szabolcsi 1994). The split-question forms in (8) suggest that in the grammar of these English-speaking children, the *wh*-operator *who* can move out of a possessive NP, although the possibility of extraction is restricted to long-distance questions. The nonadult question forms produced by English-speaking children are therefore compatible with Universal Grammar. Because this phenomenon is a matter of parametric variation, it is consistent with the Modularity Matching Model. It poses a further challenge, however, to the Input Matching Model.

5.5 Implications for Input Matching

The Input Matching Model would be hard pressed to provide an alternative account of the production data reported in this chapter. What must be explained is why children insert extra *wh*-elements into their long-distance questions, as in (1), and why they insert an extra auxiliary into their negative questions, as in (2)–(4). It is noteworthy that several of these nonadult forms involve the *insertion* of material, rather than its deletion (chapter 21 discusses the tendency by both children and adults to use reduced forms). Moreover, the Input Matching Model is hard pressed to explain why some children split full *wh*-phrases like *whose porridge* into *who*, *'s*, and *porridge* in forming long-distance *wh*-questions like (8), moving only the *wh*-operator *who* to sentence-initial position.

One way to salvage the Input Matching Model would be to allow the contents of two templates to overlap.[3] For example, consider how a template for an "auxiliary-doubling" question like (11) (= (5)) could be formed. Its formation would combine the template for a *wh*-question like *What does the Spaceman like?* and the template for one of its declarative counterparts, for example, *The Spaceman doesn't like beans*. The process is illustrated in (12). In fact, this process does not yield the kind of question forms that children actually produce (i.e., (11)). Rather, it would yield the ungrammatical question in (13). This kind of question, with a "moved" *wh*-phrase but with an N left behind, is not attested as far as we know (see Crain and Fodor 1987; but also see Wilson and Peters 1984). As noted, the kind of *wh*-question in (13) is not produced by those children who split *whose*-N phrases in long-distance *wh*-questions.

(11)   What does the Spaceman doesn't like?

(12)   a.   what does the Spaceman like
      b.   the Spaceman doesn't like beans

(13)   What does the Spaceman doesn't like beans?

Unless some other way can be found to explain children's medial *wh*-questions, their "auxiliary-doubling" negative questions, and their split *wh*-phrases in long-distance questions with *whose*-N, these examples of nonadult productions by English-speaking children appear problematic for the Input Matching Model. We suggest that they arise simply because children have not yet converged on the final state, the adult grammatical system.

5.6 Continuity in Semantics: *Donkey Sentences*

So far in this chapter, we have presented three instances of children's nonadult productions that are unexpected on the Input Matching Model. In section 5.7, we continue our case against the Input Matching Model, using evidence from children's comprehension of sentences. The findings from children's acquisition of semantics are important for another reason. The fact that children and adults understand certain sentences differently reveals a virtue in the study of child language; it shows how child language can be informative about basic linguistic principles. As we will show, it turns out that children sometimes draw linguistic distinctions even more clearly than adults do. This state of affairs arises from the following considerations. First, adult judgments about the alternative interpretations of (ambiguous) sentences may be easily manipulated by real-world knowledge and beliefs. Real-world knowledge requires real-world experiences, and these take time to gather. Because children have only limited experience, they have more limited pragmatic resources than adults do. To the extent that adults come to rely on real-world knowledge and beliefs in making decisions about the interpretation of ambiguous sentences, they may have lost contact with certain syntactic and semantic distinctions that remain available to children. This makes children's judgments potentially more revealing than those of adults regarding the contributions of syntactic and semantic principles (as opposed to pragmatic principles) in deriving the representations of sentences.[4]

The present example concerns the interpretation of so-called *donkey* sentences. There are two types of *donkey* sentences. One type contains a universal quantifier, which has scope over a relative clause, as in (14); the second type is a conditional, either with no overt quantifier or with an adverb of quantification, such as *always*, as in (15). Notice that (15) has the same interpretation with or without the adverb.

(14) *Relative clause*
Every farmer who owns a donkey feeds it.

(15) *Conditional*
If a farmer owns a donkey, he (always) feeds it.

Both types of *donkey* sentences admit of two interpretations, called the *strong* and the *weak* reading. On the strong reading, (14) and (15) are true only if every farmer feeds every donkey that he owns. On the weak interpretation, each farmer must feed at least one of the donkeys he owns; he may feed them all, but this is not necessary for the sentence to be true.

Beginning with Heim 1982 and Kamp 1981, and continuing through current versions of Discourse Representation Theory (e.g., Kamp and Reyle 1993), linguistic analyses of *donkey* sentences have had two main goals. One goal has been to provide a semantics that assigns the same truth conditions to both relative-clause *donkey* sentences like (14) and conditional *donkey* sentences like (15). A second goal has been to ensure that the truth conditions for sentences of both kinds correspond to the strong reading, according to which every farmer feeds every donkey that he owns (also see Groenendijk and Stokhof 1991).

Chierchia (1995) has questioned both of these goals. On Chierchia's account, relative-clause *donkey* sentences are interpreted using the same mechanisms of *dynamic binding* that underlie discourse anaphora (e.g., the relation between an indefinite NP in one sentence and a pronoun in a later sentence). According to Chierchia's theory, these mechanisms establish the weak interpretation for relative-clause *donkey* sentences like (14), which is true if all of the farmers feed at least one of the donkeys they own. By contrast, the interpretation of conditional *donkey* sentences like (15) is not primarily determined by the mechanisms of dynamic binding but, to a larger degree, is influenced by pragmatic factors, the strong interpretation being more readily available in many cases.

If there are distinctions to be drawn between relative-clause and conditional *donkey* sentences, as Chierchia suggests, then children may draw them more clearly than do adults, for the reasons cited above. On the Input Matching Model, by contrast, children would not be expected to make fine distinctions about sentences like these, which are surely not abundant in the primary linguistic data.

Children's understanding of both relative-clause and conditional *donkey* sentences was investigated in a series of experiments designed in collaboration with Laura Conway (Conway 1997; Conway and Crain 1995a,b; Crain, Conway and Thornton 1994). In the main experiment, children were presented with either a relative clause or a conditional *donkey* sentence in a context that was consistent with the weak reading, but not the strong reading.

The findings support Chierchia's theory of dynamic binding. First, children did not interpret relative-clause *donkey* sentences like (14) and conditional *donkey* sentences like (15) in the same way; as a group, children rejected the weak reading of conditional *donkey* sentences significantly more often than they rejected the weak reading of relative-clause *donkey* sentences. As individuals, children tell an even more interesting story. Some children consistently rejected the weak reading of conditional *donkey* sentences, but no children behaved in this fashion in response to relative-clause *donkey* sentences.

If we interpret these findings as evidence that young children initially assign the weak reading to relative-clause *donkey* sentences, then this is evidence that children's earliest hypothesis corresponds to the dispreferred option for adults (if we accept the claim in the literature that adults prefer the strong reading for both types of *donkey* sentences). It is evidence, therefore, against the Input Matching Model.

5.7 *Inalienable Possession*

Further evidence of children's nonadult linguistic analyses was uncovered in Conway and Crain's study of *donkey* sentences. The *donkey* sentences in that study were divided along an interesting semantic dimension. On half of the trials, including both relative-clause and conditional *donkey* sentences, the nature of the relation between the possessor and the object of possession was one of *inalienable* possession. An example of inalienable possession is the relation between parents and their offspring, as in (16) (or the relation between a car and its engine, a table and its legs, etc.). In contrast to this relation is the kind of possession expressed in sentences like (17). Because the relation between men and snowplows is not one of inalienable possession, let us call relations of this kind *alienable* possession. (A syntactic analysis of the distinction between alienable and inalienable possession is given in Hornstein, Rosen, and Uriagereka 1995.)

(16)   Every frog who has a baby takes it to the pond.

(17)   Every man who has a snowplow uses it to push snow.

Roughly half of the children (8/15) gave different responses to relative-clause *donkey* sentences depending on the relation between the possessor and the object of possession. For relative-clause *donkey* sentences, if the sentence involved inalienable possession, as in (16), these children rejected the weak reading. By contrast, if the sentence involved alienable possession, as in (17), these children accepted the weak reading. No child exhibited this distinction when the target sentences were conditional *donkey* sentences, however. With conditionals, children tended to either reject all of the test sentences, or accept them all. Adults we have interviewed on the same stimulus materials appear to be totally unaware of the alienable/inalienable distinction in interpreting *donkey* sentences of either kind. If so, then it is unlikely that this distinction is manifested in the input to children. Therefore, the Input Matching Model would be hard pressed to account for this aspect of children's linguistic behavior.

This experiment reveals an interesting difference between children and adults. Because adults come to rely heavily on real world knowledge in making decisions about the interpretation of ambiguous sentences, they apparently lose certain syntactic and semantic distinctions that remain available to children. Having accrued a sizable body of knowledge about the world, adults appear to assign sentences interpretations that are consistent with their experience. Because children have less real-world knowledge, their judgments appear to be more revealing with respect to the underlying contributions of syntactic and semantic principles in the derivation of linguistic representations. Being less contaminated by experience, children may occasionally manifest grammatical distinctions that are masked in adult performance by their wealth of extralinguistic knowledge.

5.8 Conclusion

This chapter illustrated linguistic phenomena that are difficult to reconcile with the Input Matching Model. This ends our case against the model. We now take up a different alternative to the Modularity Matching Model, namely, the Competing Factors Model. Although we disagree with several fundamental methodological assumptions of the Competing Factors Model, it remains the currently received view. Our arguments against it consume the greater part of the next seven chapters.

Chapter 6
The Competing Factors Model

According to the Modularity Matching Model, both children and adults should perform flawlessly in accessing their linguistic knowledge, all things being equal. Of course, not all things are equal when linguistic knowledge is being investigated experimentally. For example, there are sources of "noise" in any psychological task: subjects may not understand the instructions, they may be confused by the task, they may lack interest, and so on. This makes it difficult to devise a numerical test to reveal what proportion of "error" (i.e., noise) is acceptable in the assessment of linguistic knowledge. According to the Modularity Matching Model, the proper research strategy is to design linguistic tasks that hold the influence of these extraneous task demands to a minimum.

It is the purpose of this book to explain how to eliminate the influence of such factors in assessing children's linguistic competence. With extraneous task demands held in check, there should be little deviation from 100% correct performance (assuming that the subjects have the requisite linguistic knowledge). Occasionally, a small amount of experimental noise creeps in, even in studies that follow the methodological prescription we advise. As a rule of thumb, however, we suggest that if children's performance is not at least 90% accurate, then the researcher is obliged to identify the particular source of error (Crain and Fodor 1984).

6.1 Competing Factors

In chapter 5, we introduced an alternative view of the relation between mind and behavior, the *Competing Factors Model*. From the perspective of this model, no single component of the language apparatus has privileged access to the linguistic input. In particular, the principles of grammar do not take precedence over other forces that contribute to behavior. On the Competing Factors Model, linguistic behavior is assumed to be an aggregate of factors, of which linguistic knowledge is only one. Therefore, the manifestation of knowledge of linguistic principles is observed only as a statistical tendency for subjects to behave in conformity with the principles. As Lust, Chien, and Flynn (1987) put it:

> [P]erformance will never directly reflect only grammatical competence, but other factors as well. It will always be variable, even when it reflects grammatical competence. Thus we will assume that critical experimental data consists of *a pattern and range of behavioral variance* which is constrained by experimental factors to a degree significantly above chance. Such significantly constrained variance will be taken as evidence that children are accessing this aspect of their grammatical competence in the task. Thus, because of the nature of performance data,

behavioral evidence for significant grammatical factors will always involve significant contrasts of degree, not absolute success with one condition and absolute failure with another. (p. 282)

It is worth drawing out the predictions of the Competing Factors Model in more detail. As the quotation from Lust, Chien, and Flynn makes clear, this model anticipates "variance" in performance in any experimental task, rather than all-or-none linguistic behavior on at least certain tasks, as anticipated by the Modularity Matching Model. The quotation also makes another assumption of the Competing Factors Model clear: that linguistic competence is revealed by above-chance performance in experimental tasks.

There is more to say about the "nature of performance data" according to the Competing Factors Model. Most importantly, the distribution of scores should be unimodal.[1] By assumption, every subject is influenced by the same constellation of competing factors. Therefore, differences among subjects should be only a matter of degree. From a statistical point of view, the pattern of responses should approximate a normal distribution. In a normal distribution, the numerical scores given to individuals (i.e., the observations or data points) form a symmetrical "curve." This "bell-shaped" curve centers around some average (or mean) level of performance, such that observations taper off gradually in both directions away from the mean.

Any individual observation in a range of observations is taken to represent some "true" component of behavior, plus an "error" component, due to extraneous factors. In an experiment designed to investigate children's linguistic knowledge, the true component is linguistic performance that conforms to the principle under investigation; other factors contributing to behavior make up the error component. The magnitude of the error establishes a "gravitational field" for the true component. This field keeps the mean from skyrocketing, by pushing the true component to one side or the other, with equal likelihood. The result is a normal, unimodal distribution with a single peak or mode, as in figure 6.1. In the figure, the horizontal axis gives the percentage of correct responses on the hypothetical measure taken of a linguistic principle. The vertical axis gives the frequency of observations (e.g., by individual subjects) at varying points along the horizontal axis. The mean in figure 6.1 is roughly between 50% and 75% correct; the majority of observations fall within these boundaries, and the frequency of responses diminishes according to how far they deviate from the mean. According to the Competing Factors Model, if the effect of the true component (grammatical knowledge) is significantly above chance, then it can be inferred that the group as a whole knows the grammatical principle under investigation.

In addition to grammatical knowledge, which accounts for the "center of gravity" in the distribution of observed scores, each observation is influenced to some degree by various "unknown" factors. These extraneous factors cause the dispersion of scores in both directions away from the mean. Responses should vary only probabilistically (randomly) from the central tendency, however, so there should be a single "group" behavior.[2] The Competing Factors Model would not expect two patterns of behavior within a group of children or a group of adults; it would not expect a *bimodal* distribution, either by children or by adults. A bimodal distribution is illustrated in figure 6.2.

There is another expectation of the Competing Factors Model that is not shared by the Modularity Matching Model. On the Competing Factors Model, children's

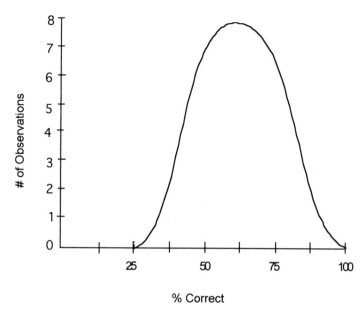

Figure 6.1
A unimodal distribution

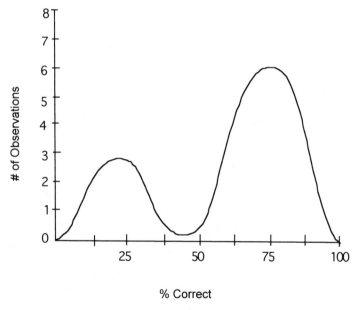

Figure 6.2
A bimodal distribution

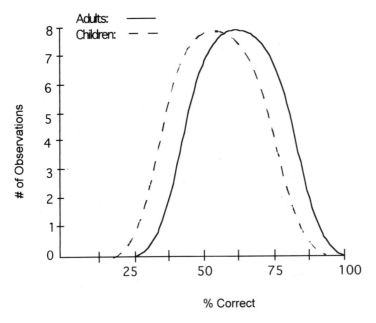

Figure 6.3
Predicted distributions of responses to crossover questions by children and adults, according to the Competing Factors Model

responses can differ from those of adults. The differences may even be statistically significant. This can happen because the precise mix of competing factors may be different for children than it is for adults, according to the model. Two factors on which children are seen to differ from adults are frequently mentioned in the literature: working memory and extralinguistic knowledge. It is widely held that children perform less successfully than adults because of their greater limitations on working memory. We evaluate this assumption in chapter 12. It is also widely believed that children perform less successfully than adults in comprehending sentences because children's linguistic analyses are more heavily influenced by general knowledge of the world. This claim is evaluated in chapter 13.

On the Competing Factors Model, these assumptions play out as follows. Even when both children and adults know the grammatical principle under investigation, there may be a *quantitative* difference in the pattern of responses by the two groups. The difference in the distributions of children's scores and adults' scores should boil down to a different "balance point." Although the factors contributing to error are rarely explicated, one thing is certain: they should be *similar* for all subjects within each group. If children's behavior differs from adults' only quantitatively, as the Competing Factors Model maintains, then the distribution of observations made by children in an experiment should retain the same "bell-shaped" curve that characterizes the distribution of observations made by adults. Figure 6.3 depicts the general pattern of responses that is expected on the Competing Factors Model.

The Competing Factors Model anticipates that the linguistic behavior of both children and adults will conform to a normal distribution. In the nineteenth century, it was generally held that the traits of all living organisms formed a normal distribution.

Although this view has been largely discredited, the statistical use of the normal distribution has continued unabated, because the assumption of a normal distribution permits one to make inferences about the population from which observations are drawn. For our purposes, it is important to recognize that the normal distribution continues to be the basis of the statistics used in investigations of children's linguistic knowledge. In chapter 7, we indicate how assuming a normal distribution can lead to erroneous inferences about children's linguistic competence.

We should add a brief disclaimer. The present discussion assumes that the linguistic knowledge under investigation is a universal principle of grammar. It is under this assumption that the Competing Factors Model anticipates a unimodal distribution of responses by both children and adults, with adults differing from children only quantitatively. If we shift the empirical question—say, to the acquisition of constructions that are subject to parametric variation—then the expectations of the Competing Factors Model would also shift. In the case of parameter setting, for example, the pattern of responses by children and adults could be qualitatively different, with adults showing a unimodal distribution of responses and children showing a bimodal distribution, assuming that the parameter had two values and that children with each setting were sampled. From a statistical point of view, however, the pattern of responses by children and adults should continue to approximate a normal distribution. In the case of parameters, children's responses would take the form of normal distributions around each mode.

6.2 Remarks on Statistics

Our position should not be construed as implying that we totally reject the use of statistics in research on language acquisition. Statistics are essential, for example, when linguistic knowledge is assessed in tasks that use nondiscrete measurements of behavior. The preferential looking paradigm is one example (see chapter 7 and Hirsh-Pasek and Golinkoff 1996). In this task, the data that are gathered are differences in the amount of time children spend attending to one or another visual display (on television monitors). Data from such measures should approximate a normal distribution. It is therefore appropriate to analyze the data using parametric statistics.[3]

Statistical tests may also be useful in ascertaining which of two readings of an ambiguous sentence is preferred by children or adults. Making such assessments is not trivial, however. For concreteness, let us suppose that we are making the assessment using a truth value judgment task. Here is how we would proceed. The experiment would be conducted in two parts. In one part of the experiment, meaning$_1$ would be true of the context, and meaning$_2$ would be false; in the second part, meaning$_2$ would be true, and meaning$_1$ false. Having conducted both parts of the experiment, we would be in a position to determine whether or not there was a statistically significant difference in the proportion of affirmative responses by subjects to meaning$_1$ (using data from the first part of the experiment) as compared to the proportion of affirmative responses to meaning$_2$ (using data from the second part). If there were significantly more affirmative responses to one reading than the other, then the conclusion would be warranted that children prefer the reading that evoked the greater proportion of affirmative responses (provided that the usual assumptions underlying the use of the particular statistical test were satisfied—for example, that both subjects and items were randomly selected).[4]

Statistical tests are also used to decide if two ambiguous sentences are analyzed in the same way. For example, as pointed out in chapter 5, there are two types of *donkey* sentences: relative-clause *donkey* sentences, such as (1), and conditional *donkey* sentences, such as (2).

(1) *Relative clause*
Every farmer who owns a donkey feeds it.

(2) *Conditional*
If a farmer owns a donkey, he (always) feeds it.

As noted, *donkey* sentences of both types admit of two interpretations: the strong reading and the weak reading. On the strong reading, every farmer feeds every donkey that he owns; on the weak reading, every farmer feeds at least one of his donkeys. Chapter 5 discussed two theories of *donkey* anaphora. According to one, both types of *donkey* sentence have the same truth conditions, corresponding to the strong reading (e.g., Heim 1982; Kamp and Reyle 1995). According to the other, the weak reading is basic for relative-clause *donkey* sentences, but the strong interpretation is basic for conditional *donkey* sentences (Chierchia 1992, 1995). To evaluate these competing accounts, Conway and Crain (1995a,b) presented children with *donkey* sentences of both kinds in contexts that were consistent only with the weak reading. Children were asked to indicate whether the test sentence matched the context. Applying a statistical test, Conway and Crain found that children accepted the weak reading significantly more often for relative-clause *donkey* sentences than for conditional *donkey* sentences, as predicted by the second theoretical account.

According to the Modularity Matching Model, these uses of statistics are appropriate because (a) the observations obtained from subjects are nondiscrete, as in the preferential looking paradigm, or (b) the observations concern ambiguous sentences. Statistics are inappropriate, according to this model, when the observations concern unambiguous sentences. For example, children's knowledge of constraints is expected to be nearly perfect, if the Modularity Matching Model is correct—it is not expected to be simply at some above-chance level of performance. That is, children are not expected to contract the verbal elements *want* and *to* in (3), and they are expected to consistently reject coreference in (4).

(3) *Who does Arnold wanna make breakfast?

(4) *He danced while the Ninja Turtle ate pizza.

At this point, it would be premature to attempt to explain the reasons behind these predictions of the Modularity Matching Model. However, we felt that we should flag these points about the use of statistics in anticipation of that discussion.

6.3 Comparing the Models

Admittedly, the Modularity Matching Model may be incorrect. Perhaps Lust, Eisele, and Mazuka (1992) are correct in assuming that subjects must "consult pragmatic context" (p. 353) and other factors in all behavioral tasks and in assuming that they do not base their responses primarily on grammatical knowledge, as the Modularity Matching Model claims. It may also turn out that there are differences in the linguistic behavior of children and adults that derive from sources within the language-processing system. For example, verbal working memory may undergo maturation. If so, the Modularity Matching Model would have to be adjusted to reflect the observed differences between children and adults. However, if children and/or adults perform poorly because they succumb to competing factors—that is, if their performance is not dictated by grammatical knowledge—then this finding would be evidence against the Modularity Matching Model.[5]

It is even possible that the patterns of observations for children and adults will prove to be qualitatively different. Instead of approximating a normal distribution, the observations made by children could turn out to be better characterized by a different class of distributions. If so, the observed differences in the patterns of responses by children and adults could be attributed to processing mechanisms, in accord with the Competing Factors Model. As we noted, however, processing explanations of observed differences between children and adults should be advanced with caution. If the processing system of a child has radically different properties from that of an adult, then the question of learnability arises: namely, how does the child attain the adult processing system?

The Modularity Matching Model skirts the problem of learnability entirely, by assuming equivalence between the mental architecture of children and that of adults. We take this to be the Null Hypothesis. By contrast, most researchers in language acquisition assume the Competing Factors Model as the Null Hypothesis. For example, consider the following statement by Lust, Eisele, and Mazuka (1992):

> Behavioral research must assume that data derived from experimental tasks are modulated to some degree (at least chance) by performance factors. Just as in adults, these factors must be expected to produce variation in children's group data.... This fact motivates the use of large samples and statistical analysis in behavioral research. (p. 340)

The Modularity Matching Model accepts the first proposition—that all tasks are susceptible to "noise." By chance, a child will make the occasional error, regardless of how tightly controlled an experiment is. However, these chance errors do not arise because performance factors are invariably at odds with grammatical knowledge; they arise because the child subject gets distracted, or fails to pay close attention to some event, and so on. As indicated, we expect only about 5% to 10% of such errors by children in response to unambiguous sentences. If errors occur more often than 10% of the time, they should not be chalked up simply to "noise"; in our view, there is something to explain.[6]

The Modularity Matching Model rejects the second proposition—that performance factors necessarily introduce variance in all experimental tasks, so much so that the experimenter's only recourse is to use statistical tests of group data. According to the Modularity Matching Model, grammatical principles are used preemptively in language processing; they are not "modulated" by performance factors in most instances. Only rarely will task demands or grammatical complexity make excessive demands on the resources of the language-processing system; in such cases, of course, production or comprehension will be curtailed. Ordinarily, however, critical thresholds in processing are not exceeded, so linguistic behavior is expected to approach 100% accuracy. Aside from the minimal intrusion of "noise," linguistic performance will be 100% accurate if appropriate experimental precautions have been followed. On the Modularity Matching Model, a child who knows the grammatical principles under investigation will rarely make an error, so children as a group will respond with over 90% accuracy. There is one exception. If subjects are confronted with ambiguous sentences, then it is "accurate" for them to respond according to any of its interpretations. In such cases, statistical tests may be useful in evaluating subjects' behavior. According to the Modularity Matching Model, however, statistical tests of group data are usually unnecessary for unambiguous sentences.

6.4 Areas of Convergence

According to the Competing Factors Model, knowledge of a linguistic principle is observed as a tendency to behave in conformity with the principle. On this model, extraneous factors compete with linguistic knowledge and often mask it. To conclude that children know a principle, therefore, it is sufficient to observe above-chance performance in experimental tests of children's performance. Moreover, quantitative differences between children and adults are anticipated because children's performance is more likely to be impeded by these extraneous factors, because children are believed to have more severe limitations on working memory and a greater bias to analyze sentences according to their extralinguistic knowledge. On the alternative model, Modularity Matching, children should generally perform as well as adults, because children are assumed to "match" adults in processing capacity and in processing routines. In chapter 7, we critically review some findings from the literature that seem to be consistent with the Competing Factors Model and inconsistent with the Modularity Matching Model.

There are circumstances in which the Modularity Matching Model and the Competing Factors Model make similar predictions, however. In these circumstances, "performance" factors play a role in language processing, even according to the Modularity Matching Model. First, performance factors are brought into play when children (and adults) are confronted with sentences that are structurally ambiguous and when these sentences are evaluated in circumstances that are consistent with a range of interpretive options. Although such circumstances are probably rare in real life, it is essential to the design of many psycholinguistic studies to construct contexts that are appropriate for more than one meaning of a sentence. In such cases, the Competing Factors Model and the Modularity Matching Model make similar assumptions about the interpretation of children's responses to ambiguous sentences.

When principles of linguistic theory make multiple representations available for a sentence, the human sentence-processing device (i.e., the parser) may attempt to resolve the ambiguity by engaging the services of real-world knowledge, for example. On the Modularity Matching Model, however, specific context supersedes extralinguistic knowledge. If the specific context surrounding a sentence supports one reading, but not any others, then that reading will be selected regardless of its a priori plausibility. We will return to this point in chapter 12.

There is another factor that has been found to exert influence in resolving ambiguities in such special circumstances. We mentioned the idea that the sentence-processing system attempts to access a linguistic analysis that makes the sentence true in the discourse context. On the Modularity Matching Model, this "tendency" is manifested in resolving ambiguities. This results in a bias to say "Yes" to either reading of an ambiguous sentence in contexts that are compatible with both interpretations. The perceiver assumes that the speaker intends to say something that is true in the domain of discourse; accordingly, the perceiver attempts to analyze an ambiguous sentence in a way that makes it express a true proposition. It is important to appreciate, however, that this bias to say "Yes" can be overruled by other factors that exert pressure on the selection of one reading of an ambiguous sentence over the others. In many studies, it has been found that children will say "No" as often as 50% of the time, or even more often when the "No" response is associated with the preferred interpretation of an ambiguous sentence.

If there is more than one means of expressing a particular message, then still other factors may influence someone's choice among the options made available by the grammar. For example, the complementizer is optional in many constructions; therefore, it may appear only occasionally in the production of these structures. Similarly, the "*by* phrase" can be omitted from the verbal passive construction in many circumstances (as Ronald Reagan made clear when he declared that "Mistakes were made" in the exchange of weapons for hostages during his administration). A similar tendency to use "reduced" forms leads speakers of English to contract the verbal elements *want* and *to*, to form *wanna*, where contraction is not prohibited by any linguistic principle. In short, performance factors (including the a priori plausibility of the message) may intrude on linguistic processing in selecting among alternative grammatical representations, both on the Competing Factors Model and on the Modularity Matching Model.

6.5 Conclusion

To sum up, the Competing Factors Model and the Modularity Matching Model make similar predictions about the interpretation of ambiguous sentences. On both accounts, the bias to accept what one hears as true, and the inherent preference for a particular interpretation of a sentence over another, are key ingredients in a person's response. The Competing Factors Model and the Modularity Matching Model make different predictions about the interpretation of unambiguous sentences, however. On the Competing Factors Model, the same factors that influence people's decisions about the preferred interpretation of an ambiguous sentence also impinge on their decisions about the interpretation of unambiguous sentences. None of these factors weigh in the processing of most unambiguous sentences, however, on the Modularity Matching Model. If only one interpretation can be assigned to a sentence in a particular context, then it will be assigned, regardless. Additional restrictions are placed on the use of extralinguistic knowledge, according to the Modularity Matching Model. This source of information is operative only for ambiguous sentences and then only if the conversational context does not support a particular reading.

Chapter 7

Competing Tasks: Reaction Time Studies

According to the Competing Factors Model, linguistic behavior is a composite of many factors, only one of which is linguistic knowledge. On some occasions, children's access to and use of principles of grammar will remain submerged beneath the confluence of other forces, such as memory limitations and extralinguistic knowledge. On those occasions, children will make mistakes or they will produce the right responses for the wrong reasons—not because of their adherence to grammatical principles. On other occasions, the principles of grammar will surface and will determine children's responses. If the principles of grammar surface often enough, then children are credited with knowing these principles, where "often enough" means above some preestablished level of correct performance that would be expected by chance. The Modularity Matching Model rejects this argument. On this model, if children know a linguistic principle, then they should behave in conformity to it, just as adults do. This follows from the joint assumptions (a) that children have access to Universal Grammar, (b) that children use the same language-processing mechanisms as adults, and (c) that the grammars of both children and adults have priority over other factors that contribute to linguistic behavior, such as memory limitations and extralinguistic knowledge.

In contrast to the Modularity Matching Model, the Competing Factors Model makes the following methodological assumption. Suppose the research question is whether or not children know two structures that are similar but not identical. If children distinguish between sentences with these underlying structures (in the adult grammar) often enough, then they can be credited with knowing the linguistic properties of the two structures even if their performance in response to both types of sentences is less than perfect. The Modularity Matching Model rejects this methodological assumption. On this model, knowing that children treat two types of sentences differently does not prove that they assign the same grammatical properties to them as adults do; instead, it must be demonstrated that this is the case. The pattern of children's linguistic behavior must conform to the Modularity Matching Model, according to which children are expected to perform perfectly, just as adults do (up to the level of experimental noise). Like adults, children should consistently reject sentences that are ungrammatical and accept ones that are grammatical. Only then can children be credited with knowing the grammatical properties that underlie the test sentences.

7.1 Problems with Reaction Time Measures

The different methodological assumptions of the two models lead to differences in the selection of tasks for assessing children's linguistic competence. One way proponents of the Competing Factors Model have chosen to ascertain whether or not children distinguish between two structures is to use reaction time as the dependent variable. Because reaction time measures determine significant differences (in the statistical sense) between structures, their use is entirely consistent with the methodological assumptions of the Competing Factors Model.

From the vantage point of the Modularity Matching Model, however, reaction time measures should be used with caution unless they are accompanied by more direct measures of children's linguistic knowledge. To anticipate the conclusions we reach: it is ill advised to use reaction time measures to investigate children's knowledge of linguistic constraints because these measures do not reveal the syntactic and semantic properties that children assign to the sentences and discourse sequences under investigation. We take up this problem first, in discussing the difference between discrete and continuous variables.

A second problem with reaction time measures of children's knowledge of linguistic constraints is that they cannot be used to tell whether or not sentences are unambiguous for children. As we have shown, it is crucial in evaluating children's knowledge of constraints to establish that certain sentences are unambiguous for them. Reaction time measures do not provide this information.

A third reason to avoid reaction time measures in assessing children's knowledge of linguistic constraints is that the usual statistical tests that are applied to reaction time data treat subjects (and sentence types) as a group. These tests can yield significant findings even when the responses of individual children (or responses to individual sentences) do not conform to the pattern that is characteristic of the group. Because statistical analyses of reaction time measures tolerate (a limited number of) exceptions, yielding significance despite the outliers, such measures should be avoided when the research question is children's knowledge of linguistic constraints. Constraints are expected to be universal and therefore do not tolerate exceptions.

We want it to be clear that these shortcomings in reaction time measures pertain primarily to the investigation of children's linguistic competence; reaction time measures have yielded substantial profits in other areas, particularly in the study of adult sentence processing. In that area, studies using reaction time as the dependent variable have been instructive in understanding such phenomena as when various kinds of information are used in on-line sentence processing, where the loci of difficulty reside in sentence processing, and how ambiguities are resolved.

Given the impressive achievements using reaction time as a dependent variable, it might seem natural, even highly desirable, to extend the use of reaction time measures to investigate children's linguistic knowledge. We urge caution in doing so, however. Appying reaction time measures to adult sentence-processing routines is justified because it can be safely assumed that adults have all and only grammatical analyses available to them. In studies of child language development, by contrast, the research question generally concerns children's underlying linguistic competence. Reaction time measures do not set sufficiently high standards for attributing knowledge to children. From the perspective of the Modularity Matching Model, it is imprudent to relax the criteria used to assess children's competence. This is why we favor measures that tap linguistic competence more directly, such as the elicited production task and the truth value judgment task.

Once children's competence with the relevant linguistic structures is established, however, reaction time studies like those used to study adult sentence processing can be used to study related questions about children's sentence-processing abilities: how children access and use different kinds of information, where the loci of processing difficulties reside in children's on-line comprehension of sentences, how children resolve ambiguities, and so on (for discussion, see McKee 1996).

7.2 Discrete and Continuous Variables

Essentially, the trouble with reaction time measures is that they do not reveal what the specific analyses are that subjects assign to test sentences. To clarify the point, it will be useful to divide measures of language comprehension into two classes: discrete variables and continuous variables.

In experiments using discrete variables, each response by a subject is an instance of just one of a limited set of values. The truth value judgment task is one such measure, because the subjects indicate their acceptance or rejection of a sentence (i.e., "Yes" or "No") on each trial. The act-out task is another discrete measure, because subjects' responses can be differentiated by the objects that they manipulate and by the order in which they act out events. Grammaticality judgments are another discrete measure. So are children's productions, since these can be categorized in specific ways.

In experiments using continuous variables, by contrast, each response by a subject falls somewhere along a continuum. By definition, the probability of the occurrence of any exact value for a continuous variable is zero; subjects' responses assume the smooth curves that are characteristic of normal distributions. By their nature, continuous variables mask the specific linguistic analyses that subjects assign to sentences (for related discussion, see Steedman and Altmann 1989, 116–117; Gordon 1996, 212).

Reaction time is a continuous variable. Reaction time studies measure the time it takes subjects to respond to test sentences; they do not categorize responses into discrete classes. Because reaction time does not indicate the syntactic and semantic properties of the sentences that are presented to subjects, such measures are not truly informative in assessing children's linguistic competence, or in comparing the pattern of responses by children with the pattern of responses by adults (whose linguistic knowledge is not in question).

The fact that reaction time is a continuous variable becomes especially problematic when the research question is knowledge of one class of linguistic constraints, namely, constraints on the meanings that can be assigned to sentences. The problem is that reaction time measures veil an essential distinction in the assessment of children's knowledge of constraints, namely, the distinction between ambiguous and unambiguous sentences. As we have shown, children who lack a constraint should find sentences that are governed by it to be ambiguous—meanings that are ruled out by the constraint should be available to these children. Children who know the constraint, however, should not find sentences that are governed by the constraint to be ambiguous. If a test sentence is unambiguous for children, they should consistently reject it in contexts that do not match the interpretation given by their grammars. Therefore, demonstrating children's knowledge of a constraint boils down to demonstrating that sentences governed by the constraint are unambiguous for them.[1] Because reaction time studies do not indicate whether or not a sentence is unambiguous for children, they do not provide an appropriate test of children's knowledge of linguistic constraints. After discussing the third limitation of reaction time measures, we illustrate this claim by reviewing a study of children's reaction time using a technique known as the *preferential looking paradigm.* The study, by Hirsh-Pasek et al. (1995), was designed to investigate children's knowledge of Principle B.

The third limitation of reaction time measures also shows itself in the investigation of children's knowledge of linguistic constraints. According to the theory of Universal Grammar, linguistic constraints should be universal. This is a consequence of innate specification, as discussed in chapter 2. Because constraints are putatively universal, all children (and languages) are expected to adhere to them. The problem with reaction time stems from the custom of analyzing the responses of subjects as a group, using (parametric) statistical tests of the combined scores of all subjects. These statistical tests determine whether or not the subjects as a group performed significantly above some preestablished level of performance—for example, a level of performance that might result by chance 1 time in 20 ($p < .05$). A positive result obtains if a sufficient number of subjects demonstrate a consistent pattern of behavior, over and above the preestablished level that would be expected to occur by chance.[2] As noted, however, it does not suffice to show that the distribution of responses by subjects as a whole conforms to a linguistic constraint; it must be shown that all children abide by the constraint.

In this connection, we review a second experimental study using reaction time measures. The study, by McKee, Nicol, and McDaniel (1993), used a reaction time measure known as *cross-modal priming* to assess children's linguistic knowledge of Principle B. This measure was used in combination with a discrete measure of children's comprehension; therefore, the study permits us to examine how a continuous measure and a discrete measure stack up against each other.

7.3 The Preferential Looking Paradigm

Our first example of a reaction time study using child subjects is by Hirsh-Pasek et al. (1995). These researchers used a preferential looking paradigm. The dependent measure in the preferential looking paradigm is gaze duration, that is, the amount of time (in hundredths or thousandths of a second) that children spend looking at scenes depicted on video displays. The scenes are associated with auditory input that is presented while the child subject is attending to the video displays. Typically, two displays are presented at the same time. Children tend to look longer at some displays than others; for instance, children have been found to spend more time looking at displays that are consistent with the meanings they assign to sentences than at ones that are not.

The study by Hirsh-Pasek et al. investigated children's knowledge of Principle B, by recording how long children looked at scenes corresponding to the licit and illicit (in the adult grammar) interpretation of a pronoun in sentences like (1). In the adult grammar, the pronoun *him* is not able to refer to Cookie Monster in (1). This assignment of coreference is prohibited by Principle B. As noted in chapter 3, much previous research using other tasks has found that children often, but not always, assent to (1) in a situation in which Cookie Monster is turning, but is not turning someone else (e.g., Chien and Wexler 1990).

(1)   Cookie Monster is turning him.
    a.   *Cookie Monster is turning him.
    b.   Cookie Monster is turning him.

Hirsh-Pasek et al. sought to pursue the issue using the preferential looking paradigm with the hope that this technique would bear better fruit than previous tasks, because it is more "child-friendly."

In this study, one video display depicted the meaning of the test sentence that is compatible with the adult grammar; the other display depicted the meaning that is ruled out in the adult grammar. For example, one of the trials included the auditory input in (2). There were two video displays corresponding to the input. One display (the "match" display) showed Cookie Monster turning Big Bird; the other (the "nonmatch" display) showed both Cookie Monster turning and Big Bird turning.

(2)   Look at Cookie Monster and Big Bird! Cookie Monster is turning him.

Match display
Cookie Monster is turning Big Bird

Nonmatch display
Cookie Monster is turning and Big Bird is turning

On the basis of previous research findings, Hirsh-Pasek et al. reasoned that children who know Principle B should spend more time looking at the match display than at the nonmatch display.[3] Indeed, a group of older children in the study, who ranged in age from 3;2 to 3;4, looked significantly longer at the match displays than at the nonmatch displays (3.22 seconds and 2.23 seconds, respectively). On this basis, Hirsh-Pasek et al. claim to have demonstrated that children know Principle B by age 3, in contrast to other research that has shown that some children as old as 5 or 6 allow coreference between pronouns and names in sentences like (1).

This conclusion is unwarranted, however. At issue is whether children know a linguistic principle (i.e., Principle B) that prohibits the assignment of a certain interpretation to sentences. Without the constraint, children should find sentences governed by it to be ambiguous. If children lack a linguistic constraint, they should be able to assign the kind of meaning(s) that the constraint rules out. In other words, for children who lack Principle B, sentences like (1) will be ambiguous; these children will be able to assign not only the legitimate meaning, but also the meaning prohibited by Principle B. This situation can be depicted as follows:

Child $\langle$sentence, $\{$meaning$_1$, meaning$_2\}\rangle$
Adult $\langle$sentence, $\{$meaning$_1\}\rangle$

Having laid the groundwork, we can now explain why the findings of the study by Hirsh-Pasek et al. do not demonstrate young children's knowledge of Principle B. Suppose that the 3-years-olds in this study lacked Principle B. If so, then both of the displays these children witnessed would have depicted meanings that were *consistent* with their grammars. That is, both displays would have been "matches." Now, are children likely to look longer at one of the displays than the other, if both displays match a reading that is generated by their grammars? It is likely. Just as adults do, children may prefer one meaning of an ambiguous sentence over another. Children who prefer one interpretation should be expected to look longer at the display that matches that interpretation. In the present context, if children's preference favored the display that depicts the meaning associated with the legitimate (adult) interpretation, then the findings could be explained without appealing to Principle B.

In short, there is a confound between (a) children's preference for one meaning of an ambiguous sentence over another and (b) their knowledge of the linguistic principle governing the interpretation of pronouns. More generally, without adequate controls, the preferential looking paradigm cannot distinguish *in principle* between children's knowledge of linguistic principles and their preference to resolve ambiguities in favor of one reading rather than another (see Lasnik and Crain 1985, for a similar objection to the act-out task). As its name suggests, the preferential looking paradigm can be used to establish the preferences of subjects for one display over others. However, subjects' preferences to perform in certain ways do not suffice to guarantee their adherence to linguistic principles.

To deal with the potential confound between preferences and principles, studies using the preferential looking paradigm could borrow a research strategy discussed earlier, in the context of the truth value judgment task—namely, to compare children's responses to ambiguous sentences with their responses to sentences that are unambiguous, because of a linguistic constraint. (For example, we described this research strategy in chapter 3, as it was applied to evaluate children's knowledge of Principle C (also see chapter 27).) The strategy involves examining children's responses to both ambiguous and unambiguous sentences. The ambiguous sentences serve as controls. For example, in investigating Principle C, we would first find out how often children accept coreference between the name, *the Ninja Turtle*, and the pronoun, *he*, in sentences such as (3).

(3)   The Ninja Turtle danced while he ate pizza.

Then we would compare the proportion of coreference that children assign to ambiguous control sentences like (3) with the proportion of coreference that children assign to sentences like (4), where coreference is ruled out by Principle C.

(4)   He danced while the Ninja Turtle ate pizza.

Children who lack Principle C should find both sentences (3) and (4) to be ambiguous, so the coreference interpretation should be assigned equally often to both sentences. On the other hand, children who know Principle C should assign only the non-coreference, or deictic, interpretation of (4); this sentence should be unambiguous for these children, just as it is unambiguous for adults.

Nothing prevents us from applying the same research strategy to study children's knowledge of Principle B using reaction time as the dependent variable. To demonstrate children's knowledge of Principle B, for example, the first step would be to record the average length of time children look at two different displays—ones that correspond to the alternative interpretations of ambiguous sentences, such as (5).

(5)   The Ninja Turtle tried his pizza.
    a.   The Ninja Turtle tried <u>his</u> pizza
    b.   <u>The Ninja Turtle</u> tried his pizza.

Presumably, children would spend more time looking at one display than another. If fortune shines, children could prefer, and therefore look longer at, the display corresponding to the coreference interpretation of the pronoun, (a), than at the display corresponding to the deictic interpretation, (b). Having established children's gaze durations in response to ambiguous sentences, the next step would be to present sentences governed by Principle B, such as (6).

(6)   The Ninja Turtle covered him.

    a.   *The Ninja Turtle covered <u>him</u>.
    b.   The Ninja Turtle covered him.

As in the truth value judgment task, the displays for (6) would correspond to both the reading that is permitted by the adult grammar, the deictic reading (b), and the reading that is ruled out by Principle B, the coreference reading (a). If children lack Principle B, the amount of time they spend looking at displays corresponding to the coreference reading of sentences such as (6) should be similar to the amount of time they spend looking at displays corresponding to the coreference reading of the ambiguous control sentences, such as (5). If children know Principle B, then they should spend significantly more time looking at displays corresponding to the deictic interpretation for test sentences than they do looking at displays corresponding to the deictic interpretation of ambiguous control sentences.

Although the study just outlined would overcome the objection leveled against the study by Hirsh-Pasek et al., we would still have qualms about concluding that Principle B is innate based on such a study. As noted, one hallmark of innateness is that a linguistic principle should be accessible to all children. Even if there is a significant difference in gaze duration by subjects as group in response to the displays corresponding to the coreference interpretation of (5) and (6), we recommend caution in interpreting the findings as evidence of innateness. Here is how Crain and Wexler (forthcoming) put the point:

> Suppose, for example, that subjects frowned more often when they heard one sentence than when they heard another sentence. There is no reason to think that the difference in behavior represents a difference in grammatical status of the two sentences. It may simply be that children failed to understand one of the sentences. Knowing that two sentences are not treated in the same way by subjects does not tell us about the grammatical properties they assign to each type of sentence.
>
> To take another example, suppose that children showed a difference on the same two types of sentences in an experiment using a different dependent measure, say reaction time. All that we could conclude would be that there is a difference for the children between the two types of sentences. We would not conclude that children know the syntactic and semantic properties of the sentences.... In order to demonstrate children's knowledge of UG principles, it must be established that their pattern of responses conforms to the model; that is, to the relevant principles of UG. To conclude that the constraint ... is innate ... it must be shown that all (or at least the vast majority of) children who are tested adhere to the constraint.

In the next section we follow up on the last point made in this quotation: that reaction time studies in particular, and continuous variables in general, often conceal individual differences in performance.

7.4 Cross-Modal Priming

Another example of the use of reaction time measures to investigate child language is a study by McKee, Nicol, and McDaniel (1993). These researchers investigated children's processing of coreference relations between ordinary pronouns (e.g., *him, her, them*) and their linguistic antecedents, and between reflexives (e.g., *himself, herself, themselves*) and their antecedents. They adapted a technique frequently used to investigate sentence processing in adults: cross-modal priming. In a cross-modal priming study, sentences are presented auditorily. As the sentence unfolds, subjects are asked to respond to a display that is presented visually. In many studies, the visual display is a string of letters, and the subjects' task is to indicate whether or not the string of letters constitutes a word. Subjects are instructed to respond "Yes" or "No" by pressing the appropriate response key. In studies of "on-line" sentence processing, subjects are requested to respond (as quickly as possible) while they continue to listen to the remainder of the stimulus sentence. If subjects respond quickly enough, responses come as the sentence unfolds in real time (i.e., before the sentence has been heard in its entirety). This makes it possible to examine the influence of specific properties within a sentence on subjects' responses to the visual display.

In the cross-modal priming technique used in the study by McKee, Nicol, and McDaniel, 17 children aged 4 to 6 (and a larger number of adult controls) listened to sentences over headphones and, for each sentence, responded to a picture that was displayed at a critical juncture in the sentence. The picture depicted an animate or inanimate object, for example, a leopard. The subjects' task was to indicate whether the depicted object was "alive" or "not alive." Subjects indicated their decision by pressing one of two response keys.

A "Yes/No" judgment task was also administered to the subjects. The judgment task was a picture verification procedure, in which subjects were asked to indicate whether or not a test sentence accurately described a picture. This was an "off-line" task, because subjects listened to sentences in their entirety before responding to the corresponding pictures.

In the cross-modal priming portion of the study, the critical manipulation was the alternation of an ordinary pronoun (e.g., *him*) with a reflexive pronoun (e.g., *himself*) or with a definite description (e.g., *the girl*). One of these items appeared in each test sentence. To form a complete set for a given sentence, the same picture was displayed immediately following each of these items (as indicated by the word [LEOPARD]). An example is (7).

(7)   The alligator knows that the leopard with green eyes is patting him/himself/the girl [LEOPARD] on the head with a soft pillow.

McKee, Nicol, and McDaniel reasoned as follows. If children and adults process sentences in the same way, subjects in both groups should respond fastest to the version of the test sentences that contain a reflexive pronoun. This prediction is based on previous research with adults, where it was found that pronominal elements reactivate, or "prime," the meaning of words that subjects associate with their linguistic antecedent. In the present study, then, the reflexive pronoun was expected to prime the preceding NP *the leopard* since this NP *is* the linguistic antecedent of the reflexive pronoun. What about ordinary pronouns? Assuming that subjects associate the pronoun, *him*, in (7) with an NP that is mentioned in the sentence, the pronoun should share its reference with the NP *the alligator*. If so, there should be no advantage in response times to the picture of a leopard when the critical word was an ordinary pronoun. In short, the prediction was that response times indicating that the picture of the leopard depicted an object that was "alive" would be faster to the reflexive, *himself*, than to the pronoun, *him* (assuming that children have the same linguistic knowledge as adults do, including knowledge of Principle B). The definite description *the girl* does not involve reactivation of any NP at all; this version of the test sentences serves only as a yardstick for comparison with the other two types of NPs.

There is a catch, however. As noted earlier, some children tolerate coreference between an ordinary pronoun and an immediately preceding NP, where adults do not. For example, some children appear to allow the pronoun *him* to corefer with the NP *Papa Bear* in a sentence like (8) (see chapter 3). For these children, then, (8) may take on the meaning "Papa Bear covered himself", as well as the meaning assigned by adults on which the pronoun *him* is interpreted deictically.

(8)   Papa Bear covered him.

Returning to the study by McKee, Nicol, and McDaniel, consider (7) again. It is conceivable that some children in the study would allow coreference possibilities that are excluded by adults. If these children associate the pronoun with an NP that is mentioned in the sentence, then the pronoun could be coreferential with either of the preceding NPs, *the alligator* or *the leopard*. For these children, then, the ordinary pronoun *him* might sometimes prime the immediately preceding NP *the leopard*. Lacking Principle B, some children might respond as quickly to the pronoun *him* as they do to the reflexive *himself*. The result would be faster responses to the picture of a leopard for both ordinary pronouns and reflexive pronouns, as compared to the definite descriptions. The fastest responses would presumably be to the reflexives, because these *always* refer to the NP corresponding to the object depicted in the picture. The exact pattern of responses to ordinary pronouns cannot be predicted in advance, because the pronouns may, but need not, refer to the depicted object.

Here are the essential findings. Both children and adults responded faster to the reflexive pronouns than to either the ordinary pronouns or the definite descriptions. Response times to the pronoun and the definite description did not differ significantly, for either group.

7.5 A Closer Look

What should we conclude from the observation that children show the same overall pattern of linguistic behavior as adults do? Should we conclude that children and adults have the same linguistic principles? Not necessarily. Although there was a statistically significant difference between reflexives and the other NPs for children analyzed as a group, the statistical test applied to the behavior of the children considered as a whole. This could obscure different patterns of responses by subtypes of individuals within the overall group. As Crain and Wexler (forthcoming) remark:

> Even if the pattern of reaction time differences by children mimicked that of adults, it would be ill-advised to attribute the same underlying knowledge to children without additional confirmation from more direct tests of grammatical knowledge.

The remark was prophetic of the situation that arose in McKee, Nicol, and McDaniel's study. Although children and adults produced similar patterns of responses as a group, on further analysis it turned out that there were differences between the groups in their patterns of responses. The need for further analysis of the reaction time data became evident, however, only when McKee, Nicol, and McDaniel considered the results of the picture verification task.

On the basis of the picture verification task, it was determined that 7 of the 17 children did not make adultlike judgments for sentences with ordinary pronouns. The behavior of these 7 children was quite unlike that of children examined in previous studies, however. These 7 children treated ordinary pronouns as if they were reflexives. That is, the exceptional group of children in McKee, Nicol, and McDaniel's study *rejected* the direct reference (deictic) interpretation of pronouns. The finding that is consistent with earlier research is that these children accepted coreference between ordinary pronouns and an immediately preceding referential NP.

A post hoc examination of the reaction time data of these 7 children was quite revealing; McKee, Nicol, and McDaniel found that both reflexive pronouns and ordinary pronouns showed priming effects, as compared to the definite descriptions. The remaining 10 children showed a priming effect only for reflexives. Thus, the reaction time data mirrored the judgment data, when the children were divided into subgroups on the basis of the results from the judgment task. The similar pattern of results in both tasks is important, because it means that reaction time studies can be revealing about children's linguistic processing, if their grammatical knowledge is documented by an independent assessment, based on a discrete measure of linguistic competence. Without the judgment task, McKee, Nicol, and McDaniel would have had no cause to examine the responses of subgroups of children. On the basis of the similar overall pattern of response times for both groups, the wrong conclusion could have been drawn: that children and adults have the same sentence-processing abilities. To put the matter differently, if only reaction time data had been used, it might have been inferred that the children and adults in the study had similar grammars. But this inference is warranted only if it is reasonable to assume that the pattern of response times by both children and adults is a reflection of their grammatical knowledge. If this assumption were correct, then the finding that children and adults showed a similar pattern of behavior would license the inference that they have similar grammars. However, the study by McKee, Nicol, and McDaniel amply demonstrates that this assumption is incorrect.

Having criticized the use of reaction time measures to study language development, we should say again why the use of such measures is justified in studies of adult sentence processing. The reason is that linguistic competence is not at issue in studies with adults. Because it is assumed that all adults have the correct grammatical analyses available to them, tasks may be used that only indirectly tap their grammatical competence, such as measures of reaction time. Clarity is sacrificed in looking at the particular syntactic and semantic properties of sentences, for example, to determine the time course of the availability of alternative sources of information. As Gordon (1996) remarks:

> A major difference in the aims of language acquisition studies and those of adult studies is that the latter tend to test for performance variables where reaction times are used to make inferences about the structure of and access to existing knowledge. (p. 212)

In studies of children's language development, "existing knowledge" is precisely what is at issue. As we have argued, the discovery that children and adults treat sentences in the same way does not entail that both groups analyze sentences in the same way. In order to demonstrate children's knowledge of particular principles of Universal Grammar, it must be established that their pattern of responses conforms to those principles. Once this has been established, however, the findings of the study by McKee, Nicol, and McDaniel become important, because they suggest that further questions about the availability of different sources of information in children's processing of linguistic information may also be open to empirical investigation.

The findings of the study by McKee, Nicol, and McDaniel are quite instructive. They suggest that the processing routines of both children and adults are intimately tied to their grammatical knowledge and that these routines may be equivalent for both children and adults, as anticipated by the Modularity Matching Model. The downside of using reaction time studies should also be evident. In the absence of more direct tests of children's linguistic knowledge, measures that are essentially nondiscrete, such as reaction time, can sometimes obscure important aspects of children's linguistic knowledge, by obscuring individual differences among children.

To conclude our discussion of the study by McKee, Nicol, and McDaniel, we wish to tie up a few loose ends. First, we wish to underscore a point we will raise in chapter 9 regarding the imitation task. The relevant finding is that both children and adults show priming effects for reflexive pronouns. This finding invites the inference that people actively attempt to establish the referents of NPs in the sentences they hear, even when sentences are presented outside of any context.

Another point worth making also anticipates later discussion. The point concerns how the referents of NPs are determined in the absence of a conversational context (i.e., in the so-called null context). In the absence of context, as in both of the tasks used by McKee, Nicol, and McDaniel, the direct reference interpretation of ordinary pronouns seems to be unavailable. This was the case with the 7 children who allowed coreference too liberally; these children showed comparable priming effects with ordinary pronouns and reflexive pronouns. Presumably, this is simply an artifact of the tasks; an anaphoric link can be made to a linguistically established antecedent, but no such link can be made to a referent that has not been established in the domain of discourse. The priming effects with ordinary pronouns could be expected to be diluted if extrasentential referents are available. In fact, intersentential anaphora may not be preferred if there is a choice between inter- and extrasentential reference. If the goal is to understand normal language-processing routines, then the cross-modal priming technique is likely to present a distorted picture of children's sentence-processing routines. This is a consequence of using a task that requires children to construct sentence meanings in the absence of contextual support.

7.6 Conclusion

This chapter discussed three limitations to using reaction time measures in the study of children's linguistic knowledge. One limitation is that such measures cannot be used to establish whether or not a certain type of sentence is unambiguous for children. We discussed this problem in the context of the preferential looking paradigm. In this task, children are asked to respond to the same test sentence in two different contexts, one that is consistent with the unique adult interpretation of the sentence and one that requires a nonadult interpretation. The finding of the study we discussed was that children generally responded faster in the context that supported the adult interpretation. The experimenters concluded on this basis that children have access to the adult reading of the target sentence, but not to the other reading. This conclusion was unwarranted, however, because there was another interpretation of the findings: that children accessed both readings, but simply preferred the adult reading.

Another limitation of reaction time measures is that they do not reveal the nature of the linguistic representations children assign to sentences. This limitation was discussed in the context of a study using the cross-modal priming technique. In that study, children showed a difference in reaction time to two types of sentences, just as adults did. It could not be inferred that children knew the syntactic and semantic properties of the test sentences, however, even though their pattern of reaction time differences mirrored that of adults.

The final limitation of reaction time measures is that they lump all subjects together and ask about their performance as a group. The performance of individuals and subgroups can be washed out if the majority of children behave in a particular way. To underscore this point, we noted that when a more direct test of grammatical competence was undertaken, the initial reaction time data were shown to be misleading. In the light of the additional measurement, the study revealed differences among children in reaction time that were obscured by the initial analysis of the findings. The lesson to be learned is that one can be confident that children's responses are based on linguistic knowledge only if they produce a targeted linguistic construction in appropriate circumstances, or consistently and correctly judge sentences to be grammatical or ungrammatical, just as adults do.

Reaction time measures are useful in finding out if subjects produce different patterns of responses to different sentence types or if they produce different patterns of responses to the same sentence type in different contexts. In both cases, statistical tests are used to argue for or against the claim that subjects' responses are influenced by a "true" component of behavior, such as linguistic knowledge. On the Competing Factors Model, significant differences in response times by children might be construed as evidence of linguistic knowledge. According to the Modularity Matching Model, however, reaction time data alone do not provide a reliable basis for making inferences about children's grammatical competence. In the absence of independent assessments of children's linguistic knowledge, based on discrete measures such as the elicited production task or the truth value judgment task, the results of reaction time studies must be interpreted with caution.

The next two chapters test the Competing Factors Model in a different way, as it has been applied in interpreting the findings of studies that use other research methodologies. Chapter 8 examines the act-out task and chapter 9 examines the imitation task.

Chapter 8

Competing Tasks: The Act-Out Task

This chapter continues our discussion of the Competing Factors Model. The Competing Factors Model anticipates that children will sometimes perform less well than adults. Evidence of this would seem to be abundant. Children often fail to perform as well as adults do in many psycholinguistic tasks, and they sometimes produce different responses than adults when they confront the same linguistic materials. The Modularity Matching Model maintains that both the linguistic and performance components of the language apparatus of children and adults are basically the same; this leaves the Modularity Matching Model with little room to maneuver in explaining why children sometimes perform with less accuracy than adults on certain tasks and why they sometimes produce systematic nonadult responses. In chapters 2 and 4, we noted one source of differences between children and adults that is consistent with the Modularity Matching Model: differences that arise because children adopt distinct grammatical hypotheses. However, the problem of generally decreased performance by children, as compared to adults, remains to be addressed.

This chapter and the next examine findings that seem, on the face of it, to be inconsistent with the Modularity Matching Model and supportive of the Competing Factors Model. The findings are less than perfect linguistic behavior by children on two tasks: act-out and imitation. The recalcitrant data do not force us to abandon the Modularity Matching Model, however. The tasks that have evoked less than perfect performance are highly unnatural and consequently do not accurately assess children's linguistic competence. In many (but not all) experimental tasks, linguistic behavior is at the mercy of irrelevant task demands. The research designs that have evoked errors from children are typically ones that are especially sensitive to irrelevant nonlinguistic factors, as well as being sensitive to grammatical competence. This underscores the need to design experimental paradigms that are free from the effects of confounding influences. One of the overarching goals of this book is to illustrate how to rid tasks of the influence of extraneous and confounding factors. First, however, let us look more closely at the problems that can arise with tasks that are frequently used in assessing children's linguistic competence. This chapter examines findings from the act-out task. Chapter 9 examines findings from the imitation task.

For illustrative purposes, we will cite two examples of research studies using the *act-out* (or *figure manipulation*) task. In this task, the experimenter presents a sentence to the child subject and instructs the child to act out ("Do what I say") the sentence using toys and props that are present in the experimental workspace. We will argue that the results of this task can seriously underestimate children's linguistic knowledge.

The first study was mentioned already, when we pointed out the suggestion that young children attempt to interpret constructions in an "order-of-mention" fashion. This study investigated children's understanding of temporal terms like *before* and *after*. In comprehending two-clause constructions that are tied together by these temporal conjunctions, even children as old as 5 were found to be much more successful in responding to instructions like (1) than in responding to instructions like (2).

(1)   After you touch your nose, touch your ears.

(2)   Before you touch your nose, touch your ears.

Having noted that the event mentioned first in (1) should be acted out first, but that there is a conflict between order of mention and the correct conceptual order in (2), researchers concluded that children lacked the grammatical resources for interpreting sentences containing subordinating temporal conjunctions. It was claimed that, lacking grammatical knowledge, children relied on order of mention as a strategy for interpretation (e.g., Amidon and Carey 1972; Clark 1971). This strategy gives the right results for (1), but the wrong results for (2).[1]

The conclusion that children lack grammatical competence sits poorly with the Modularity Matching Model. Fortunately, however, another source of children's errors was identified by Crain (1982) and further pursued by Gorrell, Crain, and Fodor (1989). These authors argued that children found the instructions in (1) and (2) odd, because these sentences have presuppositional content that was flouted in the experiments that evoked high error rates. The presupposition is that the person being addressed has already expressed an intention to perform the action mentioned in the subordinate clause. To satisfy the presupposition, all that is required is a lead-in sentence like the following: "In the next game I want you to touch some part of your face." As the game unfolds, the child is asked to say what part of her face she plans to touch. For a child who says, "I'm going to touch my nose," either (1) or (2) would be an appropriate request. When the presupposition was met in this way, children's correct responses climbed to 82% accuracy in Crain's study. This figure excludes an "other" response that accounted for almost half of the errors: that of acting out only the main clause. Intuitively, this may also be a "correct" response; see Hamburger and Crain 1982 for discussion. In any event, it is apparent that children are extremely sensitive to a presupposition that is subtle enough to have been entirely overlooked by numerous experimental psycholinguists.

A second example of children succumbing to infelicity appeared in research on the acquisition of restrictive relative clauses. In several early studies on this construction, children were found to commit errors in interpretation. The errors resulted from experiments using an act-out methodology to assess children's comprehension of sentences with relative clauses. In several such studies, children committed systematic errors in comprehending sentences like (3)–(6). The differences among these construction types are indicated by the two-letter code preceding each example; the first letter in the code identifies the grammatical function of the NP that bears the restrictive relative clause, subject (S) or object (O) of the main clause; the second letter indicates the grammatical function of the "gap" within the relative clause. For example, an OS sentence is one in which the relative clause modifies the main-clause direct object (O), and the relative clause has a gap in subject position (S).

(3)   SS: The dog that jumped over the pig pushed the sheep.

(4)   OO: The dog pushed the sheep that the pig jumped over.

(5)   SO: The dog that the sheep pushed jumped over the pig.

(6)   OS: The dog pushed the sheep that jumped over the pig.

Several studies found that 4- and 5-year-old children consistently acted out these sentences in a nonadult fashion (Sheldon 1974; Tavakolian 1981). One type of sentence was particularly likely to evoke errors: the OS sentence. When asked to act out the meaning of the OS sentence in (6), many children had the dog push the sheep and then jump over the pig. For adults, the sheep is the agent of the action expressed in the relative clause in (6). Children's nonadult enactment led Tavakolian (1981) to claim that they assigned sentences like (6) a structure appropriate for conjoined clauses, as if (7a) had the meaning of (7b). Accordingly, Tavakolian called her proposal the *conjoined-clause analysis* of relative clauses.

(7) a.   The dog pushed the sheep that jumped over the pig.
     b.   The dog pushed the sheep and jumped over the pig.

According to Tavakolian, children initially lack the principles needed to interpret relative clauses in an adultlike fashion. Therefore, when they interpret sentences with relative clauses, they are compelled to borrow syntactic and semantic principles from Universal Grammar that are used for other grammatical structures (i.e., for conjoined clauses). These linguistic principles apply to some sentences better than to others, however. The conjoined-clause analysis was able to account for 63% of children's responses to OS sentences in Tavakolian's study, but it accounted for only 19% of children's responses to OO sentences. In total, the conjoined-clause analysis explained 48% of all of children's responses to the four types of relative clauses.

Later, using other experimental procedures, it was demonstrated that English-speaking children and Italian-speaking children have mastery of sentences with a relative clause even before their third birthday (but see Labelle 1990, where French-speaking children's difficulty in producing standard adultlike relative clauses in some types of sentences is documented; also see Guasti and Shlonsky 1995, Guasti et al. 1995). The modified procedures were motivated by the observation that sentences with relative clauses often bear two kinds of presuppositions. Consider the OS sentence in (8).

(8)   The dog pushed the sheep that jumped over the pig.

The relative clause in this example modifies the NP *the sheep*, forming the constituent *the sheep that jumped over the pig*. Felicitous use of this phrase presupposes, first, that at least two sheep are present in the conversational context. If there is only one sheep, there is no need to use the relative clause at all; the speaker could just as well say, "The dog pushed the sheep." In short, a restrictive relative clause is felicitous when some restricting needs to be done. With only one sheep present in the experimental workspace, the restrictive relative clause *that jumped over the pig* is superfluous; the sentence therefore violates one of the Gricean maxims of manner: "Avoid Unnecessary Prolixity" (Grice 1975).

The second presupposition of (8) is that the event mentioned in the relative clause (the sheep jumped over the pig) took place prior to the assertion (the dog pushed the sheep).[2] Given that the past tense form of the verb is used, the event mentioned in the relative clause should have occurred before the sentence was uttered.

In the research that evoked high error rates from children, neither of these presuppositions was satisfied. Only one sheep was present in the experimental workspace for (8), and no event occurred before a test sentence was presented; the child's task was simply to "act out" the meaning of the test sentences from scratch, using the available objects.

To investigate the possibility that experimental infelicities, and not lack of linguistic competence, were responsible for children's comprehension errors, Hamburger and Crain (1982) made the apparently minor change of adding more sheep to the experimental workspace for a sentence like (8). This simple change resulted in a much higher percentage of correct responses by children, including children much younger than the ones tested previously. However, the most compelling evidence that young children command the structural knowledge underlying relative-clause formation, came in a second experiment, using an elicited production task. Pragmatic contexts were constructed in which the presuppositions of restrictive relatives were satisfied; then children were instructed to ask someone who was blindfolded to identify one toy from a set of identical toys. In such circumstances, even children as young as 2;8 consistently produce well-formed subject and object relative-clause constructions (Crain, McKee, and Emiliani 1990).

In our view, young children's conjoined-clause interpretation of sentences with relative clauses is simply the result of their attempt to behave in a manner consistent with their knowledge of pragmatic principles (see Sperber and Wilson 1986). This is why children's level of correct performance approximates that of adults when the pragmatic felicity conditions are satisfied.

Why do older children and adults not fall victim to pragmatic infelicities to the same extent as young children do? We believe it is simply because older children and adults have learned to "see through" misleading circumstances in which test sentences are presented. To be successful in previous studies, subjects were required to accommodate the presuppositional failures in the experiment. It seems that older children and adults are capable of the necessary mental gymnastics, at least for unambiguous sentences (we have more to say about this later); but many younger children are apparently unable to perform the necessary accommodations as rapidly or as successfully.

It should be understood that we are not condemning all studies using an act-out methodology. The task is not inherently defective; there are places where it could be put to good use. It has a major drawback, however, because it introduces sentences in the so-called null context. Later, we describe the inner workings of a different comprehension technique, in which context is under the experimenter's control. This alternative technique for assessing children's comprehension of sentences is the truth value judgment task, to be discussed in part III.

Chapter 9

Competing Tasks: Imitation

There is another task in which the linguistic behavior of children and adults differs: the *imitation task*. In experiments using the imitation task, children have been found to perform in a characteristically nonadult fashion. The idea behind the imitation task is to see whether children can correctly repeat sentences presented to them, or whether they change the input sentences in some way. It is anticipated that the changes children make will indicate how their underlying grammar differs from that of an adult. In this chapter, we review some representative findings from studies using the imitation task, to determine the extent to which the findings challenge the Modularity Matching Model or can be explained by it.

9.1 Previous Findings

In some imitation tasks, young children have been found to omit whole chunks of linguistic material. For example, in a study by Phinney (1981), 3- to 5-year-old children were asked to repeat sentences with overt complementizers, such as (1).

(1)   The bear said that the turtle tickled the horse.

Many of the youngest children's "repetitions" consisted only of simple sentences, whereas older children successfully repeated both clauses; but many of the older children nevertheless failed to reproduce the complementizer in Phinney's study.

Assuming that adults do not experience difficulty with this task, the findings from Phinney's study seem once again to challenge the basic tenets of the Modularity Matching Model. We disagree. First, the omission of optional lexical material, such as the complementizer *that* in (1), is not problematic for the Modularity Matching Model; this omission by children could be the result of a parsing tendency that is also characteristic of adults, namely, the tendency toward using reduced forms. We therefore disagree with Phinney, who interpreted this finding as indicative of a nonadult grammar. Our own view is confirmed by the results of elicitation experiments, where it is found that children even younger than the ones in Phinney's study can reliably produce complementizers in linguistic contexts in which they are highly preferred, for example, in questions that begin "Is it true that ..." (Thornton 1990).

What appears problematic for the Modularity Matching Model, however, is the main finding: that young children omit whole chunks of linguistic material in the imitation task. Of course, it would be easy to say that they failed to understand the task, or that they didn't see any point to it. But taking the finding at face value, there are at least two ways to explain children's nonadult behavior, short of abandoning the Modularity Matching Model. First, some of children's incomplete repetitions may be attributable to problems in lexical access. If children do not rapidly access the meanings of the lexical items they are asked to repeat, the working memory system may overload. The result could be fragments of unanalyzed material in the working memory buffer. It is therefore important to make sure that children have ready access to all of the vocabulary items they are presented with in an imitation task. If children have not learned to retrieve all of these words with sufficient speed, their ability to perform the steps in syntactic and semantic processing needed to repeat an entire sentence may be hindered.

9.2 Problems with the Task

Even if this step is taken, children may experience difficulties with the task beyond those experienced by adults. In chapter 8, we reported children's misunderstanding of sentences with a restrictive relative clause in the absence of context, because the so-called null context does not satisfy the pragmatic "felicity conditions" associated with this construction. The same is true of the imitation task. Because sentences are pre-sented in the so-called null context, the task is highly unnatural; it also fails to satisfy any presuppositions the test sentences might have. Consider example (1): *The bear said that the turtle tickled the horse.* The use of definite NPs—*the bear, the turtle, the horse*—presupposes that some bear, turtle, and horse have been introduced into the conversational context.[1] If children (and adults) are required to (mentally) establish the referents of these definite NPs in order to produce the sentence, then this process could interfere with verbatim recall.

Chapter 12 discusses how the process of adding referents to one's mental model of the context associated with a sentence is costly for adults, too, in certain cases. For adults, the ease of setting up alternative referents is revealed in their preferences for interpreting ambiguous sentences in one way versus another, when ambiguous sen-tences are presented in the absence of linguistic or nonlinguistic context. Our sug-gestion is that children, even more than adults, find it highly unnatural to perform tasks that require them to analyze sentences in the so-called null context. This has little, if anything, to do with children's linguistic knowledge, on the assumption that the accommodation of presuppositional failures is an ability that develops in children over time, as they gather more experience with the conventions of conversation.

The imitation and act-out tasks may be unnatural for children for this reason. The conclusion reached by Hamburger and Wexler (1973) is that the primary linguistic data for grammar formation must consist of ⟨sentence, meaning⟩ pairs; these authors proved that grammars cannot be learned without their associated meanings (i.e., on the basis of sentences alone). It has often been suggested that sentence meanings are inferred by children from the discourse context, although no one denies that the pro-cesses by which such inferences take place are poorly understood (see Wexler and Culicover 1980, Pinker 1984, and Gleitman 1990 for discussion of this assumption). For our purposes, the point is this. Because children are in the process of language learning, they may rely on immediate context to support sentence meaning to an ex-tent that is not characteristic of adults. Therefore, children's relatively poor perfor-mance on the imitation task and the act-out task may not directly tap the normal language-processing routines of either children or adults; somehow, older children and adults have learned to compensate for the absence of context. Poor performance on these tasks by young children is, therefore, not inconsistent with the Modularity Matching Model.

9.3 Comparing Tasks

Now that we have discussed the act-out and imitation tasks in some detail, it will be useful to look at how the results from experimental studies using these tasks have been interpreted by advocates of the Competing Factors Model. Between-task comparisons have been made both in first language acquisition (Lust, Chien, and Flynn 1987) and in second language learning (Flynn 1986a,b).

Both lines of research have reached similar conclusions. One conclusion is that production (i.e., the imitation task) provides a more direct assessment of underlying linguistic competence than does comprehension (i.e., the act-out task). First, production is seen to be influenced to a lesser degree than comprehension by extralinguistic knowledge. The availability of extralinguistic cues makes it possible for people to comprehend sentences accurately without actually constructing a full structural representation of the input sentence, according to Flynn (1986b):

> In comprehension, the lack of a fully developed structural competence is not as critical as in production. Other extralinguistic knowledge and information available to the subject can be used to make a coherent interpretation of the stimulus sentence. (p. 154)

> [W]e can hypothesize that comprehension can be achieved with a minimal structural analysis. The role of pragmatic context and extralinguistic knowledge is more likely to be helpful here than in production. A subject could easily achieve accurate performance on a comprehension task. (p. 138)

There is a second difference, according to Flynn: production (i.e., the imitation task) directly taps structural knowledge without requiring a full semantic interpretation:

> [I]mitation does not necessarily require establishing the referents or generating a complete representation of sentence meaning. (p. 138)

> Given the requirements of an elicited imitation task, we might expect the results of such a test to demonstrate that we are tapping ... structural knowledge. (p. 140)

> [W]e can conclude that while production (elicited imitation) and comprehension (act-out) both elicit data that can be evaluated for evidence of linguistic competence, the degree to which each accesses this knowledge differs significantly. Specifically, ... elicited imitation more directly evaluates a learner's structural knowledge. (p. 154)

In sum, on Flynn's view there are fewer factors competing with structural knowledge in the imitation task; the factors that compete with structural knowledge in the act-out task often result in appropriate linguistic behavior, but right answers arise for the wrong reasons in that task.

With these points in mind, it will pay to look more closely at the findings that are said to support them. The imitation and act-out experiments in question were designed to test for the relative ease of processing right-branching (RB) sentences like (2) and (4), as compared to left-branching (LB) sentences like (3) and (5).

Imitation task

(2) The man answered the boss when he installed the television. (RB)

(3) When he delivered the message, the actor questioned the lawyer. (LB)

Act-out task

(4)   The yellow square touched the red triangle when it turned around. (RB)

(5)   When it turned over, the blue triangle touched the red circle. (LB)

In Flynn's study, the "directionality" factor was significant in the analysis of the results of the imitation task, but not for the act-out task; right-branching constructions evoked fewer errors in the imitation task. However, the act-out task resulted in fewer errors overall than the imitation task, although the difference was not statistically significant. The fact that subjects performed better on the act-out task was interpreted by Flynn as evidence that "even without a fully developed syntactic competence, subjects can productively rely on and use pragmatic context and knowledge in comprehension to an extent not helpful in production" (p. 149).

In each task, certain responses were counted as correct and others were counted as incorrect. In the act-out task, a response was considered correct if either the subject or the object of the main clause was selected as the referent of the pronoun. Because the pronoun is "free" in sentences like (3) and (5), it can corefer with either NP. Among the responses that were considered incorrect in the act-out task were (a) acting out the two clauses of a sentence in the wrong order, and (b) acting out the content of only one of its clauses.

There was another manipulation within the act-out task: the presence or absence of a "pragmatic lead." The pragmatic lead drew attention to the direct object NP in the test sentence that followed. For example, (6) illustrates the way sentence (5) was introduced in the pragmatic lead condition.

(6)   I am going to tell you a sentence about the red circle.
      When it turned over, the blue triangle touched the red circle.

With a pragmatic lead, there was a significant reduction in responses in which the pronoun and the subject of the main clause had the same referent. This makes sense, because the pragmatic lead mentioned the referent of the *object* NP in the main clause of the sentence that followed.

In the imitation task, a sentence had to be repeated verbatim by subjects to be counted as correct. Among the incorrect responses were "anaphora errors." Anaphora errors were found in previous studies of first language acquisition (e.g., Lust 1981). Anaphora errors are responses in which "a subject might reverse the order of the direction of anaphora" (p. 145), as when sentence (7) is converted to sentence (8).

(7)   When he was at school, John rode the bike.

(8)   When John was at school, he rode the bike.

In Lust's study, anaphora errors occurred in 44% of the sentences produced by the younger children (2;6–3;5) and in 28% of the sentences produced by the older children (3;6–5;7).

We are now in position to evaluate the conclusions drawn by Flynn. Let us look first at the claim that the imitation task directly taps structural knowledge because "imitation does not necessarily require establishing the referents or generating a complete representation of sentence meaning" (Flynn 1986b, 138). As noted by Lasnik and Crain (1985), the fact that children make anaphora errors in the imitation task entails that they do establish the referents of the NPs in the test sentences. An anaphora error like (8) is a paraphrase of (7); the two sentences express the same meaning using different word order. In light of the fact that anaphora errors rearrange NPs in a way that preserves the gist of the original sentence, we would conclude that such errors occur only if the referents of the NPs in the original sentence had been established.

Anaphora errors indicate that children understood the meaning of sentences like (7) as involving backward anaphora. On the basis of the anaphora errors, some researchers have concluded that children experience difficulty with backward anaphora (e.g., Solan 1983). The backward anaphora interpretation cannot be too difficult for children to construct, however, because sentences like (7) need not involve anaphora at all. An alternative would be to interpret the pronoun as referring "directly," to someone who is not mentioned in the sentence. The high proportion of anaphora errors shows that the backward anaphora interpretation is frequently favored over the "deictic" (or "direct reference") interpretation; if children had consistently adopted the deictic interpretation, they would have avoided anaphora errors and would have repeated the test sentences *correctly*.

The availability of the backward anaphora reading in the imitation task is interesting, because the deictic interpretation does appear to be favored by children in the act-out task. For example, two-thirds of the children studied by Tavakolian (1978) acted out sentences like (7), in which a pronoun preceded a lexical NP, by interpreting the pronoun as referring to a figure present in the experimental workspace, but not mentioned in the sentence.

Why, then, is the deictic interpretation of the pronoun suppressed in the imitation task? In our view, this is the consequence of presenting sentences outside of context, that is, in the so-called null context. In the act-out task, (toy) figures are present in the experimental workspace. These figures establish potential referents for the NPs of the test sentences.[2] In the imitation task, by contrast, there are no potential referents other than those denoted by the lexical NPs contained in the test sentences. Therefore, for a pronoun to refer to someone other than the referent of an NP mentioned in the sentence, its referent would have to be conjured up by the hearer. In chapter 12, we provide evidence that even adults avoid interpretations of ambiguous sentences that refer to entities that have not been introduced into the conversational context. The finding that children and adults adopt similar strategies for interpreting ambiguous sentences is expected on the Modularity Matching Model.

With respect to the construction of a complete representation of sentence meaning, we would draw the same conclusion as Potter and Lombardi (1990), who investigated verbatim recall of sentences by both children and adults:

> [I]mmediate recall involves regeneration of the sentence from a conceptual representation[,] ... a representation that is based on the deepest, message level. [Immediate] Memory is (nearly) verbatim not because of a special short-term representation of the surface sequence, but because the regeneration process of recall makes use of recently activated ... entries in the lexicon to express the ideas in the sentence, using the normal mechanisms of sentence production. (p. 650)

Further evidence for this conclusion is provided by Martin (1993), who reports the findings of a battery of linguistic tests administered to a patient, E.A., who has an auditory memory span of two, as assessed by serial recall of auditorily presented words. Despite a severe limitation in immediate memory, E.A. was able to repeat the gist of two-clause sentences in an imitation task. Here are two examples (from Martin 1993, 180):

(9)   After eating dinner, the man walked the dog.
      E.A.   "After supper, the man took his dog for a walk."

(10)   Before calling her mother, the girl had a cup of tea.
      E.A.   "The girl drank some hot tea before she went to talk to her mother."

Notice that in repeating (10), E.A. converted a left-branching construction to a right-branching one. This is interesting, because it is the kind of "error" based on directionality that children were found to make in the studies by Lust (1981). The fact that E.A. correctly paraphrased (10), however, shows that she processed the syntactic and semantic structure of (10). This counts against Flynn's (1986b) claim that the imitation task directly taps syntactic processing, but does not require the construction of sentence meaning. Martin notes:

> Most of E.A.'s attempts at repetition were paraphrases that either preserved the meaning of the original sentence (50% of the sentences) or were only slightly different in meaning (10% of the sentences). (p. 180)

Along with Martin (1993) and Potter and Lombardi (1990), we would conclude, therefore, that the imitation task requires the formation of both a syntactic and a semantic representation and includes establishing the referents of the NPs in the target sentences, Flynn's claim notwithstanding.

We also question Flynn's second conclusion: that extralinguistic knowledge artificially inflates the level of correct performance in the act-out task. It seems unlikely that people have formed opinions about the plausibility of the events mentioned in the sentences used in Flynn's study, where sentences were about circles touching squares, triangles turning over, and so forth. Therefore in the interpretation of such sentences, extralinguistic knowledge is unlikely to increase the proportion of correct responses.

This leaves us to consider the possible contribution of the pragmatic lead to subjects' responses. Performance did not improve in the pragmatic lead condition; in fact, it plummeted. There were 65% correct responses in the absence of a pragmatic lead, but only 49% correct responses when a pragmatic lead was supplied. This shows that subjects were not aided by the pragmatic leads; they were confused by them for some reason. The overall decrease in comprehension with pragmatic leads is not inconsistent with the observed decrease in coreference between the pronoun and the subject NP in the pragmatic lead condition; presumably, this reduction occurred on trials where subjects were not confused.

Nor is the drop in correct responses in the pragmatic lead condition inconsistent with the observation that there were more errors overall in the imitation task than in the act-out task. Our account of the (nonsignificant) difference in performance on the two tasks is quite simple: more kinds of responses were counted as errors in the imitation task than in the act-out task. Superior performance in the act-out task is interpreted by Flynn as evidence that "subjects can productively rely on and use pragmatic context and knowledge in comprehension to an extent not helpful in production" (p. 151). As noted, the pragmatic lead sentences were actually detrimental to performance in Flynn's study. It seems likely, also, that extralinguistic knowledge was simply irrelevant.

9.4 Conclusion

Where do things stand? As we see it, the imitation task and the act-out task both induce artificially high error rates, in large part because they present sentences outside of context. If this is correct, then it lets the Modularity Matching Model off the hook. The question remains whether tasks can be devised that produce results in keeping with the Modularity Matching Model, or whether, as the Competing Factors Model maintains, all tasks are influenced to a greater or lesser degree by a host of factors in addition to grammatical competence. Adopting the Competing Factors Model, Flynn (1986b) infers that the factors that impede the imitation task and the act-out task will also impede performance on other tasks:

> [O]ther commonly used tasks, such as grammaticality judgment tests, ... yes/no answers to comprehension questions, are all mediated by a set of extralinguistic factors that could significantly attenuate access to a learner's structural knowledge of a language or produce results seriously confounded by the task requirements themselves. (p. 155)

Not necessarily, according to the Modularity Matching Model. If there are tasks that do not impose extraneous demands on language processing, performance should be nearly perfect. Later, we will describe two such tasks: the elicited production task and the truth value judgment task.

Chapter 10

Judgment Tasks and Competing Factors

This chapter compares the predictions of the Competing Factors Model and the Modularity Matching Model as they pertain to experimental studies of child language using "discrete" measures, such as yes/no judgments. The research designs we discuss in this chapter investigate children's knowledge of linguistic principles that prohibit the assignment of certain meanings to sentences—that is, with ⟨sentence, *meaning⟩ pairs. Therefore, these research designs attempt to assess the range of meanings that subjects can assign to the test sentences.

In chapter 7, we noted a problem in interpreting the findings from nondiscrete (= continuous) measures such as reaction time, when the issue is whether or not sentences are ambiguous for children. In responding to ambiguous sentences, children (like adults) might exhibit a preference for one interpretation over its competitors. It could turn out, however, that children favor the interpretation that corresponds to the only interpretation that adults assign to a sentence. That is, the sentence could be unambiguous for adults and ambiguous for children, and yet children could *favor* the adult interpretation and therefore respond to it in the same way as adults do. This scenario limits the utility of quantitative measures in assessing children's linguistic knowledge. We are therefore led to seek measures that ascertain when a meaning is authorized or proscribed by children's grammars, not preferred or dispreferred. Because linguistic constraints proscribe meanings, reaction time measures are of limited application in the study of children's knowledge of constraints (unless they are augmented by measures that directly reflect the linguistic analyses that children assign to sentences).

At first glance, it might seem that judgment tasks do not suffer from the same limitations. In this chapter, we will show that there is more to the matter than meets the eye. The same kinds of problems that confront nondiscrete measures of behavior arise with judgment tasks, depending on the level of successful performance that is taken as evidence of linguistic knowledge. According to the Modularity Matching Model, if children can parse a sentence and relate it appropriately to the context, then they will know ("cognize" in the sense of Chomsky 1981) whether or not the representation they assign to the sentence is grammatical or violates a principle of grammar. If children understand the experimental task and are cooperative, they will perform perfectly, or nearly so. Because the Competing Factors Model accepts less than perfect performance as evidence of linguistic knowledge, it is difficult on this model to ascertain when children find sentences ambiguous and when they find them unambiguous. But, as we have shown, this is crucial in deciding whether or not constraints are operative in children's grammars.

Putting aside the issue of how data should be interpreted, we note that two basic research designs have been implemented in the use of judgment tasks. In one procedure, the same sentence is presented in different contexts; one context favors one interpretation of the sentence and the other context favors an alternative interpretation. In the other procedure, two different sentences are presented in the same context, to determine whether or not the sentences can be associated with the same meaning. With the context held constant, the observation that subjects respond to the test sentences differently can be informative about differences in their underlying grammatical knowledge. Similarly, the observation that subjects respond in the same way to different sentences, with the context held constant, can be informative about their grammars. Although similar designs are used both by advocates of the Modularity Matching Model and by advocates of the Competing Factors Model, the models differ in certain features of design as well as the interpretation of findings. We defer discussion of the differences in design features to part III; here, we focus on the interpretation of research findings.

10.1 Manipulating the Context

This section continues to consider research strategies stemming from the Competing Factors Model, but ones that utilize the research strategy of matching sentences against different contexts: one corresponding to the sentence meaning that is prohibited by a linguistic constraint, and the other corresponding to the sentence meaning that is permitted by the adult grammar.

The experiment we focus on is by Grimshaw and Rosen (1990). This study was also designed to test children's understanding of sentences containing ordinary pronouns. As noted in chapter 9, the interpretation of ordinary pronouns, such as *him* and *her*, is syntactically constrained, by Principle B (see chapters 31–33). One restriction on the interpretation of pronouns is illustrated in (1).

(1) Ernie patted him.
  a. *Meaning$_1$ (coreference interpretation): <u>Ernie</u> patted <u>him</u>.
  b. Meaning$_2$ (deictic interpretation): <u>Ernie</u> patted him.

Each trial of Grimshaw and Rosen's experiment consisted of a short video clip in which puppets were acting out a scene; then a hand puppet controlled by the experimenter said what it thought had happened in the video. There were two trials for each target sentence. The puppet's commentary for one trial is given in (2).

(2) Big Bird was standing with Ernie. Big Bird hit him.

In the video for (2), Big Bird was standing near Ernie, but Big Bird was hitting himself, not Ernie. If a child accepted the puppet's commentary on these trials, then the child was interpreting the sentence incorrectly, allowing the pronoun to be anaphorically linked to Big Bird. We will refer to this illicit interpretation as *meaning₁*, or the *coreference interpretation*.

Sentences like (3) were also presented.

(3) I saw Big Bird doing something with Ernie. Big Bird patted him.

The video corresponding to (3) showed Big Bird patting Ernie. Therefore, the test sentence was a grammatically correct description of the video if the child interpreted the pronoun as referring to Ernie. We will call this interpretation *meaning₂*; this meaning gives the *deictic interpretation* of the pronoun.

The finding was that children said "Yes" to (3) in the second situation a higher proportion of the time than they said "Yes" to (2) in the first situation. To put it another way, children accepted the deictic interpretation (meaning$_2$) when it was a correct description of a situation more often than they accepted the coreference interpretation (meaning$_1$) when *it* was a correct description of a situation. On the basis of these findings, Grimshaw and Rosen conclude that children know the linguistic constraint governing the assignment of reference to pronouns. They contend that the "difference" in children's correct responses to similar sentences in different situations is sufficient to guarantee that children know the constraint.

Here is their argument. Suppose that children lack the grammatical principle instructing them that the test sentence is ungrammatical on meaning$_1$. If so, then meaning$_1$ and meaning$_2$ are both possible interpretations for children. On the basis of the proportion of children's "Yes" responses to the sentence in a situation that makes it true on meaning$_2$, a "best guess" estimate can be derived about the proportion of "Yes" responses that are expected in a situation that makes the sentence true on meaning$_1$. If children go out of their way to reject the sentence significantly more often on meaning$_1$ than is expected according to the "best guess" estimate, then something children know must be responsible for the different pattern of behavior in the two cases. The most likely candidate is the principle governing the interpretation of pronouns, which prohibits meaning$_1$.

In Grimshaw and Rosen's study, children accepted the test sentences 83% of the time on meaning$_2$, the meaning that is consistent with the adult grammar. According to Grimshaw and Rosen, children who lacked the grammatical principle that prohibits meaning$_1$ should have accepted meaning$_1$ the same proportion of the time (i.e., roughly 83% of the time). This did not happen, however. Children gave "Yes" responses to meaning$_1$ in the relevant situation only 42% of the time. The difference between 83% and 42%, Grimshaw and Rosen conclude, is due to children's knowledge of the grammatical principle prohibiting meaning$_1$.

We disagree with this conclusion. Its validity hinges on two assumptions: that the Competing Factors Model is basically correct and that children can recover either meaning of an ambiguous sentence with equal ease. According to Grimshaw and Rosen, the assignment of either meaning$_1$ or meaning$_2$ simply depends on which interpretation makes the sentence true in the experimental context. This is what made their study seem to have more promise than the preferential looking paradigm—children were actually rejecting the illicit interpretation some proportion of the time.

Let us walk though the situation a bit more slowly. We are attempting to evaluate the hypothesis that children lack the constraint, that is, Principle B. If this hypothesis is correct, then the second sentence in (2)—namely, (4)—is ambiguous for children.

(4)   Big Bird hit him.

Suppose, now, that this hypothesis is correct, namely that (4) is ambiguous for children. But suppose further that children do not have equal access to the alternative interpretations of an ambiguous sentence, as Grimshaw and Rosen suppose. That is, children might have a *preference* for one interpretation over the other. If so, then at least one other factor contributes to children's responses, in addition to the bias to access the interpretation that makes an ambiguous sentence true in the context. This additional factor is the preference to resolve the ambiguity in one way rather than in other ways.

With two (or more) factors at play, however, we must consider the possibility that one of the factors could outweigh its competitors. It is possible, for example, that the parsing preference for the deictic interpretation of the pronoun in (4) outweighs the bias to accept the interpretation that makes (4) true in the conversational context—the coreference interpretation. If children's responses show greater consistency with the parsing preference than with the bias to access an interpretation that makes a sentence true, then the children will respond correctly more often than not, despite the absence of Principle B in their grammars. Finally, it should be noted that it does not suffice to rule out this scenario to establish that children assign the deictic interpretation to a larger extent in contexts that make the sentence true on this reading. If, as we are supposing, the deictic interpretation is preferred, then the fact that this reading is also consistent with the bias to say "Yes" should boost the availability of this reading even higher.

We have been drawn back into the same predicament as with Hirsh-Pasek and Golinkoff's study; the possibility of a parsing preference for the correct interpretation throws a wrench into Grimshaw and Rosen's argument. The problem is clear: if there are inherent preferences for resolving ambiguities in favor of one meaning over its competitors, then children should not be expected to produce the same pattern of responses to these alternative interpretations. Moreover, according to the Modularity Matching Model, children should exhibit exactly the same preferences as adults, who are known to favor one reading of an ambiguous sentence over the others in many instances (these preferences are discussed in chapter 12). From the vantage point of the Modularity Matching Model, then, Grimshaw and Rosen's analysis confuses children's preferences in interpreting ambiguous sentences and their knowledge of linguistic principles. We will explain this in more detail in chapter 11.

10.2 Preferences versus Principles

It should be apparent that a great deal hinges on children's parsing preferences. For example, the data from Grimshaw and Rosen's study can be taken as evidence of children's knowledge of Principle B only if it can be independently demonstrated that children who respond incorrectly to sentences like (4) nevertheless favor the coreference interpretation of pronouns in ambiguous sentences. So far, the jury is out on this question. There is little help for Grimshaw and Rosen's account in the observation that the coreference interpretation of pronouns may be preferred in certain tasks (e.g., in the imitation task). In our view, this preference is simply the consequence of presenting sentences to children outside of context, in the so-called null context. To support this conjecture, we would point to findings from a different task, the act-out task, where children appear to favor the deictic interpretation of pronouns. Presumably, the results from the two tasks differ because the act-out task establishes potential referents for the NPs of the test sentences in the experimental workspace.[1] The imitation task, by contrast, does not; for a pronoun to refer to someone other than the referent of an NP mentioned in the sentence, its referent has to be mentally conjured up by the child. In chapter 12, we provide evidence that adults avoid interpretations of ambiguous sentences that refer to entities that have not been introduced into the conversational context. The finding that children adopt similar strategies for interpreting ambiguous sentences is therefore expected on the Modularity Matching Model.

The final difficulty with Grimshaw and Rosen's study is the low success rates by children who, they conclude, have mastered the linguistic knowledge being investigated. Such low levels of accuracy are accepted by researchers who adopt the Competing Factors Model, because they view children's linguistic behavior as an aggregate of linguistic and nonlinguistic factors, their expression of linguistic knowledge sometimes being suppressed by extraneous factors. Because the Modularity Matching Model assumes that children and adults share the same cognitive mechanisms, the observation that adults correctly comprehend sentences with ordinary pronouns, but children do not, is inconsistent with the model.

Children's poor performance with sentences governed by Principle B (i.e., roughly 50% acceptance of Principle B violations) does not sit well with the Modularity Matching Model. Even if children's failures do not stem from a lack of grammatical competence, but are due to limitations in processing capacity or the lack of certain principles of pragmatics, as several researchers have claimed (Grodzinsky and Reinhart 1993; Chien and Wexler 1990), the differences are not anticipated by the Modularity Matching Model (but see Thornton and Wexler, forthcoming, for an account of children's errors that is consistent with the model). Therefore, the model would have to be amended in appropriate respects, depending on how the controversy is resolved. However, amending the model is preferable to abandoning it altogether, in our view. As we said, maximizing the similarities between children's cognitive systems and those of adults is responsive to the general problem of language learnability—why all children successfully converge on an adult linguistic system despite the considerable latitude in their linguistic experience. To the extent that the cognitive mechanisms of children and adults are similar, learnability problems are circumvented. This is why we assume equivalence as the Null Hypothesis. By contrast, the Competing Factors Model abandons the Null Hypothesis from the start. On this model, children differ from adults in language processing. This adds unwanted degrees of freedom, by tolerating a wide range of processing explanations of differences between children and adults. Moreover, it leaves a new question to be addressed for each such account: how does the processing system of children change, so as to converge on the adult system?

10.3 Implications for Research Design

In experiments with children, the contexts that researchers construct are made to be consistent with more than one interpretation of the test sentences. One interpretation that is suited to the context is the adult interpretation. As the graphic below indicates, this will be referred to as $meaning_2$. Presumably, $meaning_2$ is also available to children. If children lack the linguistic principle being investigated, however, they will *also* be able to assign the interpretation that is prohibited by the principle: $meaning_1$. That is, children will have access to an interpretation of test sentences that is not available to adults. Experimental contexts are devised to see whether or not children access the nonadult interpretation, $meaning_1$. In designing this hypothetical experiment, let us suppose that the experimenter decided to make the test sentences false in the context if $meaning_2$ was assigned to them; and let us suppose that the contexts were also constructed such that the sentences were true if $meaning_1$ was assigned to them. In chapter 27, we explain when this particular design is appropriate.

Child	Adult	
$\langle$sentence, meaning$_1\rangle$	$\langle$sentence,* meaning$_1\rangle$	Ruled out
$\langle$sentence, meaning$_2\rangle$	$\langle$sentence, meaning$_2\rangle$	

If children consistently rejected the test sentences in these (ambiguous) contexts, their behavior would be compelling evidence that the only interpretation available to them is the adult interpretation, meaning$_2$, the interpretation of the sentence that makes it false in the context. The conclusion would be that children, like adults, find the test sentence unambiguous, by virtue of knowing the linguistic principle under investigation. Suppose, however, that the outcome is less conclusive, with children responding "No" to the test sentences only 60% of the time.

Input		Response
$\langle$sentence, context$\rangle$	meaning$_1$, true	"Yes" 40%
	meaning$_2$, false	"No" 60%

The Competing Factors Model maintains that such a level of performance is sufficient to infer knowledge of the linguistic principle. All that is required to demonstrate children's linguistic competence is above-chance performance in response to sentences testing the linguistic principle; the 40% "errors" may be attributed to "performance factors." We take this to be the viewpoint advanced by Grimshaw and Rosen (1990), for example.

There is another possibility to consider, however. On this scenario, children lack the linguistic principle. In this case, the test sentences will be ambiguous for them: both meaning$_1$ and meaning$_2$ will be accessible. But now suppose that children have a strong preference for the interpretation that is permissible in the adult grammar (i.e., meaning$_2$). This preference could be quite strong, say, by a factor of 3:1. If there were no other influences on a particular child's decision, then, the child would access meaning$_2$ 75% of the time, and meaning$_1$ 25% of the time. Because the sentence is false on meaning$_2$ in the experimental context, the result would be 75% "No" responses by children. However, children's preference for one interpretation of the sentence over another is not the only factor that influences their decisions. In addition, they exhibit a tendency to select a reading that makes the speaker's sentence true in the context. In the present experimental setup, this bias favors meaning$_1$, the reading that is true in the context (but ungrammatical for adults). It seems reasonable to conjecture that this bias could boost the availability of meaning$_1$ by 15%, such that meaning$_1$ is adopted 40% of the time, rather than 25% of the time—the result that would have been obtained in its absence. There will be a corresponding drop in "No" responses, from 75% to 60%.[2]

In short, on both of the scenarios we have considered, children give "No" responses 60% of the time. The reasons underlying this low rate of rejection are different on the two scenarios, however. In one case, children know the principle under investigation but do not display this knowledge perfectly; their low level of correct performance is attributed to competing factors. In the other case, children lack the principle, and their low level of performance is attributed to parsing preferences for one interpretation of an ambiguous sentence. Since both accounts explain the findings, it would clearly be unwarranted to infer from children's less than total rejections that they command the linguistic principle under investigation.

This discussion points out the main problem in adopting the methodological stance of the Competing Factors Model. Because the alternative interpretations of ambiguous sentences are not necessarily equally easy to access, children's occasional or even substantial rejection of sentences on an interpretation that is prohibited by a constraint is only circumstantial evidence that the constraint is part of their grammars. The possibility exists that the sentences are ambiguous for children, but that they prefer the interpretation associated with the "No" response (i.e., the adult interpretation).[3] Therefore, if we adopt the methodological stance of the Competing Factors Model, we may confuse behavior that reveals preferences among alternative interpretations with behavior that reveals knowledge of linguistic principles.[4]

To avoid this confound of parsing preferences and grammatical knowledge, the Modularity Matching Model advocates a different research strategy: an experimenter can infer that children know a linguistic principle only if they perform with near total accuracy, as adults do. Fortunately, it follows from the basic architecture of the Modularity Matching Model that it is reasonable to expect near perfect performance by children, as well as by adults. Both children and adults have grammatical modules, processing modules, and perhaps other modules. When a child or an adult is confronted with sentences that are ambiguous, the processing and "other" modules can create preferences for one reading or another. But neither children nor adults will assign an incorrect analysis to an unambiguous sentence; as long as the correct analysis is felicitous in the context, the pressures to interpret the sentence by means other than grammatical knowledge will be resisted. The reason is that the grammatical components preempt these other factors; they do not compete with them.

One might object that, even on the Modularity Matching Model, there is also no way *in principle* to distinguish principles from preferences. Pursuing the same line of reasoning that we brought to bear against the Competing Factors Model, one might counter that children could find a test sentence ambiguous, but favor the interpretation associated with the "No" response to such an extent that they display the same pattern of behavior as adults do (i.e., near total rejection of the test sentences), even though they lack the linguistic knowledge that underlies adult behavior. Similarly, the interpretation of the findings of production studies might be called into question on the grounds that children's consistent production of sentences conforming to one structural analysis does not entail that other structural analyses are not compatible with their grammars—the alternative analyses may simply be less preferred.

Although such a state of affairs may seem unlikely (in light of the inherent bias to analyze ambiguous sentences in a way that makes the speaker's statement true), we take this objection seriously, because it points to a potential limitation on the effectiveness of both of the methodologies we will introduce. We will therefore mention experimental maneuvers that can be instigated to overcome this potential confound. For the moment, let it suffice to underscore the importance of distinguishing principles from preferences in the design of experimental studies of child language. In our view, the distinction between principles and preferences looms larger than any other in the construction of appropriate experimental methodology.

10.4 Conclusion

In this chapter, we have argued against the research strategy of the Competing Factors Model. According to this model, all that is required to demonstrate knowledge of a linguistic principle is conformity to the principle at a level significantly above chance. From a theoretical standpoint, the problem with the Competing Factors Model is that it introduces additional degrees of freedom beyond those of the Modularity Matching Model. The Competing Factors Model views language as a large set of "tendencies," so that knowledge of language amounts to certain statistical tendencies in behavior. Therefore, showing that the statistical behavior of children is different for different constructions shows that they have learned adult capacities of grammar. The Competing Factors Model claims that grammar is just one linguistic ability that competes with other linguistic abilities to yield a statistical portrait of behavior. In the next chapter, we review three more studies, the findings of which appear to support the Competing Factors Model, in order to draw out the differences between this model and the Modularity Matching Model. Reasons for the alternative claims of the Modularity Matching Model are presented in chapters 12 and 13.

Chapter 11

Context and Competing Factors

In the use of judgment tasks, two basic research designs have been implemented within the Competing Factors framework. One procedure was discussed in the previous chapter. The procedure involved presenting the same sentence in different contexts: one context favoring one interpretation of the sentence and the other context favoring an alternative interpretation. In this chapter, we discuss another research design. In studies adopting this design, different sentences are presented in the same context, to determine whether or not the sentences can be associated with the same meaning. With context held constant, the observation that children respond differently to different sentences serves as a basis for inferences about children's underlying grammatical knowledge (similarly, if they respond in the same way to different sentences, with context held constant). Results from studies using such a design have led some researchers to reach conclusions that are inconsistent with the Modularity Matching Model. Therefore, it is necessary to evaluate these studies, if we are to retain the model. As always, we will examine actual studies, beginning with an investigation of Principle C of the binding theory, by Lust, Eisele, and Mazuka (1992).

11.1 Principle C

Principle C prohibits anaphoric relations between pronouns and names. Consider examples (1)–(3), adapted from the study by Lust, Eisele, and Mazuka (1992). As before, the intended interpretation of the sentence is indicated by underlining; if two NPs are underlined, then they are taken to have the same reference.

(1) *He ate the apple when Big Bird touched the pillow.

(2) When he ate the apple Big Bird touched the pillow.

(3) Big Bird touched the pillow when he ate the apple.

Principle C prohibits coreference between the pronoun, *he*, and the name, *Big Bird*, in (1), but does not prohibit coreference between these same elements in (2) or in (3).

Principle C is a linguistic constraint; it prohibits coreference in certain sentences. To assess children's knowledge of this constraint, Lust, Eisele, and Mazuka presented pictures to children and had them judge whether the sentences were, or were not, accurate descriptions of the pictures. In one of the pictures corresponding to (1)–(3), there were two characters, Big Bird and Oscar the Grouch. Big Bird was holding a pillow and eating an apple. Oscar the Grouch was in a garbage can, just observing. Lust, Eisele, and Mazuka call this the *coreference picture*. Children who know that coreference is blocked in (1), but not in (2) or (3), would be expected to accept (2) and (3) as accurate descriptions of the coreference picture. By contrast, children who know Principle C should indicate that (1) is not an accurate description of the picture: Principle C dictates that the pronoun, *he*, cannot refer to Big Bird; the only other potential referent is Oscar, but Oscar is not eating the apple.

Sentences (2) and (3) performed another service in this study. Notice that in these sentences, the linear order of the pronoun and the name differs. Sentence (2) is an instance of backward anaphora, because the pronoun precedes the name, whereas (3) is an instance of forward anaphora. Lust, Eisele, and Mazuka call this difference *directionality*. By comparing the rates at which children accepted (2) and (3) in response to the coreference pictures, Lust, Eisele, and Mazuka attempted to measure the effect of directionality. One of the findings of their study was a statistically significant effect of directionality: children were found to accept forward anaphora sentences like (3) more often than they accepted backward anaphora sentences like (2), in response to the coreference pictures (83% and 57% acceptances, respectively). Of course, it is not "incorrect" for children to reject either (2) or (3), because the grammar permits a direct reference (deictic) interpretation of the pronoun in both sentences. And on the direct reference interpretation, these sentences are not true descriptions of the coreference picture.

Because Lust, Eisele, and Mazuka advocate the Competing Factors Model, they assume that the directionality effect will influence children's responses to unambiguous sentences like (1), as well as to ambiguous sentences like (2) and (3). Moreover, they assume that directionality will influence children to a similar extent in interpreting sentences like (1), as compared to ones like (2). But, in contrast to sentences like (2), sentences like (1) are also subject to Principle C, the grammatical constraint that prohibits coreference between the pronoun and the name. In short, the directionality factor and Principle C conspire to promote the direct reference interpretation of the pronoun in sentences like (1), whereas only the directionality factor is operative in sentences like (2).

Therefore, to test children's knowledge of the constraint, Lust, Eisele, and Mazuka proposed that children must reject sentences like (1) significantly more often than they reject sentences like (2) in response to coreference pictures. This was indeed what happened. Children rejected sentences like (1) 68% of the time; they rejected sentences like (2) 43% of the time. The significant difference in the rates of rejection was attributed to knowledge of the grammatical constraint.[1] Children's less than perfect performance (i.e., the 32% erroneous acceptance rate for sentences like (1)) was blamed on "performance factors."

In an earlier study, Lust, Loveland, and Kornet (1980) sought to determine whether or not children "consult" pragmatic context in deciding upon the semantic interpretation of sentences like (1) and (2). To answer this question, they compared children's responses to such sentences with and without a pragmatic lead. The pragmatic lead was presented before each test sentence, for example, "I am going to tell you a story about Big Bird. He ate the apple when Big Bird touched the pillow." As this example illustrates, the pragmatic lead sometimes invites children to initially assign Big Bird as the referent of the pronoun in sentence (1); this turns out to be incorrect, however, once the name is encountered. Therefore, during on-line sentence parsing the pragmatic lead sometimes conflicted with the linguistic constraint under investigation. Lust, Loveland, and Kornet found that "children did allow the presence of a pragmatic lead to modulate their coreference judgments to some extent ..., increasing the percentage of coreference judgments" (Lust, Eisele, and Mazuka 1992, 338). The pragmatic lead resulted in a 35% reduction in correct responses for sentences like (1)

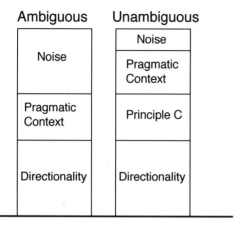

Figure 11.1
Predictions of the Competing Factors Model for ambiguous and unambiguous sentences

and a 59% reduction in coreference judgments for sentences like (2). Again, the difference was significant. Interpreting the findings of Lust, Loveland, and Kornet's study, Lust, Eisele, and Mazuka remark that "... the pragmatic context appears to interact with the knowledge that distinguishes [these] sentences on independent, presumably (grammatical) linguistic and structural grounds" (p. 338).[2]

The studies we have just reviewed are typical of one research strategy used by proponents of the Competing Factors Model. Therefore, it is important to compare the methodological assumptions of these studies with those of the Modularity Matching Model. According to the model assumed by Lust, Eisele, and Mazuka, children's responses to ambiguous sentences like (2) and (3) depend on two factors: directionality and the pragmatic context. In response to unambiguous sentences like (1), an additional factor interacts with directionality and the pragmatic context, namely Principle C. Added to these interacting factors is some level of "noise," contributed by uncontrolled factors. We illustrate these assumptions in figure 11.1. As the figure indicates, the Competing Factors Model simply adds linguistic knowledge as another factor to the equation for unambiguous sentences, as compared to ambiguous sentences.

The Modularity Matching Model is not "additive" in this way. On this model, factors like directionality, pragmatic context, and other factors we have discussed, sometimes play a role in children's understanding of ambiguous sentences; however, these factors do not play a role in the interpretation of unambiguous sentences, such as (1). Figure 11.2 illustrates the assumptions of the Modularity Matching Model.

Comparing the two figures, we see that the difference between the two models can be pinned on the analysis of unambiguous sentences. According to the Modularity Matching Model, unambiguous sentences are not subject to "performance factors," except for a small level of "noise" that is present in any experimental context. The reason for this is that the (partial) syntactic and semantic representations that are assigned to unambiguous sentences are completed *before* these other factors enter the picture. Therefore, grammatical principles alone dictate children's responses.

The differences between the models have consequences for research design. In contrast to proponents of the Competing Factors Model, proponents of the Modularity Matching Model are not content with less than nearly perfect performance by children on sentences like (1), *He ate the apple when Big Bird touched the pillow.*

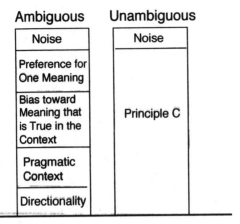

Figure 11.2
Predictions of the Modularity Matching Model for ambiguous and unambiguous sentences

Ambiguous sentences like (2), *When he ate the apple Big Bird touched the pillow*, are useful as controls because they establish a baseline level of performance for the particular interpretation that is not governed by the linguistic constraint in question. Suppose that children manifest a strong preference for an interpretation that is not governed by the constraint, when they are asked to respond to ambiguous sentences. If so, then the fact that they reject this interpretation for unambiguous sentences like (1) is compelling evidence of linguistic knowledge—in the present case, knowledge of Principle C. To put the point another way, children's responses to the ambiguous controls are used primarily to rule out an alternative explanation of their responses to the unambiguous test sentences. As noted earlier, if a linguistic constraint is absent from children's grammars, sentences governed by the constraint would be ambiguous for them. Nevertheless, they might have a preference for one interpretation over the others. Moreover, their preference might be consistent with the constraint under investigation; that is, they might prefer for the adult interpretation. If factors conspire in this way, children could produce responses that would be counted as correct, even though they lacked the constraint under investigation. In short, children would give the right answers for the wrong reasons. Ambiguous control sentences enable an experimenter to rule out this explanation of children's (seemingly) correct behavior.

In the best of all possible worlds, children will prefer to interpret ambiguous control sentences like (2) by assigning coreference between the pronoun and the name, but they will not tolerate this interpretation of test sentences like (1). If these are the findings, then it may be unnecessary to perform statistical tests of the differences in children's performance in the two conditions; "eyeball" statistics may suffice in drawing conclusions about children's knowledge of the constraint. Suppose, however, that children assign coreference in the control condition less than half of the time. In this case, it may be necessary to establish that there is a statistically significant difference between children's responses to the ambiguous control sentences and the test sentences. According to the Competing Factors Model, a positive finding resolves the issue; the hypothesis that children lack the constraint can be rejected. On the Modularity Matching Model, by contrast, there is an additional consideration, namely, the proportion of children's correct responses to the test sentences. If children truly find test sentences like (1) to be unambiguous, then they should respond correctly to them nearly 100% of the time. The Competing Factors Model does not impose this additional requirement in order to draw conclusions about children's linguistic knowledge.

The Modularity Matching Model therefore cannot accept the results of Lust, Eisele, and Mazuka's study at face value. Because children are assumed to know Principle C, they are expected to perform better than this. It is incumbent on the Modularity Matching Model to explain *why* children, who are assumed to know Principle C, make 32% errors in interpreting unambiguous sentences like (1). We take up this matter in part III, where we discuss the design features of the truth value judgment task. Our purpose here is to provide examples of research conducted within the Competing Factors framework and to expose the critical differences between that model and the Modularity Matching Model.

11.2 Principle C in Questions

This brings us to a second experiment that adopts the research strategy of holding the meaning/context constant, while comparing children's responses to different sentences. The experiment was conducted by McDaniel and McKee (1993) and is discussed in greater detail in chapter 29. These researchers asked children and an adult control group to indicate the "appropriateness" of an answer given by one puppet to a question asked by another puppet. On different occasions, the puppet who asked the questions produced either a question like that in (4) or one like that in (5). The answer provided by the second puppet was the same in both cases.

(4) Q: Who said he has the best smile?
     A: He did and he did.

(5) Q: Who did he say has the best smile?
     A: He did and he did.

These questions and their corresponding answers followed a short story in which two characters performed a similar action. In the stories associated with (4) and (5), there were two characters who each said that he, himself, had the best smile. The answer, *He did and he did,* is an appropriate response to the first question in this context, but not to the second. Principle C dictates this, as we will explain in chapter 29.

To see if subjects know Principle C, McDaniel and McKee compared their judgments about whether the same answer is appropriate for the two different questions in (4) and (5). Both children and adults indicated that this answer was appropriate to the question in (4) significantly more often (according to a statistical test) than to the question in (5). McDaniel and McKee inferred that the findings demonstrated children's knowledge of the grammatical principle under investigation.

It turned out, however, that the absolute level of performance by both children and adults was not very good. Both groups correctly rejected the answer as inappropriate to the question in (5) only about half the time, although, admittedly, neither group rejected the answer as inappropriate to (4) very often. On the basis of the greater acceptance rate to question/answer pairs like (4) than to ones like (5), McDaniel and McKee nevertheless concluded that both groups know the grammatical principle under investigation. Here is their argument:

> Overall, both the children and the adults clearly differentiated between the ... cases. The extent to which the adult group made this distinction shows how the

grammatical principle ... is expressed in this particular performance task. The fact that the children made the distinction to the same extent as the adults ["whose grammars we presumably know about" (p. 278)] shows, therefore, that their grammars also contain the principle.... (p. 287)

Although this argument and its conclusion are consistent with the Competing Factors Model, they are not consistent with the Modularity Matching Model. According to the Modularity Matching Model, both children and adults should systematically reject question/answer pairs like (5). On this model, it does not suffice for there to simply be a statistically significant difference in the rates of acceptance between different sentence types, even if "the children's distinction between types ... [is] ... significant and as great as the distinction made by adults" (p. 289).

The findings of this study permit us to make another point. In discussing the results of the cross-modal priming study by McKee, Nicol, and McDaniel (1993) in chapter 10, we showed that a group mean can obscure individual differences within groups. The same point can be made using the study by McDaniel and McKee. A close inspection of the data from this study reveals that the distributions of responses by children and adults to question/answer pairs like (5) do not conform to the expectations of the Competing Factors Model. This model predicts a unimodal distribution of responses to constructions that are generated by children's grammars. In the present study, however, the distribution of responses by both children and adults was not unimodal, but more closely approximated the kind of bimodal pattern described earlier. One group accepted the answer "He did and he did" as appropriate to questions like (5), so these subjects did not distinguish questions like those from ones like (4). A second group of subjects were successful at the task; their responses to questions like (5) fell under a different mode than their responses to ones like (4).

The difference in the proportions of correct responses to (4) and (5) was due to the group of children and adults who were successful at the task. Because many children and adults responded incorrectly to the test sentences, however, the findings of McDaniel and McKee's study are inconsistent with the Modularity Matching Model. The point here is that the pattern of responses was also inconsistent with the Competing Factors Model. Therefore, we must look elsewhere for an explanation of the pattern of responses by both children and adults. We discuss the range of possibilities open to the Modularity Matching Model in chapter 15, and we discuss our particular view of the results from McDaniel and McKee's study in chapter 29.

11.3 Universal Quantification

We now discuss a third example of an experiment, within the Competing Factors framework, that adopts the research strategy of holding the meaning/context constant, in order to compare children's responses to different sentences. The topic of this experiment was children's interpretation of sentences with universal quantification.

For at least 30 years, it has been widely believed that even children as old as 4 or 5 often misunderstand simple sentences with a universal quantifier, such as (6) and (7).

(6)   Is every farmer feeding a donkey?

(7)   Is a farmer feeding every donkey?

The basic finding has been replicated with many children and across several languages. If shown a picture like that in figure 11.3, which we will call the *extra* object

NO, NOT THAT ONE

Figure 11.3
The extra object condition

condition, many 3- to 5-year-old children who are asked the question "Is every farmer feeding a donkey?" will respond by saying "No." When asked to explain this answer ("Why not?"), children point to the unfed donkey as the reason (e.g., Philip 1991, 1995; Roeper and de Villiers 1991a; Takahashi 1991). Similarly, when asked the question in (7), if there are farmers who are not feeding donkeys in the context, children will say "No" and point to the "extra" farmers. It seems that children are interpreting (6) and (7) in the same way, as demanding symmetry between farmers and donkeys. These responses by children have therefore been called the *symmetrical response*. Children appear to reject any asymmetry between donkeys and farmers—the mapping must be one to one.

Inhelder and Piaget (1964) attempted to explain children's symmetrical interpretation of sentences like (6) and (7) in nonlinguistic terms, as the result of their inability to distinguish part-whole relationships among sets. Recently, however, a linguistically based account of the symmetrical interpretation, called the *Symmetrical Account*, has been advanced in the literature on language acquisition within the generative framework (Roeper and de Villiers 1991a; Philip 1991, 1995). The Symmetrical Account contends that children hypothesize a nonadult linguistic representation for sentences with a universal quantifier.[3] According to this representation, the quantifier has scope over both nominals, *farmer* and *donkey*, in (6) and (7).

The Symmetrical Account attempts to explain a highly complex array of facts, including children's adultlike behavior in responding to sentences that are not amenable to the symmetrical interpretation. In particular, experimental studies are presented in which children respond to questions like (8) in a variant of the extra object condition

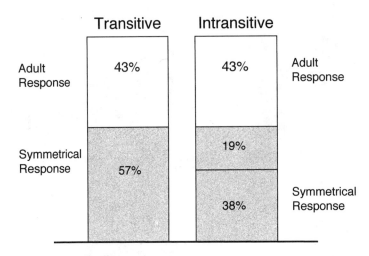

Figure 11.4
Proportion of correct and incorrect responses for transitive and intransitive sentences

where every cat is waving, and every cat is in a box, but where there is an "extra" box with no cat in it. A symmetrical response would be to reject (8) because there is a box without a cat in it.

(8) Is every cat waving?

Questions like (8) do not fall within the purview of the symmetrical interpretation, because (8) has only one noun for the universal quantifier to bind. Therefore, the Symmetrical Account anticipates that children will give significantly fewer symmetrical responses for sentences like (8). This is exactly what happens. Subjects who meet the criteria of being "pure cases" of a symmetry child give significantly fewer symmetrical responses to questions like (8), than to questions with transitive verbs, such as (6) and (7).

Only advocates of the Competing Factors Model would conclude that these results support the Symmetrical Account. From the perspective of the Modularity Matching Model, the results are troublesome. It turned out that there was only a 19% reduction in the proportion of symmetrical responses to sentences with intransitive verb phrases, such as (8), as compared to responses to sentences with transitive verb phrases, such as (6). Symmetrical responses were given by children on 38% of the trials for sentences like (8), even though they lack the ingredients (*two* NPs) essential to forming the linguistic representation that underlies the Symmetrical Account. These erroneous responses by children were chalked up to "response strategies" (Philip 1995, 107), "strong carry-over effects [that] were observed to confound the performance of all subjects" (Philip 1995, 124), and "the similarity of the picture-types across all experimental conditions" (Philip 1995, 109). However, the proportion of the data attributed to "carryover" effects is roughly twice that of the data supporting the experimental hypothesis, according to which the "pure symmetry child" adopts a nonadult linguistic analysis of quantificational sentences with transitive verb phrases. Figure 11.4 summarizes the findings.

High errors rates like this are tolerated by researchers who view linguistic behavior as an aggregate of linguistic and nonlinguistic factors, the expression of children's linguistic knowledge often being overcome by unknown factors. Assuming that adults correctly comprehend sentences like (8), the acceptance of such high error rates by children would be tantamount to surrendering a fundamental assumption of the Modularity Matching Model: that children and adults share the same cognitive mechanisms. A high proportion of errors in response to sentences that are structurally quite simple does not comport well with the Modularity Matching Model and must be explained. It will be, in chapter 35. We postpone discussion until then, however, because the source of children's errors is quite subtle and can be properly understood only after an extended discussion of methodological issues.

Chapter 12

Language Processing

This chapter and the next discuss two factors that researchers have proposed to be in competition with grammatical knowledge in tasks that assess children's linguistic competence: memory and extralinguistic knowledge. On the Competing Factors Model, such factors are expected to exert an influence on performance, to some degree, in any task. According to this model, extralinguistic knowledge can be either harmful or helpful, depending on its affinity with the representation generated by the grammar: if grammatical principles and extralinguistic knowledge agree, performance is improved; if they conflict, performance is depressed. By its perceived nature, on this model, memory is detrimental to performance.

On the Modularity Matching Model, by contrast, memory demands and extralinguistic knowledge play a much more limited role in language processing. In this chapter, we will argue that the influence of memory demands is felt only in certain tasks and on certain linguistic constructions.

In the next chapter, we make similar claims about extralinguistic knowledge. On the Modularity Matching Model, extralinguistic knowledge is used only as a last resort. It is engaged only when children (and adults) are confronted with sentences that are structurally ambiguous and when the specific context in which the sentence is introduced is consistent with more than one of its readings.

Because of the minimal contributions of factors such as memory and extralinguistic knowledge on the Modularity Matching Model, performance is expected to accord, first and foremost, with a person's grammatical knowledge. This leads to the expectation that children will perform (nearly) as well as adults in tasks that tap their linguistic knowledge, such as the elicited production task and the truth value judgment task.

12.1 Competence versus Performance

According to the Modularity Matching Model, the linguistic performance of children and adults should be (close to) perfect in properly designed experimental studies, provided that children know the relevant points of the adult grammar. According to some advocates of the Competing Factors Model, by contrast, perfect performance is an "idealization." These advocates of the model assume that this follows from the basic distinction between competence and performance, as Lust, Chien, and Flynn. (1987) make clear:

> [P]erformance will never directly reflect only grammatical competence, but other factors as well. It will always be variable, even when it reflects grammatical competence.... Thus, because of the nature of performance data, behavioral

evidence for significant grammatical factors will always involve significant contrasts of degree, not absolute success with one condition and absolute failure with another. (p. 282)

Of course [Universal Grammar] will never be directly evidenced in any particular behavior.... (p. 279)

Psycholinguistic research is specifically empirical in the sense that it pursues the assessment of language knowledge through the measurement and analyses of various modes of language behavior, principally speaking and understanding. The language functions which these behaviors reflect, viz., language production and comprehension, constitute language performance. Each performance function involves language competence, but it also involves various other aspects of language knowledge related to the specific behaviors of each performance function. Evidence of language competence ... is thus always mediated by the processing factors involved in each behavioral instance of each language function, as well as by the basic variance assumed in any sampling of performance data. (p. 273)

This view of the interrelation of competence and performance is not the only one, however. One's view of the relation between them depends on a specific set of assumptions about the role of grammar within the performance system. Few researchers in child language make clear their basic assumptions about the theory of performance or the position of grammar within it. Admitting that useful theories of performance are generally ones that incorporate theories of grammar, most researchers are content to draw the immediate inference that grammar is just one factor among many, with the consequence that all performance is less than optimal. In this chapter, we indicate why our own conception of verbal working memory does not adhere to this expectation of the Competing Factors Model.

12.2 The Role of Working Memory in Sentence Processing

As Chomsky (1965) concludes, to gain insight into the performance system, it is instructive to look at the specific grammatical devices that exceed the resources of the system, as well as at those that do not. According to the model of the performance system we endorse, linguistic behavior ordinarily begins to degrade only when specific boundaries of the system are exceeded or when specific processing routines are utilized.

When certain grammatical devices are exploited by the performance system, the result is unacceptable. One device that is known to result in unacceptability is repeated self-embedding. This characteristic of the human sentence-processing mechanism explains the difficulty people experience with multiply center-embedded sentences like (1) (Chomsky and Miller 1963; Chomsky 1965).

(1)   The cheese that the rat that the cat chased ate is on the table.

Ambiguity gives rise to unacceptability in certain instances. An example is the classic garden path sentence, *The horse raced past the barn fell.* We will discuss the reason for the unacceptability of this kind of sentence in chapter 13.

The human sentence-processing mechanism also has a bounded memory. However, the consequence of a finite memory for acceptability is not as pronounced as it is in the case of sentences that contain repeated self-embedding or ones that evoke garden path effects. This is attested by the acceptability of multiply right-branching structures, as in (2).

(2) This is the cat that caught the rat that ate the cheese that is on the table.

Further evidence that memory limitations are not always detrimental to linguistic performance comes from the literature on language breakdown. Studies of brain-damaged patients with severe memory deficits reveal that these individuals are often able to process sentences of considerable length, and ones that involve grammatical devices that are structurally complex, according to a pretheoretical metric of complexity. For example, Martin (1993) reported that her patient, E.A., who has a severe immediate-memory limitation, could successfully comprehend simple active and passive sentences, as well as several kinds of center-embedded relative-clause structures. In addition, E.A. was 90% accurate in detecting gender mismatches, as in (3), where the antecedent and the reflexive are separated by over 10 words.

(3) The girl fell down the stairs at least once a week and often hurt himself.

12.3 Acceptability and Processing Difficulty

If the goal is to discover the operating characteristics of the performance system, then a good research strategy is to examine the relative acceptability of different grammatical devices, such as self-embedding, branching direction, and ambiguity (see Chomsky 1965). It also makes sense to utilize experimental measures that are extremely sensitive to processing difficulty. In this way, the researcher will not overlook factors that help or hinder linguistic processing, but do not cause unacceptability. Earlier we mentioned one such technique: the cross-modal priming paradigm.

Another useful tool is eye-movement recording (eye-tracking). Recording the length of eye fixations during reading has been used effectively to assess processing difficulty in studies of adults. These studies amply demonstrate that acceptable sentences may impose measurable processing difficulties at certain junctures. It has been found that the eyes pause longer in specific regions of certain types of sentences and that they regress from certain regions of the sentence to earlier regions. Such studies have added to researchers' understanding of the nature of the performance system by indicating the relative amount of computation that occurs at various points during sentence comprehension. We will describe two experiments using eye-movement recording in chapter 13, in an empirical demonstration that extralinguistic knowledge does not compete with linguistic principles in the construction of structural representations for sentences.

The observation that there are nonlinguistic constraints on performance should not lead one to infer that a generative grammar does not also underlie linguistic performance. As Fodor and Pylyshyn (1988) remark, the fact that performance improves as memory constraints and the like are lifted is evidence that linguistic knowledge is also accessed in language processing:

> [T]here are a number of considerations, which suggest that, despite de facto constraints on performance, one's knowledge of one's language supports an unbounded productive capacity in much the same way that one's knowledge of addition supports an unbounded number of sums. Among these considerations

are, for example, the fact that a speaker/hearer's performance can be improved by relaxing time constraints, memory constraints, increasing motivation, or supplying pencil and paper. It seems very natural to treat such manipulations as affecting the transient state of the speaker's memory and attention rather that what he knows about—or how he represents—his language. But this treatment is available only on the assumption that the character of the subject's performance is determined by interactions between the available knowledge base and the available computational resources. (p. 802 in Goldman 1993)

As we have shown, the "interaction" between the knowledge base and the computational resources is not so great as to impede performance in most sentences. Moreover, in certain experimental tasks, performance constraints can be relaxed, such that children's (and adults') grammatical knowledge is revealed on nearly every trial. This is important in studies of child language, where the goal is to determine the nature of the grammar embedded in the performance system. For such studies, then, it makes sense to seek tasks that are not influenced to an appreciable degree by factors that contribute either to unacceptability or to subtle processing difficulties.

Granting the basic distinction between grammaticality and acceptability, the goal of empirical research in child language boils down to determining which sentences children find acceptable. As a simple example, consider (4).

(4) Him left.

Suppose some children consistently produce such sentences (in contexts where adults say *He left*). It would be reasonable to conclude that such productions directly reveal the grammatical competence of these children. It would not be reasonable to conclude that such productions are performance errors, unless the model of performance that is being assumed is quite unlike that being assumed for adults. For adults, as noted, memory effects begin to impede processing only with certain grammatical structures and only after a certain threshold has been surpassed. This does not mean, of course, that memory is not used in processing sentences like (4), just that the limits on the memory system do not interfere with successful production or comprehension to any appreciable degree in such sentences.

As an analogy, consider another resource-limited device, the airplane. In flight, airplanes consume fuel. Fuel consumption depends on several factors, including headwinds, cargo weight, the number of stops, the course, and so on. If enough of these factors conspire against it, the airplane may run out of fuel before it reaches its destination. Fortunately, airplanes carry enough fuel most of the time; so, despite an inherent limitation in resources, they successfully reach their destinations most of the time. Of course, luggage is another matter. The intent of the analogy should be clear; human language processing is similarly constrained by resource limitations such as memory and attention. Nevertheless, this does not entail that performance is negatively affected most of the time. On those occasions where factors conspire against it, the language-processing system does break down, as in processing multiply self-embedded constructions, garden path sentences, and the like. Most of the time, however, people succeed in producing sentences with the meanings they intend to convey, and they successfully understand sentences that are produced by others.

To summarize, the nature of the grammar that is incorporated in the performance system can only be examined by looking at linguistic behavior, that is, performance.

In assessing grammatical knowledge, however, it is necessary to present an explicit model of the interrelation of grammar and other components of performance, such as memory. As the case of E.A. makes clear, linguistic constructions of considerable complexity (from a pretheoretical point of view) can be produced and understood by people with extremely limited memory capacity, as measured by memory span tasks.

It follows that measures of memory span do not tell us all that we need to know about the human verbal memory system. The system must be more than a short-term storage buffer, as suggested by the name "short-term" memory. Let us therefore use another name to refer to the memory system used to process language: *verbal working memory*.

12.4 Verbal Working Memory

On our conception of verbal working memory, the memory system has two working parts. The first component of memory is a storage component that holds linguistic input briefly, between a second or two, in phonological form. It is this component of verbal working memory that is used in tests of memory span. Given its limited capacity, only short stretches of unstructured linguistic input can be maintained in this component of verbal working memory. To overcome the limitations of the phonological storage buffer, linguistic input must immediately be recoded into a more durable form and then transferred upward through the system. This is the function of the second component of working memory: the control mechanism.

The control mechanism transfers structural descriptions of the linguistic input between the different levels of linguistic representation within the language-processing system: the phonology, the lexicon, the morphology, the syntax, and the semantics. The control mechanism operates at several levels simultaneously. However, its computational resources are also limited. Therefore, once the linguistic input has been assigned a *partial* structural analysis at any level of linguistic representation, the result is immediately transmitted to the next higher level. The lower-level information can then be discarded, so that additional material can be assimilated. The control mechanism ensures that the results of computations at lower levels of representation are transferred upward through the system quickly enough to promote the on-line extraction of meaning from the linguistic input.

As long as the control mechanism of the working memory system remains intact, even people with a severely limited phonological storage buffer, such as Martin's patient E.A., should be expected to understand sentences of considerable length and complexity. However, if the partial structural analysis at any level within the system cannot be immediately integrated into the structural representation that has already been computed at that level, the assimilation of further input will be blocked. This can curtail linguistic processing in patients with limited short-term memory capacity, but only for certain linguistic devices—for example, constructions that require the results of linguistic analysis to be maintained at one level for subsequent use at the next higher level. (See Crain et al. 1990 for a more detailed description of this model of the verbal working memory system and for empirical findings consistent with the model.)[1]

For the vast majority of sentences, however, this conception of verbal working memory leads us to expect linguistic behavior to be almost flawless. As long as neither the sentences nor the task exceeds the limitations of the system, both children and adults should be expected to exhibit linguistic behavior that is consistent with their underlying grammar. This expectation does not hold on the Competing Factors Model, however. This model assumes that performance factors always weigh in against grammatical knowledge. No sentences or tasks are exempt from processing demands such as memory limitations.

We have now sketched the role of memory in language processing, according to the Modularity Matching Model. The topic of the next chapter is extralinguistic knowledge. According to the Competing Factors Model, extralinguistic knowledge contributes to all linguistic behavior, just as memory does. The influence of extralinguistic knowledge is more complex, however. Like memory, extralinguistic knowledge sometimes interferes with children's responses, reducing the number of correct responses (i.e., ones consistent with their grammars). At other times, however, extralinguistic knowledge inflates the number of correct responses; if extralinguistic knowledge and grammatical knowledge both give rise to the correct response, then this response will increase beyond the level that would be attained by grammatical knowledge alone. Because the Modularity Matching Model disagrees with the Competing Factors Model's assessment of the role of extralinguistic knowledge in language processing, it is worth examining this role more closely.

Chapter 13

Extralinguistic Knowledge

Since parsing considerations loom large in both the Modularity Matching Model and the Competing Factors Model, we will dwell a little longer on the characteristics of the human sentence-processing device (i.e., the parser). The topic of this chapter is the role that extralinguistic knowledge plays in sentence processing. We focus first on the characteristics used in resolving structural ambiguities. When the parser (a child's or an adult's) is confronted with a sentence that is structurally ambiguous, extralinguistic knowledge (i.e., a priori plausibility) may be engaged, but only if the sentence appears in a circumstance that is consistent with more than one of its readings. In this limited set of circumstances, the Modularity Matching Model and the Competing Factors Model make similar predictions.

However, the models make different predictions about how children and adults process unambiguous sentences. On the Modularity Matching Model, extralinguistic knowledge may not supersede specific context. If the specific context in which a sentence is produced supports one reading of the sentence, but not any others, then the reading that is supported by the context is selected regardless of its a priori plausibility. The Competing Factors Model is more permissive, allowing extralinguistic knowledge to influence the processing of unambiguous sentences.

13.1 Resolving Ambiguity

On the Modularity Matching Model, the architecture of the parser is adapted from what is known as the *Referential Theory* (Crain and Steedman 1985; Altmann and Steedman 1988; Ni, Crain, and Shankweiler 1996; Crain, Ni, et al. 1996). According to this model, the alternative analyses of ambiguous sentences are processed in parallel. As soon as an ambiguous fragment of a sentence is encountered, the (partial) syntactic analyses are shunted to the semantic/pragmatic component, where the current discourse representation is checked. One strategy for resolving ambiguity is to pick the reading that best fits the discourse representation. This strategy is called the *Principle of Referential Success* by Crain and Steedman (1985).

> *Principle of Referential Success*
> If there is a reading that succeeds in referring to entities already established in the perceiver's mental model of the domain of discourse, then it is favored over one that does not. (p. 331)

The Principle of Referential Success unquestionably underwrites most cases of ambiguity resolution. Ordinarily, when an ambiguous sentence is presented in context, only one reading of the sentence is felicitous. Consider the linguistic chestnut *Flying planes can be dangerous*. This sentence may describe the hazards of flying an airplane or the hazards of standing too near a runway, for example. Despite the ambiguity outside of context, only one reading will successfully match the conversational context in ordinary circumstances; the speaker/hearer will either be flying an airplane or standing too near a runway, but not both.

Concerning the influence of plausibility and general world knowledge, Crain and Steedman propose another parsing principle:

> *Principle of A Priori Plausibility*
> If a reading is more plausible in terms either of general knowledge about the world, or of specific knowledge about the universe of discourse, then, other things being equal, it will be favored over one that is not.... In case of a conflict between general and specific knowledge, then the latter must clearly take precedence. (p. 330)

The final sentence pertains to the issue of modularity. If one reading of an ambiguity is more plausible according to general knowledge of the world, but another reading is consistent with the conversational context, then the reading that matches the conversational context will be selected. This insulates the language-processing system from the influence of extralinguistic sources of information, which cannot serve as the basis for the parser's decisions in resolving ambiguities, as long as there is a specific context. Adopting a similar stance, Fodor (1984) compares a modular parser with what he calls a "New Look" parser, in which extralinguistic factors infiltrate language processing:

> In the extreme case, a New Look parser can bring to the process of assigning structural descriptions *anything that the organism knows* (or believes, or hopes, or expects ... etc.).... [B]y definition, a New Look parser tends to hear just what it expects to hear.... [T]his ... suggests one of the reasons why encapsulated perceptual modules might be quite a good thing for an organism to have: background beliefs, and the expectations that they engender, from time to time prove *not to be true.* (p. 132 in Goldman 1993)

Fodor's argument is familiar, but it bears repeating. Extralinguistic knowledge had better not infiltrate the initial operations of the parser; if it did, the parser would tend to disregard analyses that lead to the unexpected, according to one's previous experience. This would wreak havoc in exceptional circumstances, where "deviant" sentences turn out to be true (although they would be false in more usual circumstances). It does not follow, however, that a priori plausibility (i.e., general knowledge of the world) is never used in parsing, just that its role is quite limited: it is accessed only *after* the alternative structural analyses of an ambiguous sentence have been computed and then only if specific contextual information has not already resolved the ambiguity.

13.2 Resolving Ambiguity in the So-Called Null Context

Crain and Steedman (1985) suggest another parsing principle for sentences that are presented outside of context. When sentences are presented in the absence of context, as in most studies on adult sentence processing, the perceiver actively attempts to construct a mental model of a context that would make the sentence felicitous. The relative complexity of constructing the alternative mental models dictates which interpretation prevails:

Principle of Parsimony
If there is a reading that carries fewer unsatisfied presuppositions or entailments than any other, then, other criteria of plausibility being equal, that reading will be adopted as most plausible by the hearer, and the presuppositions in question will be incorporated in his or her model. (p. 333)

The Principle of Parsimony is quite general. First, it covers cases of structural ambiguity, such as the classic garden path sentence in (1).

(1)   The horse raced past the barn fell.

It is well known that people find it nearly impossible to access the reduced-relative-clause analysis of this sentence. The ambiguity arises because the verb *raced* is morphologically ambiguous; it is both the past participial form and the simple past tense form of the verb. There is an overwhelming preference for interpreting *raced* as a simple past tense form, however, outside of context. This preference results in a main-clause analysis of *the horse raced past the barn*. Having opted for this analysis, the parser has been led down the garden path, because the verb *fell* is incompatible with the structural analysis that has been constructed. If the verb *raced* had been analyzed as a passive participle, however, the verb *fell* would be a natural completion of the reduced relative clause: *the horse (that was) raced past the barn*....

The preference for the main-clause analysis of the ambiguity follows from the Principle of Parsimony. On the main-clause analysis, just one horse must be added to the perceiver's mental model of the discourse, and one event must be added, in which the horse races past the barn, as depicted in figure 13.1. On the reduced-relative-clause reading, by contrast, the mental model must be extended further. In addition to one (most salient) horse that races past the barn, the mental model associated with the reduced-relative-clause analysis must contain several other horses; these other horses are being contrasted with the one racing past the barn (otherwise the speaker would have said, "The horse fell"). In addition, the horse that is most salient is being raced by someone, as in figure 13.2.

Comparing these figures makes it clear that the mental model corresponding to the reduced-relative-clause reading of the ambiguous phrase *the horse raced past the*

Figure 13.1
Mental model for the main-clause analysis of *The horse raced past the barn ... fell*

Figure 13.2
Mental model for the reduced-relative-clause analysis of *The horse raced past the barn ... fell*

barn ... is more complex; it contains everything in the mental model corresponding to the main-clause analysis, and more. Therefore, the mental model corresponding to the reduced-relative-clause analysis is more costly to set up. Because of the greater inherent difficulty in constructing the discourse representation associated with that analysis, the main-clause analysis is selected. As a consequence, the perceiver experiences a garden path effect on encountering the verb *fell*.

In the so-called null context, the parser continues to assign syntactic and semantic representations. Tasks that require the parser to function in the so-called null context, such as the act-out task and the imitation task, do not shed additional light on its syntactic operations because its semantic operations are shut down, as suggested by Flynn (1986b). In chapters 7 and 8, we suggested that such tasks are likely to evoke artificially high error rates. Now it is clear why. When children are presented sentences without contextual support, they are required to establish the referents and the semantic relations mentioned in the test sentences by *accommodation*, that is, by augmenting the mental model to include the semantic elements mentioned in the sentence. It seems likely that children must learn the process of accommodation as they grow, so to speak. It is not a cognitive skill that comes for free, as part and parcel of Universal Grammar.

By contrast, processing language in context seems to be within the capabilities of quite young children. Perhaps children even have innate principles relating contexts and sentence meanings, which would explain why languages are learnable from ⟨sentence, meaning⟩ pairs, but not from sentences alone (Hamburger and Wexler 1973; Wexler and Culicover 1980). In any event, many of the semantic elements of the mental model already exist, if sentences are presented in a discourse context.

These elements are already in the mental model of the child, having been introduced by the preceding sentences. Therefore, they can be accessed in interpreting a new sentence. In short, presenting sentences in the null context may impede children's normal processing routines, as compared to presenting sentences in a specific context.

There is another negative implication of presenting sentences in the null context: loss of experimental control. As Crain and Steedman (1985) put it:

> [T]he so-called null context is in fact simply an *unknown* context.... [T]he set of assumptions under which the subject constructs a context are not under control. Any processing preferences that are observed may therefore be due to facts about the construction of that context, rather than about the structural properties of the different readings.
>
>   It is therefore necessary to control context in a much fuller sense, offering the target sentences in a matrix of preceding sentences [or *situations*] that unambiguously establish a known set of assumptions under which the subject will approach the target sentence. (p. 338)

Both tasks described later in the book take this advice to heart. The design features of these tasks are concerned with manufacturing specific contexts that are felicitous for the linguistic constructions under investigation.

13.3 Memory and Modularity

According to the Modularity Matching Model, the human sentence-processing device is a parallel processing system. When structural ambiguity is encountered, the control mechanism of verbal working memory relays partial structural descriptions of each of the alternative analyses for evaluation and resolution by the semantic processor. The analysis that best fits (the perceiver's mental model of) the discourse context is the one that is selected. If none of the alternatives succeeds in referring to entities in the perceiver's mental model, then a reading is selected based on the number and kinds of accommodations that must be made to the mental model. If the ambiguity still cannot be resolved, information outside the language faculty (i.e., extralinguistic knowledge) can be consulted in order to resolve it. In short, the Modularity Matching Model conceives of the language-processing system as hierarchically organized and encapsulated from the influence of nonlinguistic sources of information. Following Fodor (1983), we can refer to this last architectural feature of the model as the *Modularity Hypothesis*.

Recent research with Weijia Ni and Donald Shankweiler has produced empirical evidence that is consistent with the Modularity Hypothesis. The data suggest that syntactic and semantic structures are used for ambiguity resolution earlier than extralinguistic knowledge (a priori plausibility). These conclusions rest on experiments in which subjects were divided into groups according to differences in verbal working memory. It will be instructive to sketch the experiments as a way of clarifying the role of memory and extralinguistic knowledge in language processing.

We will report on the findings of two experiments. Both experiments exploit the technique of eye-movement recording (eye-tracking). By monitoring subjects' eye movements during reading, we are able to obtain two measures of processing difficulty: first-pass reading times (i.e., the total duration of all fixations in each region of a sentence) and incidence of regressive eye movements. It has been our working hypothesis, and that of others, that first-pass reading times reflect on-line processes; these responses reflect the influence of information that is immediately assimilated by the reader. Regressive eye movements are another indicator of processing difficulties that readers encounter during their first pass through the sentence. In contrast to first-pass reading times, regressive eye movements testify to the reader's failure to use information on-line for interpretation.

Subjects in both experiments were also assessed for verbal working memory capacity, using a memory span test adapted from Daneman and Carpenter 1980. For purposes of analysis, subjects were put in two groups of equal size: subjects with higher scores on the memory test were put in one group, called the *high-span group*, and subjects with lower scores were put in another group, called the *low span group*.

Given our conception of the role of verbal working memory, we did not expect differences in memory capacity among the subjects to influence sentence processing as long as the information needed for recovering from a misanalysis was structural. Structural principles are accessed *within* the language-processing system and should be costly of memory resources only in unusual circumstances, as discussed in chapter 12. If this is correct, then the eye-movement profiles of subjects in the high- and low-span groups should not differ in resolving ambiguities as long as the disambiguating information was structural.

We did expect, however, that individual differences in memory capacity would be relevant when extralinguistic knowledge was needed in order to resolve an ambiguity. It is assumed that querying extralinguistic knowledge taxes working memory, especially when the alternative analyses of an ambiguous phrase must be maintained until the ambiguity is resolved. The combined effort of these computations is likely to create processing difficulties that can place high demands on memory resources. Therefore, we expected the eye-movement profiles of subjects in the high- and low-span groups to differ when the task involved resolving ambiguities using extralinguistic knowledge.

Each eye-tracking experiment presented a different set of sentences, but the sets had certain features in common. In both sets, a semantic property of the test sentences was manipulated, by alternating the definite determiner *the* and the focus operator *only*. The first set of sentences involved the main-clause/reduced-relative-clause ambiguity characteristic of the classic garden path sentence *The horse raced past the barn....* The second set involved an ambiguity in the site of attachment of a prepositional phrase; the prepositional phrase could attach either to the preceding noun or to the preceding verb, as in ... *spotted the man with binoculars*. On one reading, the man was spotted by someone using binoculars; on the other reading, the man with binoculars was spotted.

An important difference between the sentence types was the type of information that *disambiguated* the sentences. In the first set of sentences, a misanalysis could be detected on the basis of structural information; test sentences varied in the presence or absence of the conjunction *but*, as a signal of the misanalysis. In the second set, misanalyses were signaled by the subject's general knowledge of the world: for example, the fact that it is implausible to paint using large cracks, or for doors to have new brushes.

According to the Modularity Matching Model, the alternation between the definite determiner *the* and the focus operator *only* should result in a different analysis of the ambiguity in each experiment. The predictions of the model, as they pertain to acceptability, are as follows:

> Experiment 1: Structural disambiguation
> *Acceptable*
> a. The horses raced past the barn but were unable to clear the jump.
> b. Only horses raced past the barn were unable to clear the jump.
> *Unacceptable*
> c. The horses raced past the barn were unable to clear the jump.
> d. Only horses raced past the barn but were unable to clear the jump.
>
> Experiment 2: Disambiguation by extralinguistic knowledge
> *Acceptable*
> a. The man painted the doors with new brushes before the festival.
> b. The man painted only doors with large cracks before the festival.
> *Unacceptable*
> c. The man painted the doors with large cracks before the festival.
> d. The man painted only doors with new brushes before the festival.

To see why the sentences with *only* and *the* should be analyzed differently, consider the on-line derivations of the meaning representations (i.e., the mental models) in the first set of sentences. First, the initial NPs, *the horses* and *only horses*, compel the parser to establish a set of horses in the mental model. We have already explained why the main-clause analysis of the (a) and (c) versions, with the definite determiner, is preferred over the reduced-relative-clause analysis. The consequence of this is a garden path effect for the (c) version, but not for the (a) version. It remains to explain why the reduced-relative-clause analysis is preferred over the main-clause analysis for the (b) and (d) versions, leading to the opposite pattern of acceptability.

The focus operator *only* requires the parser to check the mental model for a contrast set corresponding to the head noun it is in construction with—in the present example, *horses*. However, no contrast set has previously been established, because these sentences are presented in the absence of context. The only entities in the mental model are the horses, which have just been incorporated into it. According to the Principle of Referential Success, the parser favors a reading that succeeds in referring to entities already established in the perceiver's mental model of the domain of discourse over one that does not. Therefore, the parser should attempt to resolve the ambiguity, if possible, by adopting a reading that refers to the horses in the mental model. Consequently, the parser should choose to resolve the ambiguity by using the ambiguous phrase, *raced past the barn*, as a way of modifying the preceding NP, *only horses*. The resulting semantic interpretation establishes a contrast set, as required by the focus operator. The contrast set is formed by partitioning the horses into ones that were raced past the barn and ones that were not.[1]

Having analyzed the ambiguous phrase as a reduced relative clause, the parser should not experience a garden path effect when the verb phrase continuation (*were unable ...*) is encountered, as in (b). On the other hand, a garden path effect should arise in (d), because the reduced-relative-clause analysis is inconsistent with the main-clause continuation (*but were unable ...*). Similar differences are expected to turn on the alternation of *the* and *only* in the ambiguities involving the attachment of a prepositional phrase, as in the sentences from experiment 2. The presence of the focus operator *only* should cause the prepositional phrase to attach to the preceding NP in the (b) and (d) versions. The NP that is created in the (b) version is *doors with large cracks*; it is plausible for someone to paint such doors. A pragmatic anomaly results in the (d) version, however, because the phrase that is created is *doors with new brushes*, a nonsensical reference set.

We are ready to consider the experimental findings. They are just as expected by the Modularity Matching Model. The eye-movement patterns of both high-span and low-span subjects were virtually identical in experiment 1, where misanalysis of an ambiguous sentence was signaled by structural information. That is, there were no between-group differences in subjects' responses to the test sentences. There was no evidence of garden path effects for the (a) and (b) versions either in the first-pass reading times or in the incidence of regressions, for either high-span or low-span subjects. Both groups of subjects experienced garden path effects for the (c) and (d) versions, however. This is attested by elevated first-pass reading times for both groups; the incidence of regressions was not significant for either group.

The patterns of eye movements by high-span and low-span subjects diverged in experiment 2, however, where the misanalysis of the ambiguity was signaled by extralinguistic knowledge. High- and low-span subjects exhibited a similar pattern of responses for the (a) and (b) versions, which were expected to be acceptable, on the Modularity Matching Model. The patterns of eye movements were also similar for both groups for the (c) versions, which contained the definite determiner *the*. Both high-span and low-span subjects had higher first-pass reading times at the point of disambiguation for these sentences than at the corresponding regions in the (a) or (b) versions. Where the subject groups differed was in response to the (d) versions.

For these sentences, high-span subjects exhibited different kinds of eye-movement patterns than low-span subjects. High-span subjects were able to recover from misanalyses on-line, although recovery led to inflated first-pass reading times. High-span subjects made few regressions to earlier regions, however. The pattern of responses for low-span subjects was exactly the opposite. Low-span subjects were largely unable to recover from misanalyses on the first pass through the (d) versions. This resulted in the finding that low-span subjects had faster first-pass reading times in the disambiguating region for these pragmatically anomalous sentences, although the difference between groups was not significant. The impact of the anomalies took a different form for these subjects; they made frequent regressions from the disambiguating region to earlier regions. In processing the (d) sentences, it seems that the memory resources of low-span subjects had been exhausted by the time the anomaly was detected, so they were forced to deal with it by returning to earlier portions of the sentence. The eye-movement patterns of low-span subjects suggest that, although they were aware of the anomaly, their limitation in verbal working memory did not allow them to recover on-line from a misanalysis; they had to look back in order to reanalyze the ambiguity.[2] In short, low-span subjects were unable to use extralinguistic knowledge as effectively as high-span subjects, who were able to recover on-line from misanalyses signaled by semantic plausibility.[3]

Taken together, the findings of these experiments are evidence that the processing of extralinguistic knowledge lags behind syntactic and semantic processing. This explains the absence of individual differences when structural information signaled that an ambiguity had been misanalyzed, and the appearance of group differences when extralinguistic knowledge was needed to infer that the wrong analysis had been assigned. The findings suggest that the operations of the syntactic and semantic components occur within the language-processing system and do not exceed the capacity of verbal working memory. Differences in memory capacity begin to matter, however, when the disambiguating information comes later, from outside the language-processing system. If all of this is correct, then the evidence from these experiments supports both the Modularity Hypothesis and the Modularity Matching Model.

13.4 Children's Parsing Strategies

So far, we have been discussing the parsing strategies of adults. Of course, according to the Modularity Matching Model, these same parsing strategies should also be manifested by children, as long as children's parsing decisions are tested in similar ways. As noted earlier, however, the experimental contexts in which children are asked to respond to ambiguous sentences are not the same as those in which adults are asked for their judgments. In experimental investigations with children, contexts are often designed to be appropriate to more than one reading of a sentence. The contexts are specifically constructed so that the test sentence is true in the discourse context if one analysis is assigned, and false in the context if a different analysis is assigned. Crucially, then, both of the relevant interpretations of the sentence must be *felicitous* in the context. Although such contexts are undeniably rare outside the laboratory, they are necessary elements for evaluating children's grammatical knowledge. Little is known, however, about the strategies that guide the parsing decisions of children or adults in circumstances in which both readings of an ambiguity are felicitous.

In our experience with children, we have been able to identify several factors that conspire to determine which reading of an ambiguous sentence is selected.[4] First, children pick the reading that makes an ambiguous sentence true in the context, assuming that both readings are consistent with the context. On the basis of this finding, many researchers assume that children should always access the reading that makes the sentence true (see Grimshaw and Rosen 1990). However, there are other influences on children's parsing decisions in "ambiguous" contexts. Another is the structure of the context itself—for example, the order in which events take place. If one reading corresponds to the final event in the context, that reading will be favored over readings that refer to events that occurred previously.

Finally, there seem to be inherent biases for one reading or another of an ambiguous sentence. We have already indicated some preferences by adults to interpret an ambiguity in one way rather than another. The same holds true for children. For example, children have been found to prefer the direct reference (deictic) reading of the pronoun in questions like (2)—that is, the reading on which the pronoun refers to some salient male individual in the conversational context.

(2)   I know who thinks he has a hat.

The alternative, bound variable interpretation of the pronoun allows *he* to refer to more than a single individual (although it need not). It is noteworthy that many children continue to assign the direct reference interpretation of the pronoun, rather than the bound variable interpretation, even if the direct reference reading makes the sentence false in the context.

The preference for the direct reference interpretation of the pronoun in sentences like (2) is not fully general, however. For example, this preference does not extend to the VP-ellipsis construction in (3).

(3)   Snoopy thinks he has the best hat, and Mickey Mouse does too.

In interpreting (3), children generally assign the reading on which the pronoun *he* refers to both Snoopy and Mickey Mouse, and not to a third character (say, Donald Duck). The accessibility of the bound variable interpretation (the so-called sloppy reading) in sentences like (3), but not in sentences like (2), must apparently be chalked up to a construction-specific parsing preference (see Thornton 1990).

13.5 Unambiguous Sentences

According to the Modularity Matching Model, but not the Competing Factors Model, the principles used in deciding among competing discourse representations do not hold sway over the parser's interpretation of *unambiguous* sentences. In the comprehension of unambiguous sentences, according to the Modularity Matching Model, factors such as plausibility and general knowledge of the world play no role whatsoever. If the principles of grammar made only one reading available, then that reading is parsed, even if it would be highly dispreferred had it been pitted against another reading.

To help reinforce this point, it will be useful to return to the classic garden path sentence, *The horse raced past the barn fell.* Notice that the difficulty inherent in the reduced-relative-clause analysis of this sentence is not experienced by the perceiver in processing its unambiguous counterpart in (4).[5]

(4)   The horse ridden past the barn fell.

In understanding (4), there is no conscious difficulty associated with constructing the discourse representation corresponding to the reduced-relative-clause analysis, because there is no "simpler" alternative analysis. Therefore, the sentence is assigned the correct, reduced-relative-clause analysis without conscious effort. Given that children have essentially the same parsing apparatus as adults, which is the basic tenet of the Modularity Matching Model, children too should have no difficulty analyzing unambiguous sentences, even if they are compelled to assign an analysis that would be highly dispreferred if the sentence had another interpretation.

A further example may be helpful. As mentioned earlier, both children and adults attempt to access the interpretation of an ambiguous sentence that makes it true in the discourse context, all other things being equal. According to the Competing Factors Model, this "parsing strategy" also holds sway over children (and adults, to a lesser extent) in processing unambiguous sentences. On the Competing Factors Model, then, even unambiguous sentences are subject to the vagaries of performance factors. As a consequence, children who know a linguistic principle can nevertheless perform less than perfectly in response to sentences governed by it. The model maintains that less than perfect performance is sufficient to indicate the effect of a linguistic principle. Proponents of the Modularity Matching Model take issue with this way of assessing knowledge of linguistic principles. On this model, if the sentence is false in the discourse context on the interpretation assigned by the grammar, then children (and adults, to a similar extent) will reject the sentence; they will not attempt to reanalyze it in a way that makes it true. Therefore, the Modularity Matching Model maintains that only near perfect performance is sufficient to indicate the effect of a linguistic principle, either for children or for adults.

13.6 Conclusion

The Competing Factors Model and the Modularity Matching Model diverge in their expectations about the influence of memory and extralinguistic knowledge. On the Competing Factors Model, these factors play a role in processing sentences of all kinds. On the Modularity Matching Model, they play a much more limited role. In the resolution of ambiguity, extralinguistic knowledge is relevant only if the mental model of the domain of discourse cannot be engaged in deciding among the alternative readings.

The Competing Factors Model and the Modularity Matching Model also diverge in their predictions about children's responses to sentences for which there is only a single grammatical analysis (i.e., unambiguous sentences). According to the Competing Factors Model, the kinds of factors that influence children's interpretation of ambiguous sentences may also influence their interpretation of unambiguous sentences. By contrast, according to the Modularity Matching Model, if linguistic principles eliminate all but one semantic representation, leaving a sentence unambiguous for children, then they will have no difficulty interpreting the sentence correctly.

To repeat the main point, the Modularity Matching Model predicts that both children and adults will invoke the same parsing strategies to resolve ambiguity. This follows from the basic architecture of the model. Children and adults differ in one important respect, however; until two or three years after they begin to speak, children lack full linguistic competence. In the next chapter, we show that even this brief delay in acquisition has consequences for the Modularity Matching Model and implications for the Modularity Hypothesis.

Chapter 14

When Principles and Preferences Collide

This chapter presents further evidence in support of the Modularity Hypothesis. The evidence comes from a set of experiments with children and adults, designed to investigate children's understanding of sentences that are ambiguous for adults. It is possible, even likely, that the alternative meanings of an ambiguous sentence are acquired piecemeal by children. If so, the order in which alternative meanings are acquired could be instructive. Unlike adult preferences for one reading over others, which are based on semantic principles, the order of acquisition of various meanings may be determined by the LAD. Assuming that the LAD is governed by principles of learnability, and not by parsing principles, it could turn out that the initial meanings children assign to sentences are not the readings that adults prefer. This finding would offer empirical support for the kind of modular mental architecture that underlies the Modularity Matching Model. The proper interpretation of the data is seen to hinge on the observation that the modules of children and adults are different, because children but not adults have access to principles of learning (i.e., the LAD).

14.1 One Substitution

The question is whether children ever interpret sentences that are ambiguous for adults by initially giving them the interpretation that adults prefer least. Consider (1).

> (1) The big elephant is the only one playing the guitar.
>   a.   The only thing playing the guitar is the big elephant.
>   b.   The only elephant playing the guitar is the big elephant.

This sentence is ambiguous for adults. The ambiguity involves the interaction of the focus operator *only* and the linguistic phenomenon known as *one* substitution. This refers to the use of the proform *one* to refer back to the contents of a nominal element previously mentioned in a sentence. If more than one referent for the proform *one* is possible, semantic ambiguity results, even though the sentence has only one structural analysis. The ambiguity turns on what is taken as the contrast set for the focus operator *only*. There are two possible contrast sets. On the (a) interpretation, everything in the domain of discourse is in the contrast set. On the (b) interpretation, the contrast set is the set of elephants in the domain of discourse.

Experimental studies of both children and adults revealed the following: Adults prefer the (b) interpretation of (1). For (1) to be true for adults, the big elephant must be the only elephant playing a guitar, but another animal (say, an octopus) might be playing one as well. This preference is dictated by the Principle of Parsimony, discussed in chapter 12. The pattern of responses by children was not the same as that of adults, however. Most of the 3- to 5-year-old children we interviewed consistently rejected sentence (1) if any character other than the big elephant was playing a guitar. That is, children adopted the (a) interpretation of (1).

On the face of it, children's nonadult responses to (1) invite the inference that children have internalized a parser with different operating characteristics than the adult parser. It looks as though children are not using the Principle of Parsimony to resolve the ambiguity, as adults are. There is another interpretation of the findings, however. On this interpretation, certain semantic representations that are initially adopted by learners on learnability grounds are dispreferred by the sentence-parsing mechanism once additional representations have been acquired. Putting it the other way around, certain linguistic representations that are preferred by the sentence-parsing mechanism are ones that would create problems of learnability if learners initially adopted them. Therefore, children's initial representation is one that adults disprefer, but once children add additional representations themselves, they respond using the same parsing principles as adults do.

Here is the argument in a bit more detail. First, recall the relevant operating principle of the parser, Crain and Steedman's (1985) Principle of Parsimony:

> *Principle of Parsimony*
> If there is a reading that carries fewer unsatisfied presuppositions or entailments than any other, then, other criteria of plausibility being equal, that reading will be adopted as most plausible by the hearer, and the presuppositions in question will be incorporated in his or her model. (p. 333)

Crain and Hamburger (1992) suggest that the Principle of Parsimony is ultimately motivated by the need to minimize cognitive effort. To conserve effort, unnecessary extensions to the mental model are avoided whenever possible. The advantage of this "least effort" strategy for ambiguity resolution is to reduce the risk of making commitments that will need to be changed later on. In other words, the parser is a "minimal commitment" device.

Adopting the minimal commitment strategy, whenever the parser confronts a structurally ambiguous phrase or sentence fragment, it begins to construct discourse representations corresponding to all its structural analyses. Being unable to maintain multiple discourse representations in working memory for long, however, it must rapidly abandon all but one representation. The decision about which representation to keep and which to discard is made by considering the sets of circumstances that make the sentence true on each discourse representation. Sometimes, these alternative sets of circumstances (corresponding to the alternative discourse representations) form a subset/superset relation; that is, the set of circumstances that make the sentence true on one discourse representation is a superset of the circumstances that make it true on another representation. Whenever this state of affairs holds, the parser selects the discourse representation that makes the sentence true in the largest set of circumstances.[1]

To illustrate this operating characteristic of the parser, we turn back to sentence (1), with its alternative interpretations (a) and (b).

(1)   The big elephant is the only one playing the guitar.
    a.   The only thing playing the guitar is the big elephant.
    b.   The only elephant playing the guitar is the big elephant.

It is immediately apparent that sentence (1) is true on interpretation (a) only in a limited set of circumstances, as compared to interpretation (b). That is, (a) is true only in circumstances where the only guitar-playing animal is the big elephant. On the other hand, (b) is true in circumstances in which the big elephant is the only elephant playing the guitar, regardless of whether or not other animals are playing the guitar as well. In short, the circumstances corresponding to the (a) interpretation of (1) constitute a subset of the circumstances that make (1) true on the (b) interpretation. That is, the (a) reading is the subset reading, and the (b) reading is the superset reading

In formal terms, the subset/superset distinction boils down to an entailment relation between the alternative readings of the ambiguity. The relevant notion of entailment can be stated as follows:

> A reading Q of a sentence entails another reading R if and only if every circumstance in which Q is true is also a circumstance in which R is true.

To say that the (a) reading of (1) entails the (b) reading, then, amounts to the claim that every circumstance in which "the only thing playing the guitar is the big elephant" is true is also one in which it is true that "the only elephant playing the guitar is the big elephant." This relation among circumstances does indeed hold; therefore, the (a) reading entails the (b) reading. The converse relation does not hold, however; if the big elephant is the only elephant playing the guitar, it may still not be the only thing playing the guitar. Therefore, the (b) reading does not entail the (a) reading. Now we can state the subset/superset relations among the readings of certain ambiguous sentences:

> If reading Q entails reading R, but R does not entail Q, then Q is the subset reading and R is the superset reading.

By this definition, (a) is the subset reading of (1), and (b) is its superset reading. The upshot is this: the minimal commitment strategy (the Principle of Parsimony) dictates that the parser will favor the reading that is true in the *broadest* set of circumstances. The interpretation that is true in the broadest set of circumstances is the superset reading. That is why people prefer the (b) interpretation of sentences like (1): (b) is the superset reading. The preference for the superset reading of an ambiguous sentence plays an important role in the design of contexts for the truth value judgment task (see chapter 33).

To see which reading you prefer, we propose the following test: Try to imagine a context in which someone tells you (1), *The big elephant is the only one playing the guitar,* but in which that statement is *false.* Now, write down the aspect of your mentally constructed situation that makes the statement false. As predicted by the Principle of Parsimony, when adults perform this task, they generally write down things like *A little elephant was playing the guitar, too.* Few adults write things like *Someone else was playing the guitar too* (Crain, Ni, and Conway 1994).

14.2 The Semantic Subset Principle

Our assumptions about the operating principles of the LAD are quite different from our assumptions about the operating principles of the parser. The principles of the LAD must enable learners to converge successfully on the target grammar on the basis of the available evidence. Presumably, the evidence available to learners consists of ⟨sentence, meaning⟩ pairs—that is, sentences presented in circumstances that make them true. Sometimes, more than one interpretation of a sentence is made available by Universal Grammar.[2] To further complicate matters, these alternatives may form a subset/superset relation; that is, the circumstances that make the sentence true on one interpretation may be a proper subset of the circumstances that make it true on another interpretation. In such cases, a semantic subset problem arises if the target language includes the subset reading, but not the superset reading. To avoid semantic subset problems, the interpretive options for sentences must be ordered in the LAD by a principle instructing learners to initially choose the representation that is true in the smallest set of circumstances.[3] This is called the *Semantic Subset Principle* (Crain 1992, 1993; Crain, Ni, and Conway 1994; Crain and Philip 1993).

> *Semantic Subset Principle*
> Suppose that the interpretive component of Universal Grammar makes two interpretations, A and B, available for a sentence, S. If so, then see if S is true in a narrower range of circumstances on interpretation A than on interpretation B. If so, then A will be hypothesized before B in the course of language development.

The Semantic Subset Principle establishes children's initial semantic hypotheses; these are hypotheses that can be falsified on the basis of positive evidence from the input.[4] Just as children lack negative syntactic evidence—evidence about the ungrammaticality of sentence forms—so it seems likely that they lack the kind of evidence that would be needed to reject incorrect hypotheses about what sentences may and may not mean. Therefore, children who commit semantic overgeneration—assigning sentence meanings beyond those assigned by adults—would not recover from their errors. Although there is little empirical evidence on the matter, we think it highly unlikely that children expunge semantic errors on the basis of experience.

To avoid semantic errors in the first place, the Semantic Subset Principle arranges grammatical options to ensure that learners initially hypothesize the interpretation that makes a sentence true in the smallest set of circumstances. In this way, learners are assured of formulating falsifiable hypotheses. To make sentences true in the narrowest possible sets of circumstances amounts to making the maximal commitments about the entities and events in the domain of discourse. In short, the LAD is a "maximal commitment" component of the language apparatus.

This brings us back to sentence (1), *The big elephant is the only one playing the guitar.* Circumstances corresponding to the alternative interpretations of the sentence are depicted in figure 14.1. It is important to note that these are simply some of the circumstances that would make sentence (1) true on the alternative interpretations; these circumstances would not necessarily be ones we would use if our goal was to investigate children's awareness of the alternative meanings of (1). The (a) reading of (1) is depicted on the left of the figure. The circumstances that make (1) true on this reading are the ones without the "Ghostbuster" bar through them. It should be clear that these circumstances correspond to the maximal commitment interpretation. On this interpretation, the sentence is false if anything other than the big elephant is playing a guitar.

The (b) reading corresponds to the circumstances on the right of the figure. This set of circumstances is consistent with the minimal commitment interpretation. On this interpretation, the contrast set consists just of elephants. The illustrations show that the maximal commitment interpretation (a) makes sentence (1) true in a narrower set of circumstances than does the minimal commitment interpretation (b). In fact, on

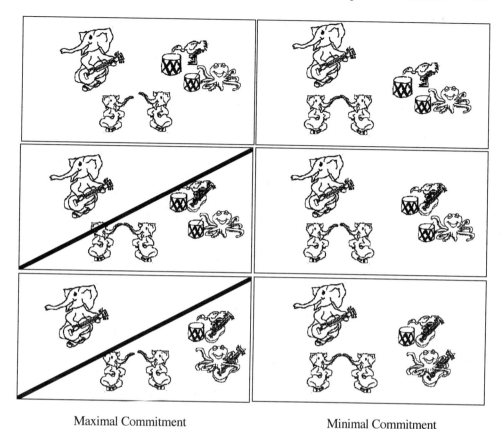

Maximal Commitment   Minimal Commitment

Figure 14.1
Sets of circumstances corresponding to the alternative readings of sentence (1)

the maximal commitment interpretation, (1) is true in only one of the circumstances depicted here.[5] For the sentence to be true on the (b) reading, however, all that is required is that no elephant besides the big elephant is playing a guitar. The activities of the octopus and the crane are not pertinent on this reading.[6]

The crucial observation here is that the (a) interpretation of (1) is true in a subset of the circumstances corresponding to the (b) interpretation. For learners, then, sentences like (1) represent a potential semantic subset problem. The circumstances in which the two readings of (1) are true fall into a subset/superset relation. The Semantic Subset Principle rescues children by compelling them to initially hypothesize the falsifiable interpretation (a), because this interpretation makes fewer commitments about who is playing a guitar (cf. Hornstein and Lightfoot 1981). For empirical results, see Crain, Ni, and Conway 1994.

14.3 Conclusion

To recap, the principles of the LAD must be responsive to demands of learnability. To achieve learnability, learners' hypotheses must be constrained so as to guarantee that linguistic representations that are not derived in the target language will not be formulated or, if formulated, can be disconfirmed by readily available evidence. Therefore, it is expected that children will adopt the "maximal commitment" reading of (1), reading (a). In contrast to the LAD, the sentence-parsing mechanism selects among the competing linguistic representations that are derived in a language. Selection is based on considerations of simplicity. Therefore, adults prefer the "minimal commitment" reading of (1), reading (b). This explains why adults and children give (1) different interpretations, letting the Modularity Matching Model off the hook.

This chapter also featured two aspects of children's linguistic behavior that substantiate our claim that children are interesting subjects for testing hypotheses concerning the inner workings of Universal Grammar. First, children are a good source of data bearing on the Innateness Hypothesis, and second, child subjects in the studies cited here produced nonadult responses that can be used as evidence germane to hypotheses that have been advanced in current linguistic theory.

Chapter 15

Performance Errors

According to the Modularity Matching Model, the language apparatus of both children and adults is organized into modules, and the inner workings of these modules are essentially the same for children as they are for adults. In chapter 12, we explained why we add the caveat "essentially the same" to describe the relation between the language-processing subcomponents of children and adults. There is one important difference between children and adults: children have access to a module that may be unavailable to adults, the LAD. In the previous chapter, we considered how children's nonadult responses might arise from the operating characteristics of the LAD.

According to the Modularity Matching Model, another viable source of children's nonadult linguistic behavior is the theory of Universal Grammar itself. It is consistent with the theory for children to sometimes hypothesize grammatical representations that are not characteristic of their target language (see chapter 5 for examples). Parameters are one source of such deviations; another possible source is maturation. On the Modularity Matching Model, however, the internal representations that children assign to sentences must be compatible with the principles of Universal Grammar. This is necessary in light of the problems of learnability that would otherwise arise. Essentially, children's grammars can differ from the target grammar only in ways that adult grammars can differ from each other. This is the Continuity Hypothesis. Put simply, the Continuity Hypothesis requires children's grammatical hypotheses to be constrained by Universal Grammar (see Crain 1991).

In certain cases, however, children produce errors that cannot be readily explained by appealing to the LAD, linguistic theory, or maturation. On the face of it, the existence of such errors might seem to compel us to reject the Modularity Matching Model and consider adopting the Competing Factors Model. The situation is not quite as grim as it might appear, however. As long as errors arise from nonlinguistic aspects of the tasks children are expected to perform, then these factors cannot count against the Modularity Matching Model. Moreover, these factors make clear one basic research strategy of the model, which is to eliminate or reduce as far as possible the nonlinguistic demands of a task. In this chapter, we discuss the nature of errors that sometimes mask children's linguistic knowledge, and we discuss ways to eliminate these sources of children's nonadult responses.

We discuss four sources of children's nonadult behavior: (a) artifacts in experimental design, (b) extralinguistic knowledge that develops over time, (c) the complexity of nonlinguistic processes that are needed to provide correct answers in a psycholinguistic task, and (d) performance factors that influence the linguistic behavior of both children and adults. It should be noted that the existence of these factors in no way challenges the fundamental precepts of the Modularity Matching Model. However, these factors are important to the investigation of child language, so they should be afforded the proper respect; we will want to eliminate them or at least reduce them as much as possible in designing tasks to assess children's linguistic competence, because, left unchecked, these factors produce underestimates of this competence. It is important to emphasize, however, that these factors do not compete with linguistic knowledge; they merely stand in the way of progress toward an understanding of children's mastery of linguistic principles.

15.1 Extraneous Demands of the Task

Flaws in experimental design are one source of children's errors. This source of non-adult linguistic behavior clearly needs to be eliminated whenever possible. Errors are likely to occur, for example, in experimental situations that force children to violate one kind of linguistic principle or another. In these circumstances, children are forced to choose which kind of principle to violate. If children choose to violate a syntactic principle, say, in order to provide a pragmatically felicitous response, they should not be said to lack syntactic knowledge. When placed in situations that are pragmatically felicitous, children should adhere to syntactic principles and should reject sentences that do not conform to them. Typically, syntactic and pragmatic principles are at odds only in infelicitous experimental circumstances; in ordinary circumstances, they do not compete. In sum, this source of errors in children's behavior is artifactual and should not serve as the basis for a model of the language apparatus as it functions in most real-life circumstances.

Children's performance errors may stem from the nonlinguistic demands of an experimental task. Tasks that use pictures, for example, assume that children are able to interpret pictures in the same way as adults do. We find this assumption highly suspect. In several instances, we have given alternative tasks to children with the same linguistic materials (e.g., Crain, Thornton, and Murasugi 1987; Miyamoto and Crain 1991). The results from the picture versions of the experiments are consistently poorer than the results from the versions that involve vignettes acted out by the experimenter using toys and other props. We have the subjective impression that children are less proficient than adults are at "parsing" the contents of pictures. Moreover, children dislike the picture task, as compared to tasks based on stories.

Pictures are limited because only "snapshots"—not ongoing records—of events can be depicted graphically. This constrains the kinds of verbs that can be used in test sentences and the kinds of predicates that can be investigated. For example, individual-level predicates (which refer to properties that persist over time) such as being intelligent, or being a car-driver, are difficult to portray in a drawing. Therefore, errors that children make in interpreting sentences in response to pictures could inaccurately reflect their grammars; instead, errors could result from their lack of a nonlinguistic skill, one that takes some time to master.

15.2 Cognitive Complexity

Besides picture tasks, other tasks can cause nonlinguistic errors. Many psychological tasks require building and executing a variety of cognitive algorithms, only some of which are linguistic. In some circumstances, the complexity of the nonlinguistic com-

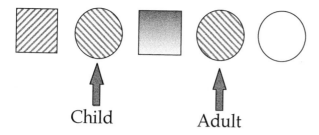

Figure 15.1
Array used to test children's interpretation of prenominal modifiers. Children were instructed to "Point to the second striped ball."

ponents of the task may exceed the child's cognitive ability. This can happen, for example, if the child must formulate a highly complex response plan in order to "act out" the meaning of a sentence with the props available in the experimental workspace. In such circumstances, analyses that have been made within the language module may be obscured by the complexity of nonlinguistic processes. As with experimental design flaws, errors that derive from this source should not be weighed in assessing children's linguistic knowledge or in modeling their language-processing system. In this case, the reason is that the components of the language apparatus are not permitted to contribute to the child's behavior as they would normally. Even consistent nonadult responses in such circumstances cannot be construed as evidence of children's nonadult language processing (e.g., within the syntax). If the goal is to investigate child syntax, then it is important to strip away extraneous sources of errors such as those due to response planning. This is accomplished by reducing the complexity of the cognitive algorithm (or "plan") the child is required to formulate in the task. Only then can it be determined whether or not the child's analysis of the linguistic input is similar to that of an adult.[1]

We can illustrate the point with an actual error committed by children that arose from the complexity of the response plan, and not from the children's lack of grammatical knowledge. The error appeared in studies by Matthei (1982) and Roeper (1972), who found that many children failed to correctly execute instructions containing sequences of prenominal modifiers, including an ordinal, such as "Point to the second striped ball." Having been trained to count objects from left to right, many children who were given the instruction to "Point to the second striped ball" in an array like that in figure 15.1 pointed to the ball in second position (the object in the array that is *second* and *striped* and a *ball*). Adults point to the second of the striped balls. This nonadult response was interpreted by Matthei as evidence that children adopted a "flat" syntactic representation, rather than the correct adult representation. Based on the conviction that children assign the same syntactic representations as adults do, there is an alternative account of children's errors, however. Children could have difficulty forming the cognitive algorithm that is needed to correctly execute instructions in which an ordinal selects and counts members of one subset of objects in the array, while disregarding the members of another subset of objects. If this nonlinguistic account of children's errors is correct, then children's performance should improve if aspects of the cognitive algorithm could be formulated in advance, by allowing children to partition the objects into subsets before they were placed in the array. The pretrial exercise can be quite simple; children can simply be asked to hand sets of objects to the experimenter, one set at a time. Hamburger and Crain (1984) found that children's performance dramatically improved once they had performed this pretrial task. Because the "error" of interpretation was almost entirely eliminated, syntax was exonerated as the culprit in evoking nonadult responses in earlier studies.

15.3 Performance Errors

In sentence processing, the linguistic knowledge of both children and adults can be obscured by performance *errors* such as slips of the tongue, repetitions of words, and mispronunciations. Even more relevant to the assessment of children's knowledge of syntax are errors caused by limitations in computational capacity, for example, limitations in verbal working memory. Since both children and adults have restricted memory capacity, performance errors may arise in circumstances that place excessive demands on memory. The Modularity Matching Model assumes as the Null Hypothesis, however, that the memory capacity of children matches that of adults.[2]

The finding that children and adults show similar patterns of behavior is a good diagnostic of performance errors. If limited working memory capacity is a contributing factor underlying an error, then the error can be expected to appear in testing both children and adults. Moreover, errors are anticipated only for constructions that require subjects to maintain linguistic material in the working memory buffer in unstructured form for an unusual amount of time (albeit only tens of milliseconds). Although it is generally believed that errors occur as a function of the length of a sentence, "length effects" are probably a hallmark of performance errors only when the additional lexical material cannot be rapidly integrated into the syntactic representation that is under construction. This leads us to expect length effects with "flat" phrase markers rather than with "tall" ones; length effects are also associated with maintaining linguistic material (e.g., a "filler" *wh*-phrase) in the working memory buffer until an appropriate "gap" is identified. This is presumably why *wh*-questions involving extraction from object position are more difficult than ones involving extraction from subject position.

More practical considerations also lead to errors. Even in circumstances where the materials and experimental design are not at issue, errors may appear. Errors can be expected at the beginning and end of an experimental session with children. Presumably, errors occur at the beginning of a session because children are attempting to figure out the task and to mentally calculate what construction or analysis yields the right results. At the end of the task, children may become tired and their attention may begin to wander. Errors arising from these sources should be sporadic, however, appearing only a relatively small proportion of the time. As a rule of thumb, we expect such errors to account for 10% or fewer of children's responses in an experiment. Children's responses should represent their competence in the main; only a limited number of errors due to "warm-up" and "fatigue" effects should be manifested.

15.4 Parsing Preferences

Another influence on language processing by both children and adults is parsing preferences. These are assumed to derive, at least in part, from the architecture of the component of the language-processing apparatus that accesses linguistic principles (syntactic and semantic) and resolves ambiguities that arise when more than one representation is consistent with the input (both the test sentence and the discourse context). Basically, a parsing preference is exhibited when the architecture of the system favors one linguistic representation over others. Given the assumption of the Modularity Matching Model, we should expect the same preferences to appear in both children and adults (see chapter 12; Crain and Fodor 1984, 1993).

To give a concrete example, the "Avoid Pronoun" principle (Chomsky 1981) can be thought of as a parsing preference. The tendency to avoid pronouns may in fact be just one of the manifestations of the more general strategy to use "reduced forms" wherever possible (see Lasnik 1990).[3] In pro-drop languages, such as Italian, the "Avoid Pronoun" strategy reflects the preference to use null subjects except when an overt pronoun is needed for emphasis or contrast. In languages such as English, by contrast, the adult grammar excludes the pro-drop option, so the parsing preference to drop subject NPs cannot be followed, at least according to the Modularity Matching Model. There is evidence, however, that pro-drop is a viable option in the grammar of young English-speaking children (Hyams 1986; Rizzi 1993/1994; Roeper and Weissenborn 1990).[4] According to the Modularity Matching Model, null subjects should not occur in children's productions as soon as the pro-drop parameter has been set to the "minus," non-pro-drop value. Adopting a Competing Factors stance, Bloom (1990, 1993) offers a performance account of the early stage of English-speaking children's grammars, the stage at which there are missing subject NPs. Bloom contends that children at this stage have the correct parameter setting (minus pro-drop) but override this for performance reasons. This is a further illustration of the key difference between the Modularity Matching Model and the Competing Factors Model. The difference concerns unambiguous sentences: on the Competing Factors Model, unambiguous sentences can be influenced by parsing preferences and other performance factors; on the Modularity Matching Model, they cannot (Crain and Wexler, forthcoming).

So far, we have discussed children's errors of performance and possible sources of their nonadult responses. We presented two new kinds of circumstances where children and adults could be expected to perform differently, but where we would not therefore infer that children differ from adults in linguistic knowledge per se; the differences in behavior could be ascribed (a) to experimental artifacts or (b) to non-linguistic demands of the task. For the moment, then, we are able to retain the Modularity Matching Model even in the face of certain circumstantial evidence against it. In the remainder of the chapter, we delve further into possible sources of differences in the linguistic behavior of children and adults, and we examine other nonadult responses by children that are ultimately consistent with the Modularity Matching Model.

In the paragraphs that follow, we consider whether there is evidence that children's linguistic behavior is under the influence of parsing preferences and/or performance factors in ways that the linguistic behavior of adults is not. This would be compelling evidence against the Modularity Matching Model and in favor of the Competing Factors Model. We examine instances of children's nonadult linguistic behavior. In each case, we conclude that the Modularity Matching Model stands up to the challenge, because there are other sources of children's nonadult responses in psycholinguistic tasks. For example, such responses arise in certain instances because children are language learners and do not yet have the full repertoire of grammatical knowledge that adults do.

15.5 Repetition of the Auxiliary in Yes/No Questions

Sometimes, children's nonadult linguistic behavior seems to meet several criteria for a performance error, but also seems to resist such an explanation. One such study was conducted by Crain and Nakayama (1987), who attempted to investigate children's adherence to the structure-dependence constraint. The task was designed to elicit yes/no questions with embedded relatives like "Is the boy who is being kissed by his mother happy?" In this study, several of the younger children produced some ungrammatical questions with an extra auxiliary verb, such as (1).

(1) Is the boy who is being kissed by his mother is happy?

In a follow-up study, Nakayama (1987) showed that, in addition to the fact that the errors were made predominantly by younger children, the majority of errors of this type occurred in questions with a long relative clause (containing a transitive verb and its complement); the number of errors was reduced in the child subjects' production of questions with relative clauses containing an intransitive verb. Also, these responses occurred more often when children attempted to ask questions containing a relative clause with an object gap than when they attempted to ask ones with a subject gap. This could also be considered to be a "length effect," since the distance between the "filler" and the "gap" is greater in object gap relative clauses. Such a length effect is also reported in the literature on other populations with notable working memory deficits: aphasic patients (Grodzinsky 1990) and children with reading disabilities (Bar-Shalom, Crain, and Shankweiler 1993).

In sum, children's productions included the insertion of lexical material, a property that is not characteristic of performance mistakes. On the other hand, the addition of material by children was influenced by phrase length, a property of sentences that is correlated with performance mistakes. Our view of the matter is this. Children are not inserting linguistic material to make processing easier. Rather, they are responding to increases in processing load by reverting to a grammatical representation that is consistent with Universal Grammar but is not part of their current grammatical system (cf. Lebeaux 1988). Further evidence of this came from an elicited production study where children were attempting to produce bound variable questions such as (2), but instead produced nonadult forms such as (3). Although (3) has completely grammatical counterparts in Italian, this use of a null subject is not grammatical in adult English (see Thornton and Crain 1989; Thornton 1990).

(2) Who thinks he has the best smile?

(3) Who thinks ____ has the best smile?

Children's deviant questions like (3) appeared, however, only in their initial attempts to produce questions. This "warm-up" effect is known to limit performance, just as is the effect of "fatigue." We contend that children's search space of grammatical representations is sometimes influenced by performance factors, but that this happens because they are still in the throes of language learning, where these alternative representations are available and may emerge when sentences impose processing demands. It should be kept in mind, however, that processing demands do not cause children to adopt grammatical analyses that are not made available by Universal Grammar. Moreover, the same processing demands are experienced by adults. Adults do not respond in the same way as children do, however, presumably because adults no longer have access to earlier grammatical representations. For adults, then, processing difficulty must be evaluated using more sensitive experimental techniques, such as the measurement of eye movements (see, e.g., Frazier and Rayner 1982; Tanenhaus and Trueswell 1995; Ni, Crain, and Shankweiler 1996).

Chapter 16

Methodological Preliminaries

Every experiment begins with two hypotheses: the experimental hypothesis and the null hypothesis. The *experimental hypothesis* will be labeled H_1. In the experiments that we will discuss, the experimental hypothesis will be that children's grammatical competence includes the principles of the theory of Universal Grammar. The experimental hypothesis is contrasted with an opposing hypothesis, called the *null hypothesis* and labeled H_0. The null hypothesis will be that children lack the principle of Universal Grammar under investigation. This use of *null hypothesis*, which we put in lowercase, describes the expected outcome of an experiment if the experimental hypothesis is not confirmed; it should not be confused with the uppercase term *Null Hypothesis*, which describes the set of working assumptions that follow from one's specific model of the language apparatus.

In chapter 2, we introduced the notion of constraints. Many of the experiments we discuss are designed to investigate children's knowledge of a constraint. As mentioned in chapter 2, the absence of a constraint entails that children's grammars will permit meanings that the target grammar does not permit. For example, one linguistic constraint prohibits *He thinks the Joker has the best smile* from having the meaning that the Joker thinks he, himself, has the best smile. The constraint does not prohibit the interpretation according to which someone else—say, Robocop—thinks that the Joker has the best smile. In testing children's knowledge of the constraint, then, the null hypothesis (i.e., the hypothesis that children lack the constraint) is that such a sentence has both the interpretation that the (adult) grammar allows and the interpretation that is ruled out by the constraint. In short, the null hypothesis is that such a sentence is ambiguous for children, but not for adults. The experimental hypothesis is that children's grammars render the test sentences unambiguous, as adults' grammars do. Returning to our example, on the experimental hypothesis, children should not permit the sentence *He thinks the Joker has the best smile* to mean that the Joker thinks he, himself, has the best smile.

16.1 Avoiding Type I Errors

When designing an experiment, it is important to make sure that the design guards against concluding that the experimental hypothesis is correct (that the child knows the constraint) when, as a matter of fact, the null hypothesis is correct (the child lacks the constraint). One of the main goals of any experiment is to avoid conclusions of this kind, which are called *type I errors*. To avoid type I errors, the experimental design must constitute a conservative test of the experimental hypothesis, H_1. A test is conservative to the extent that it reduces the risk of concluding that children adhere to a constraint when in fact the constraint is missing from their grammar; that is, a good experiment defends the null hypothesis, H_0, by stacking the cards against the experimental hypothesis, wherever possible.

To be conservative, care must be taken to avoid tasks that present test sentences in situations where subjects will give correct answers for the wrong reasons. Type I errors contrast with *type II errors*, which occur when valid hypotheses are rejected. Obviously, making this type of error can hurt one's career, but it is less damaging to the field of inquiry.

We can illustrate the choice of the null hypothesis and how type I errors can be avoided using the truth value judgment task. Recall that this task can be used to investigate whether children's grammars contain linguistic constraints on the meanings that can be assigned to sentences. When children's knowledge of constraints is being tested, the null hypothesis is that children lack the constraint. By contrast, the experimental hypothesis is that children know the constraint.

According to the null hypothesis, children should be able to assign the kind of meaning that the constraint rules out. Therefore, sentences governed by the constraint should be ambiguous for children, whereas they will be unambiguous for adults. The truth value judgment task is able to pit the null hypothesis against the experimental hypothesis. Taking the null hypothesis as the starting point, the experimenter designs a context to ensure that the meaning ruled out by the constraint is available for each test sentence. In the context, certain aspects of the story correspond to the meaning of the sentence that is illicit for adults, and other aspects correspond to the alternative meaning—the one that both children and adults license. On one meaning, the sentence is true, and on the other meaning, it is false. The children's task is to indicate whether they accept or reject the test sentence. They simply respond by saying "Yes" or "No" depending on whether they judge the sentence to be true or false.

But which meaning should be associated with the "Yes" response (i.e., true in the context), and which should be associated with the "No" response (i.e., false in the context)? Following the counsel to "be conservative," the meaning that eludes the constraint should correspond to the "No" response. Only this meaning should be accessed by children who know the constraint. Associating the "No" response with this meaning ensures that the test of the experimental hypothesis is conservative; that is, it reduces the risk of making a type I error. Because subjects have a bias to say "Yes" (i.e., to access the interpretation of an ambiguous sentence that makes the speaker's statement true), the experimental hypothesis—that subjects know the principle under investigation—should be associated with the "No" response. If the correct answer corresponds to a "No" response, then a correct response is more compelling evidence for the experimental hypothesis than it would be if it were associated with a "Yes" answer.

There are other ways to stack the cards against the experimental hypothesis, in order to avoid type I errors. One is to associate the final event in the context with the meaning that is ruled out by the constraint. As just noted, this meaning is already associated with the "Yes" response; the sentence is true on this meaning. If this meaning is also associated with the final event, then it should be relatively easy for children to access, if their grammars do not rule it out. Therefore, adopting this as a research strategy further lessens the likelihood of committing type I errors.

16.2 General Features of Experimental Tasks

We conclude part I by pointing out several other features of experiments that are important to keep in mind when working with children. Some of these features may seem quite banal, but we have found them to be important for the success of a study. Foremost among them is the child's comfort in the experimental workplace. With any kind of experiment involving young children, a key ingredient of successful data collection is to make sure that children enjoy the time they spend in the lab. In our view, higher priority should be given to the child's enjoyment than to one's own experimental goals. A child who does not enjoy the time spent in one experiment will not be a willing participant in future experiments. The "fun factor" is especially important in elicited production studies, since children are being asked to express themselves using constructions that are not always totally familiar to them. If children are comfortable in the experimental setting, however, they want to participate over and over in these "games," for sessions lasting 30 minutes or more. Attention to children's well-being also enhances parents' and teachers' confidence in the research program, fostering the kind of productive working relationship that is most conducive to research.

So that children will find an experiment optimally interesting, it is crucial for the experimenters to know the children well. Generally, the experimenter should have interacted extensively with each child participating in the study in the classroom setting and on the playground (or at the child's home). These interactions take place in the weeks before children are invited to "play the game." If the experiment requires taking the child to an unfamiliar research room, it is often worthwhile to invite the child to preview the room and the "game." The child can be given a short introduction to the puppet and the game. This practice session should be fun, so that the child will want to return to play in the real testing session. For a child who is hesitant to leave the familiar classroom setting, it is sometimes helpful to invite the teacher to accompany the child to a practice session.

Each child should receive training on the task. It is best to have a separate training session for each child, using stories and sentences that are closely related to those that will be used in the real session. On occasion, we hold group training sessions, as part of the child care facility's summer program, for example. Children trained in these sessions are briefly retrained individually before the main testing sessions begin. Children who are unable to understand the task, or who are unwilling to participate in the study, are excused from further participation. Usually only a small percentage of children (less than 10%) do not participate, but a record should be kept on these children, with any relevant information.

Our experience indicates that it is often valuable to recruit a friend or colleague to help with the experiment. This allows a much greater degree of experimental control. Usually, one experimenter manipulates toys and props, and the second experimenter plays the role of a puppet. The main reason for including a puppet is that children are often more willing to interact with a puppet than with an adult (even though they know that an adult is posing as the puppet character). This means they are more likely to be verbal in an elicited production task and are more willing to offer corrections in a truth value judgment task. Including a puppet also makes the elicited production task and the truth value judgment task similar, so that children associate the two tasks.

There is a more important reason for using a puppet, however. This makes the session more enjoyable for the child. It often takes time to set up a story, and this momentarily takes the experimenter's attention away from the child. An experimenter working alone would have to ask the child to just sit quietly. Instead, the puppet engages the child between trials, assuming the role of an interesting character who tells jokes, gets easily mixed up, is shy, and so on. The puppet also entertains the child between scenarios, while the first experimenter puts away props from one trial and prepares the props that are needed for the next trial. The result is that the child enjoys the interludes between trials, as well as the stories that make up the trials.[1]

Once a trial is in progress, the puppet's role changes. The puppet helps keep the child's attention focused on the story. During this part of the "game," then, the puppet does not entertain the child subject, but attends to the story along with the child. With her free hand, the experimenter playing the role of the puppet may also monitor the audio equipment, change audiocassettes, do a limited amount of scorekeeping and notetaking, and so on.

To make the game fun for children, we often have the child reward the puppet for saying the right thing, and give it a reminder when it says the wrong thing, "to pay closer attention." Children love to feed the puppet, so we use (plastic) food as rewards and reminders. The child is allowed to choose which item will serve as the reward and which will serve as the reminder. If children are reluctant to say that the puppet said the wrong thing, then it may be because they want to feed the reward to the puppet more than they want to give it the reminder. The food items can be adapted to make administering the admonition more fun for the child. For example, the puppet can ask the child for a little (pretend) salt on the reminder to make it taste better. Or the experimenter can suggest to the child that the puppet can eat two items if it is right, but only one if it is wrong, or the puppet can volunteer to do push-ups if it is wrong, and so on. Sometimes the system of rewards and reminders just gets in the way for certain children and even for certain experimental designs. It can also simplify certain experimental designs—for example, where the experimental sentences are conditionals (e.g., "If every troll crossed over a bridge, then feed Kermit a cookie").

16.3 Practical Tips

In this section, we suggest a few practical tips for conducting experiments. These points are relevant for both of the experimental techniques we discuss: the truth value judgment task and the elicited production task.

We cannot emphasize enough the importance of establishing rapport with the teachers and administrators at the child care facility where you will be working. It may be useful to show them a video of a "typical" experimental trial. The video demonstrates the experimental methodology and underscores the fact that children thoroughly enjoy participating in studies using these experimental methods. It must seem mysterious to teachers and their aides to see children disappear into a research room and to hear them later relate their experience witnessing stories and interacting with a puppet. We volunteer to talk with the teachers and administrators about our research, to attend meetings, and to answer questions they may have about research. Each facility will have its own list of protocols for researchers, although sometimes these protocols are not written down. Some of the protocols simply amount to common courtesy: asking the teacher for permission to interview each child, informing the teacher that the child has returned to the classroom or to the outside activities area. Others are more subtle: not using toy weapons, not casting monsters as characters in the stories.

It is essential to audiotape every session with every child, using high-quality and reliable equipment. This allows the experimenters to focus their attention on the child and not on the data being collected. Children are not usually bothered by a tape recorder and microphone sitting on the table. If they are curious about the equipment, they are usually satisfied with the explanation that a tape is being made to listen to later on. Wires should be taped down so that they will not cause accidents. It is very important to check that the equipment is working properly (i.e., that a tape has been inserted into the tape recorder and that the microphone is working) before the child is brought into the research room so that the experimenters can devote their full attention to interacting with the child.[2]

It is important that both experimenters work as a team to lead the child through a successful experimental session. When the child is brought into the room, the experimenter should mention the child's name to the puppet ("Amy has come to see you"), to guarantee that the audiotape can be correctly catalogued for later transcription and to remind the experimenter playing the role of puppet, in case the child's name has slipped her mind. From the moment the child enters the room, the puppet is "on duty," keeping the child interested in the events.

16.3.1 Constructing Stories

Making up stories for use in experimental tasks comes more easily to some people than to others. But experience spawns inspiration. Sometimes, ideas for appealing stories do not flow. When searching for inspiration, it is often helpful to lay out all of the available toys. Sometimes, interesting combinations of characters and props present themselves. Making up stories in the abstract while sitting in front of the computer frequently leads to frustration. When it comes time to assemble the toys for the experiment, inevitably, some of the needed ones are missing.

There are several ingredients to a good story. It should be short and simple (so that there's enough time to tell all of the stories planned for the experimental session). At the same time, it needs to include some action that gets resolved in some way. And the action needs to capture the child's interest—perhaps because the story is funny or fantastic, or because it is near to the child's own experience. It is a good idea to mix up unusual combinations of characters in stories, so that children do not have preconceived ideas about how certain characters should act. Children are rarely bothered if Superman, Robocop, and Goldilocks all feature in the same story.

Using odd combinations of characters also gives the potential to create novel and unusual stories. Many people seem to assume that children lean heavily on their knowledge of the world in responding to sentences. It seems to be a common belief that children will base their responses on what is semantically plausible and that they will reject sentences that depict implausible events or relations among characters. So, for example, one might speculate that a child would reject a sentence that said that an elephant ate ice cream, on the grounds that elephants eat peanuts or hay, but not ice cream. However, we have argued against the view that children base their responses on general knowledge of the world. If the Modularity Matching Model is correct, stories containing implausible events need not cause concern. Recall that, on the

Modularity Matching Model, understanding of the specific context overrides general world knowledge; because children encounter specific events, which they are asked to relate to the test sentences, they should not use their general knowledge of the world in making decisions about the match or mismatch between a test sentence and its associated context.

For any experiment, there should be several items that test the same structure. As a rule of thumb, we suggest that there should be a minimum of four items for each construction being investigated. The stories for these four items should all have the same basic design, however. The stories should all contain the same number of characters; corresponding characters should perform actions in the same order across stories; and so on. It is important, however, that children not recognize the commonalities. So that all the stories will seem different, each story should have a different "theme." For example, as the toys for each story are set up, the experimenter can say, "This is a Halloween story" or "This is a story about a dinosaur's picnic." The plots within the stories will, of course, be identical.

Children do not enjoy seeing the same story twice; they remember having seen a story before, and they will often tell you how things turned out. Children are also quick to tell you if you repeat a story, as we have found when we try to make a demonstration videotape of our experiments, for example. However, as long as new characters are substituted, children are usually satisfied that the story is also new, even if the storyline or plot is identical to the one they heard before.

"Filler" trials should be interspersed with the test trials. If the correct answer to the test sentences is "No," then the filler trials can be "Yes" trials, to ensure that children are not responding correctly to the test trials for the wrong reason—for example, because they enjoy giving the reminder to the puppet. Children's responses to the follow-up question "What really happened?" also attest to their understanding of the stories. The filler trials should be similar in complexity to the test trials.

16.3.2 Presentation of Stories
The best way to keep all of the toys together for particular stories is to sort them into resealable plastic bags. These should all be laid out, ready, before the child is brought into the room. In this way, there is no delay in finding the toys at the beginning of each experimental trial. A disorganized storyteller puts an unfair burden on the experimenter playing the part of the puppet, who then has to step in for long periods between trials to entertain the child.

At the start of the experimental session, encourage children to watch the stories and not pick up the toys during the narration. If it becomes clear that a child wants to handle the toys, offer to let the child handle them *after* the story is finished. At the end of a story, children often like to help put the toys away by making them "fly" into the bag. Having the child choose the next story is a convenient way of ensuring a random presentation order if this is the design of the experiment. The child simply picks the bag that looks interesting. Often this means getting up to inspect the selection of possibilities set out next to the experimenter. For children who have a lot of energy and find it hard to sit still, this provides a chance to use up a little physical energy.

Another pitfall to avoid is asking children if they want to do another story: "Would you like to see another story?" Because this is a yes/no question, children can say "No." Instead, tell children that they *get to* play another game or see another story: "Let's do another story," "I have another story that I know you will like." Have a positive attitude, and the session will be more enjoyable for the child and for you.

As the toys and props are brought out of the bag for a particular trial, the experimenter introduces them and checks with the child to see if the characters are familiar. Either the child or the puppet can be asked, "Do you know what this is?" If the child has his own name for a character, it is advisable to use that name in the story and in the test sentence. Or, if the child is not familiar with a character's name, it may be better to use a more descriptive name. For example, if a child has never heard of "the Incredible Hulk," then it may be better to call him "the strong guy."

As the toys are introduced, they can be set up in the workspace, ready for the start of the story. Use toys that stand upright—ones with a base or with large feet. Toys that keep falling down are a distraction and waste precious time, particularly if the child wants to take on the challenge of getting them to stand up. Toys that fall down can also impede the momentum of a story that is underway. Besides, the experimenter needs both hands to manipulate other toy characters that are "talking" in the story.

The experimenter manipulating the toys is the "voice" for all the characters that talk in the story. To avoid any confusion about which character is talking, it is often a good idea to move a character up and down slightly as it speaks. Experimenters are often tempted to narrate the story. But in fact, the stories are much more dynamic if the characters do the talking. Having the characters do the talking has another important advantage: the stories don't take so long to complete. For example, as the narrator, you would have to say, "And then the Incredible Hulk came into the room, carrying a pizza, and he said, 'Would you like some pizza?'" Instead, simply move the Incredible Hulk to center stage, with his pizza, and say, "Would you like some pizza?"

It is frequently useful to write down the order in which events are to take place in each story—particularly at the start of an experiment, before the stories become ingrained in memory. For example, a recent experiment investigating children's comprehension of questions like "What didn't every rabbit buy?" included a story about three rabbits going to a spare parts store, where spare noses, tails, eyes, ears, and so on, were for sale. Three actions took place in the story. The following notes served as a reminder of the events and their order:

Sentence: "What didn't every rabbit buy?"

1. every rabbit buys a gold heart
2. no rabbit buys spare elephant ears
3. 2 of the 3 rabbits buy a spare tail

At the end of a story, the characters and props should be arranged so that the alternative interpretations are as clear as possible. We will make this point in more detail in part III, when we discuss the truth value judgment task. There, we will note other aspects of each story that are critical to the experiment. To anticipate, one critical feature of the experiment is the lead-in, that is, the linguistic material that precedes the target sentence. The lead-in has several purposes. First, it lets the child know that the story is over. Second, it draws the child's attention to the puppet, rather than to the experimenter who acted out the story. Finally, it establishes any linguistic antecedents that may be needed for the test sentence to be felicitous on the intended reading (e.g., if it contains a pronoun). A typical lead-in, then, would be:

> "Sammy. I know what happened in that story. That was a story about Grover and Big Bird."

The stories should be told exactly the same way to each child subject (as near as possible). This takes some effort. You should rehearse the stories aloud, either to yourself (before, and as you drive to the children's school, for example) or to friends. This practice step irons out potential problems and ensures that you will present the stories smoothly during testing. It is always a good idea to test older children before moving to younger subjects. Older children are more patient if you happen to fumble and frequently will tell you what is confusing about a story.

Each session with a child should last no longer than 20 to 30 minutes. If children enjoy an experimental task, the time will pass quickly for them and they will want to come back for more. The opposite is also true. If children do not enjoy a task, they will be reluctant to participate in further studies.

16.3.3 Handling the Data

As soon as a child's session is finished, label the audiotape and its container, identifying the child's name and age, the testing date, and the topic under investigation. Even by the end of a single session, it is surprisingly difficult to remember which children were tested and the order in which they were tested. This step also prevents careless mistakes such as taping over another child's session or losing a child's data. If possible, the audiotapes should be transcribed the same day. This task is much easier if the session is fresh in your mind. The task is also easier if it is done in small doses.

The experimenter playing the role of the puppet can take notes, when possible, in addition to audiotaping. A score sheet is needed to record the child's name, age, birthdate, and the name of the child care facility where testing took place; it also provides a ready tally of the child's "Yes" and "No" responses. For experiments using the truth value judgment task, it is essential to have a score sheet so that the puppet knows what target sentence to utter at the end of the story. It is also useful to record any comments of interest that a child may make on particular trials. This helps the experimenter pinpoint the place on the audiotape later. A sample score sheet is illustrated in figure 16.1.

Every response by the child should be accepted as a good response, whether or not it was what the experimenter expected or wanted to occur. The experimenter should always be upbeat, so that children do not feel that they said or did anything wrong. Experiments can be, and should be, positive experiences for children. And for you, the experimenter.

16.4 Conclusion

It is easy to get poor results from children. Interpretable results, whether they conform to the experimental hypothesis or not, are obtained only by thinking through all aspects of the task, by piloting and repiloting (which requires constructing entirely new stories), and by practicing. Only through experience can the "art" of being an experimentalist be mastered.

```
┌─────────────────────────────────────────────────────────┐
│                                                           │
│        Scope of Negation Experiment                       │
│                                                           │
│                                                           │
│  Child's Name:    Sammy           Age:      4;6           │
│  School:          Sunny Hill      Birthdate: 5/9/92       │
│  Test Date:       11/17/96                                │
│                                                           │
│  Targets                          Response                │
│  1.  What didn't every rabbit buy?        ears            │
│                                                           │
│  2.  What didn't every troll eat?         bananas         │
│                                                           │
│  3.  What didn't every mermaid take home?   flowers       │
│                                                           │
│  4.  What didn't every horse jump over?   chair           │
│                                                           │
│  Fillers:                                                 │
│  5.  What did the pig roll in?            mud             │
│                                                           │
│  6.  What did Papa Bear ride on?          dinosaur        │
│                                                           │
│  7.  What did the spaceman crash into?    wall            │
│                                                           │
│  Comments:                                                │
│        -paid attention well                               │
│        -said "Every horse didn't jump over the fence"     │
│               (meaning 'not every horse')                 │
│                                                           │
└─────────────────────────────────────────────────────────┘
```

Figure 16.1
A sample score sheet

The remainder of the book will provide guidelines for constructing stories for experiments using the elicited production task and the truth value judgment task. We cannot emphasize enough how much effort goes into the design of a successful experiment—one in which children base their responses on their grammatical knowledge and not on strategies that they devise because they are confused or frustrated.

This concludes part I of the book. In part II, we consider the methodological desiderata for eliciting sentences from children.

PART II

The Elicited Production Task

Chapter 17

Elicited Production

More and more, it seems that the literature on child language development has come to rely on transcripts of children's spontaneous speech. Fewer in number are experimental investigations of children's comprehension of sentences. Less common still are experimental investigations that attempt to elicit sentences from children. This is surprising, because the elicited production method would seem to be more suitable than other research methods in many, perhaps most, cases. For one thing, productions can be elicited in carefully controlled contexts. There are obvious benefits to controlling the context. Most importantly, this eliminates many of the difficulties that arise in attempting to interpret a child's intended meaning, a frequent problem when examining transcripts of children's spontaneous productions.

Despite the virtues of the elicited production technique, spontaneous production has one advantage over elicited production. Longitudinal data are sometimes available in transcripts of children's spontaneous speech. The elicited production task can be used to elicit data over a period of time, but with some effort—the results are not instantaneous.

17.1 Why Elicited Production

Elicited production is preferable to searches of children's spontaneous productions in many instances, however. Many linguistic phenomena of theoretical interest are only sparsely represented in the transcripts of children's spontaneous productions, if they appear at all. Presumably, these complex linguistic forms are scarce because the situations that call for particular linguistic constructions occur only rarely in children's experience. The elicited production technique overcomes this obstacle. It enables researchers to gather data involving linguistic constructions that children produce rarely, if ever, in their spontaneous speech.[1]

In addition, the elicited production technique allows the experimenter to gather a robust data sample of the targeted structure within a single experimental session. Sufficient data can be collected to draw solid conclusions about the child's grammar at a particular point in time. This is often not true of searches of children's spontaneous speech transcripts. Researchers frequently have to search files that cover months or years in order to collect a sufficiently large sample of a linguistic phenomenon. This leaves open the possibility that important grammatical stages may be missed. A child's longitudinal course of development can be established with elicited production, by repeated elicitation sessions every week or every few weeks.

The elicited production technique also overcomes many of the limitations inherent in comprehension studies. For one thing, it offers a more direct way to assess children's emerging linguistic competence. A comprehension task that relies on "Yes" versus "No"' responses by children must take steps to ensure that nonadult patterns of responses by children truly reflect their grammatical knowledge and are not an artifact of the task. One general advantage of production data is that they reveal the child's grammar without the need to make inferences from "Yes" and "No" responses, as in a comprehension measure such as the truth value judgment task. Production tasks tap children's grammars more directly than comprehension tasks. Correct combinations of words do not come about by accident. As long as the possibility of imitation is excluded, the successful production of even a single target utterance in an appropriate context is a compelling argument for competence with the relevant structure.

Productions are revealing about children's grammars because they contain so much information about children's linguistic competence, including (a) word order, (b) which words are grouped together, (c) the appearance of "displaced" groups of words in one position of a sentence and superficially "missing" words in another position, and so on. If a particular sequence of words appears in children's speech, the sequence is very probably generated by their grammars. It is unlikely that children accidentally put words together in the ways that they do without consulting their mental grammars. It is even more unlikely that children accidentally put words together in exactly the same way as adults do, in the same contexts that adults do, unless they have access to the same grammatical principles as adults do. Therefore, children's adultlike productions permit us to infer that children and adults have similar grammars, as expected on the Modularity Matching Model.

17.2 What's the Problem?

Despite the advantages of the elicited production paradigm, it is easy to understand why the technique has for the most part remained on the shelf. As Ferreiro et al. (1976) remark, the problem is identifying a *uniquely* appropriate context for the linguistic phenomenon of interest:

> Experiments in which children are asked to produce sentences seem on the whole to be free of the hazards of comprehension studies. However, once again, we come up against an obstacle that is due to the nature of language itself; how to construct a situation that will obligatorily give rise to a certain sentence pattern? No such situations exist: thanks to the very rules that make language what it is, perfectly adequate and grammatically correct descriptions in many different forms can be given for any event or situation. (p. 231)

In this part of the book, we will provide instructions for devising contexts that are uniquely felicitous for several linguistic constructions, including ones that have significant bearing on learnability in the absence of linguistic experience. The trick will be to ensure that the contexts used to elicit sentences from children are not amenable to alternative ways of describing the context. We will prove that it is in fact not impossible to construct uniquely felicitous contexts. This chapter contains some general remarks about the elicited production task and a review of previous research (also see Thornton 1996). First, though, we consider the place of production data in the broader framework of the Modularity Matching Model.

17.3 Production and Modularity Matching

The expectations of the Modularity Matching Model extend to children's productive abilities. As noted in part I, the Modularity Matching Model makes two fundamental assumptions. The first is that the architecture of the mental faculty for language processing is modular. The second is that the language-processing system of children is essentially the same as that of adults; more specifically, the principles within any submodule of the language apparatus are the same for both children and adults. Maximizing the similarities between the cognitive systems of children and adults helps to explain children's universal mastery of language—the fact that all children successfully converge on an adult grammar despite impoverished input and a great latitude in experience with language. To the extent that the cognitive mechanisms of children and adults are similar, the problem of learnability does not arise.

On the Modularity Matching Model, the similarities between children and adults —in grammatical knowledge and in the processing mechanisms used to access that knowledge—clearly apply to the language production system. There will be differences in the productions of children and adults, and these will have to be explained. As illustrated in chapter 5, children's nonadult productions are a major source of evidence for the Modularity Matching Model and against one version of the Competing Factors Model, the Input Matching Model. For example, many children produce negative questions with two auxiliary verbs, such as "What did he didn't eat?" (Thornton 1993; Guasti, Thornton, and Wexler 1995). Since such sentences are not grammatical in the target language, it cannot be argued that children are mimicking the input, parroting back phrases that adults produce. Rather, such productions expose a difference between the child's grammatical knowledge and that of an adult.

On the Modularity Matching Model, the explanations for observed differences between children and adults are quite limited. The Modularity Matching Model requires nonadult constructions to be compatible with Universal Grammar and learnable from positive evidence. Chapter 5 examined a number of children's nonadult productions that can be explained by invoking principles of the theory of Universal Grammar. Chapter 15 discussed the kinds of errors that can arise owing to the nature of the performance system. Finally, chapter 13 showed that nonadult responses by children sometimes reflect properties of the learning mechanism: the LAD. The principles of the LAD include the Semantic Subset Principle, which determines which hypothesis children initially formulate for sentences that are ambiguous for adults.

Once children have achieved the full grammatical repertoire, they choose among the different ways of expressing a message using the same parsing strategies as adults. According to the model described in chapters 11 and 12, both children and adults adopt "least effort" (minimal commitment) strategies in resolving ambiguities, based on the complexity of the discourse representations associated with the alternative readings of the sentence. It is reasonable to assume that least effort strategies are also employed in production. When there are several ways to express the same message, the "simplest" means of expression is chosen. For example, children favor questions with extraction from subject position, as in (1), over ones with extraction from object position, as in (2), when both question forms express the same message. We will return to this preference in section 17.4.

(1) Which bug got stepped on by the elephant?

(2) Which bug did the elephant step on?

In order to assess the full linguistic competence of children using the elicited production task, the experimenter must devise situations that demand linguistic constructions that correspond to specific complex discourse representations, perhaps situations that children only rarely witness. This is one of two main design features of an elicited production task. The other is the construction of contexts that are uniquely felicitous for the structure under investigation. This enables researchers to evoke linguistic expressions that children could otherwise avoid, in favor of "simpler" means of expression.

17.4 Design Features of the Task

The elicited production method is appropriate when the question is the sentence *form* that children associate with a particular meaning. As in the truth value judgment task, a situation is acted out with toys and props in front of the child. The situation is associated with a specific sentence meaning. In addition to acting out a context that corresponds to this meaning, the experimenter produces a "lead-in" statement. The lead-in elicits the sentence form that children associate with the meaning (in their grammars) that corresponds to the situation that has been acted out by the experimenter. There are three observable phenomena: the situation, the lead-in, and the child's productions:

(3) Input   ⟨situation, lead-in⟩
     Output ⟨sentence⟩

The input side of the equation in (3) is under the control of the experimenter. The elicited production task enables the experimenter to control the meaning that is to be associated with the child's utterance, by presenting a particular scenario on each trial of the experiment. Then, the lead-in instructs the child to report the situation to a third party, often a puppet who was not able to see the story that was acted out.

As a concrete example, suppose that the research question is whether or not children can produce passive sentences with a "*by* phrase." After careful pilot work, the experimenter settles on a design that embeds the passive sentence inside a question. The child is instructed to pose questions to a puppet. In the context presented to children, the question that best conveys the intended message (for an adult) is a passive question with a *by* phrase, such as "Which bug got stepped on by the elephant?" (Crain, Thornton, and Murasugi 1987). In order to elicit this passive question, the experimenter devises a situation that includes two bugs, an elephant, and one other animal say—a walrus. The basic plot of the story is that the walrus accidentally steps on one bug, and the elephant accidentally steps on the other. (The story would be embellished to make it more interesting for children.) After the story, the experimenter addresses children with the following lead-in:

(4) *Experimenter* In that story, the elephant stepped on one of the bugs, right? Ask the puppet which bug.

Even at this point, there are several possible ways for children to form the question. The child could ask an object extraction question rather than a passive question, for example, "Which bug did the elephant step on?" The child could even reproduce the experimenter's lead-in: "The elephant stepped on a bug. Which one?" The best way to find out if children will respond with these alternative questions is to conduct pilot studies. It turns out that in the present situation, a few children ask object extraction questions, but most 3- and 4-year-old children consistently produce *get* passives with a *by* phrase, such as "Which bug got stepped on by the elephant?"

It is important to note that children do not ask the simple question fragment "Which bug?" in response to the situation/lead-in we have described. This question is infelicitous because two bugs were stepped on. The *by* phrase is necessary to differentiate between the bugs that were stepped on. Apparently, 3- and 4-year-old children are well aware of such pragmatic felicity conditions, at least enough so that they can easily be coaxed to avoid violating them. This underscores the view that young children have even complex semantic/pragmatic principles under their belts.

This example shows how the elicited production task can enable the experimenter to evoke sentences corresponding to syntactic structures that occur only rarely in children's spontaneous speech (and possibly in adult speech as well). A context that is uniquely felicitous for certain complex sentences might be quite exotic in day-to-day conversation. Moreover, ordinary contexts might not be uniquely felicitous for a given construction, such that children may avoid using the construction and choose an alternative, simpler means of expression. By presenting situations that are uniquely felicitous for the construction, elicited production can deepen understanding of the full extent of children's grammatical knowledge.

The technique of elicited production works well for children about 3 years old and older. With effort, it can be used with many children as young as $2\frac{1}{2}$. For children younger than this, however, it is difficult to maintain the appropriate degree of experimental control to reliably evoke consistent productions; for these children, some compromise between elicited and spontaneous production data is necessary. Alternatively, comprehension techniques can be used, such as the preferential looking paradigm (see, e.g., Gleitman 1990; Hirsh-Pasek and Golinkoff 1996; Naigles 1990).

Three kinds of experiments using the elicited production technique are described in part II. Two of the three experimental designs examine children's knowledge of linguistic constraints on the form of sentences. Both of these designs demonstrate that children fail to produce certain linguistic forms. On the Modularity Matching Model, this failure is expected because children know the relevant constraints. This means that the experimental hypothesis is supported by "null" findings: the absence of some behavior that might be expected to occur. It is important to point out the pitfalls in interpreting negative findings. The problem is that there are often alternative explanations—in addition to the experimental hypothesis—for the absence of specific behaviors. The experiment could be flawed, there might not be enough subjects or trials, parsing strategies could militate against the production of certain linguistic forms, and so forth.[2]

Fortunately, most of the obvious alternative explanations of the findings can be handled in the experiments we describe in part II. Chapter 17 introduces one way in which the elicited production task can use the absence of a certain kind of production to argue for children's knowledge of linguistic constraints. The particular constraint at issue is the one that prevents contraction of the verbal elements *want* and *to* to form *wanna* in certain linguistic environments. As noted in chapters 2 and 3, the ban against *wanna* contraction applies in questions like (5); as (6) illustrates, however, contraction is permitted in other linguistic environments.

(5) a.   Who does Arnold want to cook breakfast?
     b.   *Who does Arnold wanna cook breakfast?

(6) a.   Who does Arnold want to cook breakfast for?
     b.   Who does Arnold wanna cook breakfast for?

To study children's adherence to the constraint, the experimenter encourages them, through the experimental design, to produce both questions like (5) and ones like (6). Elicitation of questions like (6) establishes children's willingness to contract in constructions that permit contraction. This serves as a measuring rod against which their productions of questions like (5) can be evaluated. Their willingness to contract in (6) but not in (5) would be convincing evidence that they know the constraint.

In another type of experimental design, there is no measuring rod. For example, in a study of children's adherence to a different constraint, described in chapter 19, the experimental hypothesis anticipates the absence of certain nonadult forms in children's speech; the kind of linguistic form that should not occur is illustrated in (7).

(7)   *Is the man who sleeping is bald?

Suppose children do not, as a matter of fact, produce questions like (7). Does the absence of such productions support the experimental hypothesis? It is tempting to answer "No" on the grounds that there is no good reason to expect children to produce questions like (7), since such questions are not in their linguistic input. Presumably, the adult form of the question corresponding to (7) is (8).

(8)   Is the man who is sleeping bald?

The discussion of the Input Matching Model in chapter 5 should make it clear that children do not simply mimic the utterances that they encounter in the linguistic environment. Moreover, in the present case it turns out that children who attempt questions like (8) produce many nonadult forms. They do not produce questions like (7), however. This observation, and the fact that such nonadult forms are predicted to occur according to some models of language acquisition, must suffice to make the argument that children know the constraint that prohibits nonadult questions like (7).

So far, the discussion has concerned the uses of the elicited production task to assess children's knowledge of constraints. The other use of the task is to establish that children can in fact produce linguistic constructions that are not expected to occur according to certain models of language acquisition. The Modularity Matching Model is hard pressed to explain the absence of linguistic constructions from children's speech, especially constructions that draw heavily upon core principles of Universal Grammar, and ones that adults produce with regularity. The elicited production task is a useful tool in this regard, as we will show in chapter 18. On the Modularity Matching Model, the experimental hypothesis in that chapter is that children will successfully produce Universal Grammar–compatible linguistic forms in appropriate contexts, with the same limiting conditions applying to them as apply to adults.

This ends our general remarks on the elicited production technique. The next section begins with a discussion of previous research and briefly sketches some variations in the applications of the task, used to address particular issues. The section ends with an outline of factors that should be taken into account when planning an elicited production experiment. The chapters that follow present several elicitation experiments; in the course of these chapters, we discuss solutions to problems that one may encounter in using this methodology.

17.5 Previous Research

The elicited production task has been in service in one form or another for over 30 years. An early and much celebrated use of the task was an experiment by Berko (1958) investigating children's morphological knowledge. The aim of this study was to assess children's ability to create new linguistic forms, ones that follow from the application of rules given by the theory of Universal Grammar. To this end, Berko introduced children to novel words, which they could not possibly have heard before. Children between the ages of 4 and 7 were shown pictures of an object, such as a cartoon bird, and were told, "This is a 'wug.'" They were then shown a second picture with two tokens of the same type of object. They were told, "Now there are two of them." To elicit the target responses, children were asked to complete the experimenter's carrier phrase, "There are two _____." The carrier phrase elicited the correct form, "wugs," from most children. This was interpreted as evidence that these children had internalized the grammatical process (e.g., a rule) for supplying the plural ending to nouns. Because children produced the plural forms of novel words, it was inferred that they were not basing their productions on the input. Similar results were found for a number of other grammatical morphemes, including tense marking and possessive marking. In other words, the findings were taken as evidence against the Input Matching Model. In any event, the experimental results clearly argue against the view that children's productions of real plural nouns are the result of imitation.

Another early use of the elicited production task was reported by Bellugi (1971), who used it to probe for children's knowledge of subject-auxiliary inversion in positive and negative questions. One experimenter used a puppet who responded with the "quavering voice of an elderly puppet." The lead-in devised to elicit *wh*-questions was an indirect question. Questions like the following were elicited at various times throughout the experimental session:

(9)   *Experimenter*   Adam, ask the Old Lady what she'll do next.
       Adam   Old Lady, what will you do now?
       Old Lady   I'll fly to the moon.

(10)   *Experimenter*   Adam, ask the Old Lady why she can't sit down.
       Adam   Old Lady, why you can't sit down?
       Old Lady   You haven't given me a chair.

Notice that the lead-in preserved the word order of the declarative counterpart to the *wh*-question, giving the child no clues about subject-auxiliary inversion. Therefore, the consistent production of inverted subjects and auxiliary verbs by children would have provided compelling evidence that this process is represented in their grammars. As the examples show, Adam failed to invert the subject NP and the auxiliary verb in negative questions, but be did invert these elements in positive *wh*-questions (see Pinker 1984 for discussion and for further empirical details).

Having fallen out of fashion for some years, the elicited production task has recently resurfaced in studies of other aspects of children's grammars, in the areas of both syntax and semantics. Here is a partial list of the grammatical properties and syntactic structures that have been studied: structure-dependence (Crain and Nakayama 1987; Nakayama 1987); the *wanna* contraction and *that*-trace paradigms (Thornton 1990; Crain 1991); object agreement in Italian (McKee and Emiliani 1992); passives (Crain, Thornton, and Murasugi 1987); subject-auxiliary inversion (Erreich 1984;

Sarma 1991); negation in English questions (Guasti, Thornton, and Wexler 1995); negation in Italian questions (Guasti 1996); object scrambling in Dutch and Italian (Schaeffer 1996); properties of full versus bare *wh*-phrases in questions (Thornton 1995); relative clauses in English (Hamburger and Crain 1982); relative clauses in Italian (Crain, McKee, and Emiliani 1990); relative clauses in French (Labelle 1990; Guasti et al. 1995); control properties of infinitival sentences (Eisenberg and Cairns 1994); and universal quantification (Crain, Thornton, et al. 1996).

Although all of these studies have many features in common, there are really several elicited production techniques. The elicited production task must sometimes be modified to accomplish particular experimental goals. However, most variations of the task adopt the strategy of involving children in a game in which they interact with a puppet. Children can direct the puppet to do something (such as "Point to ..."), or they can be directed to question the puppet about scenarios acted out with toys. The task can even be used to direct children to correct a statement that the puppet makes about the scenarios. Adopting this procedure turns the truth value judgment task into an elicited production task. In studies using the truth value judgment task, this production component is typically used to establish that children are accepting and rejecting target utterances for the right reasons.

17.6 Experimental Preliminaries

Elicitation experiments involve special considerations because they require children to be quite verbal. Part of the skill of conducting a successful elicitation experiment therefore lies in effectively involving children in a game. In addition, a high level of involvement by children is important because they often experience difficulty in accessing and/or producing the words or structure at issue. It is therefore critical for experimenters to know all child subjects well, so that they will comply with their requests.

We have found that the use of puppets quickly captures the child's interest in the game. Using a puppet that pretends to be shy of grown-ups has proven quite successful in encouraging children to be verbal. The right choice of puppet also helps. We often use a snail puppet, which withdraws into its shell every time the "grown-up" experimenter gets too close or tries to ask a question. Another puppet that works well is a newborn dinosaur that has just broken out of its shell. Because these puppets are too shy to talk to grown-ups, and will only talk to kids, the experimenter explains that this poses a dilemma for her—she cannot find out what she would like to know about the puppet. To resolve the dilemma, the experimenter enlists the child's help. The child solicits the information from the puppet. One additional advantage of this research strategy is that the child isn't in a position to tell the experimenter, "*You* ask"—the puppet won't talk to grown-ups. Whatever puppet or ploy is used to involve the child, it is essential that the child have a reason to communicate with the puppet.

In the course of an elicited production experiment, children sometimes have difficulty accessing the target structure. This often demands quick thinking by the experimenter, and it probably calls for deviations from the experimental session that was planned. When a child is struggling to come up with the target structure, it is important not to frustrate him. The kind of long awkward silences that occur when the experimenter waits for the child to perform should be avoided because they can make the child feel as if he is being tested. If the child does not say anything, it is often best just to move on to the next trial. Sometimes, repeating part of the story will prompt the child to make another attempt at producing the target structure. If the experimenter decides to repeat part of a story, however, it should be clear to the child that there is a good reason for doing this. Here the puppet can come to the rescue and say something like, "That story was very hard for me. Could you do that one again?" This saves the child from feeling as if he failed to perform successfully for the experimenter. If a child does not produce the target structure on the second attempt, it is best to proceed to the next trial.

Because it is important that children should not feel as if they have failed, it is worthwhile to offer confidence-building statements such as "You're doing a great job. This is a hard game for the snail, isn't it? But you're really helping him." Depending on how a particular child reacts, it is also sometimes useful to insert a "fun" filler trial before moving on to the next test trial. Several of these filler trials should be prepared ahead of time. The fillers can be used to elicit an unrelated structure, preferably one that children will find easy to access. A successful experience with the filler item serves to renew the child's confidence and interest in the game. Such deviations from the experimenter's planned session are essential to a successful session. Failing to take all of the necessary steps to make a session enjoyable for children also jeopardizes the chances of other experimenters to work with them.

The drawback to accommodating to the child's comfort and deviating from the planned session is that some children will receive more filler trials and will hear parts of the test stories more often than other children do. Researchers may find this disquieting, feeling that they would thereby be abandoning proper research protocol. In elicited production studies, however, there is little reason to believe that such differences compromise the experiment. Unless repeating a story or adding a filler item "cues" children about the target structure, their productions are firm evidence of their grammatical knowledge. The difficulties in gathering and reporting results are offset by the richness of production data.

Chapter 18

Eliciting Relative Clauses

This chapter highlights the importance of satisfying the felicity conditions of a target construction when the goal is to elicit sentences from children. It also illustrates how satisfying the felicity conditions of a construction can result in circumstances that are uniquely appropriate for that construction. Alternative ways of expressing the same message are often eliminated once the felicity conditions are met. Failure to appreciate the pragmatic conditions that make sentences appropriate to the conversational context can lead to mistaken conclusions about the syntactic analyses children assign to them.

We begin with some general remarks about felicity conditions. Then we consider the conditions that are specifically associated with sentences that contain a restrictive relative clause. As we discussed in chapter 8, failure to attend to the conditions for felicitous usage of the restrictive relative clause has led some researchers to claim that children have a nonadult representation for relative clauses. Such claims are not compatible with the Modularity Matching Model, nor are they consistent with the empirical data that are forthcoming once the felicity conditions are satisfied.

18.1 Felicity Conditions

An essential part of designing an elicited production experiment is to understand the pragmatic conditions that are both necessary and sufficient for producing the structure under investigation. Identifying the properties of the uniquely appropriate situation for a target construction usually requires investing considerable time in conducting pilot experiments with adults and older children, before turning to younger children. The point cannot be overemphasized: pilot work is essential if the experiment is to achieve its goal. In fact, pilot work often takes more time than running the actual experiment.

Adults' intuitions about the conditions necessary for producing a particular structure are frequently dull because they have the ability to accommodate pragmatic infelicities. Adults can often fill in the missing inferential steps in response to speakers who fail to establish the presuppositions that underlie their statements. The downside of having the ability to readily accommodate presuppositional failures is that adults, including linguists, find it difficult to identify those aspects of pragmatic context that are needed to elicit a particular sentence structure.

Young children 3, 4, and 5 years old do not have the same capacity as adults to understand sentences produced in infelicitous circumstances. Apparently, children cannot accommodate presuppositional failures (see, e.g., Hamburger and Crain 1982). Presumably, this is because they do not share adults' general knowledge of the world, and not because they lack certain linguistic principles (Lewis 1979; Chierchia 1995). This means that in order to successfully elicit a structure from a child, the pragmatics must be exactly right. If an experimental context does not fulfill the presuppositions for an utterance, children are likely to have difficulty producing it. They probably won't understand what is being asked of them, and they will quickly become frustrated with the experiment and with the experimenter.

The next section presents the acquisition literature and reviews some of the structural properties of the restrictive relative clause. This will be relevant for the ensuing discussion.

18.2 Nonadult Relative Clauses

The early literature on the acquisition of relative clauses made two claims: first, that children and adults assign different syntactic representations to relative clauses, and second, that children's misanalysis results from either (a) the absence of certain rules from their grammars or (b) misattachment of the relative clause in the phrase structure that they assign. We will consider both claims. The proposals we consider all stem from experimental evidence that seemingly demonstrates children's consistent misunderstanding of a certain relative-clause construction (see Sheldon 1974; de Villiers et al. 1979; Tavakolian 1978, 1981; Goodluck and Tavakolian 1982).

The construction that was particularly problematic for children was the OS relative, so named because the relative clause modifies the noun in object position of the main clause (i.e., O), and the relative clause itself contains a superficially empty subject (i.e., S).

(1)   The dog pushes the sheep that jumps over the pig.

The experiments that evoked nonadult responses from children typically used the research methodology of the figure manipulation (or act-out) task. In these studies, the experimenter presented children with a sentence and instructed them to "make it happen" using toys and props that were present in the experimental workspace. These studies revealed that children consistently acted out OS sentences like (1) in a nonadult fashion. Many children who were asked to act out the meaning of (1) had the dog push the sheep and then jump over the pig. It is the second event that made children's responses different from those of adults. For adults, (1) asserts that the sheep, not the dog, jumps over the pig.

Children's nonadult enactment of events led different researchers to different conclusions. For example, Tavakolian (1978, 1981) concluded that children had assigned a nonadult structure to (1). On her account, the structure that children assigned to (1) closely parallels the structure underlying the sentence in (2), which has two conjoined clauses; it asserts that the dog pushes the sheep and then it, the dog, jumps over the pig. Hence, Tavakolian dubbed the account the conjoined-clause analysis of relative clauses.

(2)   The dog pushes the sheep and jumps over the pig.

For children, then, Tavakolian's account claimed that the structures underlying sentences with a relative clause, such as (1), have conjoined clauses (i.e., IPs), as in (3).

(3)

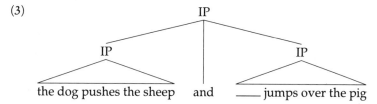

In (3), *the sheep* and *jumps over the pig* are not in the same IP.

The diagram in (4) gives the adult syntactic representation corresponding to sentence (1). In contrast to the representation attributed to children, the adult representation of (1) has, as a constituent, *sheep that jumps over the pig*.

(4)

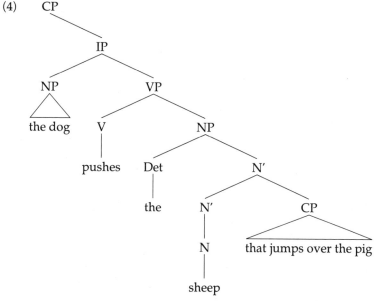

According to Tavakolian (1978, 1981), children do not have access to the (recursive) rules needed to produce the appropriate hierarchical structure for a relative clause. Specifically, she claimed that children's grammars do not have recursion within the NP; that is, they are unable to generate one NP inside another NP. Notice that in the adult structure, an entire clause (containing its own NPs) is generated below the NP containing *the sheep*. According to the conjoined-clause analysis, the inability to form recursive NP structures forces children to produce nonhierarchical, "flat" structures in interpreting sentences like (1).

At the time this "flat structure" hypothesis was formulated, phrase markers were viewed as the product of phrase structure rules. Children's intermediate grammars were assumed to comprise a *subset* of the rules and principles that characterized later stages. In children's early grammars, the rules that provide recursion within the NP were thought to be unavailable to them. This is depicted in figure 18.1. It was thought that the first recursive rule a child acquires repeats the category IP, but does not embed it under another IP. Given that this was the only recursive rule available, children were believed to generate a structure like that in (3) for a sentence with a restrictive relative clause.

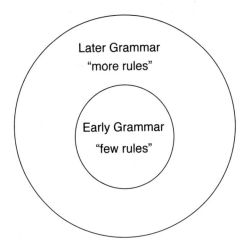

Figure 18.1
Early and later grammars in a rule-based system

There is another class of explanations for children's reputed conjoined-clause analysis of relative clauses. One alternative account, by Roeper (1982), proposes that children's nonadult responses are a function of the operating characteristics of the parser and do not reflect the absence of grammatical principles. On Roeper's account, a specific operating characteristic (or strategy) of the parser—namely, its tendency to attach constituents in a way that generates the fewest nodes—encourages the misattachment of relative clauses. This is known as the *minimal attachment* strategy (Frazier and Fodor 1978; Frazier 1978).

Although adults too are guided by the minimal attachment strategy, it is applied differently by children and adults, according to Roeper. Adults restrict its application to the resolution of structural ambiguities, whereas children also invoke it in constructing the phrasal analysis of unambiguous sentences. Application of the strategy in (1) results in a nonadult structure with the relative clause positioned high in the phrase marker, as illustrated in (5). As compared to the adult structure in (4), the structure in (5) contains fewer nodes (i.e., there are no branches between the CP containing the relative clause and the topmost IP).

(5)

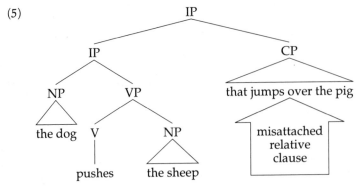

By relegating the responsibility for children's errors to a performance component of the language apparatus, Roeper's account exonerates the syntax from bearing the responsibility for children's errors. Therefore, the account is able to maintain that children's syntax is equivalent to that of adults.

Roeper's account is clearly inconsistent with the Modularity Matching Model; it is an embodiment of the Competing Factors Model. It is a fundamental assumption of the Modularity Matching Model that the grammar has primacy over the parser. According to this model, the parser cannot influence the representation generated by the grammar for unambiguous sentences.

A study by Goodluck and Tavakolian (1982) led them to conclude, like Roeper, that children's nonadvlt responses are performance errors and do not reflect a lack of linguistic competence. Goodluck and Tavakolian contended that children made non-adult responses when their linguistic processing system was overtaxed. They found that children's nonadult responses decreased when the sentence contained fewer animate nouns (e.g., *The dog pushed the sheep that jumped over the pig* vs. *The dog pushed the sheep that jumped over the fence*). Apparently, the presence of three animate nouns in the sentence burdened the processing system. Similar claims relegating children's nonadult comprehension of structures to the processing component have been made for control structures by Tavakolian (1981) and by McDaniel, Cairns, and Hsu (1991).[1]

It should be clear by now that all such performance accounts of children's "errors" are difficult to reconcile with the Modularity Matching Model. If adults are not overtaxed by the presence of three animate NPs in a sentence, then children should not be, if the Modularity Matching Model is correct. Therefore, we must look elsewhere for the source of children's nonadult behavior. Before we broach this topic, however, we would like to raise two theoretical problems faced by previous analyses of children's nonadult behavior. The first, relating to changes in linguistic theory, is of concern to the conjoined-clause analysis. The second is learnability, that is, how children's grammars or language-processing systems change, to become equivalent to those of adults.

18.3 Problems with the Conjoined Clause Analysis

The conjoined-clause analysis proposes that children lack recursion in the NP. This analysis may have made intuitive sense when it was initially formulated, within a linguistic theory that viewed grammars as sets of phrase structure rules. However, the proposal that children lack recursion in the NP makes less sense within current incarnations of linguistic theory. Recently it has been proposed that a general schema within Universal Grammar generates the phrasal structure assigned to sentences. According to the schema, phrases are hierarchically structured projections of their heads. The so-called X' (read X-bar) schema is usually written as shown in (6), where X and Y are variables ranging over any linguistic constituent: Noun (N), Verb (V), Preposition (P), Complementizer (C), Inflection (I), and so forth. This rule schema provides the building blocks for projecting hierarchical structure from the heads of phrases (X-level constituents) to phrases (the maximal projections of heads, i.e., XP-level constituents) (see Haegeman 1994 and Radford 1988 for further discussion).

(6) XP → Specifier, X'
     X' → X', YP
     X' → X, YP

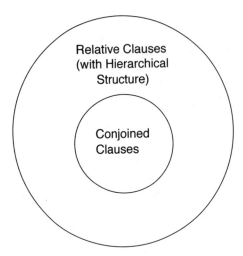

Figure 18.2
The relationship between the conjoined-clause and relative-clause interpretations

The claim that children lack recursion in the NP now would amount to the claim that children have incomplete mastery of X' theory. In the adult system, there would be a fully general X' schema that projects in the same way for every maximal projection, constructing CPs, IPs, NPs, PPs, and so on. In the child's system, by contrast, phrasal structure would presumably construct projections in one way for CPs, IPs, PPs, and so on, but in a different way for NPs. This seems inconsistent with the spirit of Universal Grammar. Children's analyses of sentences with a relative clause would be aberrant.

This brings us to the second problem. Figure 18.2 depicts the situation: Children first assign conjoined-clause interpretations to sentences (even ones that have a different meaning for adults). Later, children add to their linguistic repertoire, somehow learning to assign correct structures and their associated meaning to sentences with relative clauses.

What is wrong with this picture? The problem for children would be to find evidence from the environment that will compel them to abandon the conjoined-clause analysis. Adopting this analysis results in different meanings for sentences like (1) for children and adults. At first glance, it may seem that this poses no problem. Perhaps children simply abandon the meaning that they assign to such sentences when they encounter situations that make it clear that adults assign a different meaning. This won't work in general, however. Because many, perhaps most, sentences have more than one meaning, it follows that learners who adopted this strategy would be forced to discard many legitimate sentence meanings. It is more likely that children would add the new interpretation and keep the old one, leaving children with two meanings for a sentence that has only one meaning for adults. That is, children would find sentences like (1) ambiguous, whereas adults would find them unambiguous. This leaves the problem of unlearning the offending sentence meaning unresolved.

This problem of unlearning must be confronted by any proposal that would have children assign incorrect meanings to sentences. As noted earlier, learners must identify their errors solely on the basis of positive evidence, in the form of

⟨sentence, meaning⟩ pairs. What is needed to abandon the conjoined-clause analysis is evidence that the meaning assigned to conjoined sentences *cannot* also be assigned to sentences containing relative clauses like (1). Therefore, children whose grammars imposed a conjoined-clause analysis of sentences with relative clauses (in the adult grammar) would require access to negative "semantic" evidence; presumably, this sort of evidence is not available in the primary linguistic data.

Finally, it should be noted that the problem of learnability also confronts those accounts that attribute children's nonadult responses to performance mechanisms. If children's parsing mechanisms differ from those of adults, then we are led to ask how children's parsing mechanisms change to the adult mechanisms.

These deliberations lead us to ask whether an alternative explanation of children's errors can be found. If so, then the problems of learnability can be circumvented.

18.4 Presuppositions of Relative Clauses

What went wrong in previous comprehension experiments testing children's understanding of sentences with relative clauses? In our view, children were tested in infelicitous circumstances. A circumstance can be infelicitous if it does not attend to the presuppositional content of the sentence. In addition to what sentences assert, many sentences bear presuppositions. These are propositions that are assumed, or are presupposed to be true, by the speaker. The term *presupposition* indicates that these aspects of sentence meaning should already have been established in the conversational context, preceding the utterance of the sentence. If the propositions that are presupposed have not been previously established, then the use of the sentence is awkward at best, and in the worst case, senseless.

Restrictive relative clauses are a case in point. In many experiments, children have been found to misunderstand sentences with restrictive relative clauses. Hamburger and Crain (1982) argued that children's misunderstandings arose because the presuppositions of the restrictive relative clause were not satisfied in the experimental context. Consider the sentence *The lion licked the zebra that jumped over the fence.* Hamburger and Crain pointed out that the restrictive relative clause in this sentence (i.e., *that jumped over the fence*) has two presuppositions. First, for the relative clause to be used felicitously, there should be at least two zebras in the context. As Hamburger and Crain put it, a restrictive relative clause is felicitous only if there is some restricting to be done. The semantic contribution of the relative clause *that jumped over the fence* is to identify one particular zebra from the set of zebras present in the context. In the child language experiments that resulted in high error rates, the restrictive function of the relative clause was not met; only one zebra was present in the context.

Many relative clauses also have a second presupposition. The second presupposition requires that the action described by the relative clause took place before the sentence was uttered. That is, the information contained in the relative clause is *conceptually prior* to the information contained in the main clause. In the example, the jumping event should have taken place before the licking event. This second presupposition is particularly interesting in the present example, because as a consequence of this presupposition, the order in which events are mentioned in the sentence (first, the licking event and, second, the jumping event) conflicts with the conceptual order of events. The conceptual order of events is dictated by the presupposition of the restrictive relative clause: the event mentioned in the relative clause should have occurred before the assertion contained in the main clause. This kind of conflict between order of mention and conceptual order will prove to be important in our discussion of children's acquisition of relative clauses.

18.5   Context

Two studies by Hamburger and Crain (1982) have led to a different conclusion from previous studies about children's grammatical competence. Taking into account the different presuppositions of relative clauses, Hamburger and Crain identified a different source of children's nonadult behavior, and one that is more consistent with the Modularity Matching Model. The findings from their studies indicate that children's errors in previous experiments were neither the result of a lack of syntactic knowledge nor due to a misattachment of constituents within the phrase marker. Instead, children's errors were an experimental artifact. They arose because children were tested in circumstances that were infelicitous for the sentences that were presented to them. In experimental investigations using new methodological procedures, it has been amply demonstrated that children master the relative clause before their third birthday.

The new procedures were motivated by the observation, outlined in the previous section, that sentences with relative clauses often bear presuppositions that were not met in earlier studies. The typically poor performance by young children in these experiments was attributed to their ignorance of the linguistic properties of relative clause constructions. But suppose children did know the linguistic properties but were also aware of the associated presuppositions. Such children might be unable to relate their correct understanding of the sentence structures to the inappropriate circumstances provided by the experiment. In other words, children were put in a position that required them to ignore either their knowledge of the syntax of the relative-clause construction or to ignore their knowledge of its pragmatics. Adult subjects may be able to "see through" the unnaturalness of an experimental task to the intentions of the experimenter, but it seems unrealistic to expect this of young children.

Following this line of reasoning, Hamburger and Crain made the apparently minor change of adding more sheep to the acting-out situation for sentence (1). This simple change resulted in a much higher percentage of correct responses by children even younger than the ones tested in earlier research. The most frequent remaining "error" was made by the oldest children, who failed to act out the event described by the relative clause. Hamburger and Crain called this the *assertion-only* response, because these children acted out only the assertion in (1)—that the dog pushes the sheep—and not its presupposition—that there is one sheep that is distinguished from the others by the fact that it alone jumps over the pig. Hamburger and Crain argued, that the assertion-only response is not really an error, but is precisely the kind of response that is compatible with perfect comprehension of the test sentences. Responses of this type did not appear in previous studies presumably because these studies failed to meet the presuppositions of the restrictive relative clause.

18.6 Elicitation of Relative Clauses

The most compelling evidence that young children do not lack the structural knowledge underlying relative-clause formation comes from a second experiment in the

Figure 18.3
Context for eliciting subject gap relative clauses. (Experimenter: "If you want her to point to ... what would you say?"; Child: "Point to the kangaroo that is standing on the frog.")

study by Hamburger and Crain, an elicited production task. Pragmatic contexts were constructed in which the presuppositions of restrictive relatives were satisfied. True to the term *restrictive* relative clause, in this task children were asked to identify one toy from a set of identical toys.

As with most of the studies we have reported, two experimenters were recruited to carry out the study. One experimenter manipulated toy props and directed the child's participation in the game. A second experimenter was a blindfolded observer whose role was to follow any instructions given by the child. Children's instructions to the experimenter were always to "Point to" certain objects in the workspace. The observer was blindfolded so that children couldn't identify the object by saying, "Point to this one." (Or at least if they did, the observer could say, "I can't see! What shall I point to?") The idea was that the only way the child would be able to correctly identify the objects for the observer to point to was by using a relative clause. In order to be sure that the child would use a relative clause, a number of identical objects were placed in the workspace—say, three kangaroos. The objects were identical so that the child couldn't avoid a relative clause and use just a noun (e.g., "Point to the kangaroo"), or an adjective ("Point to the big kangaroo"), or a preposition ("Point to the kangaroo with a bow tie"). In addition to the two or three identical objects, there was one other object in the workspace—say, a frog. This object was involved in some kind of action, performed by one of the three kangaroos. To elicit a subject gap relative clause, the experimenter might have one of the kangaroos jump on the frog. The situation and protocol are shown in figure 18.3.

The experimenter who is in charge of eliciting the relative clause does not label the object that is being focused on, because doing so might cause the child to pick up on the label that the experimenter suggests. For example, if the experimenter says, "If you wanted her to point to *this kangaroo*, what would you say?", the child is likely to say, "Point to this kangaroo." Rather than encounter this situation over and over, the

Figure 18.4
Context for eliciting object gap relative clauses. (Experimenter: "If you want her to point to ... what would you say?"; Child: "Point to the kangaroo that the frog is standing on.")

experimenter gestures toward the object of interest, instructing the child as follows: "If you want her [the blindfolded observer] to point to ... [the experimenter points to the kangaroo that is jumping on the frog], what would you say?"

In order to elicit an object gap relative clause, the frog could stand on one of the kangaroos. This version of the situation is depicted in figure 18.4. The instruction to the child is the same as before, with a gesture toward the kangaroo that the frog is jumping on.

Two other points deserve mention. First, the possibility of imitation is excluded by the experimenter's care not to use any relative-clause constructions in the elicitation situation. Second, the elicitation technique has been extended to younger children (as young as 2;8) and to the elicitation of a wider array of relative-clause constructions, including gaps in oblique positions (McDaniel and McKee 1996). Some examples of relative clauses produced by young children are given in (7). Comparable findings with 2- and 3-year-old children learning Italian have also been obtained in a study by Crain, McKee, and Emiliani (1990).[2]

(7) a. Jabba, please come over to point to the one that's asleep. (3;5)
     b. Point to the one that's standing up. (3;9)
     c. Point to the guy who's going to get killed. (3;9)
     d. Point to the kangaroo that's eating the strawberry ice cream. (3;11)

18.7 Conclusion

The discovery that children understand and produce sentences with relative clauses in appropriate circumstances supports the conclusion that children's performance failures in earlier studies should not be taken as evidence that this structure is missing from their grammars.

In the past few years, several other unaccommodating findings have been reinterpreted as reflecting the influence of task factors, and not lack of structural competence. When questions about syntactic knowledge are asked in a different way, by adopting tasks that control as far as possible for the pragmatic demands of comprehension, children have been found to succeed (see Crain and Fodor 1993; Crain 1991). We conclude that the failure in previous research to control for nonsyntactic factors led to underestimates of children's grammatical capabilities in some cases. As a consequence of the new findings, the timetable for the acquisition of syntax has been brought more in line with the expectations of the Modularity Matching Model, which anticipates rapid acquisition of grammatical knowledge without numerous intermediate stages of successive approximation toward the target grammar.

Chapter 19

Asking Questions: The "Ask/Tell" Problem

In elicitation experiments designed to evoke question structures, experimenters are often plagued with what is commonly called the *ask/tell problem*. Characteristically, in situations designed to elicit a question, children respond with an answer instead. For example, if the experimenter instructs a child "Ask Kermit what he's eating," the child responds by telling the experimenter what Kermit is eating: "An ice cream." This problem can be seen as another instance of failure to satisfy felicity conditions. In general, the problem is more acute with younger children and is encountered frequently with children in the 3-year-old range. This is to be expected, since younger learners are less able to accommodate to infelicity than older ones, who have more world experience. In order to think about how to avoid the ask/tell problem, we can begin by distinguishing felicity conditions at two levels: at the level of the game, and at the level of individual experimental stimuli.

The first step is to satisfy the felicity conditions for the experiment as a whole. That is, the experiment should be designed to involve children in a game in which it makes sense to ask questions. One way is to introduce children to a puppet they have never seen before and know nothing about. This ploy is used successfully in Crain and Nakayama's (1987) experiment testing structure-dependence, to be described in chapter 20. In this experiment, children were asked to pose questions to the *Star Wars* character Jabba the Hutt. Jabba was from another planet and had never been to Earth before. The experimenter began the session by "wondering" about Jabba the Hutt to set up a lot of unknowns. The experimenter's patter went something like this:

(1) I wonder if Jabba the Hutt can walk or talk . . . I don't know. Look at his body, it's got funny bumps on it. Maybe he's part animal. Could be! I don't know. He looks quite friendly. Maybe he likes people. I wonder if he gets hungry. I have a hamburger here. I wonder if he likes hamburgers. I don't know if they have hamburgers on the planet he comes from. Maybe you could help me find out.

Having set the stage for the experiment, the experimenter can proceed to elicit individual questions. For many children, provided the game is set up in the right way, there is no danger that the ask/tell problem will arise. There are children who have more stringent requirements on question asking, however. For these children, the felicity conditions for asking questions must be satisfied for each target question in addition to the more global level of the game. Each target question must request information that the child does not already know. If the child knows the answer to the target question, the ask/tell problem reemerges, and the child provides the answer.

Continuing with the Jabba the Hutt theme, the experimenter might elicit a yes/no question, for example, by saying, "Ask him if they have hamburgers on his planet."

This lead-in would evoke the question "Do you have hamburgers on your planet?" In this case, the global setup of the experiment also satisfies the felicity conditions for an individual target item. In asking whether or not there are hamburgers on Jabba the Hutt's planet, the child is genuinely requesting new information.

It is not always simple to set up individual target questions to request new information, however. Let us suppose that among the target structures for the experiment are *wh*-questions with third person singular subjects. Now, it is no longer possible to have the child ask Jabba the Hutt a question about himself or his planet because these questions would all require a second person pronoun, taking the form "Do you ..." or "What do you ...". To elicit questions with a third person subject (i.e., "What does he ..."), the experimenter needs to ask the child to ask Jabba the Hutt about someone else. This character might be part of a scenario staged with toy props—say, one in which Fido eats a cookie but not a bone. Following this scenario, the experimenter might say, "Ask Jabba the Hutt what Fido ate." Now, the difficulty is that the question does not request new information. The child already knows that Fido ate a cookie and not a bone because this event was acted out with toys. The danger is that the child will revert to answering, not asking the appropriate question.

There are two ways to rescue the experiment. One is to do a little more work at the global level. Having asked Jabba the Hutt some questions about himself, the experimenter can suggest finding out if Jabba understands about events that take place on Earth. For example, the experimenter and the child could find out whether or not Jabba (as a creature from another planet) can pay attention and understand things about Earth, by quizzing him about the events that took place. In this way, it at least makes sense to ask Jabba a question about an event or character that doesn't relate directly to him. This step doesn't solve the problem of the child's knowing the answer to the target question, however. This problem can be solved by modifying the story. Perhaps Fido is given a bone and a cookie, and he takes them behind a wall to hide them. The child can't see behind the wall, but Jabba the Hutt can. Fido eats the cookie and buries the bone for later. In this situation, it would make perfect sense for the child to ask Jabba the Hutt, "What did Fido eat?"

For a child with an extreme ask/tell problem, it might be necessary to set up every target question so that the answer is a mystery to the child. For most children, this last step isn't necessary. As long as the experiment starts off with questions the child doesn't know the answer to, the child gets into the question game. At this point, it is usually possible to switch to stories like the first Fido scene above, without a problem.

Chapter 20

Structure-Dependence

As Chomsky (1965) notes, structure-dependence is a general constraint on the linguistic principles that children hypothesize in grammar formation. The structure-dependence constraint requires all possible syntactic operations to be stated using structural notions. A structure-dependent hypothesis contrasts with a structure-independent hypothesis that would apply to an ordered string of words, without reference to hierarchical structure. Such a structure-independent hypothesis would refer to linear relations such as "first" and "leftmost."

Given that the structure-dependence constraint is fundamental to the theory of Universal Grammar, it is also taken to be fundamental to the Modularity Matching Model. The Modularity Matching Model anticipates that children will conform to structure-dependent operations at every stage of language development. This expectation is evaluated in an experiment reported in this chapter, conducted by Crain and Nakayama (1987). The experiment investigated children's adherence to the structure-dependence constraint by examining the kinds of hypotheses children entertain about subject-auxiliary inversion in yes/no questions. As we will show, in more current linguistic frameworks, the application of structure-independent hypotheses to form yes/no questions turns out to violate a constraint, known as the head movement constraint. The particular formulation of the constraint on the formation of yes/no questions is not what is important, however. Particular formulations of the constraint will no doubt continue to change as linguistic theory progresses. The more basic question concerns the kinds of hypotheses children entertain in forming yes/no questions and other linguistic constructions. We begin the chapter by briefly presenting the relevant theoretical background. We then turn to the experiment by Crain and Nakayama, testing children's knowledge of the structure-dependence constraint.

20.1 Theoretical Background

To see how a yes/no question is formed, consider the declarative in (1). Here, the subject NP is *the man who is beating a donkey*. In forming a yes/no question, the auxiliary verb is moved past the subject NP, giving (2). Notice that it is not possible to move the auxiliary verb that is inside the relative clause (see (3)).

(1)   The man who is beating a donkey is mean.

(2)   Is the man who is beating a donkey mean?

(3)   *Is the man who beating a donkey is mean?

The ungrammatical yes/no question in (3) is compatible with a structure-independent hypothesis, however. Suppose the child hypothesized that yes/no questions are formed by moving the "first" auxiliary verb to sentence-initial position. If language is considered simply as a phonetic stream of words, this movement is apparently local; word 4 moves to sentence-initial position, as shown in (4). When hierarchical structure is taken into account, however, this movement turns out to be nonlocal. It is movement of word 8 in the phonetic stream that proves to be local movement.

(4)   The man who *is* beating a donkey *is* mean.

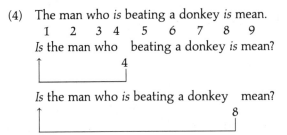

To make this clear, we must introduce some machinery from current linguistic theory.[1] According to linguists working within the generative framework, yes/no questions are formed by movement of the auxiliary verb (the head of IP) to Comp (the head of CP). Because the auxiliary verb moves across the subject (in SpecIP) to Comp, it looks as if the subject and the auxiliary verb switch positions; hence the name subject-auxiliary inversion. The movement is more accurately described as movement of Infl to Comp, however; the head of the Inflectional Phrase (IP), Infl, moves to the next higher head position in the phrase structure, Comp, the head of the Complementizer Phrase (CP). This movement process is depicted in (5).

(5)

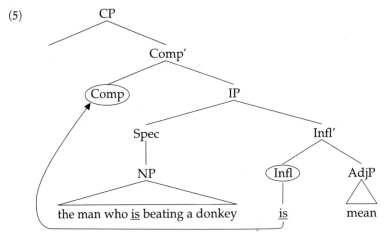

Movement of Infl to Comp is subject to the *head movement constraint*. According to this constraint, a head can only move locally, to the next higher head. If the auxiliary verb in the relative clause is moved, as in (3), it will have to move past the heads of other phrasal projections: the Comp position in the relative clause, and the head noun of the relative clause (*man*). This nonlocal movement violates the head movement constraint (Travis 1984) and results in a violation of the *Empty Category Principle* (Chomsky 1986). The movement that results in ungrammaticality is shown in (6). The intervening heads of phrases are circled in the diagram.

(6)

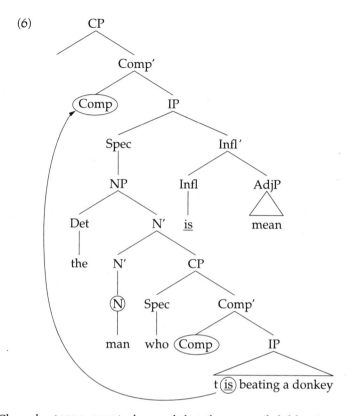

Chomsky (1971, 1975) observed that the issue of children's yes/no questions is interesting, because the structure-dependent hypothesis for yes/no question formation appears to be more complex from a pretheoretical standpoint than the alternative, structure-independent hypothesis. Moreover, as Chomsky also observed, both hypotheses are compatible with much of the input that children receive, namely, one-clause sentences. For example, in questions like (7a–b) both the structure-dependent hypothesis of Infl-to-Comp movement and the structure-independent hypothesis "Move the first auxiliary verb" yield the right results.

(7) a. Will Bill play the saxophone?
      b. Is the sky blue?

If children's initial hypotheses are limited to structure-dependent ones, then they are expected to use Infl-to-Comp movement as their initial hypothesis about the formation of yes/no questions. This precludes any kind of movement that would violate the head movement constraint (or "shortest move" or whatever takes the place of the head movement constraint in later formulations of the theory). In particular, it precludes hypotheses based on the linear position of an auxiliary verb in a sentence. This is what it means to say that children are restricted to hypotheses that are structure-dependent. Regardless of the precise formulation of the structure-dependence constraint, the central issue in investigations of Universal Grammar is whether or not children formulate a constraint that can be characterized only in structure-dependent terms.

The consequences of proposing that children entertain structure-*independent* hypotheses would not be trivial. For one thing, a learnability problem would arise.

Suppose, on the basis of simple yes/no questions compatible with both structure-dependent and structure-independent hypotheses, that children chose the structure-independent hypothesis. Eventually, on the basis of hearing complex examples containing relative clauses like *Is the man who is beating a donkey mean?* in the input, they figure out the structure-dependent rule of Infl-to-Comp movement and add it to their grammar. The problem is that adding the structure-dependent rule to the grammar does not entail purging the incorrect structure-independent one. Thus, we might expect ungrammatical yes/no questions to coexist alongside grammatical ones.

Unlike simple yes/no questions like (7a–b), which are compatible with a structure-dependent hypothesis and a structure-independent hypothesis, examples like (1), which contain a relative clause, can distinguish the two hypotheses. Children who adhere to the structure-dependence constraint (and the head movement constraint) will produce questions like (2). On the other hand, children who can entertain a structure-independent hypothesis might readily produce questions like (3). Structures like (1) containing a relative clause, then, are relevant for testing children's adherence to the structure-dependence constraint.

We are now in a position to lay out the experimental procedure for testing whether or not children adopt a structure-independent or a structure-dependent hypothesis in their initial formulation of yes/no questions. The null hypothesis is that children adopt structure-independent hypotheses. The experimental hypothesis is that children adopt only structure-dependent hypotheses. The specific grammatical and behavioral consequences of the null (H_0) and experimental (H_1) hypotheses can be summarized as follows:

- H_0: Children can entertain structure-independent hypotheses. They move the first Infl in the linear string to Comp, even if it appears inside a relative clause.
  Expected results: Children initially ask nonadult yes/no questions with sentences containing relative clauses.
- H_1: Children can only consider structure-dependent hypotheses. They always move the Infl from the main clause to Comp, regardless of its position in the string.
  Expected results: Children initially ask adultlike yes/no questions, even with sentences containing relative clauses.

According to the null hypothesis, children are not restricted to hypotheses that are structure-dependent. On this view, children might produce some sentences that are grammatical and happen to adhere to a structure-dependent hypothesis, and also some ungrammatical sentences that are not compatible with such a hypothesis. In other words, on the null hypothesis, we might expect a random pattern of errors.

20.2 *Experimental Design*

The first step in testing children's mastery of Infl-to-Comp movement in yes/no questions containing a relative clause is to identify the situations that evoke similar questions from adults. In these situations, we can observe whether children produce question forms that are compatible with the structure-dependence constraint, or whether they produce question forms that violate the constraint (as shown by **sentence*). The design can be summarized as follows:

(8)   Input   ⟨situation, lead-in⟩
       Output   ⟨sentence₁⟩
  or Output   ⟨*sentence₂⟩
             (structure-dependent violation)

There is the possibility, of course, that children could come up with question forms that are ungrammatical but do not violate the structure-dependence constraint. So, we might add

     or Output   ⟨*sentence₃⟩

Because the questions produced by children are produced in the same situations as adults' questions, we can infer that they have the same meaning. This will be true even if children's questions have a different form from those of adults. This brings us to the experiment by Crain and Nakayama on structure-dependence.

Thirty children between the age of 3;2 and 5;11 (mean 4;7) were tested in the experiment. Yes/no questions containing relative clauses were elicited from the children during the course of a game in which they posed questions to Jabba the Hutt, a creature from *Star Wars*. Jabba the Hutt was played by one of the experimenters. The second experimenter orchestrated the game. The experiment followed the usual procedure of testing children individually in a research room at the children's school.

The experimenter in charge of orchestrating the game and manipulating the experimental situations explained to the child that Jabba the Hutt was from another planet—that humans don't know about life on his planet, and he doesn't know about life on Earth. (This preliminary conversation was instrumental to avoiding the ask/tell problem discussed in chapter 19.) The game began by finding out about life on Jabba's planet. This part of the game served as a "warm-up" and to capture the child's interest in the game. Later, the focus of the game switched. Jabba the Hutt was shown some pictures, and the child's task was to find out whether he understood the events depicted there by asking him relevant questions, as directed by the experimenter. This second part of the game evoked the pretest questions and the target yes/no questions that contained relative clauses.

In order to elicit yes/no questions, the experimenter showed the child a picture, and they discussed it together. This discussion introduced the characteristics of the picture that were relevant and the lexical items that would be needed for the target question.[2] If the picture in figure 20.1 had been used, for example, the experimenter would have pointed out that it shows one man who is beating his donkey and another man who isn't beating his donkeys.[3] The lead-in for eliciting the relevant yes/no question embedded the relevant statement in a carrier, "Ask Jabba if …". A sample lead-in is given in (9). In this situation, the child has the opportunity to obey, or violate, the structure-dependence constraint.

(9)   *Protocol for eliciting yes/no questions*
    Experimenter   Ask Jabba if the man who is beating a donkey is mean.
    Child   Is the man who is beating a donkey mean? *or* *Is the man who beating a donkey is mean?

After the child formed the question, Jabba was shown the picture and responded "Yes" or "No." (Since Jabba came from another planet, he would not necessarily know whether beating a donkey was a mean thing to do.) If Jabba responded correctly, the child fed him a frog, his favorite food.

Figure 20.1
Context for eliciting yes/no questions

Notice that the lead-in provides children with all of the lexical items necessary for producing the yes/no question, without providing them with the actual target structure. All the child needs to do is transform the declarative into a yes/no question. This is important because it means that nonlinguistic demands do not interfere with the focus of the experiment: children's hypotheses about Infl-to-Comp movement.

Another feature of the task worth mentioning is that the pictures depict circumstances that are pragmatically appropriate for restrictive relative clauses. As discussed in previous chapters, this is why the drawing depicts a set of men: one who is beating a donkey, and one who is not. Furthermore, the pictures all represented action of some kind. This was to encourage children to retain the relative clause as part of their yes/no question. If the pictures could have been described by an adjective, for example, children might have been tempted to avoid a relative clause and simplify the structure of their question.

The experimental materials included three pretest sentences, which were designed to elicit simple yes/no questions, and six target sentences.

(10) *Pretest sentences*
  a.   The girl is tall.
  b.   The man is tired.
  c.   The pig next to the tree is red.
  Test sentences
  d.   The dog that is sleeping is on the blue bench.
  e.   The boy who is watching Mickey Mouse is happy.
  f.   The boy who is unhappy is watching Mickey Mouse.
  g.   The boy who was holding the plate is crying.

Table 20.1
Correct and incorrect responses by group

	Responses	Grammatical	Ungrammatical
Group 1	81	31 (38%)	50 (62%)
Group 2	87	70 (80%)	17 (20%)
Total	168	101 (60%)	67 (40%)

    h.   The boy who is being kissed by his mother is happy.
    i.   The ball that the girl is sitting on is big.

20.3 Results

The children were split into two groups for purposes of data analysis. Group 1 included the younger children, ranging in age from 3;2 to 4;7 (mean 4;3). Group 2 included the older children, ranging in age from 4;7 to 5;11 (mean 5;3). Both groups of children performed well on the pretest sentences, correctly forming grammatical yes/ no questions. The results from the test sentences were surprising, however. Among children's productions were a sizable number of ungrammatical questions. In fact, 62% of the younger children's questions were ungrammatical. The older children produced fewer errors; still, 20% of their productions were not the expected "adult" yes/no questions. Table 20.1 summarizes the results. Clearly, a thorough analysis of children's errors was necessary before any conclusions about the experimental and null hypotheses could be drawn. Unless most of the nonadult responses could be shown to be consistent with the Modularity Matching Model, the high incidence of nonadult responses in the experiment could be troublesome for the model.

    Crain and Nakayama begin their discussion of children's errors by pointing out that if children did not have innate knowledge of the structure-dependence constraint, and their ungrammatical productions represented misgeneralizations of a structure-independent hypothesis, they might be expected to make random errors *across the test items*. This did not happen, however. Certain test sentences resulted in more nonadult questions than others. For example, for group 1, items (10e), (10g), and (10h) were most problematic, evoking at most 20% grammatical sentences. On the other hand, more than half of children's responses to the other items were grammatical.

    This brings us to the crucial question. Did any of the nonadult question forms produced by the children violate the structure-dependence constraint? That is, were there any questions in which the auxiliary verb from the main clause was left in its base position, and the one from the relative clause moved to Comp, as in (11)? Or were children's nonadult questions ungrammatical for other reasons?

    (11)   *Is* the man who beating the donkey *is* mean?

There were no questions like (11). However, close examination of the errors produced by the children raised new questions. In the nonadult question type produced most frequently by the children, an auxiliary verb appeared in Comp, but there was no gap, either in the relative clause or in the main clause. An example of this kind of error is given in (12). These errors are labeled *double-Infl* errors in table 20.2.

    (12)   *Is* the man who *is* beating a donkey *is* mean?

Table 20.2
Types of errors by group

	Total	Double-Infl	Restart	Structure-independent
Group 1	50 (62%)	30 (60%)	10 (20%)	0
Group 2	17 (20%)	9 (53%)	5 (29%)	0
Total	67 (40%)	39 (58%)	15 (22%)	0

These questions did not make it possible to tease apart a structure-dependent hypothesis from a structure-independent one because it was not possible to tell which, if any, of the auxiliary verbs had "moved" or, at least, which auxiliary verb was "related" to the one in Comp. In the 1970s, errors of this sort were termed *copying-without-deletion* errors (Mayer, Erreich, and Valian 1978). Then, the idea was that the child had inserted a copy of the auxiliary verb in the Comp position, but had forgotten to delete the original one. A variant of this analysis would be to say that the auxiliary verb in (12) has been moved to Comp, and the trace of movement is "spelled out." As Crain and Nakayama point out, there is yet another analysis of questions like (12). They could be formed by simply prefixing the auxiliary *is* to the declarative. This would be much like forming questions by affixing *ka* in Japanese or prefixing *est-ce que* in French. It is not clear whether children producing questions of this sort would be applying a question formation "strategy" based on a structure-dependent hypothesis.

There was one more error type, termed *restart* errors by Crain and Nakayama. In these questions, children began with a well-formed fragment of a question and followed it with a second question containing a proform. These questions have the flavor of performance errors. The child gets underway with the question, appears to forget what she was saying, and recovers. An example is given in (13).

(13)   Is the boy that is watching Mickey Mouse, *is he* happy?

Errors made by the children are summarized in table 20.2.

As noted, the double-Infl errors could not help to distinguish a structure-dependent hypothesis from a structure-independent one since it was not possible to examine the "origins" of the auxiliary verb in Comp. Since as many as 62% of the errors made by the younger group of children were of this kind, Crain and Nakayama were not able to argue that the structure-dependence constraint was in place. They could only make a weaker argument for innate knowledge of the constraint: that children do not make errors like (3) that blatantly violate the structure-dependence constraint.

Naturally, Crain and Nakayama had not anticipated errors like (12) that would fail to disentangle structure-dependent from structure-independent hypotheses. To investigate the structure of double-Infl questions like (12), they conducted a second experiment. Ten of the children who had produced questions like (12) in the first experiment participated in the follow-up experiment. Again an elicited production task was used to further probe for the source of children's nonadult productions.

The sentences used in this experiment introduced a different auxiliary verb in the relative clause and the main clause of the lead-in sentences, as exemplified in (14).

(14)   a.   The boy who *is* happy *can* see Mickey Mouse.
       b.   The boy who *can* see Mickey Mouse *is* happy.

Statements like (14a–b) containing two different auxiliary verbs could be used to test the structure-dependence constraint, while investigating the structure of children's questions. Let us take (14a) as an example. In response to the lead-in, children could potentially produce questions with the structures illustrated in (15a–d). Only the first yes/no question, (15a), is correct, however.

(15)   *Protocol for eliciting yes/no questions with two "auxiliary" verbs*
       Experimenter: Ask Jabba if the boy who is happy can see Mickey Mouse.
       a. *Child*   Can the boy who *is* happy see Mickey Mouse?
       b. *Child*   *Is the boy who happy *can* see Mickey Mouse?
       c. *Child*   *Can the boy who *is* happy *can* see Mickey Mouse?
       d. *Child*   *Is the boy who *is* happy *can* see Mickey Mouse?

The question in (15a) is the grammatical question form that does not violate the structure-dependence constraint. The question in (15b) reflects a structure-independent hypothesis because the auxiliary verb from the relative clause has incorrectly been moved to Comp. The questions in (15c) and (15d) reveal the derivation of the double-Infl question structure. In (15c), the auxiliary verb that is doubled is the modal *can* from the main clause. Although the question is ungrammatical, the question form supports a structure-dependent hypothesis. The child clearly knows that the auxiliary verb in the main clause raises to Comp. Further, (15c) would suggest that the child is not forming questions by prefixing *is* in sentence-initial position. On the other hand, questions like (15d) do not tease apart the prefix analysis of the double-Infl questions from a structure-independent analysis. That is, questions like (15d) could have been formed by prefixing *is* to the declarative sentence, or they could have been formed by moving (or copying) the auxiliary verb in the relative clause to Comp and spelling out the trace (or failing to delete the copied auxiliary).

The second, follow-up experiment began with elicitation of two simple yes/no questions with the modal *can*. There were four target sentences: two like (14a), with the modal in the main clause, and two like (14b), with the modal in the relative clause. Two targets contained *can*, and two were designed to elicit *should*.

Children apparently had more difficulty producing questions in the second experiment than in the first. Crain and Nakayama suggest this may be because pictures are not ideally suited to eliciting questions with modal verbs. In order to make sure that the child would produce a modal verb, the description of the pictures was more abstract. Intuitively, it is harder to depict or convey the idea that someone is able or obliged to perform some action than to depict or convey the idea that someone *is* performing some action. These problems could be alleviated to some extent if the scenarios were acted out with toys and props.

Children produced a greater number of errors in the second experiment than they had in the first. For the 10 children who participated, the error rate increased from 65% nonadult questions to 79%. Altogether, the 10 children produced 34 yes/no questions containing relative clauses. Of these, 7 were grammatical, 9 could not be analyzed because they were question fragments, and 7 were "restart" errors. None of the remaining 11 responses were questions, like (15a), that clearly violated the structure-dependence constraint; in other words, there were 11 double-auxiliary questions that were open to interpretation. The results are summarized in table 20.3. Of the questions with *is* as the first auxiliary verb, 6 were like (15d); that is, they could not

Table 20.3
Analysis of double-Infl errors by sentence type

Sentence type	Rel.-clause Infl moved/copied	Prefix	Main-clause Infl moved/copied
is/modal	————————6————————		3
modal/*is*	0	————————2————————	

distinguish between the prefix analysis and a structure-independent error (e.g., *Is the boy who is happy can see Mickey Mouse?*). In another 3 questions, the main-clause auxiliary verb had clearly been moved/copied, in accord with the structure-dependence constraint. Of the questions with the modal in the relative clause, 2 could be analyzed either as being structure-dependent or as exhibiting the prefix analysis (e.g., *Is the boy who can see Mickey Mouse is happy?*) but none unambiguously supported a structure-independent hypothesis (e.g., *Can the boy who can see Mickey Mouse is happy?*).

To summarize the results: The children did not produce any questions that clearly exhibited a structure-independent operation; that is, no child produced questions like *Is the boy who happy can see Mickey Mouse?* or *Can the boy who can see Mickey Mouse is happy?* Although analysis of a few of the questions was not obvious, children's nonadult utterances were best analyzed either as prefix errors or as instances of moving/copying and spelling out the trace/failing to delete. Overall, the experiment invites the inference that children abide by the structure-dependence constraint.

In a further experiment, Nakayama (1987) showed that the double-Infl errors appeared in questions that placed more demands on children's processing systems. The auxiliary verb was doubled more in questions in which the relative clause was long and contained a transitive verb than in ones with short relative clauses and intransitive verbs. Likewise, more errors appeared in relative clauses with an object gap than in those with a subject gap. All of these factors suggest a performance explanation of the nonadult questions. As we discussed in chapter 4, the puzzle is that the double-Infl errors are errors of insertion, not deletion, which is characteristic of performance errors. Our suggestion is that children respond to increases in processing load by reverting to an earlier grammar (see Lebeaux 1988). Thus, although the children tested in this experiment produced yes/no questions with doubling of the auxiliary only when processing demands were strenuous, we assume that at an earlier stage, the doubling would have been consistent with their grammars. As it happens, the auxiliary-doubling error has been found to be consistent in another syntactic environment: questions containing negation (Thornton 1993; Guasti, Thornton, and Wexler 1995). This suggests that we are correct in thinking that this is an error that is compatible with Universal Grammar.

20.4 Conclusion

The experiments described in this chapter have shown how the elicited production technique can be used to test a constraint that rules out certain sentence forms. In this case, the technique was used to see if children produce yes/no questions that violate the structure-dependence constraint or the head movement constraint. An experimental hypothesis was set up and tested in the first experiment. However, some children produced an unanticipated form of nonadult question that made it impossible to disentangle the experimental and null hypotheses. The nonadult questions of these children were further examined in a follow-up experiment also using the elicited production technique. This experiment probed the source of the double-Infl error in order to provide evidence either for or against the experimental hypothesis.

The conclusion was that children's questions provide no evidence that can be uncontroversially explained as violating the structure-dependence constraint. A few questions could be analyzed as violating the structure-dependence constraint, but they could equally well be explained as prefix errors.

Finally, we have assumed that because children do not produce questions that violate the structure-dependence constraint, the constraint is in place in their grammars. At this point, we should raise the issue of principles versus preferences. Do children fail to produce questions with the auxiliary verb from the relative clause in Comp simply because they prefer to move the auxiliary verb from the main clause? Or does their failure to move the auxiliary verb from the relative clause indicate that their innate knowledge of the constraint prevents the illicit movement? It is not possible to prove that the ungrammatical questions fail to appear because they are prohibited by the structure-dependence constraint. On the other hand, it seems very unlikely that children are merely exhibiting a preference for moving the auxiliary verb from the main clause. Given the high number of ungrammatical questions that children produced in this experiment, we might expect the structure-independent error to have appeared. And it did not. In describing an experiment on *wanna* contraction in the next chapter, we will show how an experimental control condition can eliminate this kind of preferences-versus-principles problem.

Chapter 21

Wanna Contraction

In this chapter, we investigate the constraint that blocks contraction of the verbal elements *want* and *to* in certain *wh*-questions, first discussed in chapter 2. Children's knowledge of this constraint is examined by eliciting questions from the "*wanna* contraction" paradigm. There are two important reasons for presenting this experiment. First, it provides a very clear comparison of the Input Matching Model and the Modularity Matching Model. The two models make different predictions about the outcome of the experiment. Second, it demonstrates that an elicited production experiment can clearly adjudicate between principles and preferences. It includes an experimental control that provides a convincing test of children's knowledge of a principle of Universal Grammar; we are able to disentangle children's knowledge of a principle from their preference for a particular response.

21.1 Forming Wh-Questions

The phenomena investigated in this chapter concern the formation of *wh*-questions. For the sake of this discussion, we assume that *wh*-questions are formed by movement of a *wh*-phrase from its position at an underlying level of representation to its surface position. A further assumption is that an empty category, which we abbreviate as *t* (for "trace") is left behind as a record of *wh*-movement. The constraint of Universal Grammar that is the focus of our discussion prohibits contraction of two elements if a trace of *wh*-movement intervenes between them.[1] In English, the constraint on contraction across a *wh*-trace (i.e., a trace of *wh*-movement) plays out as a restriction on the environments in which sequences like *want to, supposed to, have to* can be contracted to *wanna, sposta, hafta*. In French, the constraint affects the environments in which liaison is possible (see Selkirk 1972). Here, we will focus on the English version of the phenomenon.[2]

First, let us examine the facts that the constraint attempts to explain. Compare *wh*-questions in which the *wh*-phrase is extracted from object position of an embedded infinitival clause with those in which the *wh*-phrase is extracted from subject position. In object extraction questions like (1), *wanna* contraction is permitted, but in subject extraction questions like (2), it is not.

(1) *Object extraction*
    a. Who do you want to kiss *t*?
    b. Who do you wanna kiss *t*?

(2) *Subject extraction*
    a. Who do you want *t* to kiss Bill?
    b. *Who do you wanna kiss Bill?

(3) *Declaratives*
     a.   I want to kiss Bill.
     b.   I wanna kiss Bill.

The theory of Universal Grammar explains the facts as follows. In (1), the *wh*-phrase *who* is moved from object position, and a trace (*t*) is left behind in this position. When the trace is in object position, it does not interfere with contraction of *want to* to *wanna*. This is not the case with (2), however. The *wh*-phrase is moved from subject position of the lower clause (cf. *You want who to kiss Bill?*), leaving a *wh*-trace between *want* and *to*. This is the environment in which the constraint rules out contraction. In declaratives like (3), there are no traces of *wh*-movement. The constraint is therefore irrelevant and contraction is not inhibited.

Consider, first, the predictions of the Input Matching Model for acquisition. On this model, children rely heavily on the input to formulate grammatical hypotheses. Questions like (1a) and (1b) provide ample evidence that contraction is possible when the lexical items *want* and *to* are adjacent in the string of words. In fact, children hear contraction frequently and should therefore develop a preference for contraction. This preference for contraction should extend to subject extraction questions, since on this model, no constraint inhibits contraction in this syntactic environment. According to this model, children monitor the input and reach the conclusion that contraction is not possible in subject extraction questions. Therefore, contraction in subject extraction questions should taper off gradually.

Until children reach the conclusion that the extraction site is relevant, however, they would be expected to contract as often in subject extraction questions as they do in object extraction questions. Note that there could be parsing pressures to encourage contraction in object extraction questions, however. The literature on aphasics and poor readers has established that object extraction questions are more difficult than subject extraction questions. If this is the case, there might be more pressure to contract in object extraction questions than in subject extraction questions. Either way, on the Input Matching Model, children are expected to produce numerous illicit contractions, like (2b), which might persist for some time, until they realize that a cell in the paradigm is missing from the language that they hear, and formulate the correct grammatical hypothesis.

Universal Grammar takes a quite different approach. Proponents of Universal Grammar assume that the constraint is innately specified precisely because mastery of it would require negative evidence; adult *wh*-questions like (1a), (1b), and (2a) inform the child which questions are permitted by the grammar, but do not inform the child that contraction is impossible when the *wh*-phrase is moved from subject position (i.e., in (2b)). Since negative evidence is thought not to be available, the solution is simple: the knowledge is innate. On the Modularity Matching Model, then, if the constraint is part of Universal Grammar, children should be steadfast in their adherence to it. Children should not mistakenly contract when they produce subject extraction questions, regardless of any conflicting parsing preference. As soon as they can be tested, all children should be found to avoid contracting *want* and *to* in their subject extraction questions.

To test children's knowledge of the constraint, we examine the hypotheses that children entertain about contraction by examining their production of questions from the *wanna* contraction paradigm. Our hypotheses will be as follows:

- H_0: Children will allow contraction in subject extraction questions (as often as in object extraction questions).
- H_1: Children will not produce subject extraction questions with contraction.

21.2 Design

The experiment discussed in this section includes an essential control that enables us to disentangle children's knowledge of the constraint from their preferences for a particular sentence form. We are able to do this by taking advantage of an interplay between the syntactic constraint and a parsing preference to produce reduced forms.

Before we proceed to the experimental design, it is instructive to review the design of the structure-dependence experiment, to see why that design is not appropriate for studying children's knowledge of the constraint on contraction across *wh*-trace. The design used in the structure-dependence experiment is represented in (4).

(4)   Input   ⟨situation, lead-in⟩
       Output   ⟨sentence₁⟩
   or Output   ⟨*sentence₂⟩

In reporting that experiment, we noted that children produced many questions that were ungrammatical but that, crucially, none of their questions clearly violated the structure-dependence constraint. From this, we concluded that children obey the constraint. Suppose we apply the same logic to the constraint on contraction. Using the design in (4), we would present children with the appropriate situation for a target subject extraction question, and we would observe whether they produced both uncontracted and contracted variants in their questions or whether they instead consistently produced the grammatical questions *without* contraction. This implementation of the design is illustrated in (5).

(5)   Input   ⟨situation, lead-in⟩
       Output   ⟨sentence₁ ... want to ...⟩
  or both Output   ⟨sentence₁ ... want to ...⟩
       Output   ⟨*sentence₂ ... wanna ...⟩

Approaching *wanna* contraction in the same way as structure-dependence would lead us to conclude from children's avoidance of the ungrammatical sentence with *wanna* that they are demonstrating knowledge of the constraint blocking contraction. There is an important difference between the two experiments, however. In the structure-dependence experiment, questions that violate the structure-dependence constraint (i.e., the head movement constraint) are always ungrammatical. In the present experiment, the form of contraction (*wanna*) that is ruled out by the constraint in subject extraction questions is permitted in different syntactic environments—for example, in object extraction questions. When extraction takes place from object position, both *wanna* and *want to* are permitted.

This raises the following dilemma. Children can choose either to contract or not to contract in object extraction questions. Suppose they consistently choose not to contract, for whatever reason; call it factor F. Factor F would presumably also apply to children's subject extraction questions. If so, then children would not contract in subject extraction questions even if this were possible in their grammars. Therefore, simply demonstrating that children do not contract in subject extraction questions would not be convincing evidence that they do so because they are obeying a constraint. They might simply prefer to avoid contraction. It must be demonstrated that there is no factor, F, pressuring children to avoid contraction whenever possible. In this experiment, then, the issue of preferences versus principles is critical.

How do we show that children's failure to contract in questions like (2b) reflects knowledge of the constraint? One possibility is to examine adults. Appealing to the Modularity Matching Model, we can say that if adults exhibit a preference to use reduced forms whenever possible, then children should exhibit this same preference. The tendency to use reduced forms flies in the face of factor F, which is the bias to use the unreduced form of *want* and *to*. Of course, this begs the question. Because we are trying to argue for the Modularity Matching Model, we cannot presuppose it.

To make a more compelling case for children's innate knowledge of the constraint, then, we would need to disprove the proposal that there is some factor, F, that compels children to avoid contraction. This is done by including object extraction questions as controls in the experiment. Since both contracted and uncontracted forms of (1) are grammatical, each individual child's preference for contraction should be assessed. If it can be shown that children prefer to contract in object extraction questions like (1b), but go out of their way to avoid contraction in subject extraction questions, we would have strong evidence that they are obeying the constraint. The design incorporating both subject and object extraction questions is shown in (6) and (7).

(6)   *Object extraction*
         Input   ⟨situation, lead-in⟩
         Output   ⟨sentence$_1$ ... want to ...⟩
and Output   ⟨sentence$_2$ ... wanna ...⟩

(7)   *Subject extraction*
         Input   ⟨situation, lead-in⟩
         Output   ⟨sentence$_3$ ... want to ...⟩
??? Output   ⟨*sentence$_4$ ... wanna ...⟩

The goal, then, is to demonstrate children's preference to contract in object extraction questions, where contraction is optional. Fortunately for this experiment, we already know that adults exhibit a parsing preference to use reduced forms (see Lasnik 1990), which leads them to favor contraction in object extraction questions like (1). Following the Modularity Matching Model, we would expect children to show the same preferences as adults, so they too should manifest a tendency to use reduced forms whenever possible. Children should therefore favor *wanna* over *want to* in their object extraction questions.

Given these observations, the first part of the experimental design is to set up situations that elicit object extraction questions from children. This will establish whether or not children exhibit the same preference as adults to use reduced forms, in this case to produce *wanna* rather than *want to*. Once children's preference to contract is established, we move to the second part of the experimental design, eliciting subject extraction questions from children. This will enable us to determine if children override their preference for contraction in their subject extraction questions.

We have discussed the importance of avoiding type I errors (improperly rejecting the null hypothesis) in conducting experiments. The null hypothesis in the present experiment is that children lack the constraint on contraction across a *wh*-trace. The experimental hypothesis is that children know the constraint and therefore will not contract in subject extract ion questions. To avoid type I errors, we should seek measures that encourage children to contract whenever they can. This ensures that the experimental hypothesis is not favored by the way the experiment is designed. One way to help avoid type I errors is to begin the experiment with the object extraction questions, where contraction is preferred, and to switch later to the subject extraction questions. More importantly, the experimenter's speech should avoid providing any clues about when contraction is and is not allowed. On the other hand, the experimental hypothesis would be favored, leading to potential type I errors, if some aspect of the experiment tempted children to avoid contraction—for example, if the puppet spoke in a staccato manner. Children might be tempted to mimic this style of speaking, leading to uncontracted forms.

21.3 *The Experiment*

The experiment tested 26 children between the ages of 2;10 and 5;5. The data from 14 of these children were used for assessing children's adherence to the constraint. These 14 children ranged in age from 3;6 to 5;5 (mean age 4;5).

The questions from the *wanna* contraction paradigm were elicited within the context of a game. The game revolved around a puppet, a rat named Ratty, who was shy of grown-ups. The role of Ratty was played by one experimenter; the other experimenter was the "grown-up." The grown-up experimenter explained that Ratty had come to live at her house, and it was a worry because she didn't know anything about him —what his favorite foods and drinks were, for example. She solicited the child's help in finding out about Ratty, and later, when he was feeling less shy, the child invited him to play a game. The session began with simple warm-up questions to find out if the rat was a boy or a girl, how old he was, where he lived, and so on. Once the child was immersed in the game, the experimenter proceeded to elicit the structures at issue in the experiment.

The object extraction questions that formed the controls assessed each individual child's tendency to contract. These questions were elicited as in the protocol in (8). In order to set up the situation for "What do you wanna eat?", the experimenter noted that Ratty had missed out on snack and was probably hungry. Various items of plastic food were laid out in the workspace and the game proceeded.

(8)   *Protocol for eliciting object extraction questions.*
       Experimenter   The rat looks kind of hungry. I bet he wants to eat something. Ask him what.
       Child   What do you wanna eat?
       Ratty   Is that pepperoni pizza over there? I'll have some of that.

Similar questions investigated what Ratty wanted to drink, what game he wanted to play, and so on. For this experiment, in general, the targets were not elicited following separate "stories" acted out by the experimenter. Rather, they were elicited as part of an ongoing discourse with the rat puppet. So, for example, after Ratty had asked for pizza to eat (as shown in the protocol), the experimenter noted that pizza often makes people thirsty, and then the protocol was repeated, substituting *drink* for *eat*.

Notice that the protocol does not include use of the *want to* sequence that is being tested. The experimenter uses *wants to* (i.e., third person), but this is not a sequence that can be contracted to *wanna*, so it provides the child with no clues about the possibility of contraction. One potential difficulty that arises in response to the experimenter's lead-in, however, is that the child simply says, "What do you want?", instead of asking a full question. This question is not useful for evaluating whether or not children contract the sequence *want to*. If this happens, the experimenter playing the role of Ratty can ask for a repetition by saying, "What?" or "Excuse me?" In most cases, this request for clarification elicits a full question.

Subject extraction questions were also elicited as part of the ongoing conversation with Ratty. For example, after Ratty had had a lot to drink and eat, the experimenter might say he should probably brush his teeth because he wouldn't want to get cavities. The experimenter put a toothbrush in the workspace, and the protocol proceeded as follows:

(9)   *Protocol for eliciting subject extraction questions*
       Experimenter   I bet the rat wants someone to brush his teeth for him. Ask him who.
       Child   Who do you want to brush your teeth?
       Ratty   You!

For the critical subject extraction questions, a more complex protocol was prepared to encourage the child to ask a full question. This was in addition to the simple protocols like the one in (9). The more complex protocol involved the child and the rat puppet in a "choosing" game. In this game, it was explained that Ratty "got to choose" what would happen. Three toys were placed in the workspace, and Ratty's task was to match each one up with one of three actions described by the experimenter. The idea was that if several potential events could take place, the child would realize that a full question was needed to distinguish among them and that the question fragment "Who do you want?" would not be felicitous.

(10)   *Complex protocol for eliciting subject extraction questions*
       Experimenter   In this game, there's a baby, a dog, and Cookie Monster, OK? And some different things are going to happen, and the rat gets to choose who gets to do those different things. Now, one of these guys gets to take a walk, one of these guys gets to take a nap, and one of these guys gets to eat a cookie. Let's do the cookie first. So, one of these guys gets to eat a cookie, right? Ask the rat who he wants.
       Child   Who do you want to eat a cookie?
       Ratty   Cookie Monster!

21.4 Analysis of the Data

In this experiment, assessment of children's adherence to the constraint rests on the experimenter's subjective recording of children's transcripts. This leaves the experiment open to the criticism that it is not scientific because the experimenter is not impartial to the outcome. A potential criticism of this sort was avoided by soliciting judgments from four linguistics graduate students and comparing them with those of the experimenters. Some of the relevant questions from five children were digitized using a *waveform-editing program* and were presented to the independent judges. To ensure that the judges could not deduce whether or not contraction was grammatical, the *wh*-phrase in initial position and the VP following the string ... *do you wanna/*

want to were omitted. The judges were thus presented with an artificial circumstance that was quite difficult to judge in isolation. For each of the five children, each judge heard four instances of what the experimenter had perceived as *wanna*, and four that the experimenter had perceived as *want to*. The crucial instances of *want to* were analyzed for agreement with the experimenter's judgments. Of the total of 80 judgments made by the four judges, 91% (73/80) agreed with the experimenter's judgments, with 6 of the 7 judgments that did not agree coming from the productions of one child. Given this high level of agreement with the experimenter's judgments, the results were considered to be valid.

It may be helpful to preface our discussion of the findings by reviewing the expectations of the null and experimental hypotheses. On the null hypothesis, children are assumed not to have any innate knowledge of the constraint, so we would expect them to contract equally often in subject and object extraction questions. How often children do contract in both question types would presumably depend on the parsing tendency to reduce forms. On the experimental hypothesis, children are expected to contract in object extraction questions, at whatever level the parsing preference dictates. By contrast, children's subject extraction questions are expected never to show contraction. The experiment is only convincing, however, if children exhibit a preference for contraction in object extraction questions.

Both the null and experimental hypotheses depend on children producing both subject and object extraction questions, so only children who produced questions of both types could be included in the analysis. In addition, only children who produced two or more questions of each type were included, since these children all produced contracted object extraction questions. These criteria selected the 14 children whose data are shown in table 21.1. These children's failure to contract in questions extracting from subject position could not be taken as a preference to avoid contraction.

Table 21.1
Data of 14 children included in analysis

Subj/Age	Object			Subject		
	Want to	Wanna	Other	Want to	Wanna	Other
KM 5;5	–	4	–	4	2	1
PM 5;1	–	3	–	3	–	–
SA 4;10	–	4	–	4	1	
TI 4;9	1	5	–	3	–	–
ST 4;8	–	5	–	4	–	–
IS 4;7	–	6	–	5	–	–
AM 4;6	–	2	–	4	–	–
BD 4;6	–	8	–	9	–	–
KE 4;4	–	2	–	5	–	–
GA 4;0	–	3	–	5	–	–
KL 3;10	–	4	–	3	3	–
SR 3;10	6	6	–	7	–	–
CA 3;7	1	5	–	7	–	–
JE 3;6	–	3	–	5	–	–
Total	8	60	0	68	6	1

Table 21.2
Data of 12 children excluded from analysis

Subj/Age	Object			Subject		
	Want to	*Wanna*	Other	*Want to*	*Wanna*	Other
MI 5;5	–	1	1	2	–	–
CA 5;4	1	1	–	2	–	–
SO 5;3	–	1	–	2	–	–
JI 5;1	1	1	–	2	–	–
KP 5;0	–	–	2	4	–	–
TT 3;9	2	–	–	2	–	–
KR 3;9	–	–	1	–	–	2
MO 3;9	–	–	4	–	–	4
RE 3;9	5	–	–	1	–	–
MC 3;7	–	3	–	–	–	8
MA 3;3	1	1	–	–	–	1
PI 2;10	–	1	–	–	–	–
Total	10	9	8	15	0	15

Overall, the 14 children whose data are shown in table 21.1 exhibited a strong preference for contraction in the control object extraction questions. Of the 68 questions elicited from this group of children, 60 (88%) showed contraction. The preference for contraction was clear in the productions of 13 of the 14 children. Just one child (SR) did not show a strong preference for contraction. She failed to contract in 6 of her 12 object extraction questions and was thus responsible for 6 of the total of 8 questions with no contraction. The 14 children produced a total of 74 subject extraction questions. Of these, 68 (92%) had no contraction. The 6 apparent violations of the constraint were produced by 3 children; 2 by KM, 1 by SA, and 3 by KL. The ungrammatical instances of *wanna* produced by KM and SA could perhaps have been misheard by the experimenter, but it is more difficult to analyze KL's productions this way, since as many as half of her subject extraction questions appear to have used the illegitimate form. Of course, no instance of contraction is easily accounted for by the theory of Universal Grammar. But it is also true that no child's responses were in accord with the null hypothesis. No child contracted in subject extraction questions as often as in object extraction questions. Even subject KL contracted in all of her object extraction questions, though she contracted in only half of her subject extraction questions.

The data from the children who did not meet the criteria for inclusion in the data analysis are presented in table 21.2. A glance at these data shows that they do not include any questions that violate the constraint on contraction across *wh*-trace. That is, there are no subject extraction questions in which children used the illicit *wanna* contraction. Most of these children were eliminated because they did not produce enough questions. Others produced enough questions but did not show a preference to contract (e.g., subjects TT and RE). Still others produced questions that were not relevant to testing the constraint. These "other" questions were irrelevant because the child used an alternative means of expression such as "What would you like to eat?" instead of "What do you wanna eat?"

21.5 Conclusion

The data from one child aside, the findings from the experiment on *wanna* contraction support the claim that the prohibition against contraction across *wh*-trace is an innate, universal constraint. Children did not make many errors initially, as the Input Matching Model would predict. On the contrary, there were almost no errors. The children whose data were not analyzed for adherence to the constraint did not produce questions that violated the principle, a result that is compatible with the Modularity Matching Model. In summary, we have provided support for an account of the contraction facts that is compatible with Universal Grammar.

Chapter 22

Long-Distance Questions and the Medial-*Wh*

This chapter shows how elicited production can be used to investigate the source of a nonadult form. The nonadult form appeared in an experiment designed to elicit long-distance *wh*-questions from children. In the course of the experiment, some children consistently produced questions with an extra *wh*-phrase in the intermediate CP; hence the term *medial-wh questions*.[1] Examples of children's medial-*wh* questions are given in (1).[2]

(1) a. Who do you think who Grover wants to hug? (TI 4;9)
    b. Who do you think who's in there, really really really? (AM 4;6)
    c. What do you think what Cookie Monster eats? (KM 5;5)
    d. What do you think what the baby drinks? (MA 3;3)

Our analysis of the error is that it is consistent with the principles of Universal Grammar. This means that it reflects a universal option that is appropriate for other languages, but that happens not to be correct for English. Using the criteria laid out by the Modularity Matching Model, we elicit a variety of structures to demonstrate that the nonadult form is the question form consistent with these children's grammars. It does not reflect a performance error.

The medial-*wh* questions appeared in an experiment designed to elicit questions from the "*that*-trace" paradigm (see Chomsky 1981). In the Principles-and-Parameters framework of Universal Grammar, this paradigm is frequently cited as showing that the constraint known as the *Empty Category Principle* (ECP) is at work.[3] The long-distance questions that make up the *that*-trace paradigm are given in (2) and (3). In this paradigm, the ECP constrains the appearance of the complementizer *that*.

(2) *Object extraction*
    a. What do you think flies eat *t*?
    b. What do you think that flies eat *t*?

(3) *Subject extraction*
    a. What do you think *t* eats flies?
    b. *What do you think that *t* eats flies?

(4) *Declaratives*
    a. I think flies eat garbage.
    b. I think that flies eat garbage.

The questions in (2), extracting from object position of a tensed embedded clause, are grammatical with or without the complementizer. In questions in which the *wh*-phrase is moved from subject position, however, the question is grammatical only when the complementizer is omitted. When the complementizer is present, as in the ungrammatical question in (3b), *that* is followed by a *wh*-trace—hence the name "*that*-trace" paradigm. The declaratives in (4) are given for comparison. The ECP is irrelevant in the declarative sentences because they contain no empty categories (such as *wh*-traces). Hence, the sentences are grammatical with or without the complementizer. The syntactic literature offers several different accounts of why the complementizer in (3b) makes the sentence ungrammatical (see, e.g., Lasnik and Uriagereka 1988; Rizzi 1990). For the present, it will suffice to note that the ungrammaticality of (3b) is due to a putative constraint of Universal Grammar.

22.1 Children's Knowledge of the Empty Category Principle

As researchers working within the framework of Universal Grammar, then, we offer as our experimental hypothesis that children have innate knowledge of the ECP. On this view, we should not expect children to make errors and produce the ungrammatical question form in (3b). The null hypothesis is that the facts of the paradigm have to be learned from the input, in which case we should expect children to make a number of errors before they realize that complementizers are grammatical in object extraction questions but not in subject extraction questions. The hypotheses can be summarized as follows:

- H_0: Children will allow complementizers in subject extraction questions as often as in object extraction questions.
- H_1: Children will not produce subject extraction questions with complementizers.

Ideally, the same logic and design that were used in the *wanna* contraction experiment reported in chapter 21 could be used for testing children's knowledge of the constraint on *that*-trace. If we follow the same logic, the argument would be that it is not sufficient to test the ECP by examining only children's production of subject extraction questions. If only subject extraction questions were elicited, we might be able to demonstrate that children never produce subject extraction questions with complementizers like (3b), but data of this kind would not answer the objection that children have a preference for omitting complementizers in their speech in general. To demonstrate children's knowledge of the constraint, one would want to show that children prefer to use complementizers when the grammar allows them, but override the preference when the grammar excludes them. This logic necessitates including object extraction questions in the design. As the *that*-trace paradigm shows, object extraction questions like (2) are grammatical with or without a complementizer. Here, we would hope to see a preference for use of the complementizer. In the ideal situation, then, questions extracting from object position could be used to assess each child's preference for using complementizers. If this control condition showed that children frequently use complementizers in their object extraction questions, but fail to use them in their subject extraction questions, we would have empirical evidence strongly supporting children's knowledge of the ECP.

In the abstract, the logic of the experiment is sound, but unfortunately it runs up against a property of the parsing system that worked in our favor in the *wanna* contraction experiment: the tendency to reduce forms. In that experiment, the tendency to reduce forms was instrumental in inducing contraction in the control object extraction questions. In keeping with the Modularity Matching Model, the tendency was operative for children as well as adults. In the present experiment, we would like to see both children and adults display a preference for using complementizers in object extraction questions. The problem is that in the adult grammar, the tendency to reduce forms encourages omission, not insertion, of complementizers. The Modularity Matching Model predicts that children should exhibit the same tendency. Pilot work indicated that this is in fact the case, with the result that this particular experimental design could not be used to provide a convincing demonstration of children's innate knowledge of the ECP—it is not possible to show that children are overriding a parsing preference in order to abide by the constraint.[4] If children use no complementizers in any of their questions, the fact that complementizers are absent from subject extraction questions is not remarkable. A preference to drop complementizers would explain the data as well as innate knowledge of the ECP.

This is not to say that the elicitation experiment cannot provide data that are relevant to probing children's knowledge of the ECP. For one thing, the medial-*wh* emerged in the course of pilot research eliciting questions from the *that*-trace paradigm, so it may well be related in some way to children's knowledge of the ECP. Part of the goal of this chapter is to show that even though it was not realistic to use the design discussed above, by comparing a range of structures elicited from children, we can find out in what circumstances the nonadult questions appear, and why. This investigation may well reveal whether or not children adhere to the ECP, and in what form it is present in their grammars.

22.2 Design

Since we have determined that the more complex experimental design used for testing the *wanna* contraction paradigm cannot succeed for testing children's knowledge of the ECP, we will assume that the goal of the experiment is simply to elicit subject and object extraction long-distance questions from children to investigate their use of complementizers and medial *wh*-phrases, should they appear. The basic design is illustrated in (5) and (6).

(5) *Object extraction*
   Input   ⟨situation, lead-in⟩
   Output   ⟨sentence$_1$ ... $\emptyset$ ...⟩
 or Output   ⟨sentence$_2$ ... that ...⟩
 ??? Output   ⟨sentence$_3$ ... wh ...⟩

(6) *Subject extraction*
   Input   ⟨sentence, lead-in⟩
   Output   ⟨sentence$_4$ ... $\emptyset$ ...⟩
 or Output   ⟨*sentence$_5$ ... that ...⟩
 ??? Output   ⟨sentence$_6$ ... wh ...⟩

This simple design explores whether children use complementizers and medial-*wh* forms equally in subject and object extraction questions. As part of our investigation of the medial-*wh*, we should compare children's long-distance questions from the *that*-trace paradigm with their questions from the *wanna* contraction paradigm. This will reveal whether or not the medial-*wh* appears in questions with infinitival embedded clauses, as well as in tensed embedded clauses.[5] If children produce medial-*wh* questions with infinitival clauses, then they should be expected to produce questions like *What do you want what to eat?* and *Who do you want who to brush your teeth?* This section of the investigation is summarized in (7) and (8).

(7)   *Object extraction*
　　　　Input   ⟨situation, lead-in⟩
　　　　Output   ⟨sentence₁ ... want to ...⟩
　　or Output   ⟨sentence₂ ... wanna ...⟩
　　??? Output   ⟨sentence₃ ... want ... wh ... to ...⟩

(8)   *Subject extraction*
　　　　Input   ⟨situation, lead-in⟩
　　　　Output   ⟨sentence₄ ... want to ...⟩
　　or Output   ⟨*sentence₅ ... wanna ...⟩
　　or Output   ⟨sentence₆ ... want ... wh ... to ...⟩

22.3 The Experiment

The protocols designed to elicit long-distance questions use the same game described for the *wanna* contraction experiment. That is, questions were elicited from children by having them find out information from the rat puppet, Ratty, who is too shy to communicate with grown-ups.

Long-distance questions from the *that*-trace paradigm were elicited by having the child invite Ratty to participate in a "guessing game." The experiment was designed as a guessing game so that Ratty could be asked his opinion in questions of the form "What do you think ...?" For the part of the game eliciting questions extracting from subject position, the child had Ratty cover his eyes. The experimenter and the child then hid a series of items (say, a toy bear, a marble, and the toy character Grover) in various places (in a box, under a blanket, and in a yogurt carton). Ratty was then allowed to uncover his eyes, and the guessing game proceeded. Here, one experimental context suffices to elicit three long-distance questions.

(9)   *Protocol for eliciting subject extraction questions*
　　　　Experimenter   ⟨in low voice to child, so that Ratty can't hear⟩ We know where all the things are hidden, right? We know that there's a marble in the box, a bear under the blanket and we know that Grover is under the yogurt carton. Let's see if Ratty can guess where we hid them. Let's do the box first, OK? We know that there's *a marble* in the box, but ask the rat what *he* thinks.
　　　　Child   What do you think is in the box?
　　　　Ratty   Can you rattle the box for me? Hmm, I think there's a marble in the box.
　　　　Child   You're right!
　　　　Experimenter   Hey, he made a good guess. Now let's do the blanket ...
　　　　⟨game continues in the same way⟩

Notice that the experimenter does not use long-distance questions. *Embedded* questions are incorporated in the protocol, and the final lead-in to the child is also an embedded question followed by an elided long-distance question. Since the crucial long-distance question is not given as overt input to the child, it cannot be said to give the child clues to the targeted structure.

The protocol for object extraction questions follows similar lines. Again, Ratty is asked to cover his eyes while the experimenter and the child set up the items for him to guess about. The experimenter might set out three characters in the workspace (say, Cookie Monster, a baby doll, and a Ninja Turtle) and then suggest to the child that Ratty guess what Cookie Monster eats, what babies drink, and what Ninja Turtles like to eat. The protocol is shown in (10).

(10)   *Protocol for eliciting object extraction questions*
    Experimenter   ⟨in a low voice to child, so that Ratty can't hear⟩ We know about all these guys, right? We know that Cookie Monster eats ...
    Child   Cookies.
    Experimenter   And babies drink ...
    Child   Milk.
    Experimenter   And Ninja Turtles like ...
    Child   Pizza.
    Experimenter   Right! Now let's find out if Ratty knows. Let's do Cookie Monster first. We know that Cookie Monster eats ⟨whispered⟩ cookies, but ask the rat what *he* thinks.
    Child   What do you think Cookie Monster eats?
    Ratty   Well, Cookie Monster is a monster, so I think he eats monsters.
    Child   No! Cookies!
    Experimenter   He's silly, isn't he? Cookie Monster eats cookies, just like you said. Let's do another one ... ⟨game continues in the same way⟩

Recall that an experiment eliciting questions must satisfy the felicity conditions that go along with a question game in order to avoid the ask/tell problem. It is often desirable to have every question request new information. That is, children should not know the answer to the question they are posing to the puppet. This is not the case in the protocols in (9) and (10). The child and the experimenter conspire, sharing knowledge of the answers; but this is a situation that is quite natural when asking someone to guess something. Even though the child knows the answer to the question, these protocols have not been found to present a problem as long as the game starts off in the right way. (In the warm-up, as described earlier, children begin by asking Ratty his name, how old he is, and so on, questions to which they don't know the answer.) If a problem were to arise with a particular child, however, it would be simple to modify the game. To elicit subject extraction questions, for example, the experimenter could hide the objects and have both the child and Ratty cover their eyes. The experimenter could then have them both guess, in turn, what was hidden in each place. The protocol could be adjusted to proceed something like this:

(11)   *Adjusted protocol for eliciting subject extraction questions*
    Experimenter   I'm going to hide some things, and then you and the rat guess. Hide your eyes! ⟨experimenter hides objects⟩ OK, you can come out now. There's something in this box, something under this blanket, and something in the yogurt carton. Let's do the box first. You guess first, and then the rat can have a turn. OK. What's your guess?
    Child   I think there's a Smurf in there.

> *Experimenter*   OK, you had your turn. You think that there's a Smurf in the box, but ask the rat what he thinks.
> *Child*   What do *you* think is in the box?
> *Ratty*   A hamburger?
> *Experimenter*   I'll show you what's really in the box. It's Grover!

In addition, "Is it true ..." questions were incorporated in the game. These questions were elicited in order to provide another angle on children's use of complementizers. In this and other factive structures, unlike in declaratives and *wh*-questions, adults generally have a preference for inserting a complementizer.[6] This seemed a likely structure to use, then, to determine whether children behave like adults in this regard. It also provided a check on their lexical choice of complementizer in another structure. To elicit this structure, children questioned Ratty about various rumors that the experimenter had heard. A protocol is given in (12).

(12)   *Protocol for eliciting "Is it true" questions*
> *Experimenter*   I've heard that rats can see in the dark. Could you find out if it's true?
> *Child*   Is it true that rats can see in the dark?

22.4 Results

The experimental findings were that a few children asked medial-*wh* questions of the form in (13c–d). The majority of the children asked questions that did not deviate from the adult forms in (13a–b).

(13)   a.   What do you think (that) Cookie Monster eats? (adult)
      b.   Who do you think (*that) is in the box? (adult)
      c.   What do you think what Cookie Monster eats? (child)
      d.   Who do you think who is in the box? (child)

Some of the children who produced medial-*wh* questions also produced occasional "partial movement" questions such as (14). In these questions, the true *wh*-phrase is found in the intermediate CP, and a dummy *wh*-phrase (which marks the scope of the intended question) appears in the matrix SpecCP. This structure will not be discussed at any length here (for details, see McDaniel 1986; McDaniel, Chiu, and Maxfield 1995; Thornton 1990).

(14)   What do you think which boy ate the cookie?

The results from the experiment eliciting long-distance questions with tensed embedded clauses are shown in table 22.1.[7] There were 2 children who consistently used a medial-*wh* (TI and MA), 2 children who consistently used complementizers (MO and TT), and other children who sporadically used these forms. As table 22.1 indicates, there were children who used complementizers in subject extraction questions who appeared to be violating the ECP. For the moment, we can put explanation of this problematic result aside and investigate the medial-*wh*. This investigation will eventually come full circle and shed some light on whether or not children's use of complementizers in subject extraction questions violates the ECP.

The "Is it true ...?" structure was designed to check children's use of complementizers. The finding was that children were much like adults. The protocol evoked the target questions from 15 of the 21 children, and 14 of the 15 produced complemen-

Table 22.1
Long distance questions extracting from tensed clauses by individual subject ($N = 21$)

Subj/Age	Object wh-questions				Subject wh-questions			
	Partial	That	Medial-wh	Adult	Partial	That	Medial-wh	Adult
KM 5;5		1	1			2	1	3
MI 5;5				4			1	3
CA 5;4		1		5				5
SO 5;3		1		7				6
JI 5;1				8				4
PM 5;1		2		6		1		10
KP 5;0				4		1		9
TI 4;9			3	2	1	1	9	
AM 4;6		3		6		2	2	6
KE 4;4				6		1		6
GA 4;0				5				4
KL 3;10		1		6				7
TT 3;9		4		1		4		
KR 3;9				5		1	2	6
MO 3;9		2	1	1		3		
RE 3;9				2				6
MC 3;7			1					1
CA 3;7	–				–			
JE 3;6	–					1	3	
MA 3;3		3		2			4	
PI 2;10	–				2		3	

tizers in this structure. Not all of the children knew that "Is it true ...?" is followed by a *that* complementizer, however. Five children used *if*; one used *so*; and another used what sounded like *it* (but this could have been a reduced form of *that*). Significantly, none of the children used a medial-*wh* in this question structure.

The children who participated in this experiment also participated in the *wanna* contraction experiment, enabling comparison across syntactic structures. The children who produced medial-*wh* questions when extracting from tensed embedded clauses never used a medial-*wh* in their questions from the *wanna* contraction paradigm, in which extraction takes place from an infinitival clause.

In the paragraphs that follow, we argue that the medial-*wh* is a form of question compatible with these children's current grammar. We do this by first showing that the medial-*wh* can be given an analysis that is consistent with crosslinguistic data. That is, these children's grammars look very similar in this respect to grammars of other languages, a finding that is in keeping with the Modularity Matching Model. In the following section, we show that the medial-*wh* does not have the characteristics attributed to performance errors in chapter 15.

22.5 Analysis of the Medial-Wh

In this section, we analyze children's nonadult medial-*wh* questions as errors compatible with Universal Grammar. Let us begin by drawing a parallel with a fact from the *that*-trace paradigm. Recall the critical contrast with respect to the ECP: *wh*-questions extracting from subject position of a tensed embedded clause are grammatical without a complementizer, but ungrammatical with one.

(15) a.   What do you think *t* eats flies?
     b.   *What do you think that *t* eats flies?

The difference between (15a) and (15b) is that Comp is filled in (15b). This prevents the *wh*-trace in subject position from being properly governed, and a violation of the ECP ensues.[8] Notice that in children's medial-*wh* questions, the same observation applies.

(16) a.   What do you think what's in that box? (MA 3;11)
     b.   Who did they say who had ants in their pants? (TI 4;9)

There are further parallels between the medial-*wh* and children's use of complementizers. We have noted that children never produce a medial-*wh* in their questions extracting from infinitival clauses. *That* complementizers do not appear in this syntactic context either.

A comparison of subject and object extraction questions was also instructive. Further follow-up testing showed that some children initially produced the medial-*wh* in both subject and object extraction questions. Later, it was found to drop out of object extraction questions but persist in subject extraction questions. This pattern was found to be the same for children who used obligatory complementizers, suggesting that the medial-*wh* and obligatory complementizers are intrinsically related.

Crosslinguistic data reveal languages showing each of the patterns found in English-speaking children's longitudinal data. Irish is similar to the first stage observed in English-speaking children's nonadult questions. According to Chung and McCloskey (1987), Irish signals that *wh*-movement has taken place by the appearance of a special complementizer in the intermediate Comp. In *wh*-questions, the complementizer changes from the declarative form, *go*, to the form *al*, which reflects agreement between the head and its specifier (i.e., spec-head agreement). Both subject and object extraction long-distance questions exhibit this change. An example of a *wh*-question extracting from object position is given in (17), from McCloskey 1979.

(17)   Cén   t-úrscéal [CP aL   mheas   mé [CP aL   dúirt sé [CP aL
       which novel   Comp thought I   Comp said he   Comp
       thuig   sé]]]?
       understood he
       'Which novel did I think he said he understood?'

In other languages, such as French, spec-head agreement causes a change in the form of the complementizer, but only when extraction takes place from subject position; this parallels the later stage in English-speaking children's grammatical development. In French, spec-head agreement causes the complementizer to change from *que* to *qui*. This alternation takes place in subject relative clauses and subject extraction questions. An example of a subject relative demonstrating the obligatoriness of a *qui* complementizer is given in (18), from Rizzi 1990.

(18)   L'homme que je crois   *que/qui viendra ...
       the man who I believe   who   will come
       'The man who I believe will come ...'

The complementizer *que* and its alternating form *qui* both also function as *wh*-words in French. This fact is important, because we will claim that the medial-*wh* is also a complementizer, even though it is more akin to a *wh*-phrase in appearance.

Rizzi (1990) argues that the change in complementizer form observed in languages such as French signals satisfaction of the ECP by a proper head governor. In long-distance questions, for example, the *wh*-phrase moves through the intermediate SpecCP, leaving a *wh*-trace. This *wh*-trace passes agreement features to the Comp, licensing it as a proper governor for the trace in subject position of the embedded clause. In languages such as Irish and French, the change in complementizer form that reflects spec-head agreement is overt. In other languages, such as English, it is argued that the process is covert. In English, for example, the same spec-head agreement process licenses the complementizer as a proper head governor for the subject trace, but the complementizer is null (that is, silent). The representation in (19) illustrates that the null complementizer can bear agreement features as a result of spec-head agreement and is thus a proper head governor for the subject trace of the embedded clause.

(19) Who$_i$ do you think [$_{CP}$ t$_i$ [$_C$ $\emptyset_{Agr_i}$ [$_{IP}$ t$_i$ will come to the party]]]?

Rizzi's theoretical framework provides a ready explanation for the structures used by English-speaking children. Children who produce medial-*wh* questions can be said to be using a form of the complementizer that signals that spec-head agreement has taken place. In the grammars of these children, the change in the form of the complementizer must be manifested overtly, as in French. Children who insert complementizers, instead of dropping them like adults, can also be said to be fulfilling spec-head agreement. The difference is that for these children the form of the complementizer signaling spec-head agreement is *that*, whereas other children take it to be a *wh*-complementizer.

Left to explain is why some children might initially express overt spec-head agreement for both subject and object extraction questions and later, just for subject extraction questions. Linguistic theory provides the answer. Adult English, like French, only requires spec-head agreement to take place in subject extraction questions, because this is the only syntactic environment where it is needed to avoid an ECP violation. In object extraction questions, for example, the *wh*-trace is properly head-governed by the verb in the embedded clause, and overt expression of spec-head agreement in the intermediate Comp might be considered "overkill." After some time during which they express spec-head agreement overtly in object extraction questions as well as subject extraction questions, children ascertain that it is only necessary for the latter.[9]

Another question is why children do not use a medial-*wh* or *that* complementizer in long-distance questions extracting from the *wanna* contraction paradigm. After all, in subject extraction questions like *Who do you want to come to the party?*, there is a trace in subject position of the embedded clause that must satisfy the ECP. According to Rizzi (1990), the subject trace is properly head-governed by the exceptional-Case-marking verb *want* in the matrix clause. Proper head government (and assignment of Case) cannot take place over a CP, suggesting that the verb *want* projects an IP and there is no complementizer position.[10]

(20) Who$_i$ do you want [$_{IP}$ t$_i$ to come to the party]?

If so, it is not surprising that children do not produce medial-*wh* or *that* complementizers in their questions from the *wanna* contraction paradigm. The medial-*wh* or *that* complementizer is not required as a proper head governor for the subject trace. Moreover, there is no Comp position in the structure.

From the fact that it is movement through the intermediate CP that triggers spec-head agreement and subsequent use of a medial-*wh* or *that* complementizer, it follows that children did not produce any instances of medial-*wh* in their "Is it true ...?" questions. Although this is a question structure, it does not involve extraction of a *wh*-phrase through the intermediate CP.

Of all the structures we have examined, the medial-*wh* or nonadult *that* complementizers appear only in long-distance questions in which a *wh*-phrase moves from a tensed embedded clause. In this syntactic environment, we have suggested that the medial-*wh* or complementizer is present to express spec-head agreement and the fact that the ECP is satisfied. In conclusion, the nonadult *that* complementizers in children's subject extraction questions do not violate the ECP, contrary to appearances.

Although we were not able to carry out a definitive experiment that by itself demonstrated children's knowledge of the ECP, we have assembled an array of facts that lead to the same conclusion. This was only possible because we were able to use elicited production to gather data crucial to the investigation.

22.6 Principles versus Preferences

The facts fit very neatly with a grammatical explanation of children's nonadult use of complementizers and of the medial-*wh*. But how can we be sure that the source of this difficulty is not language processing? It is worth reviewing the arguments in detail.

Earlier, we noted that children and adults alike have a parsing preference to reduce forms. This results in a preference to contract *want to* to *wanna* and a preference to omit complementizers in many syntactic environments.[11] Why, then, would a few children override this parsing preference and insert complementizers, if not to satisfy the grammar? If the medial-*wh* and inserted complementizers are indicative of a grammatical process, they should be obligatory, not optional. Let us take this point up first.[12]

As table 22.1 shows, the experiment revealed 2 children with a grammar that produces medial-*wh* questions and 2 children who always used complementizers. That is, these children always expressed spec-head agreement by filling the Comp, or SpecCP.[13] Let us begin by examining the data from TI, a child who produced medial-*wh* questions. All of her subject extraction questions had a filled intermediate CP (11/11 = 100%). In her object extraction questions, the intermediate CP was filled 3/5 times (= 60%). The fact that a medial-*wh* did not appear in all of her object extraction questions is not a puzzle, given the theory outlined above. Like TI, the other child, MA, used a medial-*wh* in all of his subject extraction questions (4/4 = 100%) but not in all of his object extraction questions (3/5 = 60%).

Two other children, KK and SR (who were tested later), also initially filled the intermediate CP very consistently in their questions; in later sessions, however, the frequency of occurrence dropped off. Could this be an indication that the nonadult questions are performance errors? We can illustrate the change in frequency with KK's data. In the first session, 6/7 (= 86%) of her questions had a filled CP; in the second session, 16/24 (= 66%); and in the third session, only 5/12 (= 42%).[14] The change between the second and third sessions was particularly dramatic, since the two sessions were only 10 days apart. It seems unlikely that the decrease in her tendency to use an overt element in Comp could be attributed to performance factors, such as memory limitations. It is highly unlikely that memory could mature significantly in such a short time. On the other hand, rapid change can be explained by a developing grammar (see Hamburger 1981). It may be that in the course of producing a variety of long-distance questions, these children became aware of the adult question forms, which caused them to reformulate the rule for spec-head agreement. So the drop in the medial-*wh*s or complementizers could represent a grammar in transition. In sum, these children's productions are also in keeping with a Universal Grammar–compatible explanation.

As table 22.1 shows, some children used a medial-*wh* or complementizer sporadically. Such sporadic uses do seem open to a performance explanation, particularly since they often appear as "warm-up" effects at the beginning of a session. However, we have already noted that deletions but not insertions characterize performance errors. We suggested, following Lebeaux (1988), that in times of stress (such as at the beginning of a session), children and even adults may occasionally revert to an earlier grammar. In fact, among the adult subjects who were controls for a similar experiment eliciting crossover questions was one who produced medial-*wh* questions on many trials. Two of his questions are shown in (21).

(21) a. Who did they guess who got pushed out of the bed?
      b. Who did they guess who had blue marbles?

This subject was an undergraduate male who was clearly uncomfortable at being asked to participate in an experiment designed for 3- and 4-year-old children. He admitted being somewhat confused by what was being asked of him. In this situation, it is possible that a vestige of his early child grammar appeared, causing him to produce some medial-*wh* questions. This is speculation, however, since it is not known whether the subject produced medial-*wh* questions as a child.

Another characteristic of performance errors is that they occur with a subset of items. In particular, they can appear in long sentences. The experiment eliciting long-distance questions from the *that*-trace paradigm found that length was apparently not a factor. The medial-*wh* appeared in both short and long questions, provided extraction took place from a tensed embedded clause. A clear illustration comes from MA's data.

(22) a. What do you think what's in that box? (MA, 3;3)
      b. What do you think really really really really really what's in there? (MA, 3;3)

If the medial-*wh* were a performance error, we might also expect it to appear in questions involving extraction from infinitival clauses. As noted earlier, a medial-*wh* never appeared in questions from the *wanna* contraction paradigm. The contrast is clear in (23), where TI produced a long question from the *wanna* contraction paradigm with no medial-*wh* and a short question from the *that*-trace paradigm with a medial-*wh*.

(23) a. Who do you want to help you eat the cookie? (TI, 4;9)
      b. What do you think what pigs say? (TI, 4;9)

It is also true that performance errors are more likely to occur with greater depth of embedding, presumably because this imposes greater demands on memory. This leads to the expectation that inserted complementizers or medial-*wh* elements would be more likely to occur in sentences with two embedded CP domains. However, exactly the reverse is true in the child data. In the following examples, TI and SR fill the upper CP domain, but there is no complementizer in the lower clause, because it is an infinitival clause.

(24) a. Who do you really think *who* Grover wants to hug? (TI, 4;9)
      b. What do you think *that* Ninja Turtles like to eat? (SR, 3;11)

We observed on a number of occasions that children asked fewer questions with a medial-*wh* or complementizer in their object extraction questions. This contradicts another trademark of performance errors: that they are more often associated with object extraction because there is greater distance between the *wh*-phrase and its associated gap. For example, TI filled the CP 100% of the time in subject extraction questions but only 60% of the time in object extraction questions; MA also used a medial-*wh* 100% of the time in subject extraction questions but only 60% of the time in object extraction questions; SR produced obligatory *that* complementizers 100% of the time for both subject and object extraction questions in the first two sessions, but by the fourth session the CP was filled in 73% (11/15) of her subject extraction questions but null in 100% (4/4) of her object extraction questions. This result is to be expected if our Universal Grammar–compatible proposal is on the right track. We expect children to fill the Comp in subject extraction questions as evidence that the ECP is satisfied.

Another criterion of performance errors can now be considered: that errors occur more frequently in the productions of younger children. Although questions with illegitimate complementizers and medial-*wh* questions occurred sporadically in younger children's productions, there was a subset of the older children who consistently asked these questions. For example, TI consistently used the medial-*wh* at 4;9; another child SS, used the medial-*wh* in subject position at 5;9; and JE consistently asked questions with complementizers at 5;1. It would appear, then, that age is not a good indicator of whether or not children use obligatory complementizers or medial-*wh* forms. This puts an explanation of the facts in the linguistic arena and makes a performance explanation unlikely.

It is worth pointing out that the varying age of children who use an obligatory medial-*wh* or a *that* complementizer excludes one kind of linguistic explanation of children's errors: maturation. It is highly unlikely that maturation of the grammar could account for these children's nonadult questions given that only a subset of children made the error in the first place and that their ages varied widely.

In sum, the children who consistently filled the CP give little evidence to suggest that their productions are performance errors. The same conclusion cannot be drawn for those children who produced the occasional medial-*wh* or *that*-trace violation. These ungrammatical sentences meet two criteria of performance errors: they occurred only sporadically and usually only at the beginning of a session.

Chapter 23

Why Children Make Good Subjects

The experiments reported in this chapter take advantage of the fact that many English-speaking children produce nonadult constructions. One such construction is the medial-*wh* question discussed in chapter 22. As shown there, many 3- and 4-year-olds regularly insert a *wh*-word between clauses in their long-distance questions; for example, they produce questions like (2a–b) instead of the adult (1a–b) (Thornton 1990).

(1) a. What do you think pigs eat?
    b. Who do you think eats trash?

(2) a. What do you think what pigs eat?
    b. Who do you think who eats trash?

Although structures like those in (2) are not grammatically well formed in English, they are well formed in other languages. Interestingly, even after the medial *wh*-phrase is expunged from children's object extraction questions, it persists in their subject extraction questions. This developmental sequence, too, is consistent with the theory of Universal Grammar. As suggested by Thornton (1990), the extra *wh*-phrase in children's subject extraction questions may be an overt manifestation of spec-head agreement, which is needed to ensure proper head government of the trace of the moved *wh*-phrase; such an overt "agreeing" complementizer appears in French, for example, in the familiar *que/qui* alternation (Rizzi 1990). English-speaking children's nonadult productions therefore support the Continuity Hypothesis, since both the structures themselves and the course of their development fall within the boundaries established by the theory of Universal Grammar. The Input Matching Model cannot explain this.

A second construction that will play a role in the experiments reported here is negative questions (see chapter 5). Thornton (1993) discovered that even children as old as 5 often form nonadult negative *wh*-questions and nonadult negative yes/no questions. For example, many children ask *wh*-questions like (3b) instead of the adult (3a), and many children ask yes/no questions like (4b) instead of the adult (4a) (also see Guasti, Thornton, and Wexler 1995).[1]

(3) a. What doesn't Big Bird like?
    b. What does Big Bird doesn't like?

(4) a. Doesn't Grover like the ice cream?
    b. Does Grover doesn't like the ice cream?

The (b) structures in (3) and (4) are consistent with the theory of Universal Grammar and provide compelling evidence that children are guided by it in grammar formation.

23.1 Discourse Linking: Syntactic or Pragmatic?

As pointed out earlier, children's nonadult structures are also a source of data for evaluating competing linguistic proposals. The two nonadult constructions illustrated in (1)–(4) were used to examine a theoretical controversy in the analysis of *wh*-questions. One direction that many researchers have taken emphasizes a pragmatic distinction between types of *wh*-phrases, namely, between *wh*-phrases with lexical content, such as *which boys* ("full" *wh*-phrases), and ones without lexical content, such as *who* or *what* ("bare" *wh*-phrases).

According to one viewpoint, there is no inherent (structural) distinction between bare *wh*-phrases and full *wh*-phrases. It was suggested by Pesetsky (1987) and Comorovski (1989) that the distinction is pragmatic: full *wh*-phrases are anaphorically linked to referents that have been previously established in the discourse, whereas bare *wh*-phrases are not related to such discourse entities (also see Cinque 1990; Rizzi 1990; Chung 1994; Dobrovie-Sorin 1990). Pesetsky refers to full *wh*-phrases as *discourse linked* or *D-linked*. D-linked *wh*-phrases carry the presupposition that a specific reference set has been preestablished in the discourse; bare *wh*-phrases do not.

The alternative viewpoint contends that full *wh*-phrases and bare *wh*-phrases have different structural properties. One structurally based account is presented by Thornton (1995). There are two parts to Thornton's account. First, Thornton assumes that the features of full and bare *wh*-phrases are checked in different projections. The features of full *wh*-phrases are checked in a projection above CP, which she calls *RefP*, short for *Referential Phrase* (Stowell and Beghelli 1995); the features of bare *wh*-phrases are checked within the CP at S-structure. Second, Thornton assumes that full *wh*-phrases can reach their landing site in two ways, via successive-cyclic movement or via long movement. By contrast, bare *wh*-phrases only move successive-cyclically (see Cinque 1990).

It has proven difficult to adjudicate between syntactic accounts and pragmatic accounts of the distinction between full and bare *wh*-phrases. On the one hand, there are differences in the linguistic environments in which full and bare *wh*-phrases can appear (e.g., full *wh*-phrases are more easily extracted from *wh*-islands; bare *wh*-phrases permit modification by epithets such as *the hell*).[2] On the other hand, adult judgments waver depending on the discourse context (bare *wh*-phrases behave much like full *wh*-phrases when they are embedded in contexts that establish a reference set, becoming more extractable and less tolerant of epithets). From the perspective of the structural account, the methodological desideratum is clear: with context held constant, structural differences should continue to be discernible.

Here is where child language comes into the picture. Having discovered that some children produce nonadult *wh*-questions and nonadult negative yes/no questions, Thornton (1995) investigated these children's bare and full *wh*-questions, anticipating that potential grammatical distinctions in landing sites and in movement options might be directly revealed in the structures children produce. Devising an elicited production paradigm in which questions with bare or full *wh*-phrases could be elicited in identical contexts, Thornton uncovered evidence in favor of a structural account of the distinction between bare and full *wh*-phrases.

As noted, questions with bare and full *wh*-phrases were elicited in the same experimental contexts. The only difference in the experimental setup was the lead-in sentences that followed the story. In the lead-in designed to elicit a bare *wh*-phrase, the experimenter used a bare *wh*-phrase:

Experimenter   We know that Miss Piggy kissed someone. Ask Ratty who he thinks.

In the lead-in designed to elicit a full *wh*-phrase, the experimenter used a full *wh*-phrase:

Experimenter   We know that Miss Piggy kissed one of the boys. Ask Ratty which boy he thinks.

The findings are from two groups of children: children ($N = 3$; 3;11 to 5;4) who produced long-distance medial *wh*-questions, as in (2) (group 1), and children ($N = 7$; 4;1 to 5;4) who consistently left a copy of the auxiliary verb in their matrix negative questions, as in (3b) and (4b) (group 2). Long-distance questions containing both bare and full *wh*-phrases were elicited from children in group 1. The finding was that the medial-*wh* was obligatory in both subject and object extraction questions with bare *wh*-phrases, as shown in (5a–b). In questions with full *wh*-phrases, however, it was optional for object extraction questions (see (6a–b)), but obligatory for subject extraction questions, as illustrated by the contrast in (6c) and (6d), where the symbol # indicates the absence of this construction in children's productions.

(5)   a.   Who do you think who Miss Piggy kissed?
      b.   Who do you think who kissed Miss Piggy?

(6)   a.   Which boy do you think who Miss Piggy kissed?
      b.   Which boy do you think Miss Piggy kissed?
      c.   Which boy do you think who kissed Miss Piggy?
      d.   #Which boy do you think kissed Miss Piggy?

In (5a–b) and (6a,c), Thornton argued, both the bare *wh*-phrase and the full *wh*-phrase have moved successive-cyclically, leaving a medial *wh*-phrase (agreeing complementizer) behind in the intermediate Comp. The medial-*wh* is obligatory for bare *wh*-phrases because they must move successive-cyclically (Cinque 1990). To satisfy the ECP, a medial-*wh* is also obligatory for subject extraction questions with full *wh*-phrases like (6c); the *wh*-phrase moves through SpecCP to ensure, by spec-head agreement, that there is a proper head governor in Comp for the embedded subject trace (Rizzi 1990). When extraction takes place from object position, as in (6b), there is another movement option for full *wh*-phrases: long movement, with the *wh*-phrase linked to its trace via binding. Successive-cyclic movement is not necessary in order for the trace in object position to be properly head-governed.

The object extraction questions (with negation) produced by children in group 2 usually had a doubled auxiliary verb with bare *wh*-phrases, as illustrated in (7). By contrast, other structures (in addition to doubling of the auxiliary verb) arise in the corresponding questions with full *wh*-phrases, as in (8).

(7)   What did the Spaceman didn't like?

(8)   a.   What food did the Spaceman didn't like?
      b.   What food the Spaceman didn't like?
      c.   What food that the Spaceman didn't like?

That there are more grammatical options with full *wh*-phrases in object extraction matrix questions is explained by the same theoretical assumptions used to explain the pattern of children's long-distance questions. First, full *wh*-phrases move through SpecCP *or* they proceed directly to their landing site, SpecRefP, by long movement. Bare *wh*-phrases, however, move only as far as SpecCP. Movement through SpecCP is also an option with full *wh*-phrases, as in (8a), although their final landing site is SpecRefP, not SpecCP. The difference between children and adults boils down to this: children move full *wh*-phrases to SpecRefP at S-structure; adults move them at LF. The RefP projection is detectable when the long-movement option is pursued (see (8b) and (8c)), a possibility that obtains only for full *wh*-phrases. The clearest example is (8c), where the head of CP is filled by the complementizer, *that*, which usually appears when no spec-head agreement has taken place in its projection.[3] The full *wh*-phrase has moved directly to SpecRefP, skipping SpecCP.

Group 2 children produced adultlike subject extraction questions with bare *wh*-phrases, as in (9), but exhibited additional nonadult structures with full *wh*-phrases, as in (10).

(9)   Who didn't get ants in his pants?

(10)   a.   Which clown didn't get ants in his pants?
      b.   Which clown did he didn't get ants in his pants?
      c.   Which clown it didn't get ants in his pants?

In (9), the bare *wh*-phrase has moved to SpecCP. By spec-head agreement, it provides a proper head governor for the trace of the moved *wh*-phrase, thereby satisfying the ECP. By contrast, the full *wh*-phrases in (10) terminate in SpecRefP; either they proceed there directly, or they proceed there in steps, first passing through SpecCP. In (10a) and (10b), they have moved stepwise, in order to satisfy the ECP.[4] In (10c), however, the full *wh*-phrase has moved directly from subject position to its landing site; the ECP is rendered inoperative because the child has filled the extraction site with a resumptive pronoun.

In sum, the findings from Thornton's studies of English-speaking children are interpreted as support for a structurally based distinction between full and bare *wh*-phrases. The distinctions in referentiality are borne by *wh*-phrases themselves and are not conferred on them by the surrounding context.

23.2 Conclusion

In this chapter, we have illustrated that the grammars of English-speaking children can manifest distinctions that are not manifested in the adult grammar. Children's productions, but not those of adults, make clear distinctions between bare and full *wh*-phrases. Moreover, because these productions were elicited in similar contexts, they suggest that the relevant distinction is borne by the *wh*-phrases themselves and is not bestowed on them by the context of utterance, at least for English. As a final remark, we would emphasize that children's and adults' questions have the same underlying structure. The difference between child and adult grammars is simply that children make *overt* certain syntactic processes that are *covert* in the target adult grammar. This suggests that children's nonadult productions are compatible with Universal Grammar, as expected on the Modularity Matching Model.

Chapter 24

Summary of Designs

An elicited production experiment is designed to evoke particular sentence structures from children (or adults). A particular structure is elicited by devising situations or contexts that are uniquely felicitous for the production of that structure. The context that is presented to the child is associated with a specific meaning; the experiment investigates the form of the utterance that corresponds to that meaning in the child's grammar.

(1) Input   ⟨$meaning_1$⟩
     Output   ⟨$sentence_?$⟩

One use for this simple design would be to test whether a particular syntactic structure is part of a child's current grammar. For example, it would be appropriate if we were investigating whether 3-year-old children can produce well-formed relative clauses in felicitous circumstances. To do this, we would first need to find a context that is felicitous for production of relative clauses in the adult grammar. The task would then investigate whether children produce relative clauses in the same context.

Other elicitation experiments might contrast the sentence types children produce, either in different situations or with the situation held constant. For example, suppose that the experimental hypothesis was that the referentiality of the *wh*-phrase has an effect on the form of the question in children's grammars. This hypothesis was tested in the study reported in Thornton 1995, described in chapter 23. That study contrasted *wh*-questions with referential *wh*-phrases (like *which boy* or *whose hat*) with nonreferential *wh*-phrases (like *who* or *what*). Since the experimental hypothesis is that it is the kind of *wh*-phrase that has an effect on the form of the question, the questions were elicited in the same situation, expressed as ⟨$meaning_2$⟩.

(2) Input   referential *wh*-phrase, ⟨$meaning_2$⟩ ⟨$sentence_?$⟩
             nonreferential *wh*-phrase, ⟨$meaning_2$⟩ ⟨$sentence_?$⟩

The elicited production technique is also used to test constraints on form. In this case, we want to know what sentences are *not* produced by the grammar. Let us suppose the constraint we want to test is represented as in (3) (the pairing of sentence and meaning can be represented in either order). That is, in the adult grammar, $meaning_3$ cannot be paired with $sentence_5$.

(3) ⟨$meaning_3$, *$sentence_5$⟩

To examine children's knowledge of the constraint, we could present children with a situation associated with $meaning_3$ and record what utterances they produce. If children's grammars had the constraint, they would produce the same grammatical sentences as adults. If their grammars lacked the constraint, we would expect them to produce at least some instances of the sentence form it rules out.

(4)   Input $\langle$meaning$_3\rangle$
        Output $\langle$*sentence$_5\rangle$
    or Output $\langle$sentence$_6\rangle$

This is the design used to test children's knowledge of the structure-dependence constraint (or the head movement constraint).

   To test some constraints on form, we need to take the experimental design in (4) a step further. This is because the design does not reveal whether a particular production is *excluded* from the child's grammar. It might reveal that children *do not* produce the ungrammatical sentence$_5$ in a situation associated with meaning$_3$; but it does not show that the child *cannot* produce sentences like sentence$_5$. Once again, we face the problem of principles versus preferences. Which design we use depends on the particular constraint we are testing.

   To test the constraint on *wanna* contraction, the above design is not sufficient. This is because the sentence form ruled out by the constraint in one situation is grammatical in another situation. More specifically, contraction of *want to* to *wanna* is grammatical in object extraction questions, but not in subject extraction questions. To test the constraint, the experimental hypothesis will be that children will not contract *want to* to *wanna* in subject extraction questions. Suppose we test this with the design in (4). We provide children with the appropriate situation for a target subject extraction question and observe whether they use *wanna* contraction or find some other means of expression. The problem arises with object extraction questions, where contraction is optional. Showing that children do not contract in subject extraction questions is not convincing evidence that it is the constraint that ruled out the contraction. It could have been that children simply prefer to use the no-contraction option. This complication necessitates a different experimental design, which elicits both subject and object extraction questions.

   To show that children do not produce ungrammatical cases of *wanna* contraction in subject extraction questions because the contraction is excluded by the constraint, we would first want to establish that these children use *wanna* contraction in the object extraction questions, the syntactic environment where it is possible. These questions serve as a control. That is, as a first step, we would want to establish that sentences like sentence$_5$ exist in children's grammars. For example, it could be shown that meaning$_1$ (object extraction) is associated with sentence$_5$ (*wanna* contraction). The next step would be to show that when the children are subsequently presented with meaning$_3$ (subject extraction), they never produce sentence$_5$ (*wanna* contraction). The design of this experiment is depicted in (5).

(5)   Step 1 $\langle$meaning$_1\rangle$ → $\langle$sentence$_5\rangle$
      Step 2 $\langle$meaning$_3\rangle$ → $\langle$sentence$_{5?}\rangle$

   Recent advances in linguistic theory have led to an increase in the amount of linguistic knowledge that is hypothesized to be innately specified. A linguistic property is considered likely to be innate if it appears universally and if it is mastered in the absence of evidence in the linguistic input. It is also reasonable, though not logically necessary, to expect innate properties to emerge early in linguistic development. These considerations make it important to understand why language acquisition appears to take so long. Much of the evidence for gradual acquisition comes from longitudinal studies of children's spontaneous productions. Transcripts of children's speech seem to suggest that complex syntactic structures (such as long-distance *wh*-questions) are mastered quite late. This is surprising given the strong assistance they receive from Universal Grammar.

In our view, these observations simply underscore the need for additional sources of data in assessing young children's syntactic knowledge. Focusing on the technique of elicited production, we have presented striking evidence of children's early mastery of complex syntax, including knowledge of purportedly innate constraints. These findings paint a picture of the course of language development that is in keeping with current linguistic theory. A similar conclusion about children's language comprehension will be forthcoming, as we turn to another means of assessing children's linguistic competence: the truth value judgment task.

PART III

The Truth Value Judgment Task

Chapter 25

Truth Value Judgments

This chapter begins our discussion of how child language experiments are designed and conducted using the truth value judgment task. The truth value judgment task is a research technique that measures comprehension of sentences and discourses. As discussed in chapter 1, it is often of theoretical interest to know whether children assign more than one interpretation to certain sentences. The truth value judgment task was designed to investigate which meanings children can and cannot assign to sentences (Crain and McKee 1985). That is, it can be used to examine whether sentences are ambiguous for children.

There are three main circumstances in which it is worth ascertaining whether or not a linguistic construction is ambiguous for children. First, it is sometimes of theoretical interest to know whether children assign the same interpretations as adults do. It is sometimes claimed that children analyze certain constructions *differently* than adults do; the conjoined-clause analysis of relative clauses is a case in point (see chapters 8 and 18). Second, it is sometimes of interest to know whether children assign *fewer* interpretations to certain constructions than adults do. Because children are language learners, it is conceivable that children sometimes begin by hypothesizing only a subset of the adult meanings and later extend their interpretive options to include ones that were previously absent. We looked at one such case in chapter 14, where we discussed a study of children's understanding of *one* substitution sentences. The findings of that study were interpreted as evidence in favor of the Modularity Matching Model.

Third, it is often of interest to know whether children assign interpretations *in addition to* those that adults assign. In some such cases, the theoretical issue is whether sentences that are unambiguous for adults are ambiguous for children. In testing children's knowledge, the null hypothesis is that children lack the constraint under investigation. The experimental hypothesis is that children know the constraint. According to the null hypothesis, children should be able to assign the kind of interpretation that the constraint prohibits. Therefore, sentences governed by the constraint should be ambiguous for children, though not for adults. In the syntactic component of Universal Grammar, constraints of this kind include the principles of the binding theory. In the semantic component, they include the principles that govern discourse anaphora. In the chapters that follow, we will look at experiments examining both kinds of constraint. As a matter of historical note, the truth value judgment task was specifically designed to test children's knowledge of a syntactic constraint. This task has added considerably to researchers' understanding of children's adherence to putatively universal, innately specified constraints on sentence interpretation.

25.1 Advantages

The truth value judgment task has several advantages over other methodological techniques for assessing children's comprehension. Most important is the degree of experimental control that it achieves. As stated in chapter 1, we follow Aristotle in viewing language as a mapping between sentences and their associated meanings, that is, ⟨sentence, meaning⟩ pairs. From that vantage point, the truth value judgment task can be seen as one that enables researchers to control both elements of this mapping. The test sentence is presented to the child by a puppet, so the experimenter controls the "sentence" part of the ⟨sentence, meaning⟩ equation. In addition, on each trial the experimenter acts out a story in front of the child, so the experimenter controls the context against which the puppet's sentence may be judged. There is an intimate connection between the meaning of a sentence and the set of contexts in which it is true (Davidson 1967). If a child can accurately distinguish those kinds of contexts that make a sentence true from those that make it false, one can infer with confidence that the child is interpreting the sentence in the same way as adults do. The truth value judgment task enables an experimenter to present various types of sentences to children, to see, for each, the range of circumstances in which children judge it to be true or false.

Other advantages of the truth value judgment task also deserve mention. One is that children do not feel as though they are being tested. Instead, the task is designed to make it appear that the judgments of a puppet are under investigation. This is a valuable asset. It makes the task far more enjoyable for children than many other testing procedures, especially ones in which children think they may have answered incorrectly. Since the frustration that often accompanies testing situations is eliminated, children are more relaxed and enjoy themselves, at least if they find the puppet engaging and the stories interesting. As a result, the experimenter is able to spend much more time with children, often a half an hour or even longer, in a single session. To further enhance the entertainment value of the task, children are asked to reward the puppet for correct responses and to let it know (by giving it a lesser reward) when it wasn't "paying close attention." Without the puppet, children generally give "Yes" responses, presumably because they are reluctant to say that an adult said the wrong thing. Yet these negative judgments (about what sentences cannot mean) are often the critical data.

25.2 Testing for Alternative Meanings

The truth value judgment task can be used to determine whether children have each of the alternative meanings of a sentence that is ambiguous in the target language. Other tasks are not able to achieve similar results. For example, one traditional technique that has been used to study children's interpretations of sentences is the act-out task, in which the child is asked to make toy figures perform the actions mentioned in the sentences presented by the experimenter. In this task, therefore, the experimenter controls the "sentence" part of the ⟨sentence, meaning⟩ equation, but not the "meaning" part. The experimenter must infer what meaning(s) children allow by watching and coding the actions they perform with the toys.

The actions children perform on a single trial are associated with only one interpretation of a test sentence, however. Therefore, on any given trial, the act-out task can only confirm the hypothesis that the child allows a particular interpretation. What cannot be inferred is that the child does not allow other interpretations. Moreover, it seems reasonable to suppose that even if a sentence is ambiguous for a child, in the sense that her grammar can give it more than one representation, she may have a preferred analysis. Therefore, if we use an act-out task to study ambiguous sentences, we might find that a child always, or almost always, acts out just one reading. This could be true even if the preference for one reading is slight, because this small preference might prevail on the vast majority of trials. Therefore, the act-out task might fail to give evidence for the alternative reading. Nevertheless, it would clearly be wrong to infer that the child doesn't know the alternative analysis of the sentence.

To make matters worse, it is likely that the vast majority of children have the same preferences for resolving ambiguities, so that few responses corresponding to the dispreferred interpretation of an ambiguous sentence are ever displayed in an experiment. The preference for one reading of a sentence among others may be based on a large number of different factors, for example, processing considerations, parsing strategies, situational preferences, and/or the syntactic or semantic complexity of particular readings. It is well known that adults have such preferences, at least in contexts that are consistent with more than a single interpretation. It seems reasonable to assume that the same is true of children. In situations corresponding to a single interpretation, of course, a child or adult will assign the appropriate interpretation. But in situations that are compatible with more than a single reading of a sentence, one interpretation might consistently win out. Because the "meaning" is not controlled in the act-out task, children's responses are likely to be influenced by the kinds of factors that make one reading preferred over others. The truth value judgment task is an aid in this situation.[1]

25.3 Testing Ambiguous Sentences

In this task, the child is presented with an ambiguous sentence in circumstances that make one of its interpretations true, and one false; the child's task is to indicate, by rewarding a puppet (who utters the test sentence) whether the sentence is true or false. Contexts corresponding to more than one interpretation can be presented. Suppose that the child has a preference for one interpretation over another and that the preferred interpretation corresponds to the "false" reading in the context that has been presented. It has been found that many children nevertheless give a high proportion of positive responses. The assumption is that children want the puppet to say things that are true. That is, the child prefers to say "Yes" if possible. This bias to say "Yes" is apparently enough to boost the dispreferred interpretation of an ambiguous sentence in the child's mind, thereby making it easier for the child to generate that interpretation. Especially if the preference for interpretation A over interpretation B is slight, we expect that presenting a context corresponding to interpretation B boosts its availability to the point that the child will easily be able to generate it. Thus, use of the truth value judgment task should allow us to obtain evidence for both readings, if the child's grammar makes both readings available.

The truth value judgment task involves two experimenters. One acts out stories with toy characters and props; the other plays the role of a puppet (Kermit the Frog). Following each story, the puppet says to the child what he thinks happened in the story. This is how test sentences are presented. The child's role in the experiment is to indicate whether the puppet said the right thing or not. If a child informs the puppet that it said the wrong thing, the experimenter agrees, and asks the child to explain why the puppet was wrong: "What really happened?" This is the elicitation component of the task; it enables the experimenter to tell whether or not the child understands the puppet's description of the story and is rejecting it for the right reason or for some other reason. Other probe questions are also useful.

The probe questions that follow each negative response by a child can also serve as a way of eliciting certain constructions from children. Because the puppet describes the context incorrectly, specific descriptions that explain "what really happened" are usually forthcoming. For example, the negative polarity item *any* cannot appear in the VP associated with the quantifier *every*. To test children's knowledge of this linguistic phenomenon, the puppet might make the statement, "Only two of the boys had any food," in a context that supported the following kind of correction: "No, every boy had some/*any."

25.4 Testing Constraints

The truth value judgment task can be used to investigate the possibility that children's grammars permit them to assign a sentence meaning that is ruled out by a constraint. A child who lacks the constraint should allow the meaning that the constraint prohibits.[2] It follows from the null hypothesis, according to which children lack the constraint, that children will assign a specific interpretation that adults do not assign to the test sentences. The experimental procedure is to test whether both interpretations of a test sentence are available to children. It is also useful to test a number of adults, who serve as a control group, to make sure that adults, at least, perform as expected on the experimental hypothesis. By assumption, adults have all of the linguistic constraints. Therefore, any interpretation ruled out by a constraint will not be available to adults; the test sentences will not be ambiguous for them. For children, by contrast, the null hypothesis is that the constraint is absent from their grammars and that for them, the test sentences are therefore ambiguous.

Taking the null hypothesis as the starting point, the truth value judgment task makes two alternative meanings available for each sentence on each trial. This is accomplished in the context of a story that is acted out in front of the child. On one meaning, the sentence is an accurate description of something that happened in the story that was acted out on that trial. On the other meaning, it is an inaccurate description of something that happened in the story. The experimenter constructs contexts that correspond to the meanings in question, to see if the child accepts or rejects the test sentence in such contexts. If the child rejects a sentence in contexts that correspond to the meaning that is ruled out by the constraint, but accepts it in contexts that correspond to meanings that are not ruled out by the constraint, these responses are taken as evidence that the constraint is part of the child's grammatical knowledge. On the other hand, if a child accepts the test sentence in inappropriate contexts, this response is taken as evidence that the child's grammar lacks the constraint.

The subjects' task is simply to respond "Yes" or "No" depending on whether they judge the sentence uttered by the puppet to be true or false. Earlier we indicated that the meaning that is admitted by the adult grammar should correspond to the "No" response. If children's grammar matches that of adults, as predicted by the Modularity Matching Model, they will reject the target sentence as an incorrect description of the context. Children's responses to the follow-up question "What really happened?" ensure that they are rejecting the sentence for the right reasons. The meaning that is prohibited by the constraint should correspond to the "Yes" response. This step ensures that the test of the experimental hypothesis is conservative; that is, it reduces the risk of making a type I error (concluding that the experimental hypothesis is correct when in fact the null hypothesis is correct). It is well established that subjects have a tendency to say "Yes" if they do not understand a test sentence. If the correct answer corresponds to a "Yes" response, then children's responses may be counted as evidence for the experimental hypothesis when in fact they do not understand the test sentences at all. To avoid the possibility that children will give the right answers for the wrong reasons, this bias must be circumvented. Therefore, the experimental hypothesis (that subjects know the principle under investigation) should be associated with the "No" response.

To summarize, the truth value judgment task is particularly useful in assessing children's knowledge of constraints on the meanings that can and cannot be assigned to sentences. The reason that this task is useful in investigating children's knowledge is that it enables the experimenter to control both parts of the equation, sentence and meaning.

25.5 A Disadvantage

One frustration with the truth value judgment task is the time needed to complete a study. A typical session takes about a half an hour. During this time period, an experimenter can administer 8 to 12 trials. If 1 trial is used as a warm-up, and there are 4 test trials and 4 control trials, then the allotted time is exhausted. It would be ideal to test each child on eight target sentences, or even more, and to test many subjects. However, given the practical constraints in administering the task, we sometimes limit an experiment to 4 test trials, and we test about 20 subjects. Subjects are quite consistent in their responses. Because the results are superior to those obtained with other tasks, and because the test can easily be extended to include more subjects and trials, the limitation of the truth value judgment task is only a practical one, and not an inherent problem with the task itself.

Chapter 26

Backward Anaphora

Consider the following sentence: *He thinks the Troll is the best jumper.* Every adult speaker of English knows that the pronoun *he* in this sentence does not refer to the Troll; its referent must be someone else. Linguists explain this using one of the principles of the binding theory, that component of Universal Grammar concerned with anaphoric relations among NPs. The principle that determines that a name (e.g., *the Troll*) cannot be the referent of a pronoun in certain structural configurations is Principle C. Since Principle C is a negative statement about illicit anaphoric relations, it is a constraint on meaning: ⟨sentence, *meaning⟩. The sentence itself, *He thinks the Troll is the best jumper*, is perfectly acceptable; it simply cannot receive a particular interpretation. Because Principle C is a constraint, it is a viable candidate to be viewed as an innately specified aspect of linguistic knowledge. As a result, it is anticipated to be a linguistic universal, not mastered by children on the basis of their linguistic experience. Granting these assumptions, we are led to ask whether Principle C shows up early in the course of language development. The truth value judgment task has proven to be a useful technique to address this question. In this chapter, we review the findings of previous experimental investigations of the acquisition of Principle C. First, some theoretical background.

26.1 Theoretical Background

Principle C governs the anaphoric relations between pronouns and referring expressions (e.g., names and definite descriptions). We observed that in some constructions, a referring expression (r-expression) cannot corefer with a pronoun, as in (1).

(1)   He thinks the Troll is the best jumper.

Here, the pronoun *he* cannot refer to the Troll; it must refer to someone else—Cookie Monster, perhaps. However, if the order of the pronoun and the name is switched, as in (2), then coreference between them is permitted. In (2), the pronoun can be interpreted as referring to the Troll. There is also another reading in which it refers to someone else—again, perhaps Cookie Monster.

(2)   The Troll thinks he is the best jumper.

Principle C explains why (2) tolerates an interpretation that (1) does not. Without considering further evidence, instead of Principle C, we might propose the following hypothesis to explain the facts discussed so far:

(3)   If a pronoun precedes a referential NP (an r-expression), then they cannot refer to the same thing.

In symbols, we can represent this as the following, linear prohibition:

(4)   *pro_i ... NP_i

In this representation, the fact that the two NPs (*pro* and *NP*) have the same subscript indicates that they have the same reference. As noted in chapter 20, structure-independent hypotheses like this, which treat sentences as strings of words, are not characteristic of the theory of Universal Grammar. It is therefore not surprising to find evidence that this hypothesis is incorrect. The following example will suffice:

(5)   While he_i was reading the paper, the $Troll_i$ ate a bagel.

In this sentence, the pronoun *he* can refer to the Troll. Example (5) therefore shows that in some cases a pronoun can precede a name and still be coreferential with it.

The difference between (1), on the one hand, and (3) and (5), on the other, is structural. The structural relation that determines coreference is called *c-command*, and the constraint that invokes c-command is called *Principle C*. For our purposes, the following definition of Principle C will suffice:

(6)   *Principle C*
      An r-expression R cannot be coreferential with a pronoun P that
      c-commands it.[1]

As (6) makes clear, our concern is with r-expressions that are c-commanded by NPs that are pronouns. At a coarse level of description, a pronoun c-commands an r-expression if the pronoun is positioned higher than the r-expression in the phrase structure analysis (tree diagram) of the sentence. A more precise definition is that a pronoun P c-commands an r-expression R in a phrase marker if and only if there is a path beginning at P, proceeding upward to the first branching node above P and then extending downward to R. Thus, P c-commands R in (7) but not in (8).

(7)

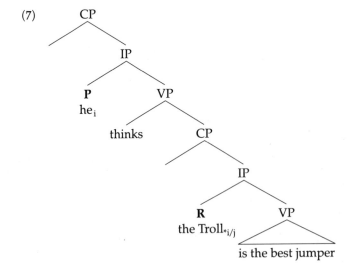

(8)

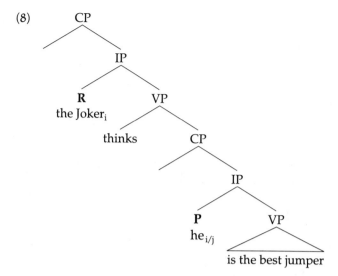

(In the indexing notation used here, which replaces the underlining notation used in previous chapters, two NPs that have different referents are given different indices $(i, j, k, \ldots)$, and two NPs that have the same referent are given the same index. *The Troll*$_{*i/j}$ and *he*$_i$ in (7) means that *the Troll* and *he* cannot refer to the same individual $(*i, i)$ but can refer to different individuals (i, j).)

When a pronoun (e.g., *he* in (7)) c-commands an r-expression (e.g., *the Troll*), coreference is not permitted; on the noncoreferential interpretation, which *is* permitted, these expressions have different indices (i, j), the result of applying Principle C. By contrast, Principle C does not apply to the structure in (8) because the pronoun does not c-command the r-expression; therefore, coreference is possible. Principle C is a negative statement; it states when coreference is not permitted. As another example, notice that in (5), *While he was reading the paper, the Troll ate a bagel*, the pronoun does not c-command the r-expression, because it is deeply embedded inside a subordinate clause, as shown in (9). Therefore, Principle C does not apply, and coreference is permitted between the pronoun and the r-expression.

(9)

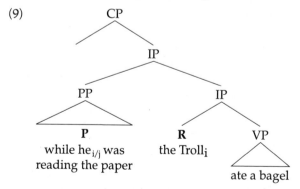

Since Principle C is a constraint within the theory of Universal Grammar, it is expected to exhibit all of the hallmarks of innate specification. It should be universal; it should emerge in the absence of linguistic experience; all children should abide by it, regardless of differences in primary linguistic data and despite its apparent complexity (pretheoretically speaking); it may appear early in the course of language development. The experiments reviewed in the rest of the chapter were concerned with the hallmark of early emergence. As we will show, several early studies of Principle C indicated that it did not bear this hallmark. Fortunately, a subsequent study using the truth value judgment task did confirm the predictions of the theory of Universal Grammar, namely, that children's grammars do include Principle C.

26.2 Previous Research

There is a large body of research on children's knowledge of coreference relations between pronouns and r-expressions. The findings of the initial studies of children's knowledge of Principle C were somewhat disconcerting. Researchers were led to conclude that, at least initially, children apply a purely linear (structure-independent) hypothesis in interpreting pronouns and r-expressions. Summarizing one such experiment, by Lust (1981), Solan (1983) concludes that children's initial hypothesis about anaphora is to prohibit coreference between a pronoun and an NP whenever the pronoun appears first. This conclusion was based on an act-out study by Tavakolian (1978) in which children were instructed to act out the meanings of sentences using toy figures and other props placed in the experimental workspace. Tavakolian found that two-thirds of the 3- to 5-year-old subjects responded in a manner that, according to Solan, indicated that children's grammars include a linear prohibition against backward coreference (cf. the directionality factor of Lust, Eisele, and Mazuka 1992).

In the figure manipulation experiment by Tavakolian, the majority of the time children selected an animal that was not mentioned in the sentence, but was present in the workspace, as the referent of the pronoun in sentences like (10a) and (10b).

(10) a. For him to kiss the lion would make the duck happy.
     b. That he kissed the lion made the duck happy.

Of the 24 subjects, 14 consistently acted out these sentences in this fashion. Solan concludes from this that "children use direction rather than structural principles in restricting anaphora, ... never allowing backward anaphora" (pp. 83–84).

This conclusion is unwarranted, for several reasons. First of all, since one-third of the subjects' responses indicated acceptance of backward anaphora, the statement that children never allow backward anaphora is too strong. But suppose that every child had chosen an unnamed referent on every opportunity. Even this would not be evidence of a prohibition against backward anaphora. The possibility exists that there is a strong preference for the deictic interpretation of the pronoun (according to which the pronoun refers to someone who is not mentioned in the sentence) over the backward anaphora interpretation (according to which the pronoun and an r-expression within the sentence are anaphorically linked).[2]

It seems more likely that the apparent lack of availability of backward anaphora was simply the result of children's preference to assign a discourse referent to a pronoun as quickly as possible, without waiting for linguistic information about the intended referent. This kind of preference, which conserves memory resources, should also show up in adult sentence processing, according to the Modularity Matching Model. The pressure to interpret constituents as rapidly as possible will be encountered by children (and adults) on every trial; therefore, we would expect to see a strong bias against backward anaphora in an act-out task. By contrast, as we will show, the truth value judgment task can be used to boost the availability of the backward anaphora interpretation. This is one of its virtues, as compared to other tasks. It is important to note that if children actually have a linear prohibition against backward anaphora, then we cannot test their knowledge of Principle C using sentences like (1). To provide evidence of children's knowledge of Principle C, we must show two things: (a) that children allow backward anaphora wherever adults allow it and (b) that children disallow backward anaphora when it is excluded by Principle C.

26.3 A Positive Finding

The question of children's knowledge of the backward anaphora interpretation of sentences was pursued in an experiment by Crain and McKee (1985). In this experiment, children encountered sentences like (11) in circumstances appropriate to the backward anaphora (or intersentential) interpretation and the deictic (or extrasentential) interpretation.

(11)   While he was dancing, the Ninja Turtle ate pizza.

The experimental procedure was the truth value judgment task. Ambiguous sentences such as (11) or its equivalent were presented on two separate occasions, in two contexts. Following both situations, the puppet, Kermit the Frog, uttered the sentence in (11). In one context for (11), the Ninja Turtle was dancing and eating pizza. This was the situation appropriate for the backward anaphora reading. Because the backward anaphora interpretation was dispreferred in previous experiments, children's knowledge of this interpretation was tested in contexts in which it was true. In the other context presented to children, someone else was dancing while the Ninja Turtle was eating pizza. The context also made (11) true. Presented in this context, the sentence was a control to check whether children would accept the deictic interpretation of the pronoun more often than the backward anaphora interpretation. Since both interpretations were presented in contexts that made the test sentences true, children's preference for one or the other interpretation could readily be assessed.

The results were that the 62 children tested (mean age 4;2) accepted the backward anaphora reading 73% of the time, in appropriate contexts. The extrasentential reading was accepted only slightly more often, 81% of the time. Only 1 of the 62 children interviewed in this way consistently rejected backward anaphora. On the basis of these findings, we can conclude that children's grammars allow backward anaphora, just as adults' grammars do. By boosting the availability of the backward anaphora reading, the truth value judgment task allowed Crain and McKee to demonstrate the existence of a reading that did not surface readily in the act-out task where children were forced to choose between interpretations.

In this study, knowledge of Principle C was tested using both one-clause sentences like "He washed Luke Skywalker" and two-clause sentences like "He ate the hamburger when the Smurf was inside the fence." It was found that children rejected coreference between the r-expression and the pronoun 90% of the time for the one-clause sentences and 84% of the time for the more complex two-clause sentences.[3] This finding underscores our contention, stated in chapter 3, that neither children nor adults find it more difficult to comprehend sentences with two clauses than sentences with a single clause.

The findings support the view that children do not rely solely on their linguistic experience in making judgments about the appropriate mappings of sentences with their meanings. Presumably, there is nothing in children's experience to tell them that certain sentence/meaning pairs are *not* allowed; therefore, they have no way to learn the structural constraint prohibiting coreference, Principle C. Nevertheless, they appear to know it at an early age. By the logic underlying the poverty-of-the-stimulus argument, we are led to conclude that children's knowledge of Principle C is innately specified.

Chapter 27

Fundamentals of Design: Principle C

Having shown that children can access backward anaphora, we are now in a position to describe how the truth value judgment task can be used to probe for children's knowledge of Principle C. In subsequent chapters, we will discuss other experiments, both real and manufactured (to make points that could not be made otherwise). In each case, experiments have been selected because they illustrate ways in which the truth value judgment task can be modified to address specific theoretical issues.

To illustrate how the truth value judgment task can test children's knowledge of Principle C, we will concentrate on sentence (1).

(1)   He thinks the Troll is the best jumper.
     a.   *He thinks the Troll is the best jumper.
     b.   He thinks the Troll is the best jumper.

By Principle C, (1) cannot be paired with the meaning in (a), according to which the Troll thinks that he, himself, is the best jumper. Let us call this meaning of the sentence $meaning_1$. The meaning in (b) is permitted by the adult grammar. On this meaning, some salient male, other than the Troll, thinks that the Troll is the best jumper. We will refer to this as $meaning_2$.

The experimental hypothesis is that children know Principle C, in which case they disallow $meaning_1$ and can assign the sentence only $meaning_2$. The null hypothesis is that children lack Principle C. If so, they should allow $meaning_1$ in addition to $meaning_2$; that is, (1) should be ambiguous for them. This chapter explains how to test children's adherence to Principle C, by probing for both $meaning_1$ and $meaning_2$. The null and experimental hypotheses, and the predictions associated with each of them, can be summarized as follows:

- H_0: Children lack Principle C.
  Expected results: Children permit both $meaning_1$ and $meaning_2$.
- H_1: Children know Principle C.
  Expected results: Children permit $meaning_2$, but not $meaning_1$.

27.1 Design Features of the Task

The general strategy "Avoid type I errors" dictates much of the experimental design of the study and many of the specific details of the stories. To avoid such errors, researchers should be conservative in designing an experiment, stacking the cards against the experimental hypothesis and in favor of the null hypothesis.

Part of the story acted out by the experimenter corresponds to $meaning_1$ of the test sentences, and part corresponds to $meaning_2$. On the null hypothesis, children have access to meaning$_1$. To be conservative, the "Yes" response should be associated with meaning$_1$, by making the test sentence *true* on meaning$_1$. The reason for associating meaning$_1$ with the "Yes" response is to avoid type I errors. It was observed in chapter 6 that both children and adults manifest a bias to give a "Yes" response when they are confused or fail to comprehend a sentence. Therefore, the part of the story corresponding to meaning$_1$ should yield the "Yes" response. If the null hypothesis is correct, children will say "Yes" in response to the puppet's assertion, either because they determine that the test sentence is true on meaning$_1$ or for some extraneous reason (e.g., they do not understand the sentence).

The part of the story corresponding to meaning$_2$ should be designed to evoke a "No" response; the test sentence should be *false* in the context, on meaning$_2$. If the experimental hypothesis is correct, children know Principle C. Because Principle C rules out meaning$_1$, children should not access that meaning. Instead, they should access meaning$_2$, which is false in the story. Children should therefore say "No" in response to the puppet's assertion.

The discussion so far is summarized in (2), where the asterisk in front of Meaning$_1$ indicates that this meaning is not allowed by the adult grammar.

(2)   *Meaning$_1$, true: The Troll thinks he is the best jumper.
      Meaning$_2$, false: He (not the Troll) thinks the Troll is the best jumper.

Having sketched these aspects of the design, we will describe how we might go about testing children's knowledge of Principle C, using sentence (1).

27.1.1 The Plot
The study centers around a series of stories, all following the same general plot. There are three protagonists, A, B, and C. They are involved in some kind of contest: for example, to see who has the best smile, or who is the best jumper. In addition to the three contestants, there is a judge, J, who determines the winner. J considers the three contestants in turn. J first tells A that he is not the winner. J then tells B that he might be the winner; but before deciding, J must consider C. Turning to C, J decides that he is the winner, and J awards C a prize. B then protests and takes a prize for himself. This ends the story.

27.1.2 Truth Values
On meaning$_1$, the reading that is ruled out by Principle C, the test sentences are accurate descriptions of the story. On meaning$_2$, the test sentences are false. On both readings, protagonist B is mentioned by name (B is the contestant who loses and protests J's choice of C as the winner). On meaning$_1$, the pronoun and the name corefer. On meaning$_2$, the referent of the pronoun in the target sentences is the judge, J.

27.1.3 The Child's Task
Following the story, the puppet, Kermit the Frog, says what he thought happened in the story (this is the test sentence). The child's task is to indicate, by reward or reminder, if Kermit's description of the story is correct or incorrect. A child who assigns meaning$_1$ to the test sentence should say "Yes" and give Kermit a reward. A child who assigns meaning$_2$ should say "No" and give Kermit a reminder.

27.1.4 The Condition of Falsification

To avoid type I errors, the experimenter should make the test sentence false on the meaning that is consistent with the adult grammar—the meaning that is not ruled out by the linguistic constraint under investigation. Take (1), for example: *He thinks the Troll is the best jumper.* To make this sentence false in the story on the adult interpretation (meaning$_2$), the judge, J, must not think that contestant B, the Troll, is the best jumper. The research strategy of making the test sentence false on a particular reading will be called the *condition of falsification*. To meet the condition of falsification, the context should make the negation of the test sentence a true description of the story: in the present case, *He doesn't think the Troll is the best jumper.* To implement the condition of falsification, the context must provide a salient male figure, besides the Troll, to be the referent of the pronoun, *he.* In the present story, this is Robocop, the judge. By the end of the story, it must be made clear to the child subjects that Robocop doesn't think that the Troll was the best jumper. This is done by having Robocop consider whether the Troll or another character, Grover, is the best jumper. After watching both characters, Robocop concludes that Grover, not the Troll, is the best jumper.

Now we can return to meaning$_1$. The story must also make the test sentence true on the interpretation ruled out by Principle C, meaning$_1$. It must be true that the Troll thinks that he, himself, is the best jumper. This is straightforward. In the story acted out by the experimenter, the Troll disagrees with Robocop's decision. He says, "You're wrong, Robocop, I am the best jumper."

27.1.5 A Record of Events

Another feature of experimental design has proven valuable in obtaining reliable results from children. At the end of the story, the characters should be situated in a way that reminds the child subjects of the events that have taken place. In the present story, for example, when Robocop judges that Grover, not the Troll, is the best jumper, Robocop ends up standing beside Grover.

The final arrangement of the props should also provide a record of the events that took place. For the story corresponding to (1), the relevant props are prizes—colored pasta. Robocop awards a prize to Grover when he judges him to be the best jumper. The Troll protests, however, and awards himself a prize. Therefore, at the end of the story both Grover and the Troll have colored pasta beside them, reminding the child that Grover was the winner, but that the Troll thought that he was the winner.

27.1.6 The Order of Events

If children access the illicit reading of the test sentence, then they should judge the test sentence to be true. Therefore, a "Yes" response is evidence that a child lacks Principle C, which rules against assigning such an interpretation. The order in which the two parts of the story are acted out is important. Specifically, we have chosen to make the event corresponding to meaning$_1$ come *last* in the context. The motivation is the same as that used in selecting meaning$_1$ to be the meaning that is true in the context (corresponding to the "Yes" response): meaning$_1$ is acted out last in order to avoid a type I error. Presumably, the last-mentioned event is the most salient, so the interpretation associated with this aspect of the context will be favored, all other things being equal.

To recap, if meaning$_1$ is available to children, then it should be readily accessible to children in the present story, for two reasons. First, it is associated with the "Yes" response, because the sentence is true in the story on meaning$_1$. Second, the story ends with the action that is expressed by meaning$_1$. If subjects indicate that the puppet said the right thing, then this counts as evidence against the experimental hypothesis. Putting it another way, children's "Yes" responses are evidence against rejecting the null hypothesis, which is the hypothesis that children find the test sentences ambiguous, allowing meaning$_1$ as well as meaning$_2$. On the other hand, if children go out of their way to consistently reject the puppet's sentence, we can feel confident that they do not permit meaning$_1$. This pattern of responses would be compelling evidence in favor of the experimental hypothesis, that the sentence means that the judge, Robocop, thinks that the Troll is the best jumper, which is false.

27.1.7 The Linguistic Antecedent

The experimental protocol should make referents available to the child for pronouns that appear in the test sentence. Again, to avoid type I errors, the order in which potential referents are introduced should not be biased toward meaning$_2$, the meaning that children should assign if they know Principle C. In the present story, Kermit would say something like, "That was a good story. It was about a jumping contest, and Robocop was the judge, because he won the contest before. Let's see. There were three other people: Grover, Cookie Monster, and the Troll. I know one thing that happened in the story." Kermit would then present the test sentence: "He thinks that the Troll was the best jumper."

27.1.8 What Really Happened

Whenever children correctly reject a test sentence, they are asked to explain to Kermit why his description of the story was inaccurate. This is done by asking them, "What really happened?" Children are told that Kermit needs to pay closer attention and that they can help him by explaining to him what part of the story he misconstrued. In the present experiment, this is accomplished by designing the story to make it clear exactly *why* the test sentence is false. Put the other way around, it must be clear why the negation of the test sentence (i.e., *He* doesn't *think the Troll was the best jumper*) is true. In the present story, this is accomplished by having Robocop consider whether the Troll or Grover was the best jumper, finally settling on Grover.

Children's explanations of what really happened are extremely useful. They provide the experimenter with a verbal report about the events that took place, and they may identify the referents of pronouns in the test sentences. For example, in the present story children would be expected to point out that Grover was the best jumper. If children do not provide revealing accounts of the story, the experimenter can follow up their responses to "What really happened?" by further questions, such as "Why does the Troll have the pasta?" and, perhaps, (a crossover question probe) "Who did he say was the best jumper?" Children's answers to these questions provide a more detailed account of how they understood the story. Children's responses to the crossover questions usually identify the character that they think is the winner of the contest, and sometimes indicate who they take to be the referent of the pronoun *he* in the test sentence. Children's answers to the question about the Troll sometimes elicit a sentence corresponding to meaning$_1$, for example, "The Troll thinks he is the best jumper."

27.1.9 The Condition of Plausible Dissent (Russell's Maxim)

Consider now what would happen if we made the following change in the experimental context. Suppose that in the story acted out in front of the child, Robocop does not judge who is the best jumper. Suppose he just stands there, for example. At first glance, one might speculate that this situation would suffice to make the test sentence false, applying the following logic: if Robocop doesn't say anything, then it should not be inferred that he thinks the Troll is the best jumper.

There is an important distinction, however, between falsity and infelicity. If Robocop doesn't say anything, then it is infelicitous, not simply false, to ask whether he thinks the Troll is the best jumper. We have found that children are confused, and make "errors," in situations like this. In our view, such errors are the result of the experimenter's putting children in the position of having to violate a grammatical constraint (e.g., Principle C) or a pragmatic one. Pragmatic constraints state the conditions under which the sentences are used in ordinary discourses. It turns out that children systematically assign the correct interpretation to sentences (and produce them) only in contexts that are pragmatically appropriate. Thus, when the goal is to assess children's comprehension of sentences, it is important to consider the pragmatic contexts in which the sentences are ordinarily used. If a child fails to perform accurately in response to some experimental task, it is conceivable that the fault lies somewhere in the experimental setup, and not in the mind/brain of the child. Crain, Thornton, et al. (1996) put it this way:

> Children make errors in experimental situations that force them to violate one kind of linguistic principle or another. In such circumstances, children are forced to choose which kind of principle to violate. However, if children choose to violate a syntactic principle, say, in order to provide a pragmatically felicitous response, they should not be said to lack knowledge of the syntactic principle.... Of course, the proof is in the pudding. To substantiate the claim that some systematic behavior by children is due to a flaw in experimental design, the claimant needs to rectify the flaw and show that the error vanishes. (p. 109)

A basic principle of pragmatics is that sentences must be relevant to the discourse in which they appear. In the context under consideration, where Robocop is just standing there, whether or not "He thinks that the Troll is the best jumper" is not pertinent to the discourse. Therefore, this context forces children to choose between violating a pragmatic constraint, "Be Relevant," and a syntactic constraint, Principle C. It is hardly surprising that children sometimes choose to violate the syntactic constraint. They may conjecture that Robocop was thinking that the Troll was the best jumper, even if he did not say so. This conjecture is consistent with the bias noted earlier, to attempt to assign an interpretation that makes the puppet's statement true.

The upshot is that it must be clear to children *why* a statement is true or false, if they are being asked to confirm or deny it. If it is not clear why a statement is false, children may end up accepting it, despite knowing the grammatical principle under investigation (cf. Wason 1980). Therefore, clarifying the reason for denying the test sentence helps guard against type II errors, rejections of valid experimental hypotheses.

We refer to this feature of the experiment as the *condition of plausible dissent*. In the present experiment, this condition is satisfied if the story makes it clear that the Troll is under consideration as the best jumper. A related point was made some years ago, by Bertrand Russell (1948), who stated that "perception only gives rise to a negative judgment when the correlative positive judgment has already been made or considered" (p. 138). In the truth value judgment task, children are asked to say whether sentences are true or false. Following Russell's observation, it is appropriate to ask children for a (possibly) negative judgment of a sentence only if the corresponding positive judgment has been under consideration. This is essentially the condition of plausible dissent (which we may call *Russell's maxim*). It is a pragmatic "felicity condition" on the use of the truth value judgment task.

Consider how the condition of plausible dissent is satisfied in the story we are developing. The condition requires meaning$_2$ to be under consideration at some point in the story. This happens when Robocop tells the Troll that he might be the winner. Subsequently, some event transpires that makes the sentence false on meaning$_2$; Robocop decides that Grover is the winner. This eventuality also makes it clear to the child subject *why* the test sentence is false in the context.

27.1.10 Background, Assertion, Possible Outcome, Actual Outcome

To see how the condition of plausible dissent is satisfied, it will be helpful to operationalize the requisite procedures. First, the test sentence can be partitioned into two parts, which we call the *background* and the *assertion*. The background is established by replacing one of the specific expressions in the sentence by a more elliptical expression. For example, a specific r-expression, such as *the Troll*, could be replaced by the more elliptical expression *so-and-so*; or a specific property that is mentioned, such as *the best jumper*, could be replaced by the more elliptical expression *such-and-such*; and so on. The specific information that has been replaced is the assertion.

More often than not there are several possible backgrounds and assertions for a test sentence. In the story we have been discussing, the background is *He (Robocop) said that so-and-so is the best jumper*, and the assertion is *the Troll*. The actual outcome is another assertion, *Grover*. There are other possibilities, but we will not discuss them here.[1]

(3) Background: Robocop thinks *so-and-so* is the best jumper.
Assertion: the Troll
Possible outcome: the Troll
Actual outcome: Grover

The actual outcome in (3) makes it quite clear to the child *why* the puppet's statement is false.

It may be useful to think of the background as a function, B, with an assertion, A, as its argument. From this perspective, the test sentence is derived by applying the background to the assertion: B(A). To place the test sentence under consideration, the application of the background to the assertion made in the test sentence should be a plausible outcome at one point in the story. This is to satisfy the condition of plausible dissent. In the present story, then, it should be a possible outcome at some point for Robocop to think that the Troll is the best jumper. To satisfy the condition of falsification, however, another event must transpire to prevent this outcome. It turns out in the story that the background applies to a different assertion: *Grover*. In the story, Robocop considers both the Troll and Grover, then decides that Grover is the best jumper. This last event, the actual outcome, indicates why the test sentence is false; Grover is judged to be the best jumper, not the Troll. It is anticipated that children will describe the actual outcome when they are asked, "What really happened?"

There is still one loose end to tie up. Do children ever assign Grover, instead of Robocop, as the referent of the pronoun in the test sentence? We have already indicated a reason for thinking that children will not make Grover the referent of the pronoun: Grover does not say anything in the story. Robocop, on the other hand, offers relevant information about who is the best jumper. In any event, if children were to assign Grover as the referent of the pronoun, they would presumably respond "Yes," in virtue of having conjured up a mental picture in which Grover thinks that the Troll is the best jumper (in order to assign an interpretation that makes the puppet's statement true). This strategy would therefore result in responses that would count against the experimental hypothesis, not for it. Hence, this assignment of reference could lead only to type II errors, not type I errors. A simple way to avoid the issue entirely is to make Robocop decide that a female character is best jumper. Then this character could not be taken as the referent of the pronoun in the test sentence.

27.2 A Summary in Pictures

This section summarizes all of the design features introduced in this chapter, in the order in which they should occur in the experiment. The summary is in the form of pictures of the story as it unfolds in real time.

27.2.1 The Jumping Competition
The characters and the setup are introduced.

Storyline

> *Experimenter*   This is a story about a jumping competition. The judge is Robocop. Last year he won the jumping competition, so this year he gets to be the judge. This year, these guys, Cookie Monster, the Troll, and Grover are in the jumping competition. They have to try and jump over this log, the barrels, and the benches over here.

Comment

The first event in the story establishes the background. Because of the particular background we have chosen (*He (Robocop) thinks **so-and-so** is the best jumper*), we have decided to make the story about a jumping contest. To make the story more interesting, Robocop is described as the judge of this year's "Best Jumper" contest, because he was the winner of last year's contest.

27.2.2   *The Prize for the Best Jumper*
The judge, Robocop, introduces the prize: colored pasta.

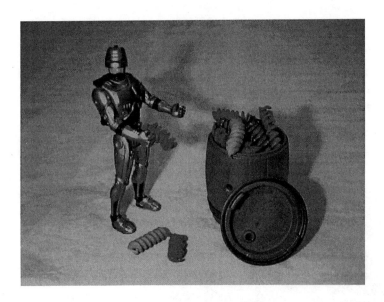

Storyline

> *Robocop*   The winner of the competition gets a great prize—colored pasta! See, it's in this barrel right here.

27.2.3   *The Competitors*
The competitors prepare for the contest.

Storyline

Robocop   Line up, everyone. Get ready to try and jump over all these things.

27.2.4 The First Competitor: Cookie Monster
Cookie Monster unsuccessfully attempts the course.

Storyline

Robocop   You go first, Cookie Monster.
Cookie Monster   OK. Here I go. I made it over the log. Now I'll try and jump over the barrels. Oh no! I crashed into them. Oh well, I'll try and jump the benches. Phew, they weren't so hard.

27.2.5 The Second Competitor: The Troll
The Troll clears the course successfully.

Storyline

> *Robocop*   Your turn next, Troll.
> *Troll*   OK. I'm a good jumper. This should be easy for me. Over the log I go. Yeah! Now I'll try the barrels. Good. I jumped over them easily. Now for the benches. Good, I didn't knock anything over!

27.2.6 The Final Competitor: Grover
Grover clears the obstacles cleanly in record time.

Storyline

> *Robocop*   OK, Grover. Your turn.
> *Grover*   I'm a good jumper, too. Watch me! See how easily I could jump over
> the log? Now I'll jump over the barrels and the benches. Great, I didn't smash
> into anything, and I was really fast.

27.2.7 Judging the Competition: The Possible Outcome

Robocop considers the performance of the first two competitors.

Storyline

> *Robocop*   All right. Line up, guys. I'm ready to judge the competition. Let's see
> who wins this great colored pasta.

> *Robocop*   Cookie Monster, I'm afraid you aren't the winner. You crashed into
> the barrels. I think you've been eating too many cookies. You better eat fewer
> cookies and lose some weight. Then you will be a better jumper.

Robocop   Troll, you jumped very well. You didn't crash into anything at all. You could be the winner. But let me judge Grover before I decide.

Comment
Robocop's statements about the Troll establish meaning$_2$ as a possible outcome: *He thinks the Troll is the best jumper*. This satisfies the condition of plausible dissent. Robocop indicates that the Troll does indeed jump very well and might turn out to be the winner, but that he will have to think about it after considering the other contestant, Grover. At this point in the story, it could turn out that the Troll is the winner of the contest, in which case the test sentence would be true on meaning$_2$.

27.2.8 The Awards Ceremony: The Actual Outcome
Grover takes the prize.

Storyline

> *Robocop*   Grover, your jumps were very good, too. You didn't knock anything down, and you were also very fast. So, I think you were the best jumper. You win the prize, this colored pasta. Well done, Grover. Great job!

Comment

To meet the condition of falsification, Robocop picks someone other than the Troll as the winner of the contest. This is the actual outcome: Robocop decides that Grover is the winner. As a record of this event, Robocop remains standing by Grover at the completion of the story. The colored pasta also serves as a record of the event.

27.2.9 The Troll Rejects the Decision

The Troll is unhappy with Robocop's choice of Grover as winner. He takes some colored pasta for himself.

Storyline

> *Troll*   No, Robocop, you're wrong! I am the best jumper. I think I should get the prize. I 'm going to take some colored pasta for myself. ⟨Troll helps himself to some of the prize⟩

Comment

The story concludes by making the test sentence true on the meaning precluded by Principle C, meaning$_1$. This is accomplished by having the Troll protest to Robocop, saying, "No, Robocop, you're wrong! I am the best jumper." Once he has said this, the test sentence is clearly true on meaning$_1$. This event comes last to boost the availability of this reading if it is consistent with children's grammars (i.e., to avoid type I errors).

27.2.10 Kermit the Frog Describes the Story

The characters are placed alongside props to remind the child of the events of the story.

Storyline

> *Kermit* Let me try to say what happened. That was a story about Robocop, who was the judge, and Cookie Monster, and Grover, and there was the Troll. I know one thing that happened. He said that the Troll is the best jumper.
> *Child* No!

Comment

The potential linguistic antecedents for the pronoun are introduced. The order of introduction is designed to avoid type I errors; the potential referent of the pronoun on meaning$_2$ (the adult interpretation) is introduced first, and the potential referent of the pronoun on meaning$_1$ (the illicit interpretation) is introduced last. If children use recency of mention to guide their selection of the referent of the pronoun, this order favors meaning$_1$.

Control sentences should be included in the experiment to ensure that children accept meaning$_1$ when the grammar permits it. One type of control would be sentences in which the pronoun and the name appear in reverse order (e.g., *The Troll said that he is the best jumper*).

27.2.11 The Child's Interpretation
Kermit the Frog checks the child's understanding of the story.

Storyline

> *Kermit*   No? Then what really happened?

27.2.12 The Child's Explanation of the Events
The child explains to Kermit the Frog that something is wrong with his version of the story.

Storyline

> *Child*   Grover was the best jumper, not the Troll!
> *Kermit*   Then why does the Troll have some pasta?
> *Child*   Because he thought he was the best jumper, but the judge didn't think so.
> *Experimenter*   OK. Let's help Kermit. That was a story about Robocop, who was the judge, Cookie Monster, Grover, and the Troll. Who did he say was the best jumper?
> *Child*   Grover.

Comment

The experimenter elicits the child's version of what really happened in the story. The potential linguistic antecedents are reintroduced before the crossover-question variant of the test sentence is presented.

27.2.13 Kermit the Frog Sees the Light

Kermit understands the child's explanation. He pays penance for saying the wrong thing.

Storyline

> *Kermit*   Oh, I see. So, I guess I don't get to eat the melon. So I have to do push-ups.

Comment

The melon is the reward, administered by the child whenever Kermit correctly describes what happened in the story. If Kermit is incorrect, he volunteers to do push-ups to wake himself up, so he can pay closer attention to the next story; this is the reminder.

27.3 Written Outline of the Story

Before constructing any real stories, it is helpful to make an outline, or even to draw pictures, of a prototypical story. Here is one outline of the features of the story under discussion:

Test sentence: He thinks the Troll is the best jumper.

- Background
  Context, part 1: There is a contest. Robocop judges who is the best jumper. (Robocop thinks *someone* is the best jumper.)
- Condition of plausible dissent: Meaning$_2$ is under consideration
  Context, part 2: Robocop could end up thinking the Troll is the best jumper. (possible outcome)
- Condition of falsification: meaning$_2$, false *or* negation of meaning$_2$, true
  Context, part 3: Robocop doesn't think the Troll is the best jumper. Robocop thinks Grover is the best jumper. (actual outcome)
- Final event: Meaning$_1$, true
  Context, part 4: The Troll protests. He says that he is the best jumper.

27.4 Conclusion

Three essential features of the truth value judgment task are worth repeating. The first concerns design. In this task, the target sentence, S, is true on one reading, meaning$_1$, and false on another reading, meaning$_2$. If children are to give negative judgments in response to sentence S on meaning$_2$, then the corresponding sentence, NOT S, must be true in the context on this reading. In a nutshell, this is the condition of falsification.

Second, it is important to make the denial of a test sentence felicitous. To accomplish this, it is essential that the sentence, on meaning$_2$, be under consideration during the trial. It is felicitous to ask whether a sentence, S, is false on a reading only if the discourse context is such that S has been under consideration on that reading. This is the condition of plausible dissent.

Third, it should be clear to the child exactly why NOT S is true, rather than S. Therefore, the experimenter must make the denial of S on meaning$_2$ as plausible as possible. This is accomplished by choosing a good background/assertion pair, namely, a pair that enables the child to explain "what really happened" with least effort. Placing the characters and props at the end of the story in such a way that they record the events is helpful in making it clear what really happened. In some cases, the exact procedures required to maximize plausible dissent depend on the particular linguistic construction(s) under investigation in the experiment. We will introduce some guiding principles for selecting background/assertion pairs in chapter 33. As a final note, we wish to emphasize that this chapter has described the design features of test sentences only; control sentences are another matter, which we take up in later chapters, especially chapter 34.

Chapter 28

What's Wrong with This Picture?

This chapter presents an alternative to the experimental design presented in chapters 26 and 27. There are several points to this exercise. First, introducing an alternative to the truth value judgment task gives us a chance to review some of the methodological prescriptions for the design of experiments using the task. Second, it enables us to reinforce the importance of satisfying the condition of plausible dissent; it also make it clear that this condition is not easily satisfied in other experimental tasks. Third, discussing a hypothetical experiment using another technique allows us to raise, yet again, the important issue of when the null hypothesis should be rejected, in favor of the experimental hypothesis.

When a reading is absent from a child's grammar, the Modularity Matching Model predicts that the child will not accept a sentence with that reading, even if the sentence is true if that reading is imposed on it. More specifically, the Modularity Matching Model predicts that when an unambiguous sentence is presented to children, they will accept the sentence (on the correct interpretation) if the correct interpretation makes the sentence true in the context, and they will reject the sentence if the correct interpretation makes the sentence false in the context. Of course, there is always some amount of noise in an experiment with children, arising from factors like inattention. In our experience, however, children succumb to these factors only slightly more than adults do. Therefore, as a rule of thumb, we expect to find performance coming close to 100% accuracy in most cases—in any event, above 90% accuracy. The fact that such levels have been achieved in many experiments (some of which are reported in this book) provides strong support for the Modularity Matching Model and leads us to apply it in other cases.

In part I, we discussed several circumstances in which children may give "incorrect" responses, despite grammatical competence. In general, this should not happen, according to the Modularity Matching Model, if the experiment that reveals such "errors" is conducted properly. The possibility exists, however, that children will sometimes respond incorrectly even to unambiguous sentences, and even when they have the grammatical competence to analyze the sentence correctly. For example, it can happen that children accept a sentence as true on a reading that is not made available by their grammars ("false positive" responses). The possibility also exists that children will incorrectly reject a sentence because they are misled into thinking that it should be interpreted in a way that is not consistent with their grammars. This will be discussed in chapter 35, where the topic is children's interpretation of sentences containing the universal quantifier *every*. For simplicity's sake, we will not consider such cases in this chapter, but it should be understood that many of the points raised here carry over to children's "false negative" responses.

Perhaps the main source of false positive responses by children is failure to construct contexts that are appropriate for a negative response. We have shown that as a
matter of research design, two experimental maneuvers are required. First, assuming
that the test sentence should be false in the context (in order to avoid type I errors),
the negation of the test sentence should be true in the context. This is the condition
of falsification. Second, it is crucial that the assertion of the test sentence is under
consideration, on the correct, adult reading. This is the condition of plausible dissent.

Suppose that the condition of plausible dissent is not met. If this condition is one
of the pragmatic felicity conditions for rejecting a sentence as untrue, then not satisfying it amounts to the violation of a pragmatic principle: "Use Sentences Felicitously" (or "Be Relevant").

The interpretation of a sentence in context requires knowledge of syntax, semantics,
and pragmatics. Even if the syntax and semantics of a sentence are correctly assigned
to it, based on its phonetic form, if the sentence is used inappropriately, then children
may not be able to assign it a grammatic representation without violating a pragmatic principle. (Similarly, it might turn out that children are forced to violate a pragmatic principle in order to accept a sentence.) In this situation, the child has to make a
choice: either ignore syntactic/semantic principles or violate the pragmatic principle.
There is no a priori reason to believe that all children will always choose to violate
just one of these kinds of conditions. When a child is forced to choose one of two
responses, each of which violates a principle, the child's response is not determined
by the Modularity Matching Model. In such a case, the child will presumably adopt
some (perhaps nonlinguistic) strategy for responding, sometimes accepting the sentence and sometimes rejecting it. It is crucial, therefore, to present sentences under
felicitous conditions in order to draw firm conclusions about children's syntactic and
semantic knowledge.

28.1 A Hypothetical Experiment

As usual, we will illustrate these points with an example. Here the example will be an
experiment that does not satisfy the condition of plausible dissent. Although this experiment is hypothetical, it is based on studies that have been reported in the literature. For example, it closely resembles the experiment by Lust, Eisele, and Mazuka
(1992), which was discussed in chapter 11.

For the hypothetical experiment, we will use the target sentence (1), which is
governed by Principle C.

(1)   He is showing Bert that the Ninja Turtle can play the trumpet.
       (a)   *Meaning₁: He is showing Bert that the Ninja Turtle can play the
              trumpet.
       (b)   Meaning₂: He is showing Bert that the Ninja Turtle can play the
              trumpet.

Principle C dictates that the r-expression, *the Ninja Turtle*, cannot have the same reference as the pronoun *he* in sentence (1). The pronoun must refer to someone not
mentioned in the sentence—say, Big Bird. As before, we refer to the meaning that is
ruled out by Principle C as meaning₁, and we refer to the meaning that is permitted
as meaning₂. Meaning₁ takes the pronoun to be coreferential with the r-expression;
meaning₂ takes it to be interpreted deictically. The null and experimental hypotheses,

Figure 28.1
The test sentence is true

and the outcomes they are associated with, can be summarized as follows:

- H_0: Children lack Principle C.
  Expected results: Children permit both meaning$_1$ and meaning$_2$.
- H_1: Children know Principle C.
  Expected results: Children permit meaning$_2$, but not meaning$_1$.

The first task of the hypothetical experiment is to test the availability of meaning$_2$. This interpretation of (1) should be available to children. To test for meaning$_2$, children could be asked if (1) is a correct description of the picture in figure 28.1. In the picture, Big Bird is pointing out to Bert that the Ninja Turtle is playing the trumpet.

So far, the experiment meets all of the methodological desiderata stated in previous chapters. Assuming that children consistently accept (1) as a description of the picture in figure 28.1, this pattern of behavior can be used as a baseline with which children's responses to another picture will be compared: namely, their responses to the same sentence (1) in a different condition, where (1) is associated with meaning$_1$

Figure 28.2
The test sentence is false

(the reading that is ruled out by Principle C). For example, the picture in figure 28.2 could be used to test the availability of meaning$_1$.

In figure 28.2, it is apparent that the Ninja Turtle is showing Bert that he (= the Ninja Turtle) can play the trumpet. This is meaning$_1$, the reading that is permitted if children lack Principle C. According to the condition of falsification, the sentence should be false on meaning$_2$. Put differently, the negation of (1), given in (2), should be a true description of the picture on meaning$_2$.

(2)   He isn't showing Bert that the Ninja Turtle can play the trumpet.

Clearly, Big Bird must again be the referent of the pronoun *he*. Therefore, (3) should be a true description of the picture. In figure 28.2, Big Bird is holding something in each hand; this prevents him from showing Bert that the Ninja Turtle can play the trumpet. Therefore, (3) is true.

(3)   Big Bird isn't showing Bert that the Ninja Turtle can play the trumpet.

The essential features of the experiment are summarized in (4).

(4)   Test sentence: He is showing Bert that the Ninja Turtle can play the trumpet.

    a.   Meaning$_1$, true
Context, part 1: The Ninja Turtle is showing Bert that the Ninja Turtle can play the trumpet.

    b.   Meaning$_2$, false
Context, part 2: Big Bird isn't showing Bert that the Ninja Turtle can play the trumpet.

We now turn to the condition of plausible dissent, which requires the truth of the test sentence on meaning$_2$ to be under consideration at some point in the trial. Subsequently, some event should occur that makes the sentence false on meaning$_2$. In the present experiment, the condition of plausible dissent dictates that sentence (1) should be under consideration in figure 28.2. That is, the proposition expressed by sentence (5) must be under consideration.

(5)   He (Big Bird) is showing Bert that the Ninja Turtle can play the trumpet.

It is here that the hypothetical experiment breaks down. There is nothing in figure 28.2 that puts the content of the test sentence under consideration on meaning$_2$. Because the condition of plausible dissent is not met, the remaining desiderata for the truth value judgment task are also flouted. Most important, because the condition of plausible dissent is not satisfied, it may be unclear to the child *why* the test sentence is a false description of figure 28.2. (Recall that the actual outcome of the story should make it clear to the child subject *why* the test sentence is false on meaning$_2$.)[1]

The failure (of the experimenter) to satisfy the condition of plausible dissent raises a problem for the child. For the child, the test sentence is a true description of the context only on an ungrammatical interpretation, meaning$_1$. The meaning on which the test sentence is grammatical, meaning$_2$, is not supported by the context, because there is nothing that can plausibly be denied. The experimental context therefore violates a pragmatic principle, namely, Russell's maxim that "perception only gives rise to a negative judgment when the correlative positive judgment has already been made or considered." According to the Modularity Matching Model, children should avoid violating syntactic and pragmatic principles, if possible. In the present circumstance, however, children have been placed in a predicament: they must choose either to violate the principles of grammar or to violate Russell's maxim. One option is to disregard the principles of grammar and select a meaning that, although ungrammatical, does not violate Russell's maxim. On this option, children must assign meaning$_1$, in violation of Principle C. Once this option is selected, though, the pragmatic condition of plausible dissent no longer applies, because the sentence is a true description of the context on this interpretation. A second option is to assign the interpretation provided by the principles of grammar, meaning$_2$, but to ignore the pragmatic infelicity of interpreting a sentence as a false description of the discourse context when the content of the sentence, on that interpretation, was not under consideration in the discourse. If children occasionally take the first route, choosing to violate their grammatical principles so as to make the sentence true in the context, this should not be held against them, in our view.

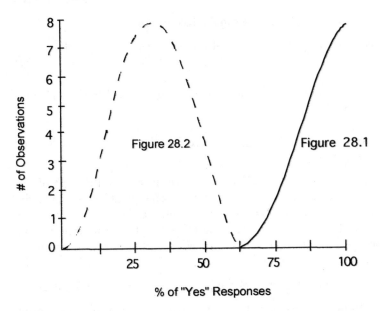

Figure 28.3
Predicted distributions of responses to pictures in figures 28.1 and 28.2 on the Competing Factors Model

On the basis of results in the literature, we feel confident in reporting the findings of the hypothetical study. In response to figure 28.2, children will give false positive responses roughly 25% to 35% of the time (cf. the 32% error rate in the study by Lust, Eisele, and Mazuka). That is, this is how often children adopt a strategy that leads them to accept ungrammatical sentences as true descriptions of contexts like figure 28.2, in violation of grammatical principles.

Children will correctly accept (1) in response to figure 28.1 much more frequently, however. The level of acceptance in that case should approach 100%. As a consequence, if enough children are tested on enough trials, the result will be a significant difference between the rates of acceptance of (1) in response to figure 28.1 and in response to figure 28.2. The distribution of responses will therefore be as shown in figure 28.3.

Now, we find ourselves in a predicament. On the null hypothesis, children should find test sentences like (1) ambiguous, permitting both meaning$_1$ and meaning$_2$. On the experimental hypothesis, children should permit only meaning$_2$. Therefore, to reject the null hypothesis, we must show that the pattern of responses in figure 28.3 is not also characteristic of the acceptance of both meaning$_1$ and meaning$_2$ for test sentences like (1). That is, we must show that the pattern of responses in the figure is not characteristic of ambiguous sentences. This is not easy to show, as we have pointed out. The problem is that it is sometimes difficult to distinguish preferences from principles—that is, whether a reading is present in the grammar but inaccessible, or absent altogether.

The confound between principles and preferences does not always get the recognition it deserves. It seems to be commonly assumed that where children can say "Yes," they will (e.g., Grimshaw and Rosen 1990). If a sentence is ambiguous, then both interpretations will be accepted in contexts that are appropriate for either reading. Therefore, many researchers maintain that if children accept a sentence on its grammatically correct interpretation significantly more often than on its ungrammatical interpretation in these contexts, then they have given evidence of their grammatical knowledge of the principle under investigation.

We disagree. Even in response to ambiguous sentences, children may exhibit a preference for one interpretation over the others in contexts that are appropriate for either reading. Of course, the relevant notion of "ambiguity" is relative to the child. A sentence is ambiguous in the relevant sense if the child has two interpretations for it, even if one of them is less accessible than the other. Suppose that meaning$_1$ is consistent with children's grammars, but that it is less accessible than meaning$_2$. The accessibility of meaning$_2$ will be further heightened in response to figure 28.1, where it is associated with the "Yes" answer. If the preference for meaning$_2$ is not sufficiently strong, however, then meaning$_1$ will also be accessed some of the time in response to figure 28.2, because there meaning$_1$ yields the "Yes" answer. This pattern is depicted in figure 28.3.

28.2 How to Satisfy the Condition of Plausible Dissent

Now let us consider how the experiment could be designed properly. The key is to meet the condition of plausible dissent. Following the methodological prescriptions of chapter 27, the task is to partition the test sentence into a background and an assertion. Recall that the background is established by replacing a specific expression in the sentence by an elliptical expression. Several possible backgrounds and assertions for sentence (1) are given in (6)–(9).

(6) Background: He (Big Bird) is showing *so-and-so* that the Ninja Turtle can play the trumpet.
Assertion: Bert

(7) Background: He (Big Bird) is showing Bert that *so-and-so* can play the trumpet.
Assertion: the Ninja Turtle

(8) Background: He (Big Bird) is showing Bert that the Ninja Turtle can *do such-and-such.*
Assertion: play the trumpet

(9) Background: He (Big Bird) is *doing such-and-such.*
Assertion: showing Bert that the Ninja Turtle can play the trumpet.

28.3 Summary

We conclude with a list of the features of the corrected experimental design. We leave it as an exercise for the reader to put these features into a story format. We have chosen the background/assertion pair in (7). For now, the goal is simply to convey the main design features of the truth value judgment task. In later chapters, we will present further complications in design, including the reasons for selecting a particular background/assertion pair.

Here is a sketch of the design features of an experiment using the truth value judgment task to test children's knowledge of Principle C, as it applies to the sentence under consideration.

Test sentence: He is showing Bert that the Ninja Turtle can play the trumpet.

- Background
  Context, part 1: Big Bird is showing Bert that *someone* can play the trumpet.
- Condition of plausible dissent: Meaning$_2$ is under consideration
  Context, part 2: Big Bird could end up showing Bert that the Ninja Turtle can play the trumpet. (possible outcome)
- Condition of falsification: Meaning$_2$, false, *or* negation of meaning$_2$, true
  Context, part 3: Big Bird ends up showing Bert that someone besides the Ninja Turtle can play the trumpet. (actual outcome)
- Final event: Meaning$_1$, true, but violates Principle C
  Context, part 4: The Ninja Turtle shows Bert that he (the Ninja Turtle) can play the trumpet.

Notice that these features of the experimental design cannot be satisfied within the confines of a static picture. At the very least, a series of pictures would be necessary, showing the transition through a number of events. In our view, telling the story in a dynamic fashion with toys and props is the easiest way to satisfy the experimental conditions.

Chapter 29

Strong Crossover

Principle C governs the interpretation of certain complex *wh*-questions called *crossover* questions. The kind of crossover questions that have been investigated with children include indirect questions like (1), for reasons that will become clear later.

(1)   I know who he thinks has the best smile.

In stating (1), the speaker presupposes that the referent of the pronoun *he* is not among the individual(s) who he thinks has the best smile. This is reminiscent of the disjoint reference between the pronoun *he* and the r-expression, *the Troll*, in the corresponding declarative.

(2)   I know he thinks the Troll has the best smile.

Assuming the trace theory of movement, we can use the same constraint, Principle C, to explain the anaphoric prohibitions in both constructions—that is, why the pronoun in (1) cannot be anaphorically related to the *wh*-phrase, and why the pronoun in (2) cannot be coreferential with the r-expression. According to the trace theory of movement, the *wh*-phrase in (1) originates in the same position occupied by the r-expression in (2).

(3)   I know he$_j$ thinks who$_i$ has the best smile
      (cf. I know he$_j$ thinks the Troll$_i$ has the best smile.)

In deriving the indirect question (1) from its underlying representation (3), the *wh*-phrase is moved, "crossing over" the pronoun, to its surface position (hence the name "crossover" question). As the *wh*-phrase moves, however, it leaves a "trace" behind at the site of origin. Given the obvious similarities between the indirect crossover question in (1) and its declarative counterpart in (2), and in light of the fact that anaphoric relations are restricted in both constructions, an attempt to unify them is warranted. Chomsky (1981) advanced the proposal that Principle C governs anaphoric relations in both constructions. To make this proposal work, only one further assumption was needed, namely, that the trace of *wh*-movement is an r-expression. If the trace in (4) is an r-expression, then it has the same status as the r-expression, *the Troll*, in (2); the trace would be subject to Principle C, which would require it to be disjoint in reference from any pronoun that c-commands it. The c-command relations can be seen in the simplified tree diagram in (4). **P** identifies the position of the pronoun, and **R** the position of the r-expression, in this case the *wh*-trace.

(4)

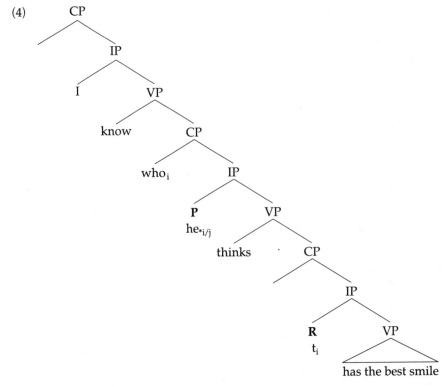

When the *wh*-trace is c-commanded by the pronoun, as it is in crossover sentences, the pronoun cannot be coindexed with *who*, as shown in (5a), because this configuration violates Principle C. The sentence is perfectly grammatical if the pronoun has a different index, as shown in (5b).

(5) a.   *I know who$_i$ he$_i$ thinks t$_i$ has the best smile.
     b.   I know who$_i$ he$_j$ thinks t$_i$ has the best smile.

The prohibition on anaphoric relations in sentences like (1), where the pronoun c-commands the trace, is stronger than it is in a related crossover configuration like (6) (where the pronoun does not c-command the *wh*-trace). Therefore, questions like (5a) are called *strong crossover questions*, whereas ones like (6) are called *weak crossover questions*.

(6) ?I know who$_i$ [his$_i$ trainer] thinks t$_i$ has the best smile.

The focus of this chapter is children's knowledge of the constraint on strong crossover questions.

29.1 Children's Knowledge of the Constraint

In asking whether children know the constraint on strong crossover, we are dealing with knowledge of the form ⟨sentence, *meaning⟩. A certain well-formed sentence cannot receive one of the interpretations that would be permitted in the absence of the constraint. As with the noncoreference facts concerning declarative sentences, it has been maintained that Principle C also constrains anaphoric relations in indirect questions like (2). More specifically, it is proposed that the trace of a *wh*-phrase is an r-expression. Granting this, we can invoke Principle C to handle crossover sentences, just as it handles declaratives. In crossover sentences, the pronoun c-commands the trace of the *wh*-phrase. If the trace of a *wh*-phrase is an r-expression, then the pronoun and the trace must be disjoint in reference, just as the pronoun and the phonetically realized r-expression in declaratives like (2) must be disjoint in reference. By transitivity, the *wh*-phrase and the pronoun are also disjoint in reference in crossover sentences. Because Principle C requires the pronoun and the *wh*-phrase (via its association with the *wh*-trace) to refer to distinct individuals, this prohibition on anaphoric relations is known as the *strong crossover effect*.

29.2 Bound Variable Questions

The constraint responsible for strong crossover effects, Principle C, does not pertain to sentences where the *wh*-phrase does not cross over the pronoun. Coreference between the pronoun and the *wh*-phrase is permitted, for example, in questions like (7). It should be noted that the pronoun in (7) can also be interpreted deictically. Nevertheless, we will refer to structures like (7) as *bound variable* structures, because they allow the other kind of interpretation as well.

(7)   I know who thinks he has the best smile.

(Compare the unambiguous question in (1), *I know who he thinks has the best smile.*) As the simplified tree diagram in (8) shows, the pronoun does not c-command the trace in the structure underlying (7). In the bound variable structure, the *wh*-phrase does not cross over the pronoun. The *wh*-phrase moves from the subject position of the embedded clause to the position for *wh*-phrases in the CP projection, leaving behind a *wh*-trace in subject position, the position labeled **R** in (8).[1]

(8)

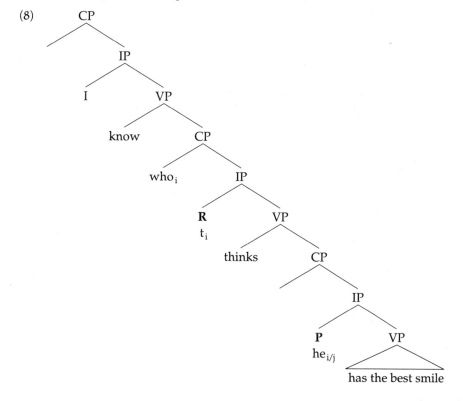

Because the pronoun does not c-command the trace, it can be coreferential with it. In sentences like this, the *wh*-phrase, *who*, and the pronoun *he* may pick out the same person, meaning I 'know who said that he, himself, has the best smile'. Another difference between the two constructions will prove important in the experiments we discuss. The crucial observation is that despite its singular form, *he* in questions like (7) can refer to more than one person. The speaker can say, without contradiction, "I know who thinks he has the best smile. The Troll, Grover, and Yogi Bear." That is, the pronoun can be interpreted as a variable, bound by the *wh*-phrase. On this *multiple referent interpretation*, (7) can be paraphrased as in (9). This is why such questions are frequently termed *bound variable questions*.

(9)   I know which *x* is such that *x* thinks *x* has the best smile.

The multiple referent interpretation is not permitted in crossover sentences. In (1), for example, the pronoun cannot be interpreted as referring to several people; this question cannot be interpreted to mean that several people think they have the best smile. The *wh*-phrase, *who*, can pick out several people, but not the pronoun. The pronoun, being singular, can refer only to one person. This difference between the possible interpretations of questions like (1) and (7) has been exploited in several experiments with children. The null hypothesis in these studies is that children will fail to exhibit strong crossover effects. If so, they should interpret questions (1) and (7) alike. On the experimental hypothesis, by contrast, children should display strong crossover effects in response to questions like (1), rejecting the multiple referent interpretation. However, they should permit this interpretation of questions like (7), to some degree. Children's level of acceptance of questions like (7), on the multiple referent interpretation, serves as a "baseline" against which to compare their responses to questions like (1) on the same interpretation. If the Modularity Matching Model is correct, children should prohibit the multiple referent interpretation of questions like (1), as should adults.

On the Competing Factors Model, the results of a (parametric) statistical test would suffice to establish whether or not children know the constraint on strong crossover. This conclusion would rest on the demonstration that children reject the multiple referent interpretation of strong crossover questions at a significantly higher rate as compared to the baseline (i.e., the rate of rejection for the bound variable questions). On the Modularity Matching Model, a significant difference in rejection rates would not suffice. This model has an additional requirement: that all children correctly reject the multiple referent interpretation of strong crossover questions 90% to 100% of the time.

29.3 *Previous Research*

Two previous studies have investigated children's knowledge of the constraint on interpreting crossover questions. These studies focused on the contrast between crossover questions, where a singular pronoun cannot refer to more than one individual, as in (10), and bound variable questions, where the pronoun can have multiple referents, as in (11).

(10)   Who does he think has a hat?

(11)   Who thinks he has a hat?

On the basis of findings from a comprehension study of the constraint responsible for strong crossover effects, Roeper et al. (1984) concluded that children interpret crossover questions and bound variable questions in the same way. According to these authors (also see de Villiers, Roeper, and Vainikka 1990), children interpret the pronoun as bound by the *wh*-phrase. This conclusion is based on the claim that children accept multiple referent answers to crossover questions like (10). However, as McDaniel and McKee (1993) observe (also see Thornton 1990; Thornton and Crain 1994; Crain 1991), careful scrutiny of the experimental results shows that few of the children tested by Roeper et al. gave multiple referent responses to crossover questions (only about 12 of the more than 100 child subjects).

A subsequent study was conducted by McDaniel and McKee (1993). They investigated children's comprehension of crossover and bound variable questions using a different experimental technique. Instead of having children evaluate the truth of the puppet's statement, they had them judge the "appropriateness" of a particular answer to both kinds of questions. On a typical trial, one experimenter acted out a scenario with toy figures and props while two puppets (played by the second experimenter) and the child looked on. After each story was acted out, the first puppet asked the second a question about what had happened. That puppet's reply, although true, was either appropriate to the question or not.

(12) a. *Bound variable*
          Who said he was under the blanket?
          Answer: He did and he did.

      b. *Crossover*
          Who did he say was under the blanket?
          Answer: *He did and he did.

The critical question/answer pairs were the crossover trials, as in (12b); the bound variable trials served as controls. As McDaniel and McKee observe, the multiple referent answer ("He did and he did") is appropriate for bound variable questions, but not for crossover questions. This is because bound variable questions can contain a bound pronoun, whereas the pronoun in crossover questions cannot be bound; that is, the crossover questions display strong crossover effects for adults. The goal of McDaniel and McKee's study was to determine whether children show strong crossover effects. Lacking the relevant constraint, they would be expected to permit a bound pronoun, hence a multiple referent answer, to both question types. Children had the opportunity to demonstrate knowledge of the constraint by rejecting the multiple referent answer ("He did and he did") as inappropriate for crossover questions, but accepting it as an appropriate answer for bound variable questions.

To summarize the main finding, the mean level of performance for children in this study was 46% correct rejections of the answer "He did and he did" to crossover questions. A control group of adults performed slightly worse than this (38% correct rejections). Despite the high rate of *overacceptance* of the multiple referent answer by both groups, McDaniel and McKee claim that the findings demonstrate that both children and adults know the constraint on strong crossover. The reason is that both children and adults accepted the same answer significantly more often for the bound variable questions (90% acceptance by children, and 96% by adults).

McDaniel and McKee argue as follows: As long as children and adults perform with a similar degree of success in distinguishing crossover and bound variable questions, it can be inferred that both groups have similar grammatical competence, whatever their level of correct performance. Adults are assumed to know the constraint on crossover questions; therefore, if children pattern like adults, it is reasonable to infer that children, too, know the constraint. Failures for both groups are attributed to performance factors and should not be taken to indicate a lack of grammatical competence.

The Competing Factors Model clearly lies at the heart of McDaniel and McKee's argument. On this model, subjects are not expected to perform perfectly. As long as the level of performance by both children and adults is similar, and both groups distinguish crossover and bound variable questions to a significant degree, it is valid to conclude that both groups know the constraint.

In assessing linguistic competence, however, performance should be compared with the model that is being assumed. On the Modularity Matching Model, children (and adults) who know a grammatical principle will perform almost perfectly, at least if the experiment is constructed properly. According to the Competing Factors Model, too, a certain pattern of linguistic responses is anticipated. As noted in chapter 6, every subject should be influenced by the same set of competing factors, to a greater or lesser degree. Therefore, the pattern of responses across subjects in an experiment should approximate a normal distribution, with a single "group" behavior centering around a mean level of performance. Individuals will deviate from the mean only probabilistically (because of extraneous factors such as fatigue or lack of attention), such that a proportion of observations will taper off gradually from the mean in both directions. The result is a unimodal distribution.

Figure 29.1 illustrates the expected pattern of responses for the two constructions, by either group, according to the Competing Factors Model. It is this pattern of behavior that serves as the basis for McDaniel and McKee's conclusion that children know the constraint on strong crossover. The argument rests on the assumption that both children and adults display the same pattern of behavior, in which they respond differently to crossover and bound variable questions, accepting the multiple referent answer (i.e., saying "Yes") significantly more often for the bound variable trials.

On the Competing Factors Model, the anticipated pattern of responses for crossover questions alone is as illustrated in figure 29.2 (figure 6.3 repeated; see the discussion of the model in chapter 6). The mean rate of correct "No" responses for both groups should be above chance, with the proportion of responses due to error tapering off in both directions away from the mean. As the figure depicts, the Competing Factors Model allows that children could have a different "balance point" from adults, because children have less resistance to extraneous factors; if so, the contribution of grammatical knowledge to their behavior will be less.

The findings of McDaniel and McKee's study were not, in fact, as predicted by the Competing Factors Model. In figures 29.3 and 29.4, respectively, we report the responses to crossover questions by children and adults. As the figures indicate, the pattern of responses by both groups more closely approximates a bimodal distribution than a unimodal distribution. There are clearly two patterns of responses within each group in response to crossover questions. Some members of each group were successful in rejecting the multiple referent interpretation of crossover questions (and therefore in distinguishing them from bound variable questions). However, other

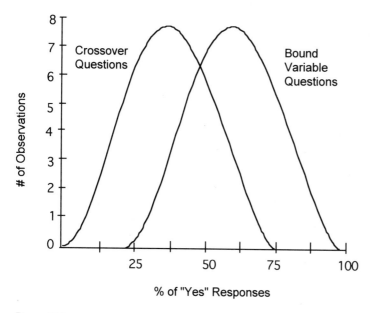

Figure 29.1
Predicted distributions of responses to crossover and bound variable questions

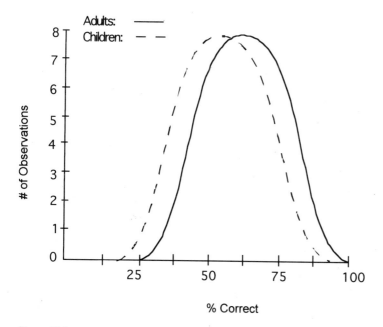

Figure 29.2
Predicted distributions of responses to crossover questions by children and adults, according to the Competing Factors Model

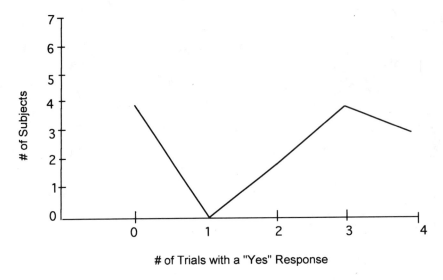

Figure 29.3
Distribution of children's responses to crossover questions

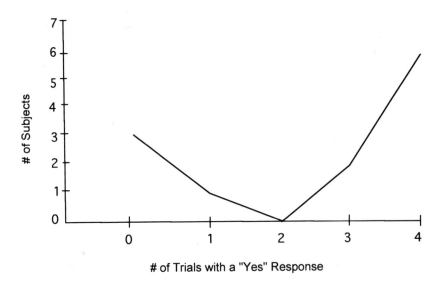

Figure 29.4
Distribution of adults' responses to crossover questions

members of each group did not, in the main, reject the multiple referent interpretation of crossover questions.

Both children and adults responded more accurately, and more consistently, to bound variable questions. However figure 29.3 indicates that 7 children accepted the multiple referent answer to crossover questions at least 75% of the time; and figure 29.4 indicates that 8 of the 12 adults accepted such an answer at least 75% of the time. Clearly, there was no substantial difference in performance by these children and adults in responding to bound variable questions and crossover questions. Although it may be reasonable to infer that the adults who performed poorly in responding to crossover questions nevertheless know Principle C, the observation that a group of children also performed poorly does not license the inference that they, too, know Principle C. Obviously, something about the task used in this study prevented even the majority of adult subjects from displaying grammatical competence.

Given the poor performance by half of the children and three-quarters of the adults, one might ask how both groups could show a significant difference in responding to crossover questions and bound variable questions. The answer is that McDaniel and McKee applied a statistic (the sign test) that discards any subject who performs at the same level of success on both constructions. Consequently, subjects were excluded if they answered "Yes" *incorrectly* to crossover questions just as often as they answered "Yes" *correctly* to bound variable questions. This left only subjects who treated the two constructions differently, and the majority of these subjects did answer "Yes" at least once more in responding to the bound variable questions than to the crossover questions. The research issue, however, is whether or not children interpret crossover questions and bound variable questions in the same way. The null hypothesis is that they do, assigning multiple referent answers to both. The experimental hypothesis, as advanced by McDaniel and McKee, is that children (and adults) analyze the two constructions differently, rejecting the multiple referent answer significantly more often for crossover questions than for bound variable questions. It is clearly inappropriate to use a statistic that discards subjects who disconfirm the experimental hypothesis.

Despite the overall similarity in the linguistic behavior of children and adults, the fact that the distribution of scores for both groups forms a bimodal distribution nullifies the validity of McDaniel and McKee's argument. The validity of the argument rests on the assumption that responses by both children and adults form unimodal distributions, as predicted by the Competing Factors Model. If this had been the pattern of results, with both children and adults successfully distinguishing between bound variable and crossover questions, then the logic used by McDaniel and McKee might have been warranted on the Competing Factors Model (but see Crain and Wexler, forthcoming).

Another feature of McDaniel and McKee's study also demonstrates their adherence to the Competing Factors Model. Acknowledging that both children and adults made a high number of errors, the authors remark:

> We think that such subjects may not be retaining the form of the question, i.e., they unconsciously change the word order of the question to match the answer. (p. 288)

The idea is that children and adults unconsciously change the word order of the crossover question, "Who did he say was under the blanket?" such that it becomes the bound variable question "Who said he was under the blanket?" Although this way of explaining data is consistent with the Competing Factors Model, the Modularity Matching Model is incapable of making such a claim. On the Modularity Matching Model, the processing of unambiguous sentences, such as the crossover questions in the present study, is not open to extragrammatical influences such as the apparent lack of fit between a question and its associated answer.

This concludes our discussion of previous research on children's knowledge of the constraint on strong crossover. The findings, which purport to support the Competing Factors Model, do not in fact support it. Neither do they seem to support the Modularity Matching Model. For this, we need to adopt a different experimental design, as described in the next chapter. As we will show, changing the experimental design leads to findings that are more in line with the predictions of Universal Grammar, and with the Modularity Matching Model.

Chapter 30

Strongest Crossover

In this chapter, we present a new experiment to investigate children's knowledge of the constraint on strong crossover. We describe the details of the entire experiment: the hypotheses, experimental design, results, and data analysis. As we lay out the experiment, we will check to see that we have satisfied all the items on our methodological checklist, in particular, the need to establish a baseline control and to fulfill the condition of falsification and the condition of plausible dissent.

The experiment presented here takes the lead from McDaniel and McKee's (1993) insightful observation that the constraint must be tested by homing in on the one place where a difference in the interpretations permitted for crossover and bound variable questions is perceivable: the possibility of a multiple referent response. McDaniel and McKee achieved this by having one puppet ask a question and a second puppet give the multiple referent answer. Children were to judge the appropriateness of the second puppet's answer. As it turned out, however, the situations were complicated, and both children and adults had a great deal of difficulty judging the appropriateness of the second puppet's responses. An important innovation that we made in the experiment described here was to simplify the experiment by using just one puppet, Kermit the Frog. By embedding the crossover question under the carrier phrase "I know who...," we were able to have the experimenter playing Kermit the Frog control both parts of the question/answer pair. That is, Kermit the Frog would say something like, "I know who he said has the best food. Grover and Yogi Bear." In addition, we introduced a truth value judgment task; children were judging whether or not the character referred to by *he* had, in fact, said that Grover and Yogi Bear had the best food.

Our new experimental design examines afresh the experimental and null hypotheses that Roeper et al. (1984) and McDaniel and McKee (1993) had tested.[1] The experimental hypothesis is that children have knowledge of the constraint on strong crossover (as stated in Principle C of the binding theory). In this case, children will not treat crossover and bound variable question/answer pairs alike. Crossover sentences will not be treated as ambiguous sentences because the constraint on strong crossover will exclude the multiple referent interpretation of the pronoun. On the other hand, bound variable questions will be ambiguous. They allow the pronoun to be treated as a bound variable, which gives rise to the multiple referent response; in addition, these questions allow a deictic interpretation of the pronoun.

    (1) *Crossover*
        I know who he said has the best food.
        a.   *I know <u>who he</u> said <u>t</u> has the best food.
        b.   I know <u>who</u> he said <u>t</u> has the best food.

(2) *Bound variable*
     I know who said he has the best food.
     a.   I know <u>who</u> said <u>he</u> has the best food.
     b.   I know <u>who</u> said he has the best food.

According to the null hypothesis, children should not distinguish the interpretations permitted for crossover and bound variable question/answer pairs. On this hypothesis, children lack the constraint on strong crossover, so nothing prevents them from assigning the multiple referent answer to a crossover question. The pronoun can be treated both as a bound variable and as a deictic pronoun. It follows from this hypothesis that both the crossover and bound variable questions will be ambiguous for children. The null and experimental hypotheses are summarized as follows:

- H_0: Children treat crossover and bound variable questions alike.
  Expected results: Children should allow the multiple referent response for both crossover and bound variable questions.
- H_1: Children distinguish crossover questions and bound variable questions.
  Expected results: Children should not allow the multiple referent response for crossover questions.

30.1 Design

As is usual in experimental studies using the truth value judgment task, the experiment described here consists of a series of trials in which a story is acted out with toys and props. The story contexts make available both the meaning ruled out by the constraint and the meaning permitted by the constraint. In the experiment, the meanings that children do and do not allow are studied by examining the answers that they allow for crossover and bound variable questions. Following the requirement that we be conservative in testing the experimental hypothesis (in order to avoid type I errors), the question/answer pair that is ruled out by the constraint on strong crossover is designed to evoke a "Yes" response from children, and the question/answer pair allowed by the adult grammar is designed to evoke a "No" response.

At issue is whether or not children allow the same interpretations for crossover and bound variable questions. Since this is the issue, it is important to make sure that the context is kept constant in our experimental test of both question types. Our test of the multiple referent response for bound variable questions should incorporate exactly the same "stories." In designing the crossover part of the experiment, we designated the multiple referent response as the "Yes" response since this is the response associated with *lack* of the constraint on strong crossover. Since we must keep the story contexts constant, the multiple referent response must also be associated with the "Yes" response in our test of bound variable questions. Both meaning$_1$ and meaning$_2$ are permitted by the grammar in this case. The design for investigating the constraint on crossover questions is as follows:

*Meaning$_1$, true: Multiple referent answers to crossover questions
Meaning$_2$, false: Deictic answers to crossover questions

There is another important reason for having the multiple referent response of bound variable questions set up as the "Yes" response. This allows us to establish a baseline for children's acceptance of the bound variable interpretation. Recall that in order to effectively demonstrate knowledge of a constraint, we need to show that children override whatever tendency they have to assign a particular interpretation, in order to obey the constraint. Here, we need to show that children have some tendency to assign the multiple referent interpretation of bound variable questions, a tendency that is absent in their responses to crossover questions. The experimental hypothesis will be supported if children say "Yes" to the multiple referent answer for bound variable question/answer pairs a significant proportion of the time, but "No" to the multiple referent answer for crossover question/answer pairs 90% to 100% of the time. If the null hypothesis is correct, children will say "Yes" to both the crossover and bound variable question/answer pairs. Children who do not easily access the multiple referent interpretation of bound variable questions will interpret the pronoun as deictic. This will cause them to reject the multiple referent answer, in which case we must eliminate their data from our evaluation of knowledge of the constraint on strong crossover.[2]

The design of the experiment allows the multiple referent response for crossover questions, the multiple referent response for bound variable questions, and the deictic response to both types of questions all to be tested following the same story. Naturally, we do not want to present children with the same story three times to test the possibilities their grammars permit. This is boring for children, and it is unlikely that they will pay close attention to Kermit's question/answer pair if the story being narrated is not novel. Instead, we want to use the same design, but change the "theme" of the stories by substituting different characters. In all essential respects, the stories are identical. This means that in principle, any story can be used for any question/answer pair. Children can pick the bag of toys that looks interesting to them, and that story can be accompanied by a crossover question/answer pair, or a bound variable question/answer pair, or a deictic crossover pair, depending on what kind of question/answer pair is needed to complete the test battery. In this way, no story can be argued to favor a particular response.

30.2   The Experiment

We now turn to specifics of the experiment. In the design we developed, each story depicts some kind of competition. Four characters are required altogether: a judge and three contestants. The judge checks all the contestants, openly rejecting two of them and settling on a "winner" of the contest. The "would-be" winners dispute the judge's decision by pointing out to him that his decision is mistaken and that they should have been chosen instead. Because the story focuses on the judge's decision, the judge is made salient as the discourse referent for *he* in the crossover question. In the typical protocol that follows, the judge, the Joker, decides which contestant has the best food.

(3)   *Protocol*

Experimenter   Last year the Joker was chosen as the winner of the best food contest. That makes him this year's judge of the best food. Here are the three people in the contest: Grover, one of the Teenage Mutant Ninja Turtles, and Yogi Bear. The Joker walks over to each contestant in turn. To Grover, "So you have a cookie. Cookies taste yummy, but they're bad for your teeth. Cookies aren't a good food." To Yogi Bear, "A hot dog. I love hot dogs, but they have a lot of bad stuff in them." Then, he looks at the Ninja Turtle and says, "Pizza. That's good. It has cheese on it. That's good for you. And it even has vegetables—green pepper and onions. You definitely have the best food." But Grover says, "Joker, you're wrong. I have the best food. Cookies are great. They give you a lot of energy." And Yogi Bear says, "No, I have the best food, Joker. Hot dogs come with ketchup and mustard. They're kind of like vegetables."

    a.   *Crossover trial*
        Kermit I know who he said has the best food. Grover and Yogi Bear.
        Child NO.
        Experimenter What really happened?
        Child The Joker said that he ⟨pointing to the Ninja Turtle⟩ has the best food.

    b.   *Deictic crossover trial*
        Kermit I know who he said has the best food. The Ninja Turtle.
        Child YES.

    c.   *Bound variable trial: Multiple referent response*
        Kermit I know who said he has the best food. Grover and Yogi Bear.
        Child YES.

    or,

    d.   *Bound variable trial: Deictic response*
        Kermit I know who said he has the best food. Grover and Yogi Bear.
        Child NO.
        Experimenter What really happened?
        Child He ⟨pointing to the Joker⟩ said that the Ninja Turtle has the best food.

Now, does the experiment satisfy the various conditions outlined in previous chapters? At issue in the story is who the Joker said has the best food. The background and assertion for this story are summarized in (4):

(4)   Background: I know who the Joker said has the best food. *So-and-so.*
        Assertion: Grover and Yogi Bear

In order to satisfy the condition of falsification, the question/answer pair must be false on meaning₂; or, put the other way around, the negation of meaning₂ must be true. So it has to be true that the Joker didn't say that Grover and Yogi Bear have the best food. This is true in the story; the Joker explicitly named the Ninja Turtle as having the best food, not Grover and Yogi Bear.[3]

(5)   Test sentence: I know who he said has the best food. Grover and Yogi Bear.

    a. Meaning₁ true
        Context, part 1: Grover and Yogi Bear each say that they have the best food.

    b. Meaning₂ false
        Context, part 2: The Joker doesn't say that Grover and Yogi Bear have the best food.

Next, let us check to make sure that the condition of plausible dissent is fulfilled. That is, the truth of the test question/answer pair should be under consideration at some point in the trial. This occurs. The Joker considers Grover's and Yogi Bear's food and says that he likes cookies and hot dogs. So the Joker might have chosen Grover and Yogi Bear; but in the end, he rejects them.

Several other features of the task deserve comment. First, some event takes place that makes the sentence false on meaning$_2$. This happens when the Joker rejects Grover's and Yogi Bear's food as not being the best. Second, there is a reason for rejecting cookies and hot dogs as the best food. The Joker goes through his reasoning in the story: cookies are bad for people's teeth, and hot dogs are full of "bad stuff" (preservatives). Third, after the Joker chooses the Ninja Turtle as the winner of the contest, the experimenter ensures that he remains beside the Ninja Turtle in the workspace. This is a record of the events that took place. Finally, the last-mentioned event in each scenario is the complaint by the two "losers" of the contest. These are the two characters named by Kermit in his explanation of the story. This event is placed last to put the pragmatic focus on these characters, so that the incorrect interpretation of the sentence is promoted, if it is consistent with a child's grammar. The question is whether children's knowledge of Principle C will cause them to override this pragmatic bias and reject the multiple referent interpretation.

30.3 Subjects and Procedures

The subjects who participated in the experiment were 12 children attending a pre-school.[4] These children ranged in age from 3;7 to 4;8 (average 4;2). The children were tested individually, in a quiet room at their school.

The experiment was divided into two sessions. In the first session, children were presented with four target crossover questions (to which they would respond "No" if their grammar included the constraint on strong crossover) and two deictic crossover controls (to which the correct response was "Yes"). The bound variable controls were tested on the same children in a separate session, so this was a within-subjects design.[5] There were two bound variable controls.

30.4 Results

The children were steadfast in rejecting the multiple referent answer to crossover questions, children accepting it on only 8% of the trials. In addition, the children had no difficulty accessing the deictic interpretation of the pronoun in crossover questions. This was accepted by all children on all trials, 100% of the time. The multiple referent interpretation of bound variable questions was accepted less often, 50% of the time when the bound variable interpretation was true in the context. These results are summarized in table 30.1.

30.5 Analyzing the Data

At first glance, it appears that the experimental hypothesis is confirmed. According to the experimental hypothesis, children should not treat crossover questions and bound variable questions alike. This was so. Crossover question/answer pairs were accepted only 8% of the time, and bound variable question/answer pairs were accepted 50% of the time. We should be wary, however, of how we interpret the 50% acceptance rate for the bound variable question/answer pairs.

Table 30.1
Group results for 12 children

Type of response	% acceptance
Multiple referent response for crossover questions	8
Multiple referent response for bound variable questions	50
Deictic response for crossover questions	100

In order to show that children have the constraint on strong crossover, we need to demonstrate that they allow the multiple referent response for bound variable questions, but not for crossover questions. To do this, it is sufficient to show that children can give the multiple referent response to bound variable questions on at least some proportion of trials.[6] Recall that the bound variable trials were ambiguous. The multiple referent response was set up as the "Yes" response, but there was another grammatical interpretation of the bound variable question. If children interpreted the pronoun as deictic, the sentence was false, and children would have said "No." Both interpretations were made available by the story context, and both constitute legitimate responses. Since the multiple referent response was set up as the "Yes" response, however, its availability should have been heightened.

An examination of the data from individual subjects showed that not all 12 children accessed the multiple referent answer of the bound variable questions. Five of the children accepted the multiple referent response on both bound variable trials, and the other 7 children rejected it on both. For the 5 children who accepted the multiple referent answer to the bound variable questions, we have good evidence that they know the constraint on strong crossover. Narrowing our attention to these 5 children, we find that they accepted the multiple referent answer to crossover questions only 5% of the time, as compared with 100% acceptance of this answer for bound variable questions. These 5 children clearly dispute the null hypothesis, that children accept the multiple referent answer for both question types.

However, closer consideration of the data from the remaining seven children is essential, to assess what bearing, if any, these data have on the experimental and null hypotheses. These children did not accept the multiple referent interpretation of either the bound variable questions or the crossover questions.[7] The data from these children cannot either confirm or disconfirm the null hypothesis, that children will accept the multiple referent interpretation of both crossover and bound variable questions.

However, there are data that can, in principle, show that even these children are not treating the two sentence types in the same way. This lends indirect support to the view that these children, too, know the constraint on strong crossover. The data come from the elicited production component of the experiment that follows children's "No" judgments. Following a "No" response, children are always prompted to explain "what really happened" in the story. In rejecting crossover question/answer pairs like "I know who he said has the best food. Grover and Yogi Bear," the children correctly explained that Kermit the Frog was wrong because the Ninja Turtle had the best food (not Grover and Yogi Bear). Children's rejection of the bound variable question/answer pairs implied that these children were accessing the alternative deictic interpretation of the pronoun, as shown in (3d). That is, these children were interpreting the pronoun "he" in "I know who said he has the best food" as referring to the winner of the contest, the Ninja Turtle. Since it was the Joker who said the Ninja Turtle had the best food, the answer Kermit the Frog provides (i.e., "Grover and Yogi Bear") was wrong. By way of explaining why they rejected the question/answer pair, children pointed out that Grover and Yogi Bear didn't say the Ninja Turtle had the best food, the Joker did. If children were treating crossover and bound variable questions alike, presumably they would have rejected both sentence types for the same reason. This did not happen. Children's responses clearly indicated that they interpreted the two sentence types differently.

Chapter 31

Principle B

The interpretation of ordinary pronouns such as *him* and *her* is syntactically constrained by the binding theory. One restriction on the interpretation of pronouns is illustrated in (1), where *him* cannot refer to Geraldo.

(1) Geraldo admires him.
    a. Geraldo$_i$ admires him$_k$.
        (i.e., Geraldo admires Regis.)
    b. *Geraldo$_i$ admires him$_i$.
        (i.e., *Geraldo admires himself.)

It should be noted that the *form* of sentence (1) is not at issue. It is a grammatical sentence of English. A certain meaning cannot be assigned to (1), however: it cannot be used with the meaning that one and the same individual is the referent of the pronoun and the referent of the name. Sentence (1) does permit another meaning, however: one that takes the name and the pronoun to refer to different individuals. In short, there is a constraint on sentences like (1) to the effect that the pronoun must refer to some male individual who is *not* mentioned in the sentence. Therefore, (1) is considered to be ungrammatical *on a particular interpretation*. The constraint in question is Principle B of the binding theory. Principle B can be stated roughly as follows:

(2) *Principle B*
    If an NP c-commands a pronoun within the same clause, they cannot be
    coindexed; hence, they cannot be anaphorically linked.[1]

A simplified phrase structure tree for (1) is given in (3); the subscripts show that the pronoun cannot refer to Geraldo.

(3)

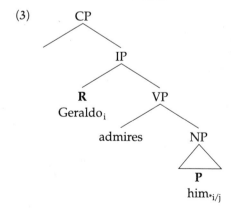

Notice that Principle B does not always prohibit pronouns from referring to individuals who are mentioned in the same sentence. In (4), for example, the pronoun
him can be used to refer to Geraldo, as in (a) (cf. (b)).

(4) Geraldo believes that Oprah admires him.
    a.   Geraldo$_i$ believes [that Oprah admires him$_{i/j}$].
    b.   *Oprah believes [that Geraldo$_i$ admires him$_i$].

Coreference is possible in (4) because the pronoun and the name *Geraldo* are in different clauses. This is illustrated in the phrase structure tree in (5). Of course, the pronoun
in (4) can also be taken to refer to some other male individual not mentioned in the
sentence, as shown by the *j* subscript on the pronoun.

(5)

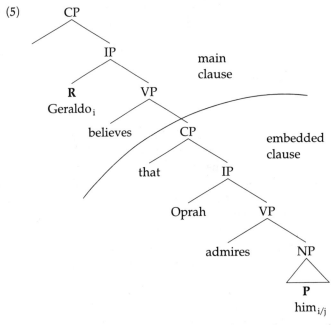

Passing over further details, we will consider another set of examples to which
Principle B applies.

(6) No talk-show host admires him.
    a.   No talk-show host$_i$ admires him$_j$.
        (i.e., No talk-show host admires Burt Reynolds, say.)
    b.   *No talk-show host$_i$ admires him$_i$.
        (i.e., No talk-show host admires himself.)
        but
    c.   No talk-show host$_i$ believes that Clinton admires him$_i$.

These examples show that Principle B also imposes a restriction on the interpretation of pronouns that co-occur with nonreferential NPs like *no talk-show host*.
Rather than referring to an individual or a set of individuals, (6) means that there is
no individual with the joint properties in question: being a talk-show host and admir-
ing some salient male person in the domain of discourse. NPs without inherent reference, such as *no talk-show host*, are called *operators* (or *quantificational NPs*). Principle B

pertains to the anaphoric relations between pronouns and operators, as well as to the anaphoric relations between pronouns and referential NPs. When a pronoun is anaphorically linked to an operator, it is called a *bound pronoun*.

One interesting property of bound pronouns, noted earlier, is that they are interpreted as variables. As a variable, the bound pronoun can range over several individuals. For example, even the singular pronoun *he* in (7) can be interpreted as a placeholder for every individual in the domain of discourse with the relevant property (possibly including females, if one uses *he* as a gender-neutral pronoun). In (7), the *wh*-phrase *who* is the operator that binds the pronoun (hence the term *bound variable question*). This bound variable question is contrasted with a crossover question like (8), in which the singular pronoun *he* can refer only to a *single male individual*.

(7)   I know who thinks he is intelligent.
      (i.e., Geraldo thinks so; Regis thinks so; ...)

(8)   I know who he thinks is intelligent.
      (i.e., Geraldo thinks Regis is.)

To help clarify matters further, we briefly sketch the semantic representation that is assigned to sentences with operators and bound pronouns. In the following examples, we use the variable x to range over individuals in the domain of discourse.

(9)   a.   I know who thinks he is intelligent.
           I know which person: x [x thinks x is intelligent]
      b.   Every talk-show host thinks he is intelligent.
           Every: x [If x is a talk-show host, then x thinks x is intelligent]
      c.   No talk-show host thinks he makes enough money.
           No: x [x is a talk-show host and x thinks x makes enough money]

31.1 An Alternative Form of Principle B

On the version proposed by Chomsky (1981, 1986), stated in (2), Principle B applies to pronouns that are c-commanded by either a referential NP or an operator. By contrast, Reinhart (1983b, 1986) has proposed a theory in which Principle B applies only to pronouns that are bound by an operator. On this account, as far as syntax is concerned, a referential NP and a pronoun in the same local context may corefer.

(10)   Geraldo admires him.
       a.   Geraldo$_i$ admires him$_k$.
            (i.e., Geraldo admires Regis.)
       b.   Geraldo$_i$ admires him$_i$.
            (i.e., Geraldo admires himself.)

On Chomsky's account, by contrast, a pronoun cannot be coindexed with a local referential NP, so only the (a) reading is possible.

Nevertheless, something in Reinhart's theory has to rule out coreference between a referential NP and a pronoun when they appear in the same local context. After all, the sentence *Geraldo admires him* has only one interpretation, at least for adult speakers. According to Reinhart, this is handled by a pragmatic rule, which she calls *Rule I*. Rule I allows speaker/hearers who are actively engaged in a conversation to figure out what coreference relations are intended by their interlocutors in cases where the syntax allows more than one option, as in (10). Essentially, Rule I instructs hearers to ascertain whether a reflexive pronoun can appear in the same position as the ordinary pronoun in a sentence; if both options are available, then the intended interpretation of the ordinary pronoun is one of direct reference (i.e., deictic).

The application of Rule I hinges on another pragmatic rule: "Avoid Ambiguity." Here is how Rule I works for sentence (10). Hearing (10), the listener reasons as follows: The speaker has chosen an ordinary pronoun, *him*, when a reflexive pronoun, *himself*, was also possible. If the speaker had intended coreference between *him* and *Geraldo*, the reflexive pronoun would have been selected, because it conveys this interpretation explicitly (without ambiguity). That is, a speaker who intended coreference would have said *Geraldo admires himself*, not *Geraldo admires him*. Since the speaker of (10) did not use a reflexive pronoun, the deictic interpretation of *him* is the intended interpretation.

This completes our remarks on the syntax and semantics of sentences accounted for by Principle B, except to add one remark about Reinhart's Rule I. Rule I is a pragmatic principle that requires the capacity to maintain two structural representations in mind at the same time. To apply Rule I to a sentence with an ordinary pronoun in it, one must maintain the representation of the actual utterance in memory long enough to decide whether another representation, with a reflexive pronoun, might have been produced instead. Grodzinsky and Reinhart (1993) contend that children know Rule I, but lack sufficient processing capacity to apply it. As children's processing capacity grows, their knowledge of Rule I becomes operative. We will return to this point below.

Now we are in a position to look at research studies on children's understanding of sentences governed by Principle B. It has been found that even children who adhere to other constraints on sentence interpretation (i.e., Principles A and C) appear to violate Principle B. This finding has been replicated in many studies and is attested in several languages (see, e.g., Avrutin and Wexler 1992; Chien and Wexler 1990; Deutsch, Koster, and Koster 1986; Jakubowicz 1984; Lee and Wexler 1987; McDaniel, Cairns, and Hsu 1990; McDaniel and Maxfield 1992b; Sigurjónsdóttir, Hyams, and Chien 1988; Thornton 1990). These findings and the research designs that were used to obtain them consume the remainder of the chapter.

31.2 Acquisition of Principle B

The research designs we discuss are concerned with investigating children's knowledge of linguistic principles that prohibit the assignment of certain meanings to sentences, that is, with ⟨sentence, *meaning⟩. Therefore, these designs attempt to assess the exact range of meanings that subjects can assign to test sentences. There are two basic procedures. In one, the same sentence is presented in different contexts; one context favors one interpretation of the sentence, and the other context favors an alternative interpretation. In the second procedure, two different sentences are presented in the same context, to see whether or not the sentences can be associated with the same meaning. With the context held constant, the observation that subjects respond to the test sentences differently can shed light on differences in their underlying grammatical knowledge. Similarly, the observation that subjects respond in the same way to different sentences, with context held constant, can also shed light on their grammars.

In the studies reviewed earlier, a sentence was matched against two different contexts: one corresponding to the sentence meaning that is prohibited by the linguistic constraint Principle B, the other corresponding to the sentence meaning that is permitted by the adult grammar. The two examples of studies using this research strategy were by Hirsh-Pasek et al. (1995) and Grimshaw and Rosen (1990) (see chapters 7 and 10). Another study of Principle B, by McKee, Nicol, and McDaniel (1993), used reaction time as the dependent variable (see chapter 7).

Probably the best-known result in the acquisition literature comes from a study by Chien and Wexler (1990) (see also Wexler and Chien 1985). In this study, children were shown pictures and were asked questions about the characters and events depicted there. In a picture designed to check children's adherence to Principle B, there were two characters: Papa Bear and a monkey. Papa Bear was shown covering himself, and the monkey was shown standing nearby, watching Papa Bear. The experimenter introduced the characters ("This is Papa Bear; this is a monkey"). Then children were asked the test question in (11).

(11)   Is Papa Bear covering him?

In response to questions like (11), many children between the ages of 3 and 6 answered "Yes," giving this answer 50% of the time or less. The correct answer is "No" for adult speakers, because the only possible referent for the pronoun in the picture is the monkey, and Papa Bear is not covering him. In other words, children are apparently able interpret the pronoun *him* as if it were a reflexive pronoun, linked to a referential NP (its antecedent). It should be noted, however, that these children are also able to assign the correct meaning to pronouns. So if Papa Bear had covered someone else, but not himself, these children would be willing to accept sentence (11) as a correct description of what happened. Because English-speaking children assign an "extra" meaning, beyond that of adult speakers, the error is one of semantic overgeneration.

This example of children's semantic overgeneration illustrates one horn of the language learnability dilemma: how children recover when they have overshot the target language. The example of children's interpretation of pronouns raises a different but corollary question: how children avoid undershooting the target language. One way to resolve this horn of the dilemma would be to claim that children are conservative, thereby avoiding the problem associated with syntactic and semantic overgeneration. As we have shown, this is not how children behave.

In sentences in which the pronoun is c-commanded by an operator, Principle B appears to be respected, however.[2] That is, the same children who accept coreference between the pronoun and the referential NP in (11), reject (12) as a description of a story in which every bear covers himself, and not the monkey.

(12)   Every bear covered him.

We are not out of the woods yet. There is still something to explain, namely, why children mistakenly permit coreference between a pronoun and a referential NP in sentences like (13) (but not between a pronoun and an overt operator in sentences like (14)).

(13)   Is Papa Bear covering him?

(14)   Is every bear covering him?

A serious learnability problem arises if one kind of explanation is pursued. For example, suppose that some children apply Principle B to bound pronouns only (see Wexler and Chien 1985). If so, these children not only assign the adult interpretation to sentences like (13), they assign a nonadult interpretation as well. This means that the evidence these children encounter will always be consistent with one of the interpretations they assign. In the absence of evidence from the environment that instructs children about what meanings cannot be assigned to sentences, these children would be hard pressed to jettison the incorrect meaning from their grammars.

An alternative explanation of children's response pattern avoids the problem of learnability. The proposal by Grodzinsky and Reinhart (1993) salvages children's grammatical knowledge by placing the blame for the problem elsewhere, in the domain of linguistic performance. Although children who respond incorrectly to sentences like (13) know pragmatic Rule I, according to this account, they lack the processing capacity to execute it. Recall that to apply Rule I to a sentence containing an ordinary pronoun, the listener must maintain the actual utterance in memory long enough to see if an alternative linguistic representation can be constructed for the sentence, one with a reflexive pronoun. According to Grodzinsky and Reinhart, some children cannot maintain the two representations in memory at the same time, so they cannot decide whether or not Rule I applies; consequently, they simply guess about the coreference relations between the pronoun and the local referential antecedent in sentences like (13). In short, on this scenario children know Rule I but lack the processing capacity to apply it. As the processing capacity of these children increases, however, Rule I becomes available for execution. Hence, the learnability problem is circumvented.

31.3 Conclusion

Even if children's failures are due to limitations in processing capacity, it should be clear by now that such differences between children and adults are not anticipated by the Modularity Matching Model. Therefore, the model would have to be amended if Grodzinsky and Reinhart's proposal turns out to be correct. Amending the model would be preferable to abandoning it altogether, of course. As we have stated, maximizing the similarities between children's cognitive systems and those of adults has the virtue of being responsive to the general problem of language learnability—the observation that all children successfully converge on an adult linguistic system despite the considerable latitude in their linguistic experience. To the extent that the cognitive mechanisms of children and adults are similar, the learnability problem is nullified. This is why we assume equivalence as the Null Hypothesis. By contrast, other models abandon the Null Hypothesis from the start. On these models, children differ from adults in language processing. Therefore, these models add unwanted degrees of freedom, by tolerating a wide range of processing explanations for differences between children and adults. In addition, they raise a new question to be addressed for each processing account: how do children modify or expunge their current processing system so as to converge on the adult system?

Chapter 32

Following Up on Principle B

The previous chapter reviewed a striking finding from the literature on language acquisition: namely, that some young children appear to violate Principle B in comprehending sentences with referential pronouns (e.g., Avrutin and Wexler 1992; Jakubowicz 1984; Wexler and Chien 1985; Chien and Wexler 1990; McDaniel, Cairns, and Hsu 1990; Thornton 1990). The result does not appear to be a methodological artifact. Even when tested in a truth value judgment task that pays attention to the condition of plausible dissent, the condition of falsification, and so forth, some children allow the pronoun *him* to refer to Papa Bear in response to sentence (1) as a description of a story in which Papa Bear covers himself.

(1)   Papa Bear covered him.

As noted, however, children appear to respect Principle B in sentences in which the pronoun is c-commanded by an operator (or quantificational element). That is, the same children who accept coreference between the pronoun and the referential NP in (1) reject (2) as a description of the same story, in which Papa Bear covers himself.

(2)   I know who covered him. Papa Bear.

A typical story that evokes this result might be as follows:

(3)   *Protocol for test of Principle B*
      Experimenter In this story, Papa Bear, Grover, and Big Bird decided to sleep outside one night, so they could see the stars. It was a very cold night, and after a while, Grover and Papa Bear began to shiver. Grover said, "Papa Bear, could you cover me with that blanket?" But Papa Bear said, "Sorry, Grover, but this blanket is not big enough for you too. I'm so cold, I will need the whole thing to keep warm. You'll have to get another blanket, Grover." "Here, Grover," said Big Bird. "You can have my blanket. I don't need it, because my feathers keep me warm. Lie down, and I'll cover you." ⟨Big Bird covers Grover⟩ Papa Bear said, "Are you all set Grover? Good. I'll lie down under my blanket, then." ⟨Papa Bear covers himself with his own blanket⟩
      a. *Kermit* I know what happened in that story. Papa Bear covered him.
      or
      b. *Kermit* I know who covered him. Papa Bear.

If children lack Principle B entirely, the test sentences in (3) should be ambiguous for them. In particular, they should be able to assign the interpretation in which the pronoun refers to Papa Bear; this interpretation would be in addition to the adult interpretation, according to which the pronoun refers to some unmentioned individual. In the story in (3), it is true that Papa Bear covered himself with a blanket. On the basis of the story, then, children who lack knowledge of Principle B should accept Kermit's assertions in (3a) and (3b). That is, it should be possible for them to interpret both "Papa Bear covered him" and "I know who covered him. Papa Bear" to mean that Papa Bear covered himself. On the other hand, if children have knowledge of Principle B, they should reject Kermit's description of the story in each case. When asked to explain what really happened, they should say something to the effect that Papa Bear didn't cover him (Grover), Big Bird did.

The finding reported in the literature is that children accept the illicit interpretation of "Papa Bear covered him," but reject the same interpretation of "I know who covered him. Papa Bear." Apparently, the difference hinges on the presence of the operator *who* in the latter. In sentences in which an operator binds the pronoun, even children who allow an illicit interpretation of certain sentences with referential NPs, in apparent disregard for Principle B, evidently obey the constraint.

A serious learnability problem arises for children who apply the constraint on the interpretation of pronouns to bound pronouns only. For these children, sentences with referential pronouns have a meaning that adults cannot assign. In other words, these children are committing semantic overgeneration. In the absence of evidence from the environment that instructs children about what meanings cannot be assigned to sentences, these children would be hard pressed to jettison the incorrect meaning from their grammars.

Several attempts have been made to explain away the learnability problem associated with children's apparent violation of Principle B in sentences like *Papa Bear covered him*. We will focus on only one: the acquisition scenario advanced by Grimshaw and Rosen (1990), responding to experimental data reported by Chien and Wexler (1990). Chien and Wexler tested children between 5 and 6 years old and found that they accepted sentences like (4a) about 50% of the time on the coreference interpretation. This contrasted with much lower acceptances, about 15% for the same interpretation, for sentences like (4b) in which the antecedent of the pronoun was an NP like *every bear*. Like the NP *no talk-show host*, the NP *every bear* does not have inherent reference and behaves like an operator.

(4) a. Papa Bear covered him.
     b. Every bear covered him.

Grimshaw and Rosen's account of Chien and Wexler's findings begins with sentences like (4a), with referential pronouns. They contend that factors such as intonation and pragmatic context may be responsible for the reduction in correct responses for some children to sentences with referential pronouns. For example, if stress is assigned to the pronoun in (4a), as in (5), then the pronoun and the name can be coreferential.

(5) Papa Bear covered HIM.

If children assigned stress to pronouns in experimental studies of Principle B, then this could have led them to make "errors" on such sentences. If so, one cannot conclude from their performance that they lack the grammatical constraint on the interpretation of referential pronouns.[1]

Still to be explained, however, is children's high rate of correct responses to sentences with pronouns that are bound by an operator, like (2) or (4b). Grimshaw and

Rosen's explanation has two parts. First, they argue that the linguistic factors (intonational and pragmatic) that may have contributed to children's poor performance in response to sentences with referential pronouns do not, by and large, apply to sentences with operators. Notice, for example, that *Every bear covered HIM* cannot mean that every bear covered himself, no matter how much stress is given to the pronoun.

Second, Grimshow and Rosen suggest that some children may have difficulty accessing the bound interpretation of a pronoun. In their view, this leads children to compute only the interpretation in which the pronoun *him* to refers to some male individual not mentioned in the sentence. In effect, sentences with operators are unambiguous for children, whereas sentences with referential NPs are ambiguous. This is why children reject sentences with operators more often than sentences with referential NPs; knowledge of Principle B is not at issue.

Let us consider what Grimshaw and Rosen's proposal means for an experiment testing children's knowledge of Principle B. In a truth value judgment task, the experimental design would be as in (6). The meaning ruled out by the constraint would be set up as true and would evoke a "Yes" response from children. This is the bound variable interpretation. The meaning that is allowed by the adult grammar would be set up as false and would evoke a "No" response.

(6) Test sentence: Every bear covered him.
   a. *Meaning$_1$, true
       Context: Every bear covered himself.
   b. Meaning$_2$, false
       Context: Every bear covered some other male.

In a truth value judgment task, we assume that children who lack Principle B will say "Yes" because they interpret the sentence to mean that every bear covered himself. A "No" response, on the other hand, is taken to mean that children *do not permit* the bound variable interpretation. Consequently, they take the only interpretation made available by the grammar. If Grimshaw and Rosen are correct, however, children's "No" responses cannot be interpreted as rejection of the bound variable interpretation (and as demonstration that the children know Principle B). Rather, children's "No" responses merely demonstrate that the only interpretation they can generate is false. In effect, the "No" responses reveal nothing about children's knowledge of Principle B. It is at least in part because these children's grammars lack the ability to form the binding relation between operators and pronouns that the children perform as well as they do.

This explanation of children's performance circumvents the learnability problem raised earlier. On this account, children's grammars do not overgenerate semantic interpretations of sentences. In fact, they undergenerate in some cases. Therefore, they will encounter the positive evidence that they need to extend their grammatical options; the evidence will consist of sentences with operators and pronouns where only the bound pronoun reading is true in the context.

Children who lack the capacity to form operator/pronoun relations will not have the full inventory of semantic interpretations for a host of constructions. For example, consider sentence (7).

(7) Every boy likes his dog.
   a. Every boy likes his own dog.
   b. Every boy likes a certain guy's dog.

For adults, (7) is ambiguous, with the interpretations paraphrased in (a) and (b). If Grimshaw and Rosen's account is correct, then some children at least will not have the bound pronoun interpretation, (7a), available to them at some stage of language development. In chapter 33, we will describe how to design a study that tests this prediction. (As far as we know, the study has not been conducted.) The design of the study proves to be quite complex. It is worth describing in detail, because it offers several valuable lessons on the appropriate use of the truth value judgment task.

Chapter 33

Sets and Circumstances

The truth value judgment task is used in this chapter to make the alternative meanings of sentences like (1) available.

(1) Every boy likes his dog.
    a. $Meaning_1$: Every boy likes his own dog.
    b. $Meaning_2$: Every boy likes a certain guy's dog.

On one meaning, the sentence (uttered by a puppet) is an accurate description of something that happened in the story that was acted out on that trial; on the other meaning, the sentence is an inaccurate description. The subjects' task is simply to respond "Yes" or "No" depending on whether they judge the sentence to be true or false. The null hypothesis is that children have both meanings available to them, just as adults do. The experimental hypothesis is that children have access only to $meaning_2$. The hypotheses take this form because we are adopting the viewpoint of Grimshaw and Rosen (1990), who maintain that children lack access to the bound variable interpretation of pronouns. In previous studies we have reviewed, children were also predicted to lack something, namely, a meaning that was ruled out by a linguistic constraint.

These considerations influence the decision about which meaning to associate with the "Yes" response (true in the context) and which to associate with the "No" response (false in the context). We continue to adhere to the research strategy of stacking the cards against the experimental hypothesis (to avoid type I errors); if it turns out that the findings favor the experimental hypothesis, the evidence they provide will be more compelling. Therefore, in the present experiment, the meaning that children are proposed to *lack*, $meaning_1$, corresponds to the "Yes" response. If the experimental hypothesis is correct, children will only assign $meaning_2$, interpreting the pronoun as referring to some salient male person not mentioned in the sentence. Therefore, the test sentence should be false in the story, evoking a "No" response on this interpretation. This part of the design is summarized in (2).

(2) Test sentence: Every boy likes his dog.
    a.   *$Meaning_1$, true
        Context: Every boy likes his own dog.
    b. $Meaning_2$, false
        Context: Every boy doesn't like a certain guy's dog.

Following these guidelines, let us construct the storyline. First, to make $meaning_1$ true in the story, we must establish that every boy likes his own dog. A child who allows this reading of the test sentence, contrary to the experimental hypothesis, should judge the test sentence to be true because of this part of the story. A "Yes" response would therefore be taken as evidence that the child is able to understand pronouns as bound pronouns. This brings us to meaning$_2$ and the condition of falsification.

33.1 *The Condition of Falsification*

The condition of falsification calls upon the experimenter to make the negation of (1) true in the context, on the interpretation that children have available to them according to the experimental hypothesis (i.e., meaning$_2$). The negation of (1) on this interpretation is (3).

(3)   Every boy doesn't like a certain guy's dog.

The problem is that (3) is ambiguous. The two interpretations are indicated in (4) and (5). In (4), the universal quantifier *every* is interpreted outside the scope of negation; in (5), negation has wide scope, as shown by the paraphrases.

(4)   Every boy is such that he does NOT like a certain guy's dog.
(i.e., All boys dislike the dog.)

(5)   NOT every boy is such that he likes a certain guy's dog.
(i.e., At least one boy dislikes the dog.)

Which of the two ways of negating the meaning of (3) should be used in the truth value judgment task? Should (4) be used as its negation, or (5)? To answer this question, imagine the thought processes of the child subject in the experiment. In part, the child might think:

Let me see. The puppet said, "Every boy likes his dog." This is either true or false. If it's false, then *every boy doesn't like his dog.*

The italicized portion of the child's thought process is ambiguous, however. The child will actually be following just one of these lines of reasoning:

(A)   The puppet said, "Every boy likes his dog." This is either true or false. If it's false, then *none of the boys likes that guy's dog.*

(B)   The puppet said, "Every boy likes his dog." This is either true or false. If it's false, then *at least one boy dislikes that guy's dog.*

It seems to us that the second line of reasoning is more likely, for reasons we take up next.

33.2 *Plausible Dissent: Choose the More General Reading*

At this point, we are considering how to satisfy the condition of plausible dissent for the sentence "Every boy likes his dog." In satisfying the condition of falsification, we are faced with an ambiguity: there are two possible ways to form the negation of the test sentence. Which of the two interpretations of (3) offers the better way to satisfy the condition of plausible dissent? We suggest that the negation of the sentence should correspond to the (B) reading, according to which at least one boy dislikes the guy's dog.

A

Every boy does not like his dog

B

Not every boy likes his dog

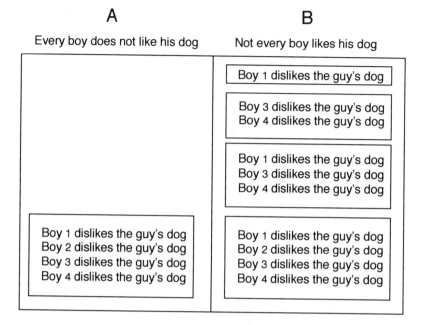

Figure 33.1
Sets of circumstances corresponding to the alternative readings of sentence (3)

To see why (B) offers the more natural way to satisfy the condition of plausible dissent, let us consider an example. In the domain of discourse, there are four boys. The (A) reading pertains to all four boys, and all of them dislike the guy's dog: boy_1 dislikes the dog, boy_2 dislikes the dog, boy_3 dislikes the dog, and boy_4 dislikes the dog. Therefore, there is just one circumstance that makes the sentence true on this reading. On the (B) reading, however, several circumstances suffice to make the sentence true. All that is required on this reading is that at least one boy dislike the guy's dog. Figure 33.1 illustrates four of the possible circumstances that could make the (B) reading true. Notice that one of them is that none of the boys like the guy's dog. That is, the (B) reading remains true even in the one circumstance that makes the (A) reading true: where all four boys dislike the guy's dog.

As noted in chapter 14, when a particular relation of entailments holds between the alternative readings of an ambiguous expression, the circumstances corresponding to the alternative readings exhibit a subset/superset relation. The relevant notion of entailment is as follows:

A reading Q of a sentence entails another reading R iff every circumstance in which Q is true is also one in which R is true.

To say that (A) entails (B), then, amounts to the claim that every circumstance in which "Every boy does not like the guy's dog" is true is also one in which "Not every boy likes the guy's dog" is true. This relation among circumstances does indeed hold. Consider the circumstances in which (3) is true on the (A) reading. In every one of these circumstances, all of the boys in the domain of discourse dislike the dog belonging to some salient male. Sentence (3) is also true on the (B) reading in all of these circumstances, because (B) requires only that one (or more) of the boys dislike the guy's dog. The point is that if every boy dislikes the dog, then at least one boy dislikes it. In short, whenever (A) is true, (B) is true also. Therefore, (A) entails (B).

The converse does not hold, however. That is, the (B) reading does not entail the (A) reading. For (B) to entail (A), it must be the case that every circumstance in which (B) is true is also one in which (A) is true. We can establish that (B) does not entail (A), therefore, by identifying some circumstance in which (B) is true but (A) is false. As figure 33.1 shows, there are three circumstances in which (3) is true on reading (B) but false on reading (A). On each of these, at least one boy dislikes the guy's dog, but not every boy does. According to the definition of entailment, then, (B) does not entail (A). In other words, if not every boy likes the guy's dog, it may nevertheless be false that every boy dislikes the guy's dog: even if not *every* boy likes the guy's dog, *some* boy might.

33.3 Entailments and Sets

In this section, we will indicate somewhat more formally how to determine which reading is the subset reading and which is the superset reading, based on the notion of entailment. First, however, a few definitions.

Ultimately, we are concerned with the meanings of one class of linguistic expressions, sentences. Another term that is used to refer to the meaning of a linguistic expression is *intension*. In addition to the intension (meaning) of a linguistic expression, many expressions have a *reference*, or *extension*. For example, the extension (reference) of an NP, such as *Bill Clinton*, is an individual, in this case Bill Clinton. The extension of a VP, such as *sleeps*, is a property that individuals have, in this case the property of sleeping. If an individual denoted by an NP has the property denoted by a VP, then the sentence consisting of that NP followed by that VP is true. For example, the sentence consisting of the NP *Bill Clinton* and the VP *sleeps* is *Bill Clinton sleeps*. This sentence is true if and only if Bill Clinton sleeps, and is false otherwise. On the basis of this observation, we will follow Frege (1893) in taking the extension of a sentence to be its truth value, either true or false.

In truth-conditional semantics, there is an intimate connection between the meaning or intension of a linguistic expression and its reference or extension. In short, the intension of a linguistic expression is a function whose value is its extension. For example, the value of the function associated with the intension of the NP *Bill Clinton* is Bill Clinton. If the extension of the function is its value, what is its argument? The argument is a set of circumstances, where a circumstance is a possible state of affairs, at a particular time. Now we can flesh out the notion of intension a little more. An intension is a function. The value of an intension is its extension, and the argument of the function is a set of circumstances. Putting the two together, it follows that the intension of a linguistic expression is a function from a set of circumstances to its extension. For example, the intension of the VP *sleeps* is a function from circumstances to properties of individuals, that is, a function that picks out the property of *sleeping* in different states of affairs and at different times (i.e., in different circumstances). Now, the NP *Bill Clinton* has the same extension in different possible states of affairs and at different times (it is a *rigid designator* (Kripke 1972)), but other NPs behave differently. For example, the NP *the president of the United States of America* has a different extension in different circumstances. Figure 33.2 summarizes this discussion. At the bottom of the figure we have separated out the intension of the special class of

Expression	Extension	Intension
NP	Individual	Circumstances ➡ Individuals
VP	Properties of Individuals	Circumstances ➡ Properties of Individuals

Expression	Extension	Intension
S	Truth Value	Circumstances ➡ Truth Values

Figure 33.2
Extensions and intensions for different kinds of expressions

Proposition = Characteristic Function of a Set

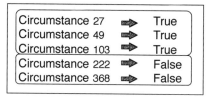

```
Circumstance 27    ➡  True
Circumstance 49    ➡  True
Circumstance 103   ➡  True
Circumstance 222   ➡  False
Circumstance 368   ➡  False
```

OR:

Proposition = Set of Circumstances

```
Circumstance 27
Circumstance 49
Circumstance 103
```

Figure 33.3
Two ways to think about propositions

linguistic expressions that we will be concerned with, sentences. Since the extension of a sentence is a truth value, the intension of a sentence is a function from circumstances to truth values. Following common usage, we will call the intension (meaning) of a sentence a *proposition*. Propositions are functions from circumstances to truth values. In other words, to know the meaning of a sentence (the proposition the sentence expresses) is to know those circumstances in which the sentence is true and those in which it is false.

Propositions can also be viewed as sets. That is, rather than viewing a proposition as a function from circumstances to truth values, one can view it as a set of circumstances, namely, as the set of circumstances in which it is true. As figure 33.3 illustrates, these two ways of looking at propositions carry the same informational content.

We are ready at last to state the relationship between entailments and sets. The definition of entailment can be revised as follows:

> A proposition Q entails another proposition R if and only if every circumstance in which Q is true is also one in which R is true.

or

> Proposition Q entails proposition R if and only if $Q \subseteq R$.

Also, we can now formally characterize the subset/superset readings of ambiguous sentences. For example, we have established that the (A) (=(4)) reading of (3) (repeated here) entails the (B) (=(5)) reading, but not vice versa.

(3) Every boy doesn't like a certain guy's dog.
     (A) Every boy is such that he does NOT like a certain guy's dog.
          (i.e., All boys dislike the dog.)
     (B) NOT every boy is such that he likes a certain guy's dog.
          (i.e., At least one boy dislikes the dog.)

Now we can state the subset/superset relation among these readings, based on the earlier definition:

> If reading Q entails reading R, but R does not entail Q, then Q is the subset reading and R is the superset reading.

By this definition, (A) is the subset reading of (3), and (B) is the superset reading.

On the basis of the joint observations that the (A) reading of (3) entails the (B) reading, but that the (B) reading does not entail the (A) reading, we can conclude that (A) is true in a subset of the circumstances that make (B) true (see figure 33.4). In some sense to be made clear, it is "easier" to make (B) true than to make (A) true. Therefore, we will call (B) the *general* interpretation and (A) the *specific* interpretation.

Having observed that (B) is a more general interpretation of (3) than (A), we can now say why people find it more natural to hypothesize (B). The reason is simply that people tend to prefer the more general interpretation of an ambiguous sentence. To explain this preference, we need only invoke an already familiar principle of

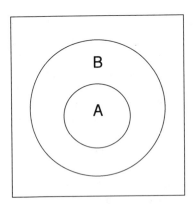

Figure 33.4
Specific and general interpretations

ambiguity resolution: the Principle of Parsimony. As mentioned in chapter 13, the Principle of Parsimony is motivated by the parser's desire to minimize the cognitive effort that is required to process sentences. Because of its inherent limitations in working memory capacity, the parser avoids unnecessary extensions to the mental model of the current conversational context, as much as possible. Thus, the principle can be seen as a "least effort" strategy for ambiguity resolution; it is designed to reduce the risk of making commitments that later need to be revised.

Adopting the strategy of minimizing commitments, the parser begins to construct discourse representations corresponding to all structural analyses of an ambiguous phrase or sentence fragment. Being unable to maintain multiple discourse representations in working memory for long, however, the parser rapidly abandons all but one representation. The decision about which representation to keep and which to discard is made by considering the sets of circumstances that make the sentence true on each discourse representation. Whenever the alternative sets of circumstances form a subset/superset relation, the parser selects the discourse representation that makes the sentence true in the largest set of circumstances. In other words, the parser opts for the more general interpretation of an ambiguous sentence. Figure 33.5 illustrates the subset/superset relations corresponding to the alternative readings of the classic garden path sentence, *The horse raced past the barn fell*. Appealing to the Modularity

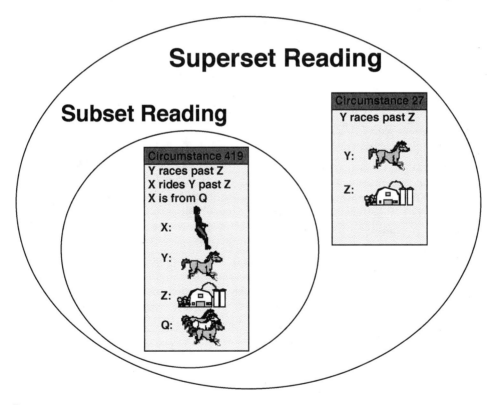

Figure 33.5
Subset and superset readings

Matching Model, we are assuming that children have the same parsing preferences as adults do. Therefore, children too should favor reading (B) as the meaning they assign to (3). Therefore, this is the reading to falsify in the experiment.

Perhaps another example will help to underscore our claim that the more general reading of an ambiguous sentence is the more "natural" interpretation. Imagine that you hear a used-car salesman on TV say, "Every car on the lot has under 100,000 miles on it." Later, you learn that the ad was taken off the air because it violated truth-in-advertising laws. Would you expect to find that the salesman had lied because in fact none of the cars on the lot had been driven under 100,000 miles? This would be the specific interpretation. Or would you expect to find that he had lied because at least some of the cars on the lot had been driven over 100,000 miles? This is the general interpretation. It seems to us that people favor the general interpretation of ambiguous sentences, that is, the reading that makes a particular sentence true in the largest set of circumstances.

33.4 Conclusion

This brings us back to the experiment. The test sentence (1) will be false on one interpretation. This means that the negation of (1) will be true. The negation of (1) is (3), which is ambiguous. Our present task is to decide which interpretation of (3) to use in the experiment, (A) or (B).

(1)   Every boy likes his dog.

(3)   Every boy doesn't like a certain guy's dog.
    (A)   Every boy is such that he does NOT like a certain guy's dog.
        (i.e., All boys dislike the dog.)
    (B)   NOT every boy is such that he likes a certain guy's dog.
        (i.e., At least one boy dislikes the dog.)

We are guided by the strategy of plausible dissent, which instructs us to identify the interpretation of (3) that children will find most natural. Because (B) is the general interpretation, it is more natural. Therefore, it will be easier for children to see why (1) is false if the (B) meaning of (3) corresponds to meaning$_2$. Since this meaning will be on children's minds, they will most easily grasp why it is incorrect, as dictated by the condition of plausible dissent. What should be true in the context, then, is that at least one boy dislikes the guy's dog (not for all of them to dislike it).

We end the discussion by adding a caveat. Our reasoning in selecting the general interpretation depends on two additional assumptions: that sentence (3) is ambiguous for children, and that children employ the same strategies for resolving ambiguities as adults do. Only if both of these assumptions are correct would we expect children to find it more plausible to deny (1) in circumstances corresponding to reading (B) of (3).

Chapter 34

Discourse Binding

Within the generative framework, many aspects of grammatical knowledge are represented as constraints, that is, as sanctions against linguistic analyses of one kind or another. Constraints are negative statements. It is safe to assume that not all children, perhaps no children, encounter evidence pertaining to constraints. The pertinent evidence would be information about which linguistic expressions and meanings are prohibited in the target language. It follows from the absence of such negative evidence in children's experience that knowledge encoded by constraints is not learned from experience. If not, then this aspect of linguistic competence must be innately specified, as part of Universal Grammar. This is the familiar argument from the poverty of the stimulus.

The poverty-of-the-stimulus argument and its conclusions are generally accepted within the domain of syntactic knowledge and have served as impetus for much research on the early emergence of syntactic principles. Similar research has recently been extended to children's mastery of semantic principles, although considerably less is known in this area. Still less is known about how knowledge of discourse principles develops. Nevertheless, certain discourse principles have been characterized as linguistic constraints and are therefore subject to the same poverty-of-the-stimulus considerations that apply to constraints within sentence grammar. In this chapter, we extend the poverty-of-the-stimulus argument to a specific discourse constraint, called the *closure constraint*. The closure constraint explains why the singular pronoun, *he* in the second sentence of discourse sequences like (1) and (2) cannot be anaphorically linked to the quantificational antecedents *no mouse* and *every mouse* in the first sentences.

(1) No mouse came to Simba's party. He was upset.
   a. No mouse came to <u>Simba</u>'s party. <u>He</u> was upset.
   b. <u>No mouse</u> came to Simba's party. *<u>He</u> was upset.

(2) Every mouse came to Simba's party. He was upset.
   a. Every mouse came to <u>Simba</u>'s party. <u>He</u> was upset.
   b. <u>Every mouse</u> came to Simba's party. *<u>He</u> was upset.

Application of the closure constraint is restricted to particular quantificational antecedents. The example in (3) shows that a singular pronoun *can* be related to an indefinite NP that appears in a preceding sentence. That is, the discourse sequence in (3) is ambiguous, unlike the sequences in (1) and (2).

(3) A bear sleepwalked into Genie's house. He ate the spaghetti.
   a. A bear sleepwalked into <u>Genie</u>'s house. <u>He</u> ate the spaghetti.
   b. <u>A bear</u> sleepwalked into Genie's house. <u>He</u> ate the spaghetti.

In addition, it is worth noting that the singular pronoun *he* can be anaphorically related to negatively and universally quantified NPs that appear within the same sentence, as (4) illustrates.

> (4) No/Every mouse at Simba's party said that he was upset.
>   a.   No/Every mouse at <u>Simba</u>'s party said he was upset.
>   b.   No/Every <u>mouse</u> at Simba's party said <u>he</u> was upset.

The closure constraint, then, restricts the range of possible antecedents of singular
pronouns in certain discourse sequences. In section 34.5, we report an experimental
investigation of children's knowledge of this constraint.

The application of the poverty-of-the-stimulus argument to principles of discourse is of special interest because these principles are commonly viewed as more
closely tied to experience than is syntactic or semantic knowledge. However, it is
important to distinguish principles of discourse that are gained through experience,
so-called real-world knowledge, from principles that take the form of linguistic constraints. Like other linguistic constraints, constraints on discourse representations
presumably cannot be learned through experience. We are therefore invited to draw
the same inferences about discourse constraints as we do for syntactic and semantic
constraints. Although discourse principles are not part of sentence grammar, they
constitute a substantive component of the language apparatus. Therefore, all things
being equal, knowledge of these principles should emerge early in the course of
language development. This conclusion is confirmed by the findings of the study
reported in section 34.5. The results support the view that the closure constraint
is part of Universal Grammar, that is, of the human biological endowment for
language.

34.1 Discourse Binding

The discourse constraint discussed in this chapter governs anaphoric relations between pronouns and quantificational antecedents. We have chosen to frame our discussion within the theory of discourse anaphora advanced by Chierchia (1995).
Because space limitations prevent us from offering more than a rudimentary sketch of
Chierchia's theory, we refer readers to his book for a more complete explication.

During a discourse with an indefinite NP, such as (5), the indefinite NP may establish a discourse referent to which a later pronoun can be anaphorically linked. In the
second sentence in (5), for example, the pronoun *he* can be interpreted as referring to
the boy introduced in the first sentence. Such anaphoric links will be represented by
underlining.

> (5) A <u>boy</u> walked in. <u>He</u> was tall.

In Chierchia's theory, each sentence in a discourse is partitioned into its usual truth-
conditional content, S, and a propositional variable, p (bound by a lambda operator,
omitted here). The propositional variable serves as a placeholder to be filled in by the
content of a subsequent sentence. The general operating principle of discourse binding is illustrated in (6): the propositional variable in one sentence in a discourse is replaced by the subsequent sentence, with its own propositional variable: q in (6).

> (6) $[S^1 \ \& \ p] \ [S^2 \ \& \ q] \Rightarrow [S1 \ \& \ S^2 \ \& \ q]$

By this process, the pronoun in the second sentence in (7) finds its way inside the scope of the existential quantifier, ∃, introduced by the indefinite NP, *a boy*, in the first sentence.

(7)   A boy walked in. He was tall.

As the logical representations in (8) and (9) indicate, the variable, x, in the second formula is brought within the scope of the existential quantifier in the first by lambda conversion; the once-free variable is now bound.

(8) $\exists x\ \lambda p[\text{boy}(x)\ \&\ \text{walked-in}(x)\ \&\ p]\ [\text{tall}(x)\ \&\ q]$

(9) $\exists x[\text{boy}(x)\ \&\ \text{walked-in}(x)\ \&\ \text{tall}(x)\ \&\ q]$

34.2 *Illicit Discourse Binding*

Referential dependence between a singular pronoun and some quantificational NPs is prohibited in discourse, however. Example (7) illustrates a construction in which a singular pronoun can be anaphorically linked to a preceding indefinite NP. By contrast, a pronoun cannot be linked to a quantificational NP in an earlier sentence, if this NP contains negation or a universal quantifier. An example of an illicit discourse sequence is given in (10).

(10)   No boy walked in. *He sat down.

Example (10) illustrates the closure constraint, which renders the scopal domain of these quantified NPs "closed" to pronominal binding. In Chierchia's system, this discourse constraint results from dynamic negation, ⌐. Dynamic negation proceeds in two steps: first, the existing propositional variable within the scope of negation is eliminated; second, a new propositional variable is generated in a different location, outside the scope of negation. These two parts of dynamic negation require two operators: ↓, which we will call the "cut" operator, and ↑, which we call the "paste" operator. The definition of dynamic negation is given in (11).

(11) $\lnot\ [S\ \&\ p] \Rightarrow {\uparrow}\lnot{\downarrow}\ [S\ \&\ p]$

Working from inside out, the "cut" operator first eliminates the original propositional variable, p, by saturating it with a tautology, T, which is subsequently dropped. This follows from the definition of ↓, the "cut" operator: $\downarrow S = S(T)$. After this operator has been applied, the "paste" operator, ↑, introduces a new propositional variable, outside the scope of negation. By definition, $\uparrow S = \lambda p\ (S\ \&\ p)$.

The dynamic interpretation of the first sentence in (10) is illustrated in (12).

(12)   No boy walked in.

$\lnot\ \exists x\ \lambda p\ [\text{boy}(x)\ \&\ \text{walked-in}(x)\ \&\ p]$	
${\uparrow}\lnot{\downarrow}\ \exists x\ \lambda p\ [\text{boy}(x)\ \&\ \text{walked-in}(x)\ \&\ p]$	by definition of ⌐
${\uparrow}\lnot\ \exists x\ \lambda p\ [\text{boy}(x)\ \&\ \text{walked-in}(x)\ \&\ p](T)$	by definition of ↓
${\uparrow}\lnot\ \exists x\ [\text{boy}(x)\ \&\ \text{walked-in}(x)\ \&\ T]$	by λ-conversion
${\uparrow}\lnot\ \exists x\ [\text{boy}(x)\ \&\ \text{walked-in}(x)]$	by law of identity
$\lambda p\ [\lnot\ \exists x\ [\text{boy}(x)\ \&\ \text{walked-in}(x)]\ \&\ p]$	by definition of ↑

When the second sentence is integrated with the first (by lambda conversion), the pronoun falls outside the scope of the quantificational antecedent. As shown in (13), the pronoun (i.e., the second occurrence of x) is free. This accounts for the fact that the pronoun in (10) cannot be anaphorically linked to the negative quantificational NP, *no boy*.

> (13)   ... He sat down.
> λp [$\neg \exists x$ [boy(x) & walked-in(x)] & p] [sat-down(x) & q]
> $\neg \exists x$ [boy(x) & walked-in(x)] & [sat-down(x) & q]

Similarly, quantificational NPs with a universal quantifier in one sentence cannot bind a pronoun that appears in a subsequent sentence in a discourse.

> (14)   <u>Every boy</u> walked in. *<u>He</u> sat down.

Anaphoric relations are prohibited in discourse sequences like (14), because the definition of dynamic universal quantification derives from that of dynamic negation: $\underline{\forall} \Leftrightarrow \underline{\neg} \underline{\exists} \underline{\neg}$.

34.3 *Discourse Constraints in Child Language*

The remainder of the chapter presents an experiment designed to examine the possibility that the closure constraint on discourse binding may be operative in the grammars of young children. The experiment was designed and conducted in collaboration with Laura Conway; indeed, she should be credited with many insights in the experimental design.

Considerations of language learnability in the absence of negative evidence invite us to expect that children will adhere to the closure constraint. In order to accept this experimental hypothesis, however, we must reject the null hypothesis, which is that children's linguistic behavior will include violations of the constraint. Turning this around, if the null hypothesis is correct, children will accept the bound variable interpretation of the pronoun in discourse sequences like (15).

> (15)   No mouse came to Simba's party. He wore a hat.
> a.   Meaning$_1$: <u>No mouse</u> came to Simba's party. *<u>He</u> wore a hat.
> b.   Meaning$_2$: No mouse came to <u>Simba</u>'s party. <u>He</u> wore a hat.

Children who lack the closure constraint will be able to link the pronoun in the second sentence of (15) to the quantificational NP in the first sentence. This will permit them to assign a reading to (15) that is not available to adults: meaning$_1$, which we will call the *bound pronoun* interpretation.

Another reading will be available to children who lack the constraint. On this reading, the pronoun refers to Simba. Since this reading, meaning$_2$, is given by direct reference, we will call it the *direct reference* interpretation. The anaphoric link between the pronoun and the r-expression *Simba* is indicated by underlining.

If children lack the closure constraint, they should find discourse sequences like (15) ambiguous. If they know the closure constraint, meaning$_1$ will not be accessible to them; the only interpretation possible for them will be meaning$_2$, just as for adults.

34.4 *Eliminating Alternative Hypotheses*

It is not straightforward, however, to reject the null hypothesis. Suppose that children consistently respond in an experimental task by assigning meaning$_2$. Although this could reflect their adherence to the closure constraint on discourse binding, we must be certain that they are not giving the "right" answers for the wrong reason. Other factors besides the closure constraint could cause children to consistently assign meaning$_2$ to discourse sequences like (15), despite the availability of meaning$_1$ in their grammars.

There are at least two alternative scenarios to consider. On both of them, children produce the "correct" pattern of responses, consistently assigning meaning$_2$ to the test discourse sequences. However, children's responses are not based on the closure constraint, but on some other strategy for interpreting pronouns in discourse. Therefore, experimental maneuvers must be engaged to untangle the effects of the closure constraint and these alternative sources of children's "correct" linguistic behavior.

One reason children might consistently analyze discourse sequences like (15) using meaning$_2$ is that, on this analysis, the pronoun in the second sentence refers to the most recently mentioned discourse referent. This kind of strategy for relating linguistic expressions is reminiscent of the Minimum Distance Principle (Chomsky 1969). Supposing that children systematically assign meaning$_2$ to discourse sequences like (15) (repeated here), we must be able to rule out this alternative explanation of their behavior.

(15)   No mouse came to Simba's party. He wore a hat.
    a.   Meaning$_1$: <u>No mouse</u> came to Simba's party. *<u>He</u> wore a hat.
    b.   Meaning$_2$: No mouse came to <u>Simba</u>'s party. <u>He</u> wore a hat.

To check for this possibility in the present study, items such as (16) were included as controls; we will call them *indefinite NP controls*. The closure constraint does not apply to the indefinite NP controls; the first sentence in (16) contains two legitimate discourse antecedents for the pronoun in the second sentence. Use of these controls therefore enabled us to identify any tendency children exhibited to interpret pronouns as referring to the closest preceding potential antecedent.

(16)   A bear sleepwalked into Genie's house. He ate the spaghetti.
    a.   *Closer antecedent*
          A bear sleepwalked into <u>Genie</u>'s house. <u>He</u> ate the spaghetti.
    b.   *More distant antecedent*
          <u>A bear</u> sleepwalked into Genie's house. <u>He</u> ate the spaghetti.

In the discourse sequence in (16), both the closer NP, *Genie*, and the more distant one, *a bear*, in the first sentence are potential antecedents for the pronoun in the second sentence. In designing the experiment, we decided to enhance the accessibility of the closer NP as the antecedent of the pronoun in the indefinite NP controls. To accomplish this, we made the referent of the closer NP the agent of the last event in the discourse context. For example, the last event in the context corresponding to (16) was performed by Genie, not by the bear. (This was not an event in which Genie ate spaghetti, however, for reasons that we will come to.) All things being equal, the interpretation associated with the last-mentioned event should be most salient; consequently, the closer potential antecedent should be favored over the more distant one in the ambiguous discourse sequences presented in the indefinite NP control condition. If children assign the more distant, indefinite NP, as antecedent for the pronoun, despite this contextual bias and despite the proximity of the other NP, then we can be confident that they are not relying solely on a parsing strategy such as the Minimum Distance Principle in assigning referents to pronouns.

All things are not equal, however. There is another important factor that biases children (and adults) toward one analysis of an ambiguous sentence rather than another. As noted earlier, (see chapters 6 and 26), children tend to resolve ambiguities by assigning whichever analysis makes the sentence true in the discourse context.

In experimental investigations with children, contexts are devised to make one meaning of a test sentence true and the other meaning false. In the present study, we adopted this research strategy, as follows: the second sentence in every discourse like (16) was false in the context if the pronoun was anaphorically linked to the closer NP; if the pronoun was linked to the more distant NP, the second sentence in the discourse was true. To the extent that subjects are influenced by the strategy of interpreting sentences in a discourse in a way that makes them true, then this should boost the availability of the representation in which the pronoun is linked to the more distant potential antecedent in the discourse (e.g., the indefinite NP in (16)).

There is a good reason for designing this part of the experiment in this way. In the test discourse sequences, the corresponding analysis that links the pronoun and the more distant NP is meaning$_1$, which is ruled out by the closure constraint:

(17)   No mouse came to Simba's party. He wore a hat.
       Meaning$_1$: No mouse came to Simba's party. *He wore a hat.

If children consistently establish anaphoric links between the pronoun and the more distant NP where this is permitted, as in (16), but refuse to do so where this is prohibited, as in (17), then we would have compelling evidence that they were adhering to the closure constraint, as long as alternative explanations of their behavior are ruled out.

There is a second reason why children might consistently assign meaning$_2$ to discourse sequences such as (15) that are governed by the closure constraint, despite the availability of meaning$_1$ in their grammars: their parsers might lead them to prefer the direct reference interpretation of pronouns over the bound pronoun interpretation. If this parsing preference exists, then children will assign meaning$_2$ on most trials; meaning$_1$ will rarely surface despite its availability in children's grammars.

One reason for thinking that children may prefer the direct reference interpretation (meaning$_2$) of discourse sequences like (15) over the bound pronoun interpretation (meaning$_1$) is that they contain an occurrence of the singular pronoun *he* rather than the plural pronoun *they* as the form of the bound pronoun. The plural pronoun serves this grammatical function in the grammars of some young children (Thornton 1990). Such children sometimes even produce agreement errors in order to use the plural form of the pronoun (e.g., "Which one thinks they are the best?"). To establish that the children in the present study could interpret the singular pronoun *he* as a bound pronoun, control sentences like (18)—the *bound pronoun controls* were included. The bound pronoun controls consist of single-sentence discourses; but it seems highly unlikely that children prefer one form of bound pronoun in sentence grammar and another in discourse.

(18)   No mouse at Simba's party said he wore a hat.
       a.   Bound pronoun: No mouse at Simba's party said he wore a hat.
       b.   Direct reference: No mouse at Simba's party said he wore a hat.

In the experiment, the control sentences were true on the bound pronoun interpretation and false on the direct reference interpretation. Therefore, children's level of acceptance of the bound pronoun interpretation of the ambiguous control sentences like (18) can be used as another baseline against which to compare their performance in response to the test discourse sequences like (15). Because the bound pronoun interpretation of the discourse (meaning$_1$) is prohibited by the closure constraint, children who adhere to the constraint must override whatever preference they manifest for assigning this interpretation to the bound pronoun control sentences. As with the indefinite NP controls, any bias children have to analyze sentences in a way that makes them true will favor the anaphoric link between the pronoun and the more distant NP. By contrast, in the test discourse sequences, only the closer NP is a legitimate antecedent, if children obey the closure constraint. Finally, the last event in the contexts associated with both the bound pronoun controls and the test discourse sequences was the same; this event corresponded to the bound pronoun interpretation. Therefore, both this bias and the bias to assign an analysis that makes the test discourse sequences true had to be overridden if children were to perform successfully on the task. Children's consistent negative judgments would therefore demonstrate a resolute adherence to the closure constraint.

There is one constant in the experiment to keep in mind, however: both the control trials and the test trials were designed such that the meaning corresponding to the "No" response was always the direct reference interpretation, in which the pronoun is referentially dependent on the closer NP.

34.5 The Experiment

To give a flavor of the technique, (19) summarizes a protocol that is typical of the bound pronoun controls. In the actual protocol, of course, the characters do most of the talking, and they do not use words like *abundance* and *assert*.

(19)   Simba the lion is hosting a party. The main attraction is an abundance of silly hats. There are three mice at the party, who are discussing who has already put on a hat at the party. Two mice assert that they did not see Simba put on a hat, so they believe that he did not wear one at the party. A third mouse disagrees, saying that Simba did put on a hat, and made a spectacle of himself. The mice then discuss their own hat-wearing, and each mouse recounts how he decided not to wear a hat because all of the hats were too silly.

Following the story, a puppet presents the target sentence:

(20)   No mouse at Simba's party said he wore a hat.

There are aspects of the context described in (19) that correspond to both readings, but the context is such that the bound pronoun interpretation is true (because none of the mice said that he, himself, wore a hat) and the direct reference interpretation is false (because one mouse did say that Simba wore a hat). As noted earlier, associating the bound pronoun interpretation with the "Yes" response facilitates assigning this interpretation. Notice, also, that this interpretation is associated with the last event in the story. Therefore if the bound pronoun interpretation is available in children's grammars, both of these aspects of experimental design should heighten its accessibility. The proportion of bound pronoun responses to these control stories therefore serves as a comparison for the experimental trials, where the bound pronoun interpretation is ruled out by the closure constraint.

Another feature of the story in (19) satisfies the condition of plausible dissent. This condition is relevant to the interpretation that is false in the story, namely, the direct reference interpretation. On this interpretation of (20), the pronoun *he* refers to Simba. For the direct reference interpretation to be felicitous, it must be clear to the child that if events had taken a slightly different turn, the response to the sentence on this interpretation would have been "Yes" rather than "No." For (20) to be true on the direct reference interpretation, all three mice would have had to deny that Simba wore a hat. This could easily have been the outcome, since two of the mice say that they did not see Simba wearing a hat. However, the third mouse disagrees, saying that he saw Simba wearing a hat. This last event makes sentence (20) false on the direct reference interpretation.

Children were also presented with two-sentence test discourses such as (21), to determine the range of interpretations they allowed for discourses that are governed by the closure constraint.

(21)   No mouse came to Simba's party. He wore a hat.

A child lacking the closure constraint should allow both the bound pronoun and the direct reference interpretations; that is, this child should treat discourse (21) as ambiguous. If so, the same factors would weigh in the child's decision about which analysis to assign; the bound pronoun interpretation should be accepted to the same extent in response to (21) as it is in response to (20).

Two modifications were required for the experimental protocols corresponding to (21). First, it was necessary to alter the truth value judgment task in order to present discourses, rather than sentences, as in previous research. Because the evaluation of a discourse is not a composite of the truth values of the individual sentences of the discourse, we could not ask children for a single response (see Groenendijk and Stokhof 1991). Instead, we had the puppet report two things about the story (the two sentences of the discourse), and children were asked to evaluate each sentence separately. If both sentences were correct, the child gave the puppet two of its favorite treats; if only one sentence was correct, the child gave the puppet only one treat.

The second design modification was introduced to satisfy the condition of plausible dissent. As with bound pronoun control sentences like (20), the truth or falsity of test discourse sequences like (21) hinges on the interpretation of the pronoun. However, in a discourse, anaphoric links are constructed in a different way. Since the pronoun is in the second sentence, only the truth or falsity of this sentence turns on the interpretation of the pronoun. It was decided, therefore, to construct contexts such that the first sentence in all of the discourse sequences was true; the second sentence was true if the bound pronoun interpretation was assigned, and false if the direct reference interpretation was assigned.

It follows that the condition of plausible dissent is relevant only to the second sentence on the direct reference interpretation. The story summary provided in (22) illustrates how plausible dissent was met for the two-sentence discourse in (21).

(22)   Simba invites his three mice friends to a party. There is lots to do, and
       special hats to put on. At the last minute, the mice conjecture that
       Simba's invitation is a trick, to lure them to his house so that he can
       eat them. Frightened by this prospect, the mice decide to go to a nearby
       rodeo. Meanwhile, the innocent Simba decides that his mice friends are

not coming to his party. To cheer himself up, he considers wearing one of the party hats, but finds that they are specially sized for mice, and will not fit a big lion like Simba. He decides, instead, to wear his new lion cape. Off at the rodeo, the mice decide to wear cowboy hats, so they will look like the cowboys at the rodeo.

The first sentence in the discourse is true: *No mouse went to Simba's party*. The second sentence, *He wore a hat*, is true if the bound pronoun interpretation is assigned, but is false if the pronoun is interpreted by direct reference. To satisfy plausible dissent, the interpretation of this sentence, with the pronoun referring to Simba, must be under consideration at some point in the story. The sentence ultimately turns out to be false on this interpretation. Finally, it is clear to children "What really happened?" on the direct reference interpretation: the hats were too small for Simba, so he put on his new cape.

One complete set of test items is provided in (23).

(23) a. Indefinite: A mouse came to Simba's party. He wore a hat.
      b. Every: Every mouse came to Simba's party. He wore a hat.
      c. None: None of the mice came to Simba's party. He wore a hat.
      d. Every: Every mouse at Simba's party said he wore a hat.
      e. No: No mouse at Simba's party said he wore a hat.

There were two trials of each item type, interspersed with up to five unrelated, unambiguous filler trials. The fillers were used to monitor for a response bias (e.g., a bias to accept whatever the puppet said as true).

Children were interviewed in two sessions. Data from 15 children ranging in age from 3 to 5 were analyzed from the items like those in (23a–c), and data from 12 children were analyzed from items like (23d) and (23e).

34.6 The Findings

The main findings were as follows. In response to discourse sequences like (23a), with indefinite NPs, children responded "Yes" 93% of the time, indicating their tolerance of an anaphoric link between the pronoun and a distant NP where this is permitted by discourse grammar. Similarly, children responded "Yes" 77% of the time to sentences like (23d–e). We interpret this as evidence that children permitted a bound pronoun interpretation (with a singular pronoun).

Did children also permit the bound pronoun interpretation in discourse sequences with quantificational elements like *none* and *every*, where the closure constraint precludes this interpretation? They did not. There was a lower incidence of bound pronoun responses to discourse sequences like (23b) and (23c); the second sentences of such discourse sequences were accepted 19% of the time, the majority of "Yes" responses being contributed by two children. Because of the responses of these two children, whose grammars remain mysterious to us for the present, the findings can be considered only suggestive. It appears that the closure constraint is part of many children's grammars, but perhaps not all. Finally, there was no systematic difference between trials like (23b), where the quantified NP contained *every*, and trials like (23c), where the quantified NP contained *none*. Children rejected both types of discourse to a similar extent.

34.7 Conclusion

The results of the study discussed in this chapter tend to support the experimental hypothesis. However, it would be premature to reject the null hypothesis in light of the finding that two children accepted violations of the closure constraint. When presented with contexts favoring the bound pronoun interpretation, though, many children responded in accordance with the closure constraint on discourse binding, rejecting the second sentence of the test discourse sequences over three-quarters of the time.

The findings from the control conditions help rule out alternative accounts of these children's correct rejections. We can eliminate the possibility that children's negative judgments were due to a parsing preference for the direct reference interpretation over the bound pronoun interpretation, and we can eliminate the possibility that children's correct responses reflect a performance strategy that makes closer NPs more attractive antecedents.

On a larger front, the successful performance by many children in this study makes it clear that knowledge of pragmatic constraints may be evinced early in the course of language development, just like knowledge of syntactic and semantic constraints. This further reinforces the poverty-of-the-stimulus argument, in yet another component of the language apparatus, where principles of discourse reside. For further discussion and empirical findings, see Conway 1997.

Chapter 35

Universal Quantification

For the past 30 years, it has been widely believed that even children as old as 4 or 5 misunderstand sentences with the universal quantifier, such as (1) and (2).

(1) Every farmer is feeding a donkey.

(2) A farmer is feeding every donkey.

English-speaking children, it is claimed, understand both (1) and (2) in the same way, to entail that every farmer is feeding a donkey and, in addition, that every donkey is being fed by a farmer (see, e.g., Inhelder and Piaget 1964; Roeper and de Villiers 1991a; Takahashi 1991). In this chapter, we present theoretical arguments and empirical evidence in favor of the view that children learning English analyze the universal quantifier just as adult English speakers do.

The basic finding is this. If shown a picture like that in figure 35.1, which we call the *extra object condition*, many 3- to 5-year-old children who are asked the question "Is every farmer feeding a donkey?" will respond by saying "No." When asked to explain this answer ("Why not?"), children point to the unfed donkey as the reason (e.g., Philip 1991, 1995; Roeper and de Villiers 1991a; Takahashi 1991). Similarly, when asked the question "Is a farmer feeding every donkey?", if there are farmers that are not feeding donkeys in the context, children will say "No" and point to the "extra" farmers. It seems that children are interpreting both (1) and (2) in the same way, as demanding symmetry between farmers and donkeys. These responses by children have been called *symmetrical responses*, because children appear to reject any asymmetry between donkeys and farmers—the mapping must be one to one.

Inhelder and Piaget (1964) attempted to explain children's symmetrical interpretation of sentences like (1) and (2) in nonlinguistic terms, as the result of their inability to distinguish part-whole relationships among sets. A linguistic account of children's comprehension failures, called the *Symmetrical Account*, has been advanced within the generative framework (Philip 1991, 1995). We will concentrate on the most recent version of this account (Philip 1995), according to which children ignore the surface position of the universal quantifier in sentences like (1) and (2).

35.1 The Symmetrical Interpretation

To explain children's nonadult interpretation of sentences with a universal quantifier, the Symmetrical Account appeals to a distinction between quantificational elements, which may function as either determiners (D-quantifiers) or adverbs (A-quantifiers). In adult English, the universal quantifier *every* is a D-quantifier. As such, it is a two-place relation; its domain of quantification (first argument) is limited to the individuals

NO, NOT THAT ONE

Figure 35.1
The extra object condition

denoted by the N' that it combines with syntactically. By contrast, the domain of quantification for A-quantifiers such as *always* and *usually* may include the contents of another clause; that is, these quantifiers can have scope over several NPs at the same time, and they may quantify over events as well as individuals (see Davidson 1967; Lewis 1975; Parsons 1990). The Symmetrical Account proposes that children treat the universal quantifier as an A-quantifier like *always*. As such, the universal quantifier ranges over both *farmer* and *donkey* in both (1) and (2). (A number of experiments in Roeper and de Villiers 1991a also point to the conclusion that children treat the universal quantifier as an adverb.)

The Symmetrical Account suggests that children disregard the position of the universal quantifier in sentences like (1) and (2); it is as though there are two universal quantifiers, one with scope over each nominal expression. As this analysis of the situation suggests, the truth conditions that children assign can be stated as in (3).

(3) $\forall(x)\exists(y)$ [farmer(x) & donkey(y) $\rightarrow$ (x is feeding y)]
& $\forall(y)\exists(x)$ [donkey(y) & farmer(x) $\rightarrow$ (x is feeding y)]

'For every farmer x, there is a donkey y such that x is feeding y, and for every donkey y, there is a farmer x such that x is feeding y.'

As (3) indicates, the truth conditions corresponding to the interpretation on which the existential quantifier has wide scope seem to be missing from the child's analysis of sentences with the universal quantifier. Assuming that some children impose the truth conditions in (3), it is clear that they do not apply the same semantic principles as adults do in deriving the truth conditions for sentences with universal quantification.

Although the truth conditions stated in (3) contain two occurrences of the universal quantifier—one ranging over *farmers* and one ranging over *donkeys*—the Symmetrical Account maintains that children hypothesize a single universal quantifier, but assign it scope over more than one nominal constituent, as if it were an *unselective binder* in the sense of Heim (1982). Although the Symmetrical Account differs from Heim's unselective binding approach in several respects, there are enough similarities between the two approaches to make it worth reviewing the mechanisms of unselective binding.

35.2 Unselective Binding

In Heim's system, indefinite NPs carry no quantificational force of their own. When an indefinite NP, such as *a boy*, appears in discourse, it is semantically represented by an open predicate with a free variable:

(4) *a boy* $\rightarrow$ boy(x)

The open predicate inherits its quantificational force in one of two ways. One pertains to indefinite NPs within the scope of a quantificational element, such as *every* or *always*. In such cases, the domain of the quantificational element is extended beyond its usual limits, so as to encompass all disenfranchised indefinite NPs. That is, the quantificational element is an unselective binder, with scope even over indefinites that it does not c-command. Alternatively, indefinite NPs can inherit quantificational force by Existential Closure, which inserts an existential quantifier to bind indefinite NPs that stand alone (i.e., with no quantificational antecedent).

An example of unselective binding occurs in conditional *donkey* sentences like (5), in which the adverb of quantification, *always*, imparts its quantificational force to both of the indefinite NPs, *a boy* and *a dog*. The semantic representation postulated by Heim for such sentences is an extension of an earlier analysis, by Lewis (1975), who was the first to observe that adverbs of quantification can take scope over several indefinites at the same time. The truth conditions that result correspond to a reading in which (5) is true only if every boy in the discourse context takes every dog that he has to the park. This is the *strong reading*.

(5) If a boy has a dog, he always takes it to the park.

In addition to the strong reading, *donkey* sentences like (5) have a *weak reading*. For (5) to be true on the weak reading, all that is required is that each boy take at least one of his dogs to the park.

Following Lewis, Heim's semantic representation of *donkey* sentences like (5) partitions them into three elements: a *quantifier*, a *restrictor*, and a *nuclear scope*. As the sample tripartite structure in (6) indicates, the domain of the quantifier is given by the restrictor and may include more than one open predicate. The quantifier binds the variables of these predicates, unselectively. The nuclear scope states conditions that must be satisfied by the quantified variables. Notice that this representation yields the truth conditions of the strong reading of the *donkey* sentence.

(6) *Quantifier*   *Restrictor*   *Nuclear scope*
     $\text{ALWAYS}_{x,y}$ boy(x) & dog(y) & has(x, y)   takes-to-the-park(x, y)
     '(Always) if a boy has a dog, he takes it to the park.'

Relative-clause *donkey* sentences like (7) receive a similar analysis in Heim's framework.

(7)   Every boy who has a dog takes it to the park.

Like the adverb of quantification *always*, the universal quantifier *every* is analyzed as an unselective binder, with scope over all open predicates inside the restrictor.

(8)   *Quantifier   Restrictor   Nuclear scope*
       EVERY$_{x,y}$ boy(x) & dog(y) & has(x, y)   takes-to-the-park(x, y)

Comparing (6) and (8), it is clear that relative-clause *donkey* sentences have the same truth conditions as their conditional counterparts: the strong reading. In short, this is how the truth conditions are derived for both conditional *donkey* sentences, such as (5), and relative-clause *donkey* sentences, such as (7). In both cases, the sentence is true on the strong reading: it is true if and only if every boy takes every dog that he owns to the park. To sum up, on the unselective binding account, both relative-clause and conditional *donkey* sentences are instances of unselective binding, and both have the truth conditions corresponding to the strong reading.

35.3 *The Symmetrical Account*

To explain children's symmetrical interpretation of sentences with a universal quantifier, Philip's (1991) Symmetrical Account has several features in common with Heim's unselective binding approach to *donkey* sentences. The Symmetrical Account maintains that, unlike adults, children interpret even simple sentences with a universal quantifier by putting both nominals (e.g., *farmer* and *donkey* in (1) and (2)) into the restrictor. That is, the universal quantifier is semantically analyzed like an adverb of quantification, and not as a Determiner. On the Symmetrical Account, children's analysis of universal quantification differs from that of adults in a second way, as well; children analyze the universal quantifier as unselectively binding (a disjunction of) event variables, rather than individual variables. Adopting the tripartite framework, the Symmetrical Account maintains that children assign the semantic representation in (9) to both the sentence *Every farmer is feeding a donkey* and the sentence *A farmer is feeding every donkey*.

(9)   *Quantifier   Restrictor   Nuclear scope*
       Every(e)   [PART(farmer(e)) or   farmer-is-feeding-a-donkey(e)
                      PART(donkey(e))]

       'For every event, *e*, in which a farmer participates or a donkey
       participates (or both), a farmer is feeding a donkey in *e*.'

In this representation, the universal quantifier *every* ranges over events, indicated by the variable *e*. The events mentioned in the restrictor form a disjunction: events in which a farmer participates, or ones in which a donkey participates, or both.[1] The test given by the nuclear scope states that the sentence is false if any such events do not have a farmer feeding a donkey in them. This explains why children who adopt this semantic representation deny the truth of the sentence *Every farmer is feeding a donkey* if there is an unfed donkey in the domain of discourse. It also explains why children deny *A farmer is feeding every donkey* if there is at least one farmer who is not feeding anything.

The Symmetrical Account predicts that children should respond differently to sentences with intransitive verb phrases, such as *Every cat is waving*. This sentence contains only one nominal, *cat*, for the universal quantifier to bind. Therefore, such sentences are not susceptible to the symmetrical interpretation. The Symmetrical Account predicts only adultlike responses to these sentences. Any residual errors must be due to experimental noise. Indeed, Philip (1995) reports a significant increase in adultlike responses to sentences with intransitive verb phrases over adultlike responses to ones with transitive verb phrases. The higher incidence of symmetrical responses to the transitive sentences is advanced as support for the Symmetrical Account.

35.4 Problems with the Symmetrical Account

At first blush the Symmetrical Account has much to recommend it. It appears to explain several intriguing linguistic phenomena, including children's apparent misunderstanding of simple sentences with universal quantification. Despite its theoretical interest, however, the account makes the wrong predictions about children's interpretation of certain sentences. On the Symmetrical Account, children should respond to both kinds of *donkey* sentences—the relative-clause and the conditional—in the same way. However, as we describe in chapter 36, the results of a study by Conway and Crain (1995a,b) show that children do not do this. As a group, children in that study tended to reject the weak reading of conditional *donkey* sentences significantly more often than they rejected this reading of relative-clause *donkey* sentences. This finding is difficult to reconcile with the Symmetrical Account.

Moreover, the evidence in favor of the Symmetrical Account is not overwhelming. Of the 276 children who were interviewed in the studies reported by Philip (1995), only 87 (32%) were "pure symmetry children" (children who prefer the symmetrical interpretation over other interpretations). This subgroup of children produced symmetrical responses only 57% of the time; an adultlike interpretation accounted for the remainder of their responses. Moreover, experimental noise accounted for roughly half of their symmetrical responses. In sum, the symmetrical interpretation accounts for only about 10% of children's overall responses in the experiments and for only about 30% of the responses by "symmetry children."

To continue our examination of the Symmetrical Account, it is instructive to look more closely at the relative proportions of three factors that contribute to children's responses to questions with transitive verb phrases and the universal quantifier: (a) the symmetrical interpretation, (b) the adultlike interpretation, and (c) the amount of experimental noise. We continue our critique of the Symmetrical Account by showing that one of the Symmetrical Account's fundamental claims, that the "symmetry child" prefers the symmetrical interpretation over an adultlike interpretation, is false.

Consider children's responses to questions with transitive verb phrases and to ones with intransitive verb phrases.

(10)   Is every farmer feeding a donkey?

(11)   Is every cat waving?

Of the 49 children who participated in an experiment comparing sentences like these, 44 children produced nonadult responses to questions with transitive verb phrases.

Included among the 44 children were 25 pure "symmetry children," according to criteria invoked by Philip 1995, which excludes a different nonadult response. The "symmetry children" produced 61% symmetrical responses to questions with transitive verb phrases, such as (10). In response to questions with intransitive verb phrases, such as (11), this figure dropped to 40%. The difference between 61% and 40% was significant by a t test ($p < .01$). On the basis of this statistical finding, Philip (1995) infers that children's symmetrical responses to sentences with transitive verb phrases are linguistic in nature.

With these figures, we can measure the relative contributions of both linguistic and nonlinguistic factors in children's responses to questions with transitive verb phrases, such as (10). The 25 "symmetry children" produced 39% adultlike responses to such sentences. On this proportion of trials, then, these children accessed an adultlike linguistic representation. The total percentage of children's nonadult responses to questions with transitive verb phrases was 61%. These nonadult responses are due to a combination of factors, only one of which can be considered to be part of children's linguistic competence (i.e., the symmetrical interpretation). The other factors are not the product of children's grammars, nor are they under experimental control; they are "uncontrolled secondary factors" (p. 109) or "generalized 'noise'" (p. 124). To calculate the proportion of nonadult responses due to linguistic knowledge (the symmetrical interpretation), we need to subtract out the noise.

35.5 Estimating Noise

To estimate noise, we look at children's responses to the control sentences. In the present study, the control sentences were questions with intransitive verb phrases, such as (11). On the Symmetrical Account, there should be no nonadult responses to these sentences; either children assign these sentences the same semantic representation as adults do, or they assign them an event-quantificational analysis that yields the same truth conditions as the adult analysis. Therefore, all 40% of the nonadult responses by children to sentences like (11) are due to noise.

Having obtained an estimate of the percentage of nonadult responses due to noise, we can now calculate the contribution of the symmetrical interpretation to children's nonadult responses to questions with transitive verb phrases. This is accomplished by subtracting the noise, estimated at 40%, from the percentage of nonadult responses to the transitive sentences, 61%. The result, 21%, is a (liberal) estimate of how often children accessed the symmetrical interpretation for questions with transitive verb phrases. To sum up, the responses by "symmetry children" to transitive questions can be partitioned as follows: these children assigned an adultlike interpretation 39% of the time; they assigned the symmetrical interpretation 21% of the time; the remaining 40% of their responses are unaccounted for.

These figures permit us to assess the relative contributions of linguistic representations and nonlinguistic factors to children's linguistic behavior in response to sentences with a transitive verb phrase. The conclusion to be drawn is that the symmetrical interpretation is not preferred to an adultlike interpretation of questions, like (10), with the universal quantifier and a transitive verb phrase: an adultlike interpretation was favored nearly 2:1 by "symmetry children" when responses to intransitive questions were used as the basis of the estimate. This casts doubt on one tenet of the Symmetrical Account: the claim that quantification over events is easier, and resides in children's grammars earlier than quantification over objects. To the extent that a preference for event quantification is deemed important for the Symmetrical Account, the account is undermined by the finding that an adultlike response is at least as accessible as the symmetrical interpretation.

35.6 Other Concerns

There are several other reasons for concern with the experimental findings. First, it turns out that uncontrolled factors account for as much or more of children's linguistic behavior than does the symmetrical interpretation. Second, it is a mystery why different proportions of children's responses are attributed to the symmetrical interpretation for different constructions (or, to put it differently, it is a mystery why there are different levels of noise across constructions). Third, the children's strong bias to say "No" in response to uncontrolled factors is troublesome. Just the opposite is usually reported in experimental investigations of both children and adults (see, e.g., Grimshaw and Rosen 1990, 190). That is, subjects generally manifest a bias to say "Yes" when they are confused or when they find sentences difficult to comprehend. The fact that the picture verification studies conducted by Philip and his colleagues evoked an unusual response bias from children is unexplained. This finding suggests that some feature of the task conflicts with children's expectations about the circumstances corresponding to the "Yes" responses on the meaning they assign to the test sentences. It is tempting to conclude that some feature(s) of the experimental design encouraged errors that would have not occurred otherwise.

A final problem with the Symmetrical Account is that it maintains that children find sentences with the universal quantifier ambiguous, whereas they are unambiguous for adults. Attributing ambiguity to children's grammars creates a serious problem for the account, however. Because children have both interpretations, they can never expunge the symmetrical interpretation. There are two ways to expunge an incorrect analysis: either parents provide correction when children assign the nonadult interpretation, or children notice that adults' behavior does not match their own. Neither source of error detection is available for the "symmetry child," however. First, correction by adults will never be forthcoming, because whenever children assign the symmetrical interpretation, they do so in circumstances that make the sentence true on the adult interpretation. (Notice that the symmetrical interpretation makes sentences with the universal quantifier true in a subset of the circumstances corresponding to the adult interpretation.) Second, the evidence children encounter will always be consistent with their preferred interpretation, the adultlike interpretation. Therefore, if the Symmetrical Account is correct, children will never converge on the adult grammar, because they cannot notice that adults allow only one of the interpretations that they allow. It follows that another tenet of the Symmetrical Account must be abandoned, in light of considerations of language learnability, namely, the view that children find sentences with a universal quantifier ambiguous.

We have established that the Symmetrical Account makes the wrong predictions about children's interpretation of relative-clause *donkey* sentences and that a good case can be made against the account as an explanation of children's nonadult linguistic behavior. Next, we ask whether there is a reasonable alternative explanation for children's misunderstanding of sentences with a universal quantifier.

35.7 An Alternative Account

The Symmetrical Account claims that children prefer a particular nonadult reading of sentences with the universal quantifier. The dispreferred reading is the meaning assigned by adults (meaning$_1$); the other reading at issue is the symmetrical interpretation (meaning$_2$).

(12) Is every farmer feeding a donkey?
  a. Meaning$_1$: Every event with a farmer or a donkey in it is an event in which a farmer is feeding a donkey.
  b. Meaning$_2$: Every farmer is feeding a donkey.

Sentence (12) should be unambiguous for those children who have the adult grammar. By contrast, according to the Symmetrical Account, (12) is ambiguous, with meaning$_1$ preferred (although we have shown that the latter claim is likely to be false).

Let us start to design an experiment from the perspective of the Symmetrical Account. On this account, children are expected to make errors. Therefore, the experimental hypothesis is that children will not assign meaning$_2$ alone; meaning$_1$ will also be accessed. The null hypothesis is that children have only meaning$_2$. Except for the experiment on bound pronouns, all of the previous experiments we have discussed associated meaning$_2$, the adult interpretation, with the "No" response. To avoid type I errors, however, an experimenter who adopts the Symmetrical Account should choose to associate meaning$_2$ with the "Yes" response. Therefore, research by Philip and others made the test sentences *true* on the adult interpretation.

As noted earlier, in this design the target sentences can be partitioned into background, assertion, possible outcome, and actual outcome. The assertion corresponds to the actual outcome (the "Yes" answer), and the possible outcome corresponds to the negative judgment (the "No" answer). For the question to be felicitous, the assertion must be in doubt at some point during the trial. Therefore, at some point during the trial, some outcome other than the actual one should be conceivable. This is a corollary of the condition of plausible dissent (i.e., one of plausible *assent*). We summarize the experimental design as follows:

(13) Background: Every farmer is feeding *so-and-so*.
   Assertion: a donkey
   Possible outcome: Some farmer feeds a dinosaur
   Actual outcome: Every farmer feeds a donkey

The experimental setup used in the studies reported by Philip (1995) did not conform to the experimental design outlined in (13). The main difference is the absence of a possible, but not actual, outcome; no alternative to the actual outcome was under consideration. Therefore, the Yes/No questions were not used felicitously. We contend that this was the source of many children's nonadult responses in the extra object condition, for example. On this scenario, children made nonadult responses because the circumstances were inappropriate for a yes/no question (or a true/false judgment) on the adult interpretation. Placed in this predicament, children were led to suppose that another interpretation was intended. On the alternative interpretation, the question concerned the numerical correspondence between agents and objects. Children who inferred that the "extra object" was relevant to their interpretation would conclude that the correct answer was "No." It would also be clear to these children that the correct answer would be "Yes" if the extra object were removed. In short, the test questions were more felicitous on the symmetrical interpretation than on the adult interpretation.

35.8 Loose Ends

Before we leave this discussion of experimental design, a few more remarks are in order. First, if the felicity conditions are satisfied, the presence of an "extra object" (e.g., a donkey that was not fed by any of the farmers) should not influence the interpretation children assign to the target sentences. Therefore, we are led to predict that children will respond correctly to the question "Is every farmer feeding a donkey?" as long as it is asked in a felicitous context, regardless of the number of donkeys in the situation. That is, if every farmer is feeding a donkey in the context, then children should respond affirmatively to the question.

We should also consider why older children and adults do not fall victim as often as younger children to flaws in experimental design. We believe the reason is that older children and adults are simply better test-takers than young children. To be successful in previous studies, subjects were required to accommodate the fact that the negation of the test sentences was not under consideration on the adult interpretation. Presumably, older children and adults have learned to "see through" misleading circumstances in which test sentences are presented, although this leads to increased processing time, as Wason (1965) has shown. Many younger children are apparently unable to perform the necessary accommodations as rapidly and as successfully as older children and adults.

One final comment on differences between children and adults: Another population of adults—namely, adults with Broca's aphasia (also known as agrammatism or nonfluent aphasia)—are also prone to exhibit abnormal response patterns in circumstances that do not facilitate normal sentence processing. For example, a nonfluent aphasic subject studied by Tyler (1985) manifested the same on-line response patterns as normal adults when presented with sentences that were both syntactically well formed and semantically coherent. However, this subject manifested an aberrant profile when he encountered sentences that were syntactically well formed but semantically anomalous. Shankweiler et al. (1989) interpret the findings as evidence that

> the syntactic processing capabilities of Tyler's patient are adequate under ordinary conditions, where both syntactic and semantic cues converge on an appropriate analysis. But in adverse conditions syntactic processing may become derailed. (pp. 26–27)

In light of the similar response patterns by children and nonfluent aphasics in "adverse" conditions, it might be expected that nonfluent aphasics would give symmetrical responses in the same situations that evoke them from children. Indeed, Avrutin and Philip (1994) found this to be the case. The observation that some young children and nonfluent aphasics produce the same responses to quantificational sentences in the same contexts suggests that the difficulty is nonlinguistic for both groups and does not derive from children's nonadult linguistic representations, as the Symmetrical Account maintains.

35.9 Conclusion

It has long been thought that children have difficulty understanding even simple sentences with a universal quantifier. Several accounts have been offered, including the Symmetrical Account, which is noteworthy because it incorporates insights from the syntax and semantics of generative grammar.

The Symmetrical Account clearly adopts the methodological assumptions of the Competing Factors Model. The conclusion that children assign the symmetrical interpretation to sentences with transitive verb phrases is based on the reduction of nonadult responses they produce with other constructions (sentences with intransitive verb phrases, sentences with bare plural noun phrases, noun-incorporated structures, etc.). The fact that children continue to produce nonadult responses as much as 40% to 50% of the time is attributed by Philip (1995) to "response strategies" (p. 109), "the effects of secondary uncontrolled variables" (p. 107), or "strong carry-over effects [that] were observed to confound the performance of all subjects" (p. 124). From the vantage point of the Modularity Matching Model, accepting the Symmetrical Account would be tantamount to surrendering the fundamental assumptions of the model: that children and adults have access to the same cognitive mechanisms.

These observations prompted us to investigate whether there was something in previous tasks, other than lack of grammatical knowledge, that might explain children's errors. We discovered that those studies that had made the strongest case for a linguistic account of children's errors had not satisfied the pragmatic felicity conditions for the task they had adopted, asking yes/no questions. In investigating children's linguistic competence, it is crucial to ensure that test sentences are presented in felicitous contexts. In the contexts for yes/no questions, felicitous usage dictates that both the assertion and the negation of a target sentence should be under consideration. In tests of the Symmetrical Account, however, the target questions were not felicitous, because nothing in the task corresponded to the negative answer to the questions on the adult interpretation. In studies that elicited the symmetrical interpretation in response to questions like "Is every farmer feeding a donkey?", children responded to pictures that led them to infer that the question of concern to the experimenter was whether or not there were equal numbers of farmers and donkeys. The answer to this was "No." From a methodological point of view, if the goal is to evoke optimal performance from children, it is important to present sentences in felicitous contexts, whatever their inherent complexity. Overly simplified contexts can actually impair children's performance, as compared to their level of performance in more complex but more appropriate contexts. (Hamburger and Crain (1982) make a related argument concerning children's performance in response to sentences with restrictive relative clauses.)

In studies that met the felicity conditions we identified, children performed about as well as adults do in interpreting sentences with a universal quantifier; moreover, like adults, children produced such sentences in appropriate contexts. For a report of the relevant findings, see Crain, Thornton, et al. 1996. On the basis of the findings from seven studies of 4- to 6-year-olds, we conclude that children do not lack grammatical competence. This opens the door for further studies of children's knowledge of universal quantification, and other aspects of quantification. We anticipate that these studies will offer additional results that are in keeping with the precepts of the theory of Universal Grammar.

Chapter 36

Donkey Sentences

This chapter concerns relative-clause *donkey* sentences like (1) and conditional *donkey* sentences like (2).

(1) *Relative clause*
Every farmer who owns a donkey feeds it.

(2) *Conditional*
If a farmer owns a donkey, he (always) feeds it.

First, some background. Beginning with Heim 1982 and Kamp 1981, and continuing through current versions of Discourse Representation Theory (e.g., Kamp and Reyle 1993), linguistic analyses of *donkey* sentences have had two main goals. One goal has been to provide a semantics that assigns the same truth conditions to both relative-clause and conditional *donkey* sentences. The other has been to ensure that the truth conditions for sentences of both kinds correspond to the strong reading, according to which every farmer feeds every donkey that he owns (see Groenendijk and Stokhof 1991). (On the weak reading, each farmer must feed at least one of the donkeys he owns; he may feed them all, but this is not required for the sentence to be true.) Heim achieves these goals by treating the universal quantifier as an "unselective binder". In relative-clause *donkey* sentences like (1), the universal quantifier is taken to unselectively bind both nominals, *farmer* and *donkey*. As a result, relative-clause *donkey* sentences receive the same reading as conditional *donkey* sentences like (2)—the desired effect.

36.1 Preferences in Interpretation

The Symmetrical Account (chapter 35) should extend to relative-clause *donkey* sentences. Children who adopt the symmetrical interpretation of simple sentences with a universal quantifier should assign only the strong reading of relative-clause *donkey* sentences. Because the analysis children assign is based on unselective binding, they should reject relative-clause *donkey* sentences in contexts that correspond to the weak interpretation. For example, they should reject (1) in a context in which every farmer feeds at least one, but not all, of his donkeys. Moreover, these children should not distinguish relative-clause *donkey* sentences from conditional *donkey* sentences; both constructions should have the same truth conditions (i.e., the strong reading).

Chierchia (1995) has challenged the assumption that relative clause and conditional *donkey* sentences have the same truth conditions (corresponding to the strong reading). On Chierchia's account, relative-clause *donkey* sentences are interpreted using the mechanisms of dynamic binding used in discourse anaphora. According to Chierchia, these mechanisms establish the weak reading for relative-clause *donkey* sentences, by the definition of the dynamic conditional, $\Rightarrow$. In the metamorphosis from the dynamic conditional to its more customary counterpart, the indefinite NP in the antecedent clause is repeated in the consequent; by dynamic binding, material in the main clause VP comes to reside within its scope. A brief sketch of the essentials of the derivation is given in (3).

(3)   Every farmer who owns a donkey feeds it.
    a. $\forall x \, [(\text{farmer}(x) \, \& \, \exists y \, (\text{donkey}(y) \, \& \, \text{owns}(x, y))) \Rightarrow (\text{feeds} \, (x, y))]$
    b. $\forall x \, [(\text{farmer}(x) \, \& \, \exists y \, (\text{donkey}(y) \, \& \, \text{owns}(x, y))) \rightarrow$
        $\exists y \, (\text{donkey}(y) \, \& \, \text{owns}(x, y) \, \& \, \text{feeds}(x, y))]$

In the final formula, (3b), the pronoun (i.e., the variable y) is bound by the existential quantifier associated with the indefinite NP in the main-clause VP; therefore, the representation corresponds to the weak interpretation. By contrast, the interpretation of conditional *donkey* sentences is not determined primarily by the mechanisms of dynamic binding but is influenced, to a large degree, by pragmatic factors, the strong interpretation being more readily available in most cases.

If there are distinctions to be drawn between relative-clause and conditional *donkey* sentences, as Chierchia suggests, then we would expect children to draw them more clearly than adults, for the following reason. Adult judgments about the alternative interpretations of (ambiguous) sentences may be easily influenced by general world knowledge. Acquiring such knowledge requires experience. Because children's experience is more limited, their judgments should not be subject to the influence of general world knowledge to the same extent as adults' judgments. If so, children's judgments may directly reflect basic principles of the language apparatus.

36.2 The Experiment

In collaboration with Laura Conway (Crain, Conway, and Thornton 1995; Conway and Crain 1995a; Crain, Thornton, et al. 1996), we conducted an experiment designed to test children's understanding of both relative-clause and conditional *donkey* sentences, using a variant of the truth value judgment task. The main innovation of the experiment was this: instead of saying what he thought had already happened in a story, Kermit the Frog tried to predict what would happen in the story. Kermit repeated the prediction at the close of the story, to remind the child what he had said would happen.

The protocols for relative-clause *donkey* sentences and conditional *donkey* sentences were exactly the same. The stories corresponded to the weak interpretation of the target sentence. If only the strong interpretation were available to children, they should have rejected the test sentences. Children were tested with four relative-clause *donkey* sentences and two conditional *donkey* sentences. The stories corresponding to both relative-clause and conditional test sentences were virtually identical. Typical lead-in and test sentences are given in (4).

(4)   a.   I know a lot about boys and dogs. Every boy who has a dog takes it to the park.
    b.   I know a lot about boys and dogs. If a boy has a dog, he takes it to the park.

Figure 36.1
Context corresponding to the weak interpretation

Although the experiment featured stories that were acted out in real time, the outcome of the story corresponding to (4), which we call a *weak context*, is statically represented in figure 36.1. The story depicted in this figure involved four boys and six dogs. One boy had one dog, one boy had two dogs, one boy had three dogs, and one boy had no dogs.[1] After the characters were introduced, but before the story was presented, Kermit uttered the test sentence, either (4a) or (4b). The experimenter then acted out the story, according to the protocol in (5).

(5)   These boys decided to take their dogs to the park because it was such a nice day. The boy with one dog prepared his dog to go to the park by putting a leash on it. The boy with two dogs put a leash on one of his dogs (the dog that was awake), but the other dog was sleeping and could not go to the park. The boy with three dogs put a leash on one of his dogs because that dog was awake, but not on his other two dogs, who were asleep. The boy without any dogs went along with the other boys to the park.

Thus, during the course of the story, each dog owner took only one dog to the park. Therefore, a child who assigns the weak reading should say that the puppet's statement is true; a child who assigns the strong reading should say that the statement is false.

Fifteen children participated in the experiment. They ranged in age from 3;7 to 5;5 (mean 4;5). Six of the children had consistently given symmetrical response to sentences with a universal quantifier and a transitive VP in an earlier experiment, using pictures. The results are as follows. Overall, children accepted (a relevant subset of)[2] the relative-clause *donkey* sentences significantly more often than the conditional *donkey* sentences, 86% (37/43) versus 46% (13/28), in contexts that were not appropriate to the strong interpretation. The difference was significant (chi-square = 6.12; $p < .05$). The 6 children who had given the symmetrical responses earlier manifested a similar distinction between the two constructions; these children accepted the weak interpretation of relative-clause *donkey* sentences more often than the weak interpretation of conditional *donkey* sentences (89% versus 60%).

The data from individual subjects provide even stronger evidence that children did not treat the two types of *donkey* sentences alike. With relative-clause targets, all children demonstrated that the weak reading was available in their grammars; no child required the strong interpretation for all relative-clause targets. By contrast, with conditional targets, 4 children always assigned the strong interpretation. In fact, with conditional targets, the responses by individual children were extremely consistent: the child either assigned the weak reading on all trials or assigned the strong reading on all trials. The availability of the strong reading for conditional *donkey* sentences is not surprising since it is widely accepted that these sentences involve unselective binding.

36.3 Conclusion

The observation that children readily accept the weak interpretation of relative clause *donkey* sentences resists explanation on an account according to which children interpret the universal quantifier roughly as if it is an unselective binder, such as the Symmetrical Account considered in chapter 35. In our view, the appropriate research strategy is to maintain the strongest view of language development that is consistent with the theory of Universal Grammar. On this view, children assign the same syntactic and semantic analyses to sentences as adults do, and they adhere to all universal constraints that govern these analyses. Here, we have attempted to support this viewpoint as it pertains to children's understanding of universal quantification. The findings of our studies demonstrate that young children correctly understand even complex quantificational sentences. This brings child language acquisition data directly in line with Universal Grammar.

Chapter 37

A Potential Drawback of the Task

There is no absolute guarantee that, if the experimenter makes an interpretation available to child subjects, they will generate that interpretation. For example, if a sentence is ambiguous for children, we cannot take consistent "No" responses to one reading as evidence that they cannot generate the reading that is associated with the "Yes" response. Rather, the preference for the alternative reading might be great enough that even the explicit presentation of the first reading does not make it readily available to children (or adults). This puts a limit on the effectiveness of the truth value judgment task in certain instances. In these cases, it is not always possible to tell whether a child's pattern of responses indicates a strong preference for one reading of an ambiguous sentence or a genuine grammatical prohibition against the other reading. In this chapter, we will illustrate the problem with an example. In the next two chapters, we will illustrate some ways to overcome the problem, in specific cases.

37.1 Preferences versus Principles

The need to distinguish preferences and principles has not taken hold, even among researchers who work within the generative framework. Perhaps the following remarks will make the importance of this distinction clear. Generally, people use ambiguous sentences in contexts that are consistent with only one of their interpretations; it is rare for a sentence to be used in a context that is appropriate for more than one of its interpretations. Although such circumstances are rare, consider an ambiguous sentence for which one interpretation would be strongly preferred if the context were consistent with both interpretations. In certain instances in ordinary life, the sentence will be used in contexts that are consistent only with its dispreferred interpretation. In such contexts, the perceiver is compelled to disregard the preferred interpretation and seek out the dispreferred interpretation. This may take some cognitive effort, but apparently it is something perceivers manage quite well for the most part. In ordinary contexts, then, the perceiver can correctly understand a sentence, whichever interpretation is intended by the speaker, although the cognitive demands may be greater in certain contexts than in others.

Children's linguistic knowledge is rarely tested in ordinary contexts, however. In experiments with children, the contexts that researchers construct are generally consistent with more than one interpretation of the test sentence. One is the adult interpretation; the other is the interpretation prohibited by the principle being investigated. Lacking the principle, children may have access to both interpretations of the test sentence, but they could still favor one over the other. Suppose that children favor the interpretation that is consistent with the adult grammar. If the sentence is false on this interpretation in the (ambiguous) experimental contexts, then children may reject it, because it is false on the interpretation that comes most easily to them. Therefore, we cannot infer from children's "No" responses that they do not command the interpretation associated with the "Yes" response. The interpretation associated with the "Yes" response may simply be less accessible.

37.2 Plural NPs

Consider an example. In a situation in which there are three octopuses, each one holding a hamburger, what is the answer to the following question?

(1) How many hamburgers do the octopuses have?

Clearly, the question is ambiguous. If the questioner intends to ask, "How many hamburgers does each octopus have?", then the answer is "One"; but if the questioner intends to ask, "How many hamburgers do the octopuses have altogether?", then the correct answer is "Three." When the plural NP the octopuses is interpreted as referring to the octopuses as a group (i.e., on the collective interpretation of the plural NP), "Three" is an appropriate answer. When the plural NP is given a distributive interpretation, however, "One" is correct.

   As child subjects listen to the test sentence in (1), they will no doubt assign one or the other interpretation of the plural NP the octopuses. It is well established that adults rapidly resolve ambiguities in context. This is surely true of children, too. However, in the real world, the context surrounding an ambiguous sentence is usually appropriate to only one of its interpretations. Therefore, listeners can ordinarily appeal to features of the conversational context to resolve ambiguity. However, in the context just described, the plural NP in the question can correctly be assigned either the distributive or the collective interpretation, Accordingly, either answer is correct. Nevertheless, if children resolve ambiguities as adults do, then they will favor one interpretation of the plural NP over the other. If there is a preference for one interpretation over the other, they might consistently give just one of the possible responses to the question in (1), because it is ambiguous. Suppose we want to know whether children have both interpretations. How would this be tested?

   To begin, we would advise adopting the research strategy used in the strong crossover experiment, in which the questions were embedded as indirect questions. This enables the puppet, Kermit the Frog, to express both the question and its answer. That is, Kermit could give either the "One" answer or the "Three" answer on different experimental trials, as in (2).

(2) a. I know how many hamburgers the octopuses have. Three.
        or
     b. I know how many hamburgers the octopuses have. One.

Embedded questions permit the experimenter to present the alternative interpretations individually for evaluation by the child. For adults, both of Kermit the Frog's statements are true. That is, both (2a) and (2b) are accurate descriptions of the situation.

   A problem remains, however. Suppose that children have a strong preference for one interpretation over the other. If they process the indirect question on-line, as adults do, then they could decide on the correct answer before Kermit produces the answer. A child's acceptance of Kermit's description of the situation depends on the correspondence between Kermit's answer and the answer the child expects Kermit to give. If Kermit gives the expected answer, the child will almost certainly say that Kermit said the right thing. However, if Kermit does not give the expected answer, then one of two events may take place in the child's mind. On the one hand, the child may be able to access the alternative interpretation. For example, if children generally favor the distributive interpretation, they may nevertheless be able to mentally regroup, with the goal of making Kermit's statement true, conforming to the bias to resolve an ambiguity in a way that makes the speaker say something true. It is easy to imagine that the collective interpretation will be readily available to children if they follow this bias, so despite their preference for the distributive interpretation, they will say "Yes"—that is, that Kermit said the right thing.

On the other hand, it is easy to imagine that children have such a strong preference for one or the other interpretation of plural NPs that they will judge Kermit's answer to be wrong. On this scenario, if children prefer the distributive interpretation, but hear Kermit give a collective answer, they may not be able to retrieve the alternative interpretation. If not, they will say "No."

Given these considerations, suppose that children are found to consistently reject one kind of answer to embedded questions like (2a–b). Such a finding presents a dilemma. We cannot tell whether the interpretation that children reject is strongly dispreferred or whether it is not available at all at a particular stage of language development.

Exactly this situation arose in Miyamoto and Crain's (1991) study the acquisition of the distributive and collective interpretation of plural NPs; it was found that the majority of children systematically rejected the collective interpretation of the plural pronoun *they* in sentences similar in form to (2a–b). In chapters 38 and 39, we describe two ways to resolve this dilemma.

Chapter 38
Resolving the Dilemma: Control Sentences

As described in the previous chapter, the truth value judgment task faces the problem of distinguishing whether children's responses reveal (a) a strong preference for one reading of an ambiguity over another possible reading or (b) the absence in children's grammars of all but one reading of what constitutes an ambiguity in the adult grammar. There are two ways to overcome this limitation in certain cases: by including the right control sentences or by varying the context in which a single test sentence is presented. We discuss these strategies in this chapter and the next, respectively.

38.1 Strong Crossover

In some of the experiments discussed earlier, we were able to avoid the problem of distinguishing preferences against a particular reading from its absence in child grammars. For example, consider the experiment on strong crossover that investigated whether or not children adhere to Principle C of the binding theory. For the experiment, the null hypothesis is that children lack Principle C. Lacking Principle C, children could interpret crossover questions like (1) and bound variable questions like (2) in the same way. That is, (1) would be ambiguous, just as (2) is. The experimental hypothesis is that (1) is unambiguous for children, just as it is for adults, and that (2) is ambiguous, just as it is for adults.

(1) *Crossover*
   I know who he thinks has the best smile. Grover and Yogi Bear.

(2) *Bound variable*
   I know who thinks he has the best smile. Grover and Yogi Bear.

More specifically, the null hypothesis maintains that the child could interpret the pronoun *he* in (1) as a bound pronoun (meaning$_1$), perhaps with multiple referents; the deictic interpretation of the pronoun (meaning$_2$) would also be possible, according to which *he* refers to a single individual. On the experimental hypothesis, the crossover question is unambiguous: only the deictic interpretation of the pronoun is allowed. The experiment was therefore set up as follows, where meaning$_1$ was associated with the "Yes" response:

- H_0: Children lack the constraint on strong crossover.
  Expected results: Children permit both meaning$_1$ and meaning$_2$.
- H_1: Children know the constraint on strong crossover.
  Expected results: Children permit meaning$_2$, but not meaning$_1$.

Suppose that questions like (1) were tested in isolation and that children consistently assigned the deictic interpretation of the pronoun. There are two ways of interpreting these data: (a) they support the experimental hypothesis, or (b) the deictic interpretation of a pronoun is preferred over the bound variable interpretation. Both possibilities are consistent with the hypothetical findings.

This is where the control questions—the bound variable questions—come into play. On the null hypothesis, these questions should be interpreted in exactly the same way as the crossover questions. In particular, since both questions are ambiguous on the null hypothesis, both types of questions should allow a multiple referent interpretation of the pronoun at least some proportion of the time. Of course, the alternative, deictic interpretation of the pronoun will also be available; the two interpretations will thus compete. This means that the proportions of responses that are allotted to one interpretation or the other will depend on the various factors that govern ambiguity resolution. Moreover, if the null hypothesis is correct, whatever pressures favor one interpretation over the other will hold for both crossover questions and bound variable questions. Therefore, if both sentences are presented in exactly the same contexts, the alternative interpretations of questions like (1) and (2) should be observed, to the same extent. For example, if the multiple referent answer is accepted 50% of the time in response to the bound variable questions, then this answer should be accepted 50% of the time in response to crossover questions.

- H_0: Children lack the constraint on strong crossover.
  Expected results:

	Deictic meaning	Bound variable meaning
Bound variable questions:	50%	50%
Crossover questions:	50%	50%

On the other hand, if the experimental hypothesis is correct, then subjects know the grammatical principle; therefore, they should never assign the interpretation prohibited by the principle (the bound variable interpretation). According to the experimental hypothesis, the crossover questions are unambiguous, in contrast to the bound variable questions, which are ambiguous. Whatever tendency there is to respond to the ambiguous bound variable questions by assigning a multiple referent interpretation of the pronoun should be overridden by the grammatical principle, Principle C, in crossover questions. Therefore, we would expect a different pattern of responses by subjects to crossover questions and bound variable questions. Subjects will give the multiple referent answer some proportion of the time to bound variable questions, but never to crossover questions. In short, whatever tendency subjects exhibit to assign the bound variable interpretation to the ambiguous control sentences will be obviated by the grammatical principle prohibiting this interpretation of crossover questions. This contrasts with the prediction of the null hypothesis: that subjects will exhibit the same proportion of bound variable responses to both types of questions. The data from the experiment can unequivocally test between these competing hypotheses, at least if subjects respond by giving the multiple referent interpretation of the bound variable questions a reasonable proportion of the time.

- H_1: Children know the constraint on strong crossover.
  Expected results:

	Deictic meaning	Bound variable meaning
Bound variable questions:	50%	50%
Crossover questions:	100%	0%

In the present case, both (1) and (2) could be presented in the same contexts, because the null hypothesis claimed that both sentences had the same range of meanings. In our presentation of the experiment, this enabled us to randomly match sentences with contexts. That is, the child could randomly decide which story to listen to on a particular trial (by choosing the bag of toys for the next story), and the experimenter could choose a sentence of one type or the other to present on that trial. This eliminated any effects, favoring one reading or another, that could be due to the context.

Also, because the same contexts could be used for either type of construction, the order of events could be held constant in all of the contexts. If the order of events favored the bound variable interpretation of one type of question, then, by hypothesis, this interpretation would be favored to the same extent for the other type of sentence.

38.2 Discourse Binding

Several factors make it impossible to achieve the same degree of control in other cases. Nonetheless, even in these cases we were able to distinguish grammatical knowledge from preferences to a large extent. Again, the strategy was to compare children's interpretations of control sentences with their interpretation of test sentences.

The study of children's adherence to the closure constraint on discourse binding is a good example of using a different structure as a control. Recall that, in a test of the closure constraint, children were presented with linguistic items like (3) and (4). The null hypothesis was that children would permit an anaphoric link between the pronoun and the quantified NP in both (3) and (4). The experimental hypothesis was that only (4) permits such linkages; they are prohibited in (3) by the closure constraint.

(3)   No mouse came to Simba's party. He wore a hat.

(4)   No mouse at Simba's party said he wore a hat.

Items like (3) and (4) cannot be presented in identical contexts, however, because (3) consists of two sentences, and (4) of only one.

In the experimental situations acted out for (3) and (4), however, the bound variable reading is associated with the "Yes" response. The order of events in both contexts also favors the bound variable reading—it is the last event acted out. If the order of events favors the bound variable interpretation of one type of sentence, then, by hypothesis, this interpretation should be favored to a similar extent for the other type of sentence. Suppose the findings of the experiment are as predicted by the experimental hypothesis; that is, children reject any link between *no mouse* and *he* in (3), but allow it in (4). Nevertheless, it could be maintained that the lack of a bound variable reading in (3) results from some unexplained difference in the properties of (3) and (4). It is logically possible that (3) does allow an anaphoric link between the pronoun and the quantified NP but that this link is highly dispreferred. There could be some hidden difference between the two sentence types that results in a stronger preference for the bound variable reading in (4) than in (3). But this would be a post hoc explanation of the pattern of responses that the experimental hypothesis predicts. Moreover, anyone advocating such a position would be obliged to explain why there are strong parsing pressures in one direction for one kind of example but in the opposite direction for the other kind of example. In the absence of independent evidence for such a state of affairs, which we judge to be highly unlikely, the pattern of results can be taken as presumptive support for the principle under investigation.

38.3 Plural NPs Reconsidered

We conclude this chapter by returning to the problematic case introduced in the previous chapter: plural NPs. In the study under discussion, children were presented with indirect questions like the ones in (5).

(5) a.   I know how many hamburgers the octopuses have. Three.
         or
     b.   I know how many hamburgers the octopuses have. One.

The puppet, Kermit the Frog, expressed both the question and its answer. Kermit gave the distributive answer, "One," or the collective answer, "Three," on different trials. In the context, there were three octopuses, and each octopus was holding one hamburger. Therefore, Kermit's question/answer pair was correct on either trial. However, many children accepted only the distributive answer, "One," and rejected the collective answer.

   Are there control sentences that could be presented to children in order to tell whether or not the collective interpretation of plural NPs is available to them? One possibility was suggested to us by Susan Carey and Gavin Huntley. They pointed out the existence of purely "collective" NPs like *army*, *family* and *forest*. These collective NPs could easily be incorporated into the experiment. For example, different trials could compare the plural NP *trees* with its unambiguous, collective counterpart *forest*.

(6) (a) I know how many kites got stuck in the trees. Four/One.
         vs.
     (b) I know how many kites got stuck in the forest. Four/One.

Suppose that the context includes a forest consisting of four trees, each with a kite stuck in it. Comparing children's responses to the alternatives in (6) would determine whether or not they had the collective interpretation of a plural NP available to them. If children continued to accept only a distributive answer, "One," with collective nouns like *forest*, then it could be inferred that they did not have the collective interpretation available to them.

Chapter 39

Resolving the Dilemma: Varying the Context

At the end of chapter 37, we were left facing a dilemma. The study of children's knowledge of the distributive and collective interpretations of plural NPs by Miyamoto and Crain (1991) was designed to investigate the availability of both interpretations of plural NPs (also see Miyamoto 1992; Avrutin et al. 1992). However, only one reading was successfully evoked on most trials. We have just discussed one way to resolve the dilemma, by means of control sentences. In this chapter, we will discuss another way: making changes in the context. This maneuver not only permits us to probe further for the availability of additional readings of ambiguities, beyond those that are preferred in ambiguous circumstances, but also allows us to return to a point made in chapter 1: that children are extremely sensitive to changes in pragmatic context.

39.1 Individual versus Collective Events

A second experiment by Miyamoto and Crain tested 24 children between the ages of 3;0 and 6;0 (mean age 4;11), using sentences like the following:

(1) They are lifting four cans.

The experimental trial corresponding to (1) involved two characters, Big Bird and Ernie. The story that was acted out had two parts. First, both characters engaged in a contest to see who could lift more cans. Each of them succeeded in lifting two cans. Kermit the Frog described what he thought happened, using the test sentence "They are lifting four cans." Here, the context favors a distributive interpretation of the sentence; it is pragmatically odd on the collective interpretation. Therefore, we will call this the *distributive condition* of the experiment. Following the distributive condition, Ernie still wanted to win the contest, so he attempted to lift all four cans by himself. The cans turned out to be too heavy and he started to drop them. At this point, Big Bird came to his rescue, and together they managed to lift the entire set of four cans. Again, Kermit described the situation with a variant of the original test sentence: "They are holding four cans." In this context, Kermit's description is pragmatically appropriate on the collective reading, but not on the distributive interpretation. Therefore, we will call this the *collective condition*.

If children are like adults in processing ambiguous sentences, then they will prefer the interpretation that matches the discourse context. This is Principle of Referential Success, described earlier.[1] Children who adhere to this principle of ambiguity resolution should assign the collective interpretation in the collective condition and the distributive interpretation in the distributive condition. This is exactly what happened in the experiment. Children responded affirmatively to the test sentences in the collective condition 89% of the time. This is not too surprising, because the sentences were both true and pragmatically felicitous in this condition on the collective interpretation.

In the distributive condition, where each character lifted two cans, Kermit's statement "They are lifting four cans" was *false* on this interpretation. Accordingly, children rejected Kermit's statement 70% of the time. This is evidence that children were guided the Principle of Referential Success. Presumably, children's mental model of the discourse context represented the two "lifting events" separately, and this caused them to decide on the truth value of the sentence on the basis of the distributive interpretation. Despite the pragmatic infelicity of the collective interpretation, there was some tendency for children to assign this interpretation, because it made Kermit's statement true. However, the match between the sentence and the children's mental model of the discourse was the main contributor to their decision about which interpretation to assign.

The findings of Miyamoto and Crain's study show that children can access both the collective and the distributive interpretations of plural pronouns, if the context is appropriate. Analyzing the data by age produced another interesting finding: children younger than 5 rejected Kermit's statement in the distributive condition 84% of the time, as compared to 70% for all children. This outcome has several possible explanations. First, younger children might differ from older ones in the strength of their bias to say "Yes," being less concerned with making a speaker's utterance true. Second, younger children might favor the distributive interpretation over the collective interpretation to a greater degree than do older children. Finally, younger children could adhere to the Principle of Referential Success with greater tenacity than older children. The last possibility seems the most likely, but further discussion of the issue would take us too far afield.

In addition, Miyamoto and Crain's findings invite us to infer that children, like adults, hypothesize a covert distributive operator (D-operator) to express the distributive interpretation of plural NPs (Heim, Lasnik, and May 1991). This is the point of departure for the experiment reported in section 39.4. The experiment, by Avrutin and Thornton (1994), owes a debt to Miyamoto and Crain for the observation that the discourse context has considerable influence on children's decisions about which interpretation to assign to ambiguous sentences.

39.2 Learnability Considerations

We should ask whether the findings from Miyamoto and Crain's (1991) study pose a learnability problem. A learnability problem would arise if the following circumstances conspire against the child. First, the sentence in question must be ambiguous for adults, but not for children. Second, the circumstances corresponding to the alternative interpretations (for adults) are in a subset/superset relation. Third, the child's initial hypothesis about the sole meaning of the sentence is the superset interpretation, according to which the sentence is true in a superset of the circumstances corresponding to the alternative interpretation.

Fortunately, the distributive and collective interpretations of plural NPs are not in a subset/superset relationship. If a child initially hypothesizes the distributive interpretation, real-world experience will provide ample evidence for the alternative, collective interpretation. For example, the child could encounter a sentence like

"Gennaro and David have 50 cents," in a context in which, say, Gennaro has 10 cents and David has 40 cents. Since the child was expecting the total to be $1.00, it will be clear that the distributive interpretation yields the wrong results for such sentence/meaning pairs. Similarly, if the child initially hypothesizes the collective interpretation, there will be ample evidence for the alternative, distributive interpretation. For example, the child could encounter the sentence "Gennaro and David have 50 cents" in a context in which Gennaro and David each have 50 cents.

39.3 Principle B Reconsidered

This chapter concludes with another example of the research strategy for studying children's grammars, according to which the context is modified while the structure of the test sentences is held constant. The example comes from a study by Avrutin and Thornton (1994) designed to test children's knowledge of a covert quantificational operator associated with plural NPs.

This study is based on the observation made by Wexler and Chien (1985) and many others that some young children incorrectly accept sentence (2) as a description of a story in which Papa Bear covers himself (with, say, a blanket), but does not cover another male character who is salient in the discourse context (and similarly for other, analogous sentences).

(2)   Papa Bear covered him.

Recall that the same children who accept (2) reject (3) in the same context, that is, when Papa Bear covers himself (Thornton 1990; also see Avrutin and Wexler 1992).

(3)   I know who covered him. Papa Bear.

Evidently, children who allow an illicit interpretation of certain sentences with referring expressions, like *Papa Bear*, adhere to the relevant constraint on interpretation (i.e., Principle B of the binding theory) when a quantificational NP and a pronoun are related, as in (3), that is, when the pronoun is bound by the NP. In other words, children distinguish between bound and referential pronouns, in that they fail to observe an adultlike restriction on the interpretation of referential pronouns. It is worth remarking that many languages make an overt distinction between referential pronouns and bound pronouns. In Spanish, for example, bound pronouns are not phonetically realized in certain syntactic contexts, whereas pronouns are overt if they are used referentially. Some children learning English have incorporated this distinction into their grammar, as well; although their grammars follow the natural seams of the theory of Universal Grammar, they are not the seams of the target language.

Pronouns are not the only linguistic elements that can be either overt or covert. Operators share this chameleon-like quality. There were overt operators in the sentences children were asked to respond to in Wexler and Chien's studies (e.g., *Every bear covered him*). In the study by Avrutin and Thornton, children responded to sentences with conjoined NPs (e.g., *The Smurf and the Troll covered him*), which are associated with a covert operator in certain cases, according to Heim, Lasnik, and May's (1991) account. A covert operator is attached to a conjoined NP when it is being assigned a distributive interpretation. A distributive interpretation, in turn, is appropriate in a context where the members of the group being referred to by the pronoun are analyzed individually. For example, consider the conjoined NP *the Smurf and the*

Troll in (4), and imagine a context in which two characters, Grover and Big Bird, ask the Smurf and the Troll to cover them.

(4)   *The Smurf and the Troll* covered them.

It would be appropriate to assign the distributive interpretation to the conjoined NP, *the Smurf and the Troll*, in a context in which the Smurf covered Grover and Big Bird with a blanket at one time and the Troll covered them at another time. In such a context, call it the distributive context, we would expect the covert distributive operator to be attached to the subject NP. The distributive operator would be absent in another context, where the Smurf and the Troll together covered Big Bird and Grover. In this context, call it the collective context, the conjoined NP *the Smurf and the Troll* is given a collective or group interpretation.

To test for the distributive operator in children's linguistic representations, Avrutin and Thornton used sentences like (4), presented in distributive contexts and in collective contexts.[2] The two contexts were alike in all essential respects. In the story that was presented to children, the Smurf and the Troll refuse to cover Grover and Big Bird, because they need their blankets for themselves. In the collective context, having refused to cover Grover and Big Bird, the Smurf and the Troll cover themselves together with a big blanket. In the distributive context, there were two separate events. In the first event, the Smurf refuses to cover Grover and Big Bird and covers himself, instead. The second event repeats this scenario, with the Troll saying he is unable to cover Grover and Big Bird and covering himself instead.

Adults' grammar prohibits *them* from referring to *the Smurf and the Troll* in (4), regardless of whether the conjoined NP is given a collective or a distributive interpretation. But we have seen that, for some children, it makes a difference whether an NP contains an operator or not. The children who accept an anaphoric relation between a pronoun and a referring expression (as in (2)), but not between a pronoun and an NP with an operator (as in (3)), are ideal candidates to test the proposal that conjoined NPs are assigned a covert operator in some instances. If the proposal that an unseen distributive operator attaches to the subject NP in (4) in a distributive context is correct, then some children should allow coreference in the collective context, but not in the distributive context. These children should prohibit *them* from referring to *the Smurf and the Troll* in the distributive context, owing to the presence of the unseen operator. This is exactly what Avrutin and Thornton found. Twelve out of 33 children were identified as relevant subjects. That is, these children were sensitive to the presence of an operator, distinguishing sentences like (2) from sentences like (3), and they demonstrated knowledge of the collective and distributive distinction in a separate control condition.[3] These 12 children accepted the collective context of (4) 93% of the time, but the distributive context only 27% of the time.[4]

Avrutin and Thornton's study underscores three points about investigating children's knowledge of linguistic principles. First, the findings demonstrate the utility of studies of child language for evaluating theoretical proposals. Second, the study illustrates children's sensitivity to variations in pragmatic context. With the sentence held constant, children assigned different linguistic analyses to the conjoined NPs depending on features of the discourse context. Third, the findings illustrate a linguistic distinction that is hidden in adult English but overtly manifested in many of the world's languages. Therefore, the findings represent another challenge for the Input Matching Model.

Chapter 40
Conclusion

Recent advances in linguistic theory have led investigators to hypothesize that more linguistic knowledge is innately specified than was previously thought. Much of this knowledge is seen to be encoded in principles and parameters. Innate linguistic principles, in turn, assist in the formation of a variety of linguistic constructions, certain properties of which must be learned from experience (see Crain, McKee, and Emiliani 1990; Crain and Fodor 1993). If not all aspects of a linguistic construction are innately given, we might expect some delay in its acquisition. However, we should expect it to emerge just as soon as the relevant learning has taken place. Unfortunately, a great many research findings do not comport well with the expectation that linguistic knowledge should emerge early in development. Worse still, apparent violations of putatively innate linguistic principles have occasionally been reported (e.g., Jakubowicz 1984; Lust 1981; Matthei 1981, 1982; Phinney 1981; Roeper 1986; Solan and Roeper 1978; Tavakolian 1978, 1981). In addition, longitudinal studies of children's spontaneous productions suggest that language develops gradually, such that many linguistic constructions—even ones that receive special assistance from innate principles—are mastered quite late.

Slow acquisition and a high proportion of errors by children in experimental studies seem out of step with recent findings in the literature on child language development, however. Children have been found to perform almost flawlessly in response to sentences that require complex syntactic and semantic representations. This has been true especially if the linguistic principles are arguably part of the child's innate linguistic knowledge, that is, if the principles under investigation are linguistic universals. In addition, apparent gaps in children's knowledge of other linguistic phenomena have often proved to be artifacts of inappropriate experimental methodology. On the basis of these findings, the Modularity Matching Model maintains not only that children have access to Universal Grammar, as adults do, but also that the principles of Universal Grammar have primacy over nonlinguistic factors for children, just as they do for adults (Fodor 1983; Crain and Steedman 1985). Owing to the modular architecture of the language apparatus, grammatical knowledge preempts nonlinguistic factors. Nonlinguistic factors do not compete with linguistic knowledge pursuant to linguistic behavior. In fact, nonlinguistic factors exert little influence on behavior. Their role is limited to circumstances in which linguistic knowledge fails to yield a well-formed and interpretable analysis of the input. Ordinarily, however, children are expected to process linguistic information as well as adults do.

High error rates continue to be accepted, however, by researchers who view linguistic behavior as an aggregate of linguistic and nonlinguistic factors. According to this viewpoint, the Competing Factors Model, the influence of factors extraneous to grammar may be enough to make ungrammatical sentences acceptable for children, or these factors may conspire to make children reject grammatical sentences. In this book, we have questioned this viewpoint and its methodological foundation. We have tried to show that apparent gaps in children's syntactic knowledge are artifacts of experimental design—the introduction of nonsyntactic demands caused children to make errors. This conclusion is supported by evidence that children's errors disappear, or are greatly reduced, when tasks that minimize the nonlinguistic burdens of language processing are used to assess their linguistic knowledge.

These observations underscore the need for a considered discussion of research strategies and empirical tools in child language studies. The research strategies and designs introduced in this book are offered in the hope that this need can eventually be met, and in the hope that they may eventually bring research findings in line with the expectations of linguistic theory. To conclude, we hope that this book will aid students and researchers in designing new experimental studies. We have tried to offer specific guidelines for research design, introducing research strategies that we believe will further advance understanding of children's universal mastery of the syntactic and semantic principles of Universal Grammar.

Notes

Chapter 1

1. For a survey of experimental methods, see McDaniel, McKee, and Cairns 1996.
2. Whether or not adults learning a second language have access to the LAD is a matter of debate that we will not take up here.
3. For an introduction to syntax within the generative framework, we recommend Haegeman 1994; Radford 1988 provides a more general introduction. For an introduction to semantic theory, we recommend Chierchia and McConnell-Ginet 1990 and Larson and Segal 1995.

Chapter 2

1. There are even caveats to this expectation. For example, it may turn out that not every language exhibits the structural prerequisites for the application of the principle in question.
2. Some constraints that meet this criterion are stated in positive terms. When they take this form, they generally indicate what *must be* the case. For example, Principle A of the binding theory states that an anaphor (e.g., a reflexive pronoun) must have a local antecedent. This is logically equivalent to the negative statement that an anaphor cannot fail to have a local antecedent. Clearly, then, the removal of this constraint from the grammar would result in an increase in sentence/meaning pairs, to include ones in which a reflexive appears without a local antecedent.
3. In later chapters, we present evidence that augmenting one's mental model in this way is quite difficult, both for children and for adults.
4. Although in most cases the grammatical knowledge of adults is not at issue, it is usually important to incorporate adult controls in an experiment, to ensure that the task is tapping linguistic knowledge (see chapter 29).

Chapter 3

1. The form in which this knowledge is encoded is subject to debate, however. For example, some researchers have argued that constraints are not statements within the theory of grammar, but are part of the architecture of the human parsing apparatus (see Fodor and Crain 1987).
2. Recall that constraints need not be stated negatively to be prohibitions against certain sentence/meaning pairs. See note 2, chapter 2.
3. To learn constraints on meaning, rather than on form, children would need negative semantic evidence; that is, they would need to be informed in some way that it is illicit to assign certain interpretations to sentences.
4. The observation about the necessity of an abundant supply of negative evidence also presents a challenge to conservative learning strategies that invoke special "cues" or "triggers." If any of the necessary ingredients for grammar formation are not abundant in the input, then some learners would not encounter them, and these learners would fall short of the target grammar.

Chapter 4

1. In parts II and III, the term *null hypothesis* is used differently, to refer to one set of possible experimental outcomes, namely, outcomes that are not expected according to the model under investigation. At that point, we will use lowercase to distinguish that use of the term from its present use.

Chapter 5

1. At least, the LAD is no longer in service in the analysis of adults' first language. There is some suggestive evidence that the LAD may be available for second language learning.
2. As expected on the Continuity Hypothesis, there is a crosslinguistic parallel to the structure in (6) in the Paduan dialect of Italian.
3. We are grateful to William Snyder for this idea, and for pointing out its negative empirical consequences.
4. Lacking real-world knowledge, children may also be more consistent in their judgments than adults are.

Chapter 6

1. A mode is a measure of central tendency, like the mean or median. A mode is a peak in the distribution of scores. The mode is a useful description of distributions of scores with more than one peak.
2. If the true component in the observations made by children is the same as the true component in the observations made by adults, then the overall distribution will be normal, although the magnitude of the error will be greater for children; hence, the contribution of the true component to children's linguistic behavior will be less. For example, in a task in which children are asked to judge whether sentences are true or false, almost no children (or adults) should indicate that all of the test items are true or all are false.
3. Parametric statistics are used to evaluate quantitative measures of distributions of observations drawn from populations that exhibit certain special characteristics, and where the sample size is sufficiently large. Parametric statistics (e.g., the t test, analysis of variance) are contrasted with nonparametric statistics (e.g., the chi-square test), which are more appropriate for populations that do not meet the assumptions underlying the use of parametric statistics, or where the sample size is small.
4. Parametric statistics may be applied to the findings of experiments adopting the truth value judgment task, provided there are enough subjects and items. This may seem surprising because the data from such a task are on a nominal scale. These data can be converted to an interval scale, however, by averaging across trials. According to the Central Limit Theorem, the resulting data approximate a normal distribution in the limit.
5. We would add the caveat that there are circumstances in which children's grammatical knowledge is overruled or goes unused. We will discuss several of these circumstances. Also, see Fodor 1984 for a related discussion of adult linguistic judgments.
6. Here we are simply following conventional wisdom, as advocated, for example, by the criterion of attributing knowledge of a grammatical process if it is manifested at least 90% of the time in obligatory contexts.

Chapter 7

1. Children's responses to ambiguous control sentences also serve an important function: they are the yardstick against which to compare children's responses to sentences within the jurisdiction of the constraint.
2. Moreover, when the results of a statistical test are significant, it is inferred that other subjects who are similar to the ones sampled by the experimenter would also be influenced by the true component of behavior in a similar test of their linguistic knowledge.
3. This expectation may seem counterintuitive to readers who are familiar with findings from the literature on adult sentence processing, where longer reaction time is usually associated with processing difficulty.

Chapter 8

1. The other order of main and subordinate clauses was tested for both temporal conjunctions in all of the studies under consideration.
2. Not all adults share the intuition that the event mentioned in the relative clause is conceptually prior to the event mentioned in the main clause. We have queried hundreds of undergraduate and graduate students, however, and most agree with this intuition.

Chapter 9

1. Moreover, it should be appropriate in the context for the bear to say that the turtle tickled the horse. We leave aside the pragmatic prerequisites for this statement by the bear.
2. Moreover, experimenters often make it clear that figures that are not mentioned in the test sentences can be used in acting out the content of the sentences.

Chapter 10

1. Moreover, experimenters often make it clear that figures that are not mentioned in the test sentences can be used in acting out the content of the sentences.
2. Of course, children would accept meaning$_1$ at rates approaching 100% if this interpretation was associated with the "Yes" response in the (ambiguous) context.
3. Adults also reject the sentences, but for a different reason; adults reject them because the constraint permits only one reading, and the context is such that this reading makes the sentences false.
4. Of course, if it can be shown that children do not prefer the interpretation that is false in the context (i.e., the adult interpretation), then the Competing Factors Model could be maintained; but advocates of the Competing Factors Model do not see the necessity of such a demonstration.

Chapter 11

1. Of course, the statistical test was performed using raw scores, not these mean percentages for the two conditions.
2. Children's judgments of coreference in response to sentences like (1) do not show that they find such sentences *grammatical*; they show only that they find them *true* (if the pronoun refers to the only linguistic antecedent provided by the context). That is, the pragmatic lead encouraged children to interpret (1) as if it meant *Big Bird ate the apple when Big Bird touched the pillow*. Although true, this sentence too violates Principle C. In experiments that provide an additional linguistic antecedent, children always interpret the pronoun as coreferring with its denotation.
3. Children hypothesize the nonadult representation in addition to an adultlike representation, according to Philip (1995).

Chapter 12

1. To evaluate this conception of the verbal working memory system, we have conducted a number of studies investigating both the kinds of unambiguous sentences that are costly of memory resources, and those sentence types that pose lesser demands on memory resources. Space does not permit us to review the relevant literature here. For discussion and empirical research on the effects of working memory differences on processing, also see Bar-Shalom, Crain, and Shankweiler 1991, Crain, and Shankweiler 1991, and Shankweiler and Crain 1986.

Chapter 13

1. Of course, using a restrictive relative clause in this way is infelicitous. It requires accommodation of the presupposition that some horses had already been raced past the barn; but accommodating in this way avoids adding new entities to the mental model, as dictated by the Principle of Parsimony.
2. Presumably, the (c) versions were easier to repair because they did not require construction of a contrast set immediately before the ambiguity was encountered; the region with the focus operator *only* resulted in elevated reading times in both experiments, as compared to sentences with the definite determiner *the*.
3. The alternative is to suppose that low-span subjects did not initially pursue the NP-attachment analysis of prepositional phrases in sentences with *only*. However, this account fails to explain the significant number of regressions by these subjects in the *only*-VP sentences.
4. Similar findings have been obtained with special populations of adults, such as Broca's aphasics.
5. In keeping with the Modularity Matching Model, Ni, Crain, and Shankweiler (1996) found that people with low working memory capacity did as well as people with high capacity in processing unambiguous sentences containing relative clauses.

Chapter 14

1. Any model of discourse that contains individuals or events whose existence is disconfirmed by new information will have to be modified appropriately, in order to bring the model of the parser in line with that of the interlocutor. Mismatches between the mental models of a speaker and a hearer, or a writer and a reader, are apt to interfere with the flow of information between them. To facilitate the transfer of information, perceivers must continuously attempt to align their mental model with that of the other participants in the discourse. Following the guidelines of the Principle of Parsimony, the strategy adopted by the parser is to avoid interpretations of ambiguous sentences that entail additional commitments about individuals and events within the domain of discourse.

2. This does not entail, however, that both options are derived in the target language. Some options of Universal Grammar may be available in the theory, but may not appear in some particular language. Such is the case with parameter settings, for example. It is important, therefore, not to confuse the state of affairs we are describing, where the child selects among competing grammatical options, with the state of affairs that confronts adults in processing structurally ambiguous sentences.

3. This argument presupposes that negative semantic evidence is not available to learners. That is, we shall assume that learners are not informed with sufficient regularity about interpretations that *cannot* be assigned to sentences in the target language.

4. Even if Universal Grammar makes alternative interpretive options available for a sentence, the sentence is not necessarily ambiguous for the child. As in parameter setting, children may have a range of options available to them in the theory, but they may nevertheless hypothesize only certain of these values at any given time. There is an important difference between parameter setting and the case we are considering, however. In parameter setting, new parameter values supplant old ones. In formulating semantic hypotheses, by contrast, children begin with a limited set of (universal) interpretive options that is then extended to include additional (language-particular) options on the basis of positive evidence.

5. It is important to observe the correlation between the size of a contrast set and the number of commitments being made: the larger the contrast set, the more commitments are being made. The consequence of a large number of commitments is maximal falsifiability.

6. This is not to say that people would necessarily judge this sentence to be a true description of the bottom right-hand picture. In a picture verification task, even adults would probably judge the sentence to be a false description of this picture. We explain why in the chapters on the truth value judgment task. Roughly, the idea is that the picture forces hearers to regard the "extra" characters as relevant to the interpretation of the sentence. For now, we refer the reader to the "test" mentioned in section 14.1, which relies on the imagination of the adult subjects.

Chapter 15

1. Children may also make errors if for some reason they cannot assign any grammatical representation to a sentence, perhaps because they cannot comprehend the sentence because it is too long or too complex. In such cases, children may well invoke nonlinguistic factors in interpreting the sentence and may attempt to assign it an interpretation that makes it true in the discourse context. It follows from the assumption of modularity matching, however, that these sources of errors will have a similar effect on adults.

2. This may ultimately turn out to be incorrect. If it is, the proportion of incorrect responses will sometimes be inflated for children, but the incorrect response made by children and adults should be similar in nature. In short, children would make more errors, but their errors would be the same kind that adults also make. From a statistical point of view, the different responses by children and adults to various linguistic constructions should appear as "main effects," but there should be no "group-by-construction interactions."

3. The tendency to use "reduced forms" also underlies people's tendency to contract, when contraction is permissible. An example from chapter 2 was the phenomenon known as "*wanna* contraction," where *want* and *to* are contracted to form *wanna*. This preference for producing contracted forms proves to be quite strong in both children and adults. Another consequence of the preference for reduced forms is the omission of optional complementizers. However, in sentences in which linguistic principles do not tolerate contraction or where complementizers are obligatory, contraction of *want* and *to* to form *wanna*, or the deletion of a null complementizer should not occur in the speech of either adults or children, according to the Modularity Matching Model.

4. It is interesting to speculate on the possibility that the parser's preferences may cause genuine performance errors, in some cases. That is, even when the grammar of a particular language does not permit

one to use a certain reduced form, the language user could, in times of stress, respond in a way that is consistent with the grammar of another language. In fact, evidence for this comes from an experiment on elicitation of bound pronouns (Thornton and Crain 1989). In the first few trials of the experiment, when children were trying to access the structure mandated by the experimental situation, some children produced null pronouns, asking questions like "Who thinks____is the skinniest?" instead of "Who thinks he is the skinniest?" The result is not a parsing preference, since the response is not a viable option in English; "Avoid Pronoun" is not a grammatical option. However, this performance error could, in some sense, be a reflection of the parser's inner workings.

Chapter 16

1. For researchers testing children's acquisition of American Sign Language (ASL), however, use of puppets is problematic, because it is very difficult to make a puppet sign. Yet, for all the reasons presented, it remains desirable to have a puppet interact with the child. To counteract this problem, Lillo-Martin and her colleagues have one of the experimenters (the one who would play the role of the puppet in tests using a spoken language) actually dress up as the character, wear face paint, and so on. This modification has been very successful. Presumably, children do not envisage the dressed-up character as an adult with this modification of the task.
2. If it is feasible, the sessions can be videotaped. In general, we do not videotape every experimental session. We do try to videotape several sessions of each experiment, however, to document the experiment and for use in classes and at conferences.

Chapter 17

1. In cases where the construction of interest occurs frequently, presumably transcripts of children's spontaneous productions can yield sufficient data for analysis.
2. Some of the alternative explanations of negative findings apply more forcefully to comprehension tasks and to the Competing Factors Model. In studies of elicited production, children's productions can be used to make inferences about their intended messages. Moreover, on the Modularity Matching Model, statistical power is not an issue, because the experimental hypothesis is the total absence of certain forms of behavior by all subjects, both children and adults. This leaves, as alternatives to the experimental hypothesis, factors such as parsing strategies and memory limitations; these will therefore be the focus of the rest of our remarks.

Chapter 18

1. On the account proposed by McDaniel, Cairns, and Hsu (1991), children have a different processing system from adults, however. They suggest that children generate a coordinate structure as a default structure, because the appropriate control structure is too complex to process.
2. This study elicited both subject and object gap relative clauses.

Chapter 20

1. The machinery we adopt is one notation that is employed by linguists to indicate the pertinent structural relationships in the examples under consideration. It is these structural relationships that are important, and not the notation itself.
2. It was important that the experimenter point out the relevant characteristics of the picture to the child so that the child did not focus on details irrelevant to the experiment.
3. This example is introduced for purposes of illustration. In practice, we avoid experimental items that suggest violence.

Chapter 21

1. More specifically, contraction is prohibited across a wh-trace that is Case-marked (Chomsky 1980; Jaeggli 1980). An alternative explanation of the facts offered by Snyder and Rothstein (1992) is that a null, Case-assigning complementizer is responsible for blocking the contraction. The details of the syntactic analysis are not important for the discussion in this chapter.

2. The constraint is most easily studied in dialects of American English, where *wanna* contraction is widespread. In British and other varieties of English, the difference between the contracted and non-contracted forms may not be so obvious. The point holds, however. Questions extracting from subject position should not exhibit contraction.

Chapter 22

1. By saying that the *wh*-phrase is in the intermediate CP, we intend to remain neutral at this point about the position of the medial-*wh* in the phrase structure.

2. The term *medial-wh* is not used here in the same way it is used in de Villiers, Roeper, and Vainikka 1990 and subsequent papers. In those works, *medial-wh* refers to the *wh*-phrase in the embedded SpecCP in questions with two *wh*-phrases such as *When did Cookie Monster know what to bake?* We use *medial-wh* only to refer to children's long-distance *wh*-questions that contain a copy of the *wh*-phrase in the embedded CP.

3. In the Minimalist Program, being developed by Chomsky since 1992, the ECP no longer has a role to play. Many of the facts previously explained by the ECP are now explained by "shortest move."

4. As we explain later, there were in fact children who always used the complementizer. We argue that this is a consequence of their grammar. Children override the parsing preference to reduce forms in order to generate syntactic representations that are in keeping with their current grammar.

5. Strictly speaking, since *want* is an exceptional-Case-marking verb, questions from the *wanna* contraction paradigm cannot shed light on the status of the medial-*wh* in all infinitival clauses.

6. The obvious question is why there should be a preference to insert a complementizer in factive structures, when there is a preference to delete complementizers in declaratives and *wh*-questions. The answer is not clear, but the Modularity Matching Model would predict that it arises for grammatical reasons. Factives are generally thought to contain a null operator in SpecCP (or some other projection) (Melvold 1991; Watanabe 1993). It may be that since the operator is null, there is some requirement that the head be overt (for this idea, see Speas 1994).

7. The column labeled "Partial" in table 22.1 indicates partial movement questions. In addition to the data summarized in table 22.1, another set of long-distance questions was elicited from each child. In these questions, the adverb *really* was inserted into the lead-in (e.g., "Ask the snail what he thinks really ..."), with the hope that this would elicit more complementizers (see Thornton 1990). The questions did not differ significantly in form from those reported in table 22.1.

8. One standard view is that in subject extraction questions, the trace in the intermediate SpecCP is a proper governor for the trace in subject position of the embedded clauses. If a complementizer is present, however, antecedent government by the intermediate trace is blocked (see Lasnik and Uriagereka 1988; Haegeman 1994).

9. There are also other possible scenarios. Children do not necessarily have to pass through the outlined stages in turn. If children are sensitive to the input in the form of adult questions, they will realize that in addition to being necessary only for subject extraction questions, spec-head agreement does not need to be expressed overtly. If they make both of these observations simultaneously, they will not pass through the second stage, in which they think English spec-head agreement is like the French version in being realized overtly.

10. It may be that the verb *want* takes a CP complement. See Snyder and Rothstein 1992 for arguments supporting this view.

11. There are certain syntactic environments in which *that*-trace effects appear to be suspended—for example, cases involving a topicalized adverb (Culicover 1991; Rizzi 1996). This is illustrated in (i) and (ii) (examples from Julien Musolino).

    (i)   *Which amendment do you think that *t* will become law?

    (ii)   Which amendment do you think that next year will become law?

12. In the dialects of German and Romanian that allow a copy of the *wh*-phrase in the intermediate CP, the structure is apparently optional. If children were to start out thinking that the medial-*wh* was optional, however, they would be faced with a learnability problem. What evidence could inform them that the medial-*wh* is not permissible? All of the positive evidence would be consistent with their hypothesized grammar.

13. We say "SpecCP" here, because we include partial movement questions as a form expressing overt spec-head agreement. But unlike medial-*wh* questions and questions with a *that* complementizer, partial

movement questions may contain the extra *wh*-phrase in SpecCP. For this reason, we sometimes refer to filled CPs rather than filled Comp positions.

14. These figures are calculated across question types and do not differentiate between medial-*wh* questions and partial movement questions.

Chapter 23

1. These structures are attested in children's spontaneous productions, but not with sufficient frequency to determine whether they represent a grammatical phenomenon. For example, in an extensive search of 1,500 negative utterances from 14 children in the CHILDES database (MacWhinney and Snow 1985), Stromswold (1990) found only eight examples of questions like those in (3b) and (4b), with two auxiliary verbs.

2. One diagnostic of D-linked *wh*-phrases is their incompatibility with certain modifications, such as *the hell* or *in the world* (Pesetsky 1987). Notice that *Who the hell broke my window?* is fine, but *Which boy the hell broke my window?* is not.

3. In children's declarative sentences, such as "I think that the Spaceman likes beans," the presence of a complementizer does not signal that spec-head agreement has taken place. However, individual children used *that* to signal spec-head agreement, as mentioned in chapter 22.

4. Stepwise movement is necessary so that there is a proper head governor for the trace in subject position.

Chapter 25

1. There are modifications to the act-out task that can overcome this deficiency, at least in some cases. For example, if an experimenter can establish that children have a preference for one interpretation of an ambiguous control sentence, but consistently avoid this interpretation in acting out a sentence that is unambiguous in the adult grammar, it would be reasonable to infer that they were overriding their preference owing to a linguistic constraint on interpretations. The same general strategy will serve as the foundation for variants of the elicited production task.

2. Caution must be used, however, in interpreting the results of experiments. It may look as though children lack a constraint when they do not. For example, it has been argued that children's apparent failure to obey Principle B results either from (a) a limitation in processing capacity (Grodzinsky and Reinhart 1993) or (b) lack of knowledge of a pragmatic principle needed to apply Principle B properly to certain linguistic expressions, namely, pronouns that are anaphorically linked to referential NPs (Chien and Wexler 1990).

Chapter 26

1. This statement of Principle C is a subcase of the more general formulation of the principle that states that an r-expression must be free (i.e., not coindexed with any c-commanding NP). There are two reasons for using the statement in (6). First, all of the relevant examples will involve pronouns. Second, there are languages that run counter to the more general formulation of Principle C but, as far as we know, not to the formulation in (6).

2. Indeed, such a preference is expected, if one accepts the claim that young children have a limited verbal working memory capacity (Crain et al. 1990). Other studies have revealed similar effects of working memory on other linguistic constructions, including restrictive relative clauses and temporal adverbial clauses. Thus, children's extrasentential interpretation of pronominals is not by itself convincing evidence that they disallow all cases of backward anaphora.

3. Fifty children participated in trials testing sentences like "He washed Luke Skywalker," and 32 children participated in trials testing "He ate the hamburger when the Smurf was inside the fence."

Chapter 27

1. Other possible background/assertion pairs are given in (i)–(iii).

   (i)   Background: Robocop thinks the Troll is *such-and-such*.
          Assertion: the best jumper

(ii)   Background: Robocop thinks *such-and-such.*
       Assertion: the Troll is the best jumper

(iii) Background: Robocop *does so-and-so.*
       Assertion: thinks the Troll is the best jumper

It is not necessarily wrong to choose one of the pairs in (i)–(iii), but the story would have to be quite different from the one we have developed in this chapter. For example, if the background/assertion pair in (i) were selected, then Robocop would think that the Troll is best at something else besides jumping—say, cooking. But, as before, at some point in the story it should be a possible outcome for Robocop to think that the Troll is the best jumper. Chapter 33 discusses reasons for selecting one background/assertion pair over others.

Chapter 28

1. The experiment is defective in yet another way. Recall that there should be a record at the conclusion of the trial indicating "what really happened" to make the test sentence false. There is no such record in figure 28.2.

Chapter 29

1. *Wh*-phrases move to a position known as SpecCP, the specifier of the CP projection. The subject is positioned in SpecIP before it moves.

Chapter 30

1. Our experiment (reported previously in Thornton 1990 and Crain 1991) was actually conducted at about the same time McDaniel and McKee were independently conducting their experiment on strong crossover.
2. As an additional experimental control, the experimenter might want to check that children have the adult interpretation of crossover questions. In the experimental design laid out, this is equated with a "Yes" response. The experimenter playing Kermit the Frog would say "I know who he said has the best food. The Ninja Turtle." For children who do not have the constraint on strong crossover, the sentence would be ambiguous, and a multiple referent answer would also be possible. Since we set up the correct adult response as the "Yes" response, however, we did not expect children to access the multiple referent interpretation.
3. Notice that in this case, we cannot simply negate the test sentence and assume it must be true. This is because the assertion "He said Grover and Yogi Bear have the best food" is embedded in a discourse consisting of a question/answer pair. The lead-in "I know who ..." is not relevant to the assertion that is being made. Kermit the Frog could have said something like, "Let me tell you what happened in the story. He said that Grover and Yogi Bear have the best food." This format would not have worked here, however, because an indirect question was needed to test the strong crossover configuration *[wh_i ... $pronoun_i$]. The negation of the assertion that is embedded in the discourse is true, however (i.e., "He said that Grover and Yogi Bear have the best food").
4. In this experiment, we tested fewer subjects than usual. This was because we tested these children on a large battery of structures related to binding. We report only the crossover part of the battery here. In normal circumstances, we would aim to test 20 subjects. As we will show, in cases where only some children can be included in the data analysis, it becomes critical to test enough children. For this reason, we are planning to conduct the experiment again with more children.
5. For discussion of within-subjects versus between-subjects designs, and the circumstance in which each is appropriate, see Gordon 1996, McKee 1996, Hsu and Hsu 1996. We generally use within-subjects designs, because each subject serves as his or her own control in such designs.
6. There is no rule-of-thumb way of knowing what the figure should be. The availability of certain readings appears to be construction-specific. We would want the "Yes" responses to be well above 10%, however, since we allow ourselves a 10% error margin.
7. Five of the 7 remaining children participated in the bound variable session. The other 2 children participated in many other sessions, including one testing children's knowledge of crossover in one-clause question structures. Unfortunately, they did not complete the bound variable control for two-clause crossover.

Chapter 31

1. We have chosen to use the term *anaphorically linked* rather than *coreferential* here because we will be discussing cases in which the preceding NP contains a quantifier, such as *every bear* or *no bear*. Since these quantificational NPs are not referring expressions, it seems inappropriate to label the relationship between these expressions and a pronoun one of "coreference."

2. This finding was made by Chien and Wexler (1990) for sentences like *Every bear is washing her*, in which the NP *every bear* is a quantificational NP. (Also see Avrutin and Wexler 1992.) The finding has been confirmed by other researchers, and by Thornton (1990) for the operator *who*.

Chapter 32

1. The force of the argument is blunted, however, by the fact that Chien and Wexler (1990) controlled for intonation (p. 234, fn. 4).

Chapter 35

1. Because the universal quantifier is downward entailing on the nominal constituent it combines with, the disjunction of nominals, *farmer* and *donkey*, in the restrictor clause entails that a *conjunction* of events must satisfy the conditions stated in the nuclear scope. Any event in which there is a farmer *and* any event in which there is a donkey must be an event such that a farmer is feeding a donkey.

Chapter 36

1. As observed by Hamburger and Crain (1982), children find restrictive relative clauses to be most felicitous when they are used to restrict from a larger set. Therefore, each trial included an extra character (a boy, in this case) who did not have the object mentioned in the relative clause. This extra character was also included on the trials in which the test sentence was a conditional.

2. The test materials were divided along another dimension, which hinged on the nature of possession.

Chapter 39

1. If children lacked this Principle of Referential Success, then their response would be dictated by the two remaining factors in the resolution of ambiguities: (a) the preference for one interpretation over another; and (b) the bias to say "Yes" (i.e., accept either interpretation when it makes a true statement about the discourse context). Assuming that both interpretations are equally available to children, they should give "Yes" responses to test sentences like "They are lifting four cans" in both the distributive and collective conditions. This is not what occurred, however.

2. Children heard exactly the same sentence presented twice, once in a distributive context and once in a collective context. So that the game would be more interesting for the children, however, the stories used to test the distributive and collective contexts did not use exactly the same characters. Nevertheless, the stories were identical in all important respects. We have used the same characters in the text just for purposes of exposition.

3. In the control condition, children were presented with contexts that were ambiguous between a collective and a distributive interpretation, but heard a test sentence appropriate for only one of these interpretations. For example, two turtles might be set out in the workspace, each with two pet bugs in front of it. Then Kermit might say, "I know how many bugs they have. Four." This particular utterance would test whether or not children could accept a collective interpretation of the context. To test the distributive context, on other trials Kermit would say, "I know how many bugs they have. Two."

4. One might ask why these children accepted the distributive context as much as 27% of the time. Presumably, this happened because the context is responsible for generating the syntactic representation that contains a distributive operator. It may have been that in some of the stories, the context was not sufficient to cause children to generate the operator. If so, it is highly unlikely that children's acceptances of (4) in the distributive context represent violations of Principle B.

References

Altmann, G., and Steedman, M. (1988). Interaction with context during human sentence processing. *Cognition, 30,* 191–238.

Amidon, A., and Carey, P. (1972). Why five-year-olds cannot understand "before" and "after." *Journal of Verbal Learning and Verbal Behavior, 11,* 417–423.

Atkinson, M. (1996). Now, hang on a minute: Some reflections on emerging orthodoxies. In H. Clahsen (Ed.), *Generative perspectives on language acquisition.* Amsterdam: John Benjamins.

Avrutin, S. (1994). *Psycholinguistic investigations in the theory of reference.* Doctoral dissertation, MIT, Cambridge, MA.

Avrutin, S., Crain, S., Miyamoto, Y., and Wexler, K. (1992). *Who knows everything about what everyone knows? (A study of quantification in child grammar).* Paper presented at the Workshop on the Acquisition of WH, University of Massachusetts, Amherst.

Avrutin, S., and Philip, W. (1994). *Quantification in agrammatic aphasia.* Paper presented at the Annual Meeting of the Linguistic Society of America, Boston.

Avrutin, S., and Thornton, R. (1994). Distributivity and binding in child grammar. *Linguistic Inquiry, 25,* 265–271.

Avrutin, S., and Wexler, K. (1992). Development of Principle B in Russian: Coindexation at LF and coreference. *Language Acquisition, 2,* 259–306.

Bar-Shalom, E., Crain, S., and Shankweiler, D. (1991). A comparison of comprehension and production abilities of good and poor readers. *Applied Psycholinguistics, 14,* 197–227.

Bellugi, U. (1967). *The acquisition of negation.* Doctoral dissertation, Harvard University, Cambridge, MA.

Bellugi, U. (1971). Simplification in children's language. In R. Huxley and E. Ingram (Eds.), *Language acquisition: Models and methodology.* New York: Academic Press.

Berko, J. (1958). The child's learning of English morphology. *Word, 14,* 150–177.

Bloom, P. (1990). Subjectless sentences in child grammar. *Linguistic Inquiry, 21,* 491–504.

Bloom, P. (1993). Grammatical continuity in language development: The case of subjectless sentences. *Linguistic Inquiry, 24,* 721–734.

Borer, H., and Wexler, K. (1987). The maturation of syntax. In T. Roeper and E. Williams (Eds.), *Parameter setting.* Dordrecht: Reidel.

Borer, H., and Wexler, K. (1992). Bi-unique relations and the maturation of grammatical principles. *Natural Language & Linguistic Theory, 10,* 147–190.

Bowerman, M. F. (1987). Commentary: Mechanisms of language acquisition. In B. MacWhinney (Ed.), *Mechanisms of language acquisition.* New York: Springer-Verlag.

Bowerman, M. F. (1988). The "no negative evidence" problem: How do children avoid constructing an overly general grammar? In J. A. Hawkins (Ed.), *Explaining language universals.* Oxford: Blackwell.

Braine, M. (1971). On two types of models of the internalization of grammar. In D. Slobin (Ed.), *The ontogenesis of grammar.* New York: Academic Press.

Brown, R., and Hanlon, C. (1970). Derivational complexity and order of acquisition in child speech. In J. Hayes (Ed.), *Cognition and the development of language.* New York: Wiley.

Cazden, C. (1972). *Child language and education.* New York: Holt, Rinehart and Winston.

Chien, Y.-C., and Wexler, K. (1990). Children's knowledge of locality conditions in binding as evidence for the modularity of syntax and pragmatics. *Language Acquisition, 1,* 225–295.

Chierchia, G. (1992). Anaphora and dynamic binding. *Linguistics and Philosophy, 15,* 111–183.

Chierchia, G. (1995). *Dynamics of meaning: Anaphora, presupposition and syntactic theory.* Chicago: University of Chicago Press.

Chierchia, G., and McConnell-Ginet, S. (1990). *Meaning and grammar.* Cambridge, MA: MIT Press.

Chomsky, C. (1969). *The acquisition of syntax in children from 5 to 10*. Cambridge, MA: MIT Press.

Chomsky, N. (1965). *Aspects of the theory of syntax*. Cambridge, MA: MIT Press.

Chomsky, N. (1971). *Problems of knowledge and freedom*. New York: Pantheon.

Chomsky, N. (1975). *The logical structure of linguistic theory*. New York: Plenum.

Chomsky, N. (1980). *Rules and representations*. New York: Columbia University Press.

Chomsky, N. (1981). *Lectures on government and binding*. Dordrecht: Foris.

Chomsky, N. (1986). *Knowledge of language: Its nature, origin, and use*. New York: Praeger.

Chomsky, N., and Miller, G. (1963). Introduction to the formal analysis of natural languages. In R. D. Luce, R. Bush, and E. Galanter (Eds.), *Handbook of mathematical psychology* (Vol. 2). New York: John Wiley.

Chung, S. (1994). Wh-agreement and "referentiality" in Chamorro. *Linguistic Inquiry, 25*, 1–45.

Chung, S., and McCloskey, J. (1987). Government, barriers, and small clauses in Modern Irish. *Linguistic Inquiry, 18*, 173–237.

Cinque, G. (1990). *Types of Ā-dependencies*. Cambridge, MA: MIT Press.

Clark, E. V. (1971). On the acquisition of the meaning of "before" and "after." *Journal of Verbal Learning and Verbal Behavior, 10*, 266–275.

Comorovski, I. (1989). Discourse-linking and the Wh-Island Constraint. In J. Carter and R.-M. Déchaine (Eds.), *Proceedings of NELS 19*. Amherst: University of Massachusetts, GLSA.

Conway, L. (1997). *Excavating semantics*. Doctoral dissertation, University of Connecticut, Storrs.

Conway, L., and Crain, S. (1995a). Donkey anaphora in child grammar. In J. N. Beckman (Ed.), *NELS 25*. Amherst: University of Massachusetts, GLSA.

Conway, L., and Crain, S. (1995b). Dynamic acquisition. In D. MacLaughlin and S. McEwen (Eds.), *Proceedings of the 19th Annual Boston University Conference on Language Development*. Somerville, MA: Cascadilla Press.

Cook, V. J., and Newson, M. (1996). *Chomsky's Universal Grammar* (2nd ed.). Oxford: Blackwell.

Crain, S. (1982). Temporal terms: Mastery by age five. *Papers and Reports on Child Language Development, 21*, 33–38.

Crain, S. (1991). Language acquisition in the absence of experience. *Behavioral and Brain Sciences, 14*, 597–650.

Crain, S. (1992). *The Semantic Subset Principle in the acquisition of quantification*. Paper presented at the Workshop on the Acquisition of Wh-Extraction and Related Work on Quantification, University of Massachusetts, Amherst.

Crain, S. (1993). *Semantic subsetutions*. Invited paper at The Center for Cognitive Science Conference: Early Cognition and the Transition to Language, University of Texas, Austin.

Crain, S., Conway, L., and Thornton, R. (1994). D-quantification in child language. In J. Fuller, H. Han, and D. Parkinson (Eds.), *ESCOL '94: Proceedings of the 11th Eastern States Conference on Linguistics*. Ithaca, NY: Cornell University, Department of Linguistics.

Crain, S., and Fodor, J. D. (1984). On the innateness of Subjacency. In G. Alvarez, B. Brodie, and T. McCoy, (Eds.), *ESCOL '84: Proceedings of the First Eastern States Conference on Linguistics*. Columbus: The Ohio State University, Department of Linguistics.

Crain, S., and Fodor, J. D. (1985). How can grammars help parsers? In D. R. Dowty, L. Karttunen, and A. Zwicky (Eds.), *Natural language parsing: Psychological, computational, and theoretical perspectives*. Cambridge: Cambridge University Press.

Crain, S., and Fodor, J. D. (1987). Sentence matching and overgeneration. *Cognition, 26*, 123–169.

Crain, S., and Fodor, J. D. (1993). Competence and performance. In E. Dromi (Ed.), *Language and cognition: A developmental perspective*. Norwood, NJ: Ablex.

Crain, S., and Hamburger, H. (1992). Semantics, knowledge and NP modification. In R. Levine (Ed.), *Formal grammar, theory and implementation* (Vol. 2). Vancouver: University of British Columbia Press.

Crain, S., and McKee, C. (1985). The acquisition of structural restrictions on anaphora. In S. Berman, J. Choe, and J. McDonough (Eds.), *Proceedings of NELS 15*. Amherst: University of Massachusetts, GLSA.

Crain, S., McKee, C., and Emiliani, M. (1990). Visiting relatives in Italy. In L. Frazier and J. de Villiers (Eds.), *Language processing and language acquisition*. Dordrecht: Kluwer.

Crain, S., and Nakayama, M. (1987). Structure dependence in grammar formation. *Language, 63*, 522–543.

Crain, S., Ni, W., and Conway, L. (1994). Learning, parsing and modularity. In C. Clifton, L. Frazier, and K. Rayner (Eds.), *Perspectives on sentence processing*. Hillsdale, NJ: Lawrence Erlbaum.

Crain, S., Ni, W., Shankweiler, D., Conway, L., and Braze, D. (1996). Meaning, memory, and modularity. In C. Schütze (Ed.), *MIT occasional papers in linguistics 9: Proceedings of NELS 26 Sentence Processing Workshop*. Cambridge, MA: MIT, Department of Linguistics and Philosophy, MITWPL.

Crain, S., and Philip, W. (1993). *Global semantic dependencies in child language*. Paper presented at the 16th GLOW Colloquium, Lund, Sweden.

Crain, S., and Shankweiler, D. (1991). Modularity and learning to read. In I. G. Mattingly and M. Studdert-Kennedy (Eds.), *Modularity and the motor theory of speech perception*. Hillsdale, NJ: Lawrence Erlbaum.

Crain, S., Shankweiler, D., Macaruso, P., and Bar-Shalom, E. (1990). Working memory and comprehension of spoken sentences: Investigations of children with reading disorder. In G. Vallar and T. Shallice (Eds.), *Neuropsychological disorders of short-term memory*. Cambridge: Cambridge University Press.

Crain, S., and Steedman, M. (1985). On not being led up the garden path: The use of context by the psychological parser. In D. R. Dowty, L. Karttunen, and A. Zwicky (Eds.), *Natural language parsing: Psychological, computational, and theoretical perspectives*. Cambridge: Cambridge University Press.

Crain, S., Thornton, R., Boster, C., Conway, L., Lillo-Martin, D., and Woodams, E. (1996). Quantification without qualification. *Language Acquisition, 5*, 83–153.

Crain, S., Thornton, R., and Murasugi, K. (1987). Capturing the evasive passive. Paper presented at the 12th Annual Boston University Conference on Language Development, Boston.

Crain, S., and Wexler, K. (forthcoming). Methodology in the study of language acquisition: A modular approach. In T. Bhatia and W. Ritchie (Eds.), *Handbook on language acquisition*. San Diego, CA: Academic Press.

Culicover, P. (1991). Polarity, inversion, and focus in English. In G. F. Westphal, B. Ao, and H.-R. Chae (Eds.), *ESCOL '91: Proceedings of the Eighth Eastern States Conference on Linguistics*. Columbus: The Ohio State University, Department of Linguistics.

Daneman, M., and Carpenter, P. A. (1980). Individual differences in working memory and reading. *Journal of Verbal Learning and Verbal Behavior, 19*, 450–466.

Davidson, D. (1967). Truth and meaning. *Synthese, 17*, 304–323.

Deutsch, W., Koster, C., and Koster, J. (1986). What can we learn from children's errors in understanding anaphora? *Linguistics, 24*, 203–225.

de Villiers, J., Roeper, T., and Vainikka, A. (1990). The acquisition of long-distance rules. In L. Frazier and J. de Villiers (Eds.), *Language processing and language acquisition*. Dordrecht: Kluwer.

de Villiers, J. Tager-Flusberg, H., Hakuta, K., and Cohen, M. (1979). Children's comprehension of relative clauses. *Journal of Psycholinguistic Research, 8*, 499–518.

Dobrovie-Sorin, C. (1990). Clitic doubling, *wh*-movement, and quantification in Romanian. *Linguistic Inquiry, 21*, 351–398.

Eisenberg, S. L., and Cairns, H. S. (1994). The development of infinitives from three to five. *Journal of Child Language, 21*, 713–734.

Erreich, A. (1984). Learning how to ask: Patterns of inversion in yes/no and *wh*-questions. *Journal of Child Language, 11*, 579–592.

Ferreiro, E., Othenin-Girard, C., Chipman, H. H., and Sinclair, H. (1976). How do children handle relative clauses? *Archives de Psychologie, 44*, 229–266.

Flynn, S. (1986a). *A parameter-setting model of L2 acquisition: Experimental studies in anaphora*. Dordrecht: Reidel.

Flynn, S. (1986b). Production vs. comprehension: Differences in underlying competences. *Studies in Second Language Acquisition, 8*, 135–164.

Fodor, J. A. (1983). *The modularity of mind*. Cambridge, MA: MIT Press.

Fodor, J. A. (1984). Observation reconsidered. *Philosophy and Science, 51*, 23–43. [Reprinted in A. Goldman (Ed.), *Readings in philosophy and cognitive science*. Cambridge, MA: MIT Press, 1993.]

Fodor, J. A., and Pylyshyn, Z. (1988). Connectionism and cognitive architecture: A critical analysis. *Cognition, 28*, 3–71. [Reprinted in A. Goldman (Ed.), *Readings in philosophy and cognitive science*. Cambridge, MA: MIT Press, 1993.]

Fodor, J. D., and Crain, S. (1987). Simplicity and generality of rules in language acquisition. In B. MacWhinney (Ed.), *Mechanisms of language acquisition*. Hillsdale, NJ: Lawrence Erlbaum.

Frazier, L. (1978). *On comprehending sentences: Syntactic parsing strategies*. Doctoral dissertation, University of Connecticut, Storrs.

Frazier, L., and Fodor, J. D. (1978). The sausage machine: A new two-stage parsing model. *Cognition, 6*, 291–325.

Frazier, L., and Rayner, K. (1982). Making and correcting errors during sentence comprehension: Eye movements in the analysis of structurally ambiguous sentences. *Cognitive Psychology, 14*, 178–210.

Frege, G. (1893). Über Sinn und Bedeutung. *Zeitschrift für Philosophie und philosophische Kritik, 100*, 25–50. [Translated as Frege 1952.]

Frege, G. (1952). On sense and reference. In P. Geach and M. Black (Eds.), *Translations from the philosophical writings of Gottlob Frege*. Oxford: Basil Blackwell.

Gleitman, L. (1990). The structural sources of verb meanings. *Language Acquisition, 1*, 3–55.

Goodluck, H. (1991). *Language acquisition: A linguistic introduction*. Oxford: Blackwell.

Goodluck, H., and Tavakolian, S. L. (1982). Competence and processing in children's grammar of relative clauses. *Cognition, 11*, 1–27.

Gordon, P. (1996). The truth-value judgment task. In D. McDaniel, C. McKee, and H. S. Carins (Eds.), *Methods for assessing children's syntax*. Cambridge, MA: MIT Press.

Gorrell, P., Crain, S., and Fodor, J. D. (1989). Contextual information and temporal terms. *Journal of Child Language, 16*, 623–632.

Grice, H. P. (1975). Logic and conversation. In P. Cole and J. Morgan (Eds.), *Syntax and semantics 3: Speech acts*. New York: Academic Press.

Grimshaw, J., and Rosen, S. T. (1990). Knowledge and obedience: The developmental status of the binding theory. *Linguistic Inquiry, 21*, 187–222.

Grodzinsky, Y. (1990). *Theoretical perspectives on language deficits*. Cambridge, MA: MIT Press.

Grodzinsky, Y., and Reinhart, T. (1993). The innateness of binding and the development of coreference: A reply to Grimshaw and Rosen. *Linguistic Inquiry, 24*, 69–103.

Groenendijk, J., and Stokhof, M. (1991). Dynamic predicate logic. *Linguistics and Philosophy, 14*, 39–100.

Guasti, M. T. (1996). Acquisition of Italian interrogatives. In H. Clahsen (Ed.), *Generative perspectives on language acquisition*. Amsterdam: John Benjamins.

Guasti, M. T., Dubugnon, C., Hassan-Shlonsky, S., and Schnitter, M. (1995). *Quelques aspects de l'acquisition des phrases relatives* [Some aspects of the acquisition of relative clauses]. Ms., DIPSCO, Milan, and the University of Geneva.

Guasti, M. T., and Shlonsky, U. (1995). The acquisition of French relative clauses reconsidered. *Language Acquisition, 4*, 257–277.

Guasti, M. T., Thornton, R., and Wexler, K. (1995). Negation in children's questions: The case of English. In D. MacLaughlin and S. McEwen (Eds.), *Proceedings of the 19th Annual Boston University Conference on Language Development*. Somerville, MA: Cascadilla Press.

Haegeman, L. (1994). *Introduction to Government and Binding Theory* (2nd ed.). Oxford: Blackwell.

Hamburger, H. (1981). A deletion ahead of its time. *Cognition, 8*, 389–416.

Hamburger, H., and Crain, S. (1982). Relative acquisition. In S. Kuczaj (Ed.), *Language development: Syntax and semantics*. Hillsdale, NJ: Lawrence Erlbaum.

Hamburger, H., and Crain, S. (1984). Acquisition of cognitive compiling. *Cognition, 17*, 85–136.

Hamburger, H., and Wexler, K. (1973). Identifiability of a class of transformational grammars. In K. J. J. Hintikka, J. M. E. Moravcsik, and P. Suppes (Eds.), *Approaches to natural language*. Dordrecht: Reidel.

Heim, I. (1982). *The semantics of definite and indefinite NPs*. Doctoral dissertation, University of Massachusetts, Amherst.

Heim, I., Lasnik, H., and May, R. (1991). Reciprocity and plurality. *Linguistic Inquiry, 22*, 63–102.

Hirsh-Pasek, K., and Golinkoff, R. M. (1996). *The origins of grammar: Evidence from early language comprehension*. Cambridge, MA: MIT Press.

Hirsh-Pasek, K., Golinkoff, R., Hermon, G., and Kaufman, D. (1995). Evidence from comprehension for early knowledge of pronouns. In E. Clark (Ed.), *The Proceedings of the 26th Annual Child Language Research Forum*. Stanford, CA: CSLI. [Distributed by Cambridge University Press.]

Hornstein, N., and Lightfoot, D. (1981). *Explanation in linguistics*. London: Longman.

Hornstein, N., Rosen, S. T., and Uriagéreka, J. (1995). Integral predications. In J. Camacho, L. Choueiri, and M. Watanabe (Eds.), *Proceedings of the 14th West Coast Conference on Formal Linguistics*. Stanford, CA: CSLI. [Distributed by Cambridge University Press.]

Hsu, J. R., and Hsu, L. M. (1996). Issues in designing research and evaluating data pertaining to children's syntactic knowledge. In D. McDaniel, C. McKee, H. S. Cairns (Eds.), *Methods for assessing children's syntax*. Cambridge, MA: MIT Press.

Hyams, N. (1986). *Language acquisition and the theory of parameters*. Dordrecht: Reidel.

Inhelder, B., and Piaget, J. (1964). *The early growth of logic in the child*. London: Routledge and Kegan Paul.

Jakubowicz, C. (1984). On markedness and binding principles. In C. Jones and P. Sells (Eds.), *Proceedings of NELS 14*. Amherst: University of Massachusetts, GLSA.

Jaeggli, O. (1980). Remarks on *to* contraction. *Linguistic Inquiry, 11*, 239–245.

Kamp, H. (1981). A theory of truth and semantic interpretation. In J. Groenendijk, T. Janssen, and M. Stokhof (Eds.), *Formal methods in the study of language*. Amsterdam: Mathematical Centre.

Kamp, H., and Reyle, U. (1993). *From discourse to logic: Introduction to modeltheoretic semantics of natural language, formal logic and Discourse Representation Theory*. Dordrecht: Kluwer.

Kripke, S. (1972). Naming and necessity. In D. Davidson and G. Harman (Eds.), *Semantics for natural language*. Dordrecht: Reidel.

Labelle, M. (1990). Predication, *wh*-movement, and the development of relative clauses. *Language Acquisition, 1*, 95–119.

Larson, R., and Segal, G. (1995). *Knowledge of meaning*. Cambridge, MA: MIT Press.

Lasnik, H. (1990). *Essays on restrictiveness and learnability*. Dordrecht: Kluwer.

Lasnik, H., and Crain, S. (1985). On the acquisition of pronominal reference. *Lingua, 65*, 135–154.

Lasnik, H., and Uriagereka, J. (1988). *A course in GB syntax*. Cambridge, MA: MIT Press.

Lebeaux, D. (1988). *Language acquisition and the form of the grammar*. Doctoral dissertation, University of Massachusetts, Amherst.

Lee, H., and Wexler, K. (1987). *The acquisition of reflexives and pronouns in Korean from the cross-linguistic perspective*. Paper presented at the 12th Annual Boston University Conference on Language Development, Boston.

Lewis, D. (1975). Adverbs of quantification. In E. Keenan (Ed.), *Formal semantics of natural language*. Cambridge: Cambridge University Press.

Lewis, D. (1979). Scorekeeping in a language game. In R. Bauerle, U. Egli, and A. von Stechow (Eds.), *Semantics from different points of view*. Berlin: Springer-Verlag.

Lust, B. (1981). Constraints on anaphora in child language: A prediction for a universal. In S. L. Tavakolian (Ed.), *Language acquisition and linguistic theory*. Cambridge, MA: MIT Press.

Lust, B., Chien, Y.-C., and Flynn, S. (1987). What children know: Comparisons of experimental methods for the study of first language acquisition. In B. Lust (Ed.), *Studies in the acquisition of anaphora* (Vol. 2). Dordrecht: Reidel.

Lust, B., Eisele, J., and Mazuka, R. (1992). The binding theory module: Evidence from first language acquisition for Principle C. *Language, 68*, 333–358.

Lust, B., Loveland, K., and Kornet, R. (1980). The development of anaphora in first language: Syntactic and pragmatic constraints. *Linguistic Analysis, 6*, 359–391.

MacWhinney, B., and Bates, E. (1989). *The cross-linguistic study of sentence processing*. New York: Cambridge University Press.

MacWhinney, B., and Snow, C. (1985). The Child Language Data Exchange System. *Journal of Child Language, 12*, 271–296.

Marcus, G. (1993). Negative evidence in language acquisition. *Cognition, 46*, 53–85.

Martin, R. (1993). Short-term memory and sentence processing: Evidence from neuropsychology. *Memory and Cognition, 21*, 176–183.

Matthei, E. H. (1981). Children's interpretations of sentences containing reciprocals. In S. L. Tavakolian (Ed.), *Language acquisition and linguistic theory*. Cambridge, MA: MIT Press.

Matthei, E. H. (1982). The acquisition of prenominal modifiers. *Cognition, 11*, 301–332.

Mayer, J. W., Erreich, A., and Valian, V. (1978). Transformations, basic operations and language acquisition. *Cognition, 6*, 1–13.

McCloskey, J. (1979). *Transformational syntax and model theoretic semantics*. Dordrecht: Reidel.

McDaniel, D. (1986). *Conditions on wh-chains*. Doctoral dissertation, City University of New York.

McDaniel, D., Cairns, H. S., and Hsu, J. R. (1990). Binding principles in the grammars of young children. *Language Acquisition, 1*, 121–139.

McDaniel, D., Cairns, H. S., and Hsu, J. R. (1991). Control principles in the grammars of young children. *Language Acquisition, 1*, 297–335.

McDaniel, D., Chiu, B., and Maxfield, T. (1995). Parameters for *wh*-movement types. *Natural Language & Linguistic Theory, 13*, 709–753.

McDaniel, D., and Maxfield, T. (1992a). The nature of the anti-c-command requirement: Evidence from young children. *Linguistic Inquiry, 23*, 667–671.

McDaniel, D., and Maxfield, T. (1992b). Principle B and contrastive stress. *Language Acquisition, 2*, 337–358.

McDaniel, D., and McKee, C. (1993). Which children did they show know strong crossover? In H. Goodluck and M. Rochement (Eds.), *Island constraints*. Dordrecht: Kluwer.

McDaniel, D., and McKee, C. (1996). Children's oblique relatives. In A. Stringfellow, D. Cahana-Amitay, E. Hughes, and A. Zukowski (Eds.), *Proceedings of the 20th Annual Boston University Conference on Language Development*. Somerville, MA: Cascadilla Press.

McDaniel, D., McKee, C., and Cairns, H. S. (Eds). (1996). *Methods for assessing children's syntax*. Cambridge, MA: MIT Press.

McKee, C. (1988). *Italian children's mastery of binding*. Doctoral dissertation, University of Connecticut, Storrs.

McKee, C. (1992). A comparison of pronouns and anaphors in Italian and English acquisition. *Language Acquisition, 2*, 21–54.

McKee, C. (1996). On-line methods. In D. McDaniel, C. McKee, and H. S. Cairns (Eds.), *Methods for assessing children's syntax*. Cambridge, MA: MIT Press.

McKee, C., and Emiliani, M. (1992). Il clitico: C'e ma non si vede. *Natural Language & Linguistic Theory, 10*, 415–438.

McKee, C., Nicol, J., and McDaniel, D. (1993). Children's application of binding during sentence processing. *Language and Cognitive Processes, 8*, 265–290.

McNeill, D. (1970). *The acquisition of language: The study of developmental psycholinguistics*. New York: Harper and Row.

Melvold, J. (1991). Factivity and definiteness. In L. L. S. Cheng and H. Demirdache (Eds.), *More papers on wh-movement: MIT working papers in linguistics* (Vol. 15). Cambridge, MA: MIT, Department of Linguistics and Philosophy, MITWPL.

Miyamoto, Y. (1992). *The collective and distributive interpretation in child grammar: A study on quantification*. General examination, University of Connecticut, Storrs.

Miyamoto, Y., and Crain, S. (1991). *Children's interpretation of plural pronouns: Collective vs. distributive interpretation*. Paper presented at the 16th Annual Boston University Conference on Language Development, Boston.

Morgan, J. L., and Travis, L. L. (1989). Limits on negative information in language input. *Journal of Child Language, 16*, 531–552.

Naigles, L. (1990). Children use syntax to learn verb meanings. *Journal of Child Language, 17*, 357–374.

Nakayama, M. (1987). Performance factors in subject-auxiliary inversion by children. *Journal of Child Language, 14*, 113–125.

Nelson K. G., Carskaddon, G., and Bonvillian, J. D. (1973). Syntax acquisition: Impact of environmental variation in adult verbal interaction with the child. *Child Development, 44*, 497–504.

Ni, W., Crain, S., and Shankweiler, D. (1996). Sidestepping garden paths: Assessing the contributions of syntax, semantics and plausibility in resolving ambiguities. *Language and Cognitive Processes, 11*, 283–334.

Parsons, T. (1990). *Events in the semantics of English*. Cambridge, MA: MIT Press.

Pesetsky, D. (1987). Wh-in-situ: Movement and unselective binding. In E. Reuland and A. ter Meulen (Eds.), *The representation of (in)definiteness*. Cambridge, MA: MIT Press.

Philip, W. (1991). Spreading in the acquisition of universal quantifiers. In D. Bates (Ed.), *Proceedings of the Tenth West Coast Conference on Formal Linguistics*. Stanford, CA: CSLI. [Distributed by Cambridge University Press.]

Philip, W. (1995). *Event quantification in the acquisition of universal quantification*. Doctoral dissertation, University of Massachusetts, Amherst.

Phinney, M. (1981). *Syntactic constraints and the acquisition of embedded sentential complements*. Doctoral dissertation, University of Massachusetts, Amherst.

Pinker, S. (1984). *Language learnability and language development*. Cambridge, MA: Harvard University Press.

Pinker, S. (1990). Language acquisition. In D. N. Osherson and H. Lasnik (Eds.), *Language: An invitation to cognitive science* (Vol. 1). Cambridge, MA: MIT Press.

Potter, M., and Lombardi, L. (1990). Regeneration in the short-term recall of sentences. *Journal of Memory and Language, 29*, 633–654.

Radford, A. (1988). *Transformational grammar*. Cambridge: Cambridge University Press.

Radford, A. (1990). *Syntactic theory and the acquisition of English syntax: The nature of early child grammars of English*. Oxford: Basil Blackwell.

Reinhart, T. (1983a). *Anaphora and semantic interpretation*. Chicago: University of Chicago Press.

Reinhart, T. (1983b). Coreference and bound anaphora: A restatement of the anaphora question. *Linguistics and Philosophy, 6*, 47–88.

Reinhart, T. (1986). Center and periphery in the grammar of anaphora. In B. Lust (Ed.), *Studies in the acquisition of anaphora* (Vol. 1). Dordrecht: Reidel.

Rizzi, L. (1990). *Relativized Minimality*. Cambridge, MA: MIT Press.

Rizzi, L. (1993/1994). Some notes on linguistic theory and language development: The case of root infinitives. *Language Acquisition, 3*, 371–395.

Rizzi, L. (1996). *The fine structure of the left periphery*. In A. Belletti and L. Rizzi (Eds.), *Parameters and functional heads*. New York: Oxford University Press.

Roeper, T. (1972). *Approaches to acquisition theory, with data from German children*. Doctoral dissertation, Harvard University, Cambridge, MA.

Roeper, T. (1982). On the importance of syntax and the logical use of evidence in language acquisition. In S. Kuczaj (Ed.), *Language development: Syntax and semantics* (Vol. 1). Hillsdale, NJ: Lawrence Erlbaum.

Roeper, T. (1986). How children acquire bound variables. In B. Lust (Ed.), *Studies in the acquisition of anaphora* (Vol. 1). Dordrecht: Reidel.

Roeper, T., and de Villiers, J. (1991a). The emergence of bound variable structures. In T. Maxfield and B. Plunkett (Eds.), *University of Massachusetts occasional papers: Papers in the acquisition of WH*. Amherst: University of Massachusetts, GLSA.

Roeper, T., and de Villiers, J. (1991b). Ordered parameters in the acquisition of *wh*-questions. In J. Weissenborn, H. Goodluck, and T. Roeper (Eds.), *Theoretical issues in language acquisition: Continuity and change in development*. Hillsdale, NJ: Lawrence Erlbaum.

Roeper, T., Rooth, M., Mallis, L., and Akiyama, S. (1985). *The problem of empty categories and bound variables in language acquisition*. Ms., University of Massachusetts, Amherst.

Roeper, T., and Weissenborn, J. (1990). How to make parameters work. In L. Frazier and J. de Villiers (Eds.), *Language proceesing and language acquisition*. Dordrecht: Kluwer.

Rosen, T. J., and Rosen, S. T. (1995). Inferring the innateness of syntactic knowledge. In E. Clark (Ed.), *The Proceedings of the 26th Annual Child Language Research Forum*. Stanford, CA: CSLI. [Distributed by Cambridge University Press.]

Russell, B. (1948). *Human knowledge: Its scope and limits*. London: Allen and Unwin.

Sarma, J. (1991). *The acquisition of wh-questions in English*. Doctoral dissertation, University of Connecticut, Storrs.

Schaeffer, J. (1996). *Object scrambling in Dutch and Italian child language*. Doctoral dissertation, University of California, Los Angeles.

Selkirk, E. (1972). *The phrase phonology of English and French*. Doctoral dissertation, MIT, Cambridge, MA.

Shankweiler, D., and Crain, S. (1986). Language mechanisms and reading disorder: A modular approach. *Cognition, 24*, 139–168.

Shankweiler, D., Crain, S., Gorrell, P., and Tuller, B. (1989). Reception of language in agrammatism. *Language and Cognitive Processes, 4*, 1–33.

Sheldon, A. (1974). The role of parallel function in the acquisition of relative clauses in English. *Journal of Verbal Learning and Verbal Behavior, 13*, 272–281.

Sigurjónsdóttir, S., Hyams, N., and Chien, Y.-C. (1988). The acquisition of reflexives and pronouns by Icelandic children. *Papers and Reports on Child Language Development, 27*, 97–106.

Snyder, W., and Rothstein, S. (1992). A note on contraction, case and complementizers. *The Linguistic Review, 9*, 251–266.

Solan, L. (1983). *Pronominal reference: Child language and the theory of grammar*. Dordrecht: Reidel.

Solan, L., and Roeper, T. (1978). Children's use of syntactic structure in interpreting relative clauses. In H. Goodluck and S. Lawrence (Eds.), *University of Massachusetts occasional papers 4: Papers in the structure and development of child language*. Amherst: University of Massachusetts, GLSA.

Speas, M. (1994). Null arguments in a theory of economy of projection. In E. Benedicto and J. Runner (Eds.), *University of Massachusetts occasional papers 17: Functional projections*. Amherst: University of Massachusetts, GLSA.

Sperber, D., and Wilson, D. (1986). *Relevance*. Oxford: Blackwell.

Steedman, M., and Altmann, G. (1989). Ambiguity in context: A reply. *Language and Cognitive Processes, 4*, (Special Issue), 105–122.

Stowell, T., and Beghelli, F. (1995). *The direction of quantifier movement*. Paper presented at the 17th GLOW Colloquium, Vienna.

Stromswold, K. (1990). *Learnability and the acquisition of auxiliaries*. Doctoral dissertation, MIT, Cambridge, MA.

Szabolcsi, A. (1994). The noun phrase. In F. Kiefer and K. Kiss (Eds.), *Syntax and semantics 27: The syntactic structure of Hungarian*. San Diego, CA: Academic Press.

Takahashi, M. (1991). Children's interpretation of sentences containing *every*. In T. Maxfield and B. Plunkett (Eds.), *University of Massachusetts occasional papers: Papers in the acquisition of WH*. Amherst: University of Massachusetts, GLSA.

Tanenhaus, M. K., and Trueswell, J. C. (1995). Sentence comprehension. In J. Miller and P. Eimas (Eds.), *Handbook of perception and cognition*. Vol. 11, *Speech, language, and communication*. San Diego, CA: Academic Press.

Tavakolian, S. (1978). Children's comprehension of pronominal subjects and missing subjects in compli-
    cated sentences. In H. Goodluck and L. Solan (Eds.), *University of Massachusetts occasional papers 4:
    Papers in the structure and development of child language.* Amherst: University of Massachusetts, GLSA.

Tavakolian, S. L. (1981). The conjoined-clause analysis of relative clauses. In S. L. Tavakolian (Ed.), *Language
    acquisition and linguistic theory.* Cambridge, MA: MIT Press.

Thornton, R. (1990). *Adventures in long-distance moving: The acquisition of complex* wh-*questions.* Doctoral
    dissertation, University of Connecticut, Storrs.

Thornton, R. (1993). *Children who don't raise the negative.* Paper presented at the Annual Meeting of the
    Linguistic Society of America, Los Angeles.

Thornton, R. (1995). Referentiality and *wh*-movement in child English: Juvenile D-linkuency. *Language
    Acquisition, 4,* 139–175.

Thornton, R. (1996). Elicited production. In D. McDaniel, C. McKee, and H. S. Cairns (Eds.), *Methods for
    assessing children's syntax.* Cambridge, MA: MIT Press.

Thornton, R., and Crain, S. (1989). *Children's use of bound pronouns.* Paper presented at the Annual Meeting
    of the Linguistic Society of America, Washington, DC.

Thornton, R., and Crain, S. (1994). Successful cyclic movement. In T. Hoekstra and B. Schwartz (Eds.),
    Language acquisition studies in generative grammar. Amsterdam: John Benjamins.

Thornton, R., and Gavruseva, E. (1996). Children's split "whose-questions" and the structure of possessive
    NPs. Paper presented at the 21st Annual Boston University Conference on Language Development,
    Boston.

Thornton, R., and Wexler, K. (forthcoming). *Children's interpretation of pronouns in Principle B and VP ellipsis
    structures.* Cambridge, MA: MIT Press.

Travis, L. (1984). *Parameters and effects of word order variation.* Doctoral dissertation, MIT, Cambridge, MA.

Tyler, L. (1985). Real-time comprehension processes in agrammatism: A case study. *Brain and Language, 26,*
    259–275.

van Hoek, K. (1995). Conceptual reference points: A cognitive grammar account of pronominal anaphora
    constraints. *Language, 71,* 310–340.

Wason, P. (1965). Contexts of plausible denial. *Journal of Verbal Learning and Verbal Behavior, 4,* 7–11.

Wason, P. (1980). The verification task and beyond. In D. R. Olson (Ed.), *The social foundations of language
    and thought.* New York: Norton.

Watanabe, A. (1993). Larsonian CP recursion, factive complements, and selection. In A. J. Schafer (Ed.),
    NELS 23 (Vol. 1). Amherst: University of Massachusetts, GLSA.

Wexler, K., and Chien, Y.-C. (1985). The development of lexical anaphors and pronouns. *Papers and Reports
    on Child Language Development, 24,* 138–149.

Wexler, K., and Culicover, P. (1980). *Formal principles of language acquisition.* Cambridge, MA: MIT Press.

Wilson, B., and Peters, A. M. (1984). What are you cookin' on a hot?: A blind child's "violation" of univer-
    sal constraints. Paper presented at the 9th Boston University Conference on Language Develop-
    ment, Boston.

Index